THE FIRST SUMMIT

Roosevelt and Churchill

at Placentia Bay 1941

THE FIRST SUMMIT

Roosevelt and Churchill

at Placentia Bay 1941

Theodore A. Wilson

Illustrated with Photographs

Houghton Mifflin Company

Boston 1969

First Printing **w**

Copyright © 1969 by Theodore A. Wilson
All rights reserved. No part of this work may be
reproduced or transmitted in any form by any
means, electronic or mechanical, including
photocopying and recording, or by any
information storage or retrieval
system, without permission
in writing from the
publisher.

Library of Congress
Catalog Card Number: 69:15032

Printed in the United States of America

The author is grateful to the following for permission to quote from their books:

Council on Foreign Relations, Inc. The Undeclared War *by W. L. Langer and S. E. Gleason, New York: Harper and Row, for the Council on Foreign Relations, 1953.*
Dodd, Mead and Company. Atlantic Meeting *by H. V. Morton.*
Duell, Sloan and Pearce. As He Saw It *by Elliott Roosevelt. Copyright, 1946, by Elliott Roosevelt. By permission of Duell, Sloan and Pearce, Affiliate of Meredith Press.*
Farrar, Straus and Giroux. Assignment: Churchill *by Walter Thompson.*
Harper and Row. Global Mission *by H. H. Arnold and* Roosevelt and Hopkins *by Robert E. Sherwood.*
Houghton Mifflin Company. The Second World War *by Winston S. Churchill.*
Princeton University Press. The Road to Pearl Harbor *by Herbert Feis.*
The Viking Press. George C. Marshall: Ordeal and Hope *by Forrest C. Pogue.*

In memory of my father and mother,
Benjamin H. and Anna L. Wilson

Preface

THE SECOND WORLD WAR witnessed a marked increase in meetings between national leaders as compared to past eras. Conferences such as Casablanca, Quebec, Teheran, and Yalta made the assembling of presidents, premiers and generalissimos normal, even expected, events. The first of these conferences on the Allied side, the dramatic sea meeting off Argentia, Newfoundland, of Franklin D. Roosevelt and Winston S. Churchill, coming as it did before formal American entry into the war, was in many ways the most novel. It determined the style and much of the agenda for subsequent meetings. Important for confirming the policy of aid to Great Britain, it sanctioned that statement of high principle afterward termed the "Atlantic Charter," and — inestimably important — was the first meeting in their official capacities of two members of the triumvirate which was to encompass the destruction of the Axis.

Although the meeting at Argentia was one of the critical events of the war, it now receives little attention in histories of the period. Occurring at a time when the United States was neither legally nor emotionally committed to full participation in the war, this encounter of Roosevelt and Churchill was an anomaly, an event which defied easy classification. Later, when Pearl Harbor had propelled the United States into the conflict, decisions reached at other "summit" conferences made the embryonic agreements of Argentia seem trivial and outmoded. Besides, Roosevelt and Churchill always were talking together somewhere.

When the Atlantic Conference was remembered, it was as one of the milestones on the road to Pearl Harbor or for the Atlantic Charter. My purpose in undertaking this study, first as a doctoral dissertation at Indiana University, was to examine the Atlantic Conference as a discrete event, largely outside of the "flow" of events leading to Pearl Harbor. I have strayed from this original aim, because, of course, investigation of such a subject without large attention to cause and effect relationships is both impossible and absurd. Nonetheless, I hope that something remains of the attempt to understand the meeting at Argentia on its own merits, not merely as yet another test case in an effort to "prove" a particular hypothesis about the success or failure of United States foreign policy before December 7, 1941. Finally, it is worth noting that differences between my exposition and those previously put forward may be the result of my not having witnessed the events about which I have written. I believe I am aware of the pitfalls thus encountered. Hopefully, the reader will find a decided gain in perspective is one benefit, at least, of the author's lack of personal experience with the period.

I welcome this opportunity to thank those whose counsel and generous assistance made possible this study. I trust they will clothe my inadequate words with the substance of the debt I owe them. I am indebted to Craig Wylie of Houghton Mifflin who provided editorial guidance and wise counsel. I am grateful to Professor Clifford S. Griffin and to William J. Wilson, both of whom read the manuscript in its entirety and made many perceptive suggestions. I want to thank Professor Charles K. Warner for reading the study and for his unselfish assistance in other ways. Many of my colleagues gave helpful criticism and encouragement, and their contributions require acknowledgment. I wish also to express my appreciation of the encouragement extended by Professor Leo F. Solt and by the former Chairman of the Department of History at the University of Kansas, Professor George L. Anderson.

To Robert H. Ferrell, I offer recognition of a debt I can never repay. Others have written of the "Ferrell treatment," and I can add little to their tributes. I will say that what there is of robust and zestful historical writing in this study, how well it conforms to the dictum that history is intended to be read, is largely due to Mr. Ferrell's patient and incisive criticism.

For assistance in my research, I wish to thank the staffs of Yale University Library, the University of Kansas Library, the Office of the Director of Naval History, the Library of Congress, the Columbia Oral History Project, and the Colindale newspaper library of the British Museum. I am especially grateful to Dr. E. Taylor Parks of the Department of State Historical Office, Miss Patricia Dowling of the National Archives and to Dr. Elizabeth B. Drewry and her able staff at the Franklin D. Roosevelt Library. Cooperation from surviving participants in the meeting was crucial. Four of the persons who responded to my entreaties, all British, deserve particular recognition: General Sir Ian Jacob, Vice-Admiral Brian B. Schofield, Air Vice-Marshal W. M. Yool, and Mr. H. V. Morton.

Financial support was in part provided by an Elizabeth B. Watkins Faculty Fellowship and a grant from the General Research Fund of the University of Kansas. For many kindnesses, I wish to thank Mr. and Mrs. Jerry C. Wilson, Mrs. JoAnn Wilson, Mr. and Mrs. V. H. Juncker, Mr. and Mrs. David A. Lawhead, and Rev. and Mrs. William A. Sexton. Mrs. Goldie L. Schlink, Mrs. Barbara L. Medford, and Mrs. Betty Artherton assisted in typing the manuscript. My wife, Judith J. Wilson, served as typist, proofreader, and critic. Most important of all, she was the balance wheel in this enterprise, quietly helping in the times of furious activity, calmly confident in the more frequent periods when my pen lay idle and the stacks of notes gathered dust.

I am deeply grateful to all who are mentioned here, and to those whose contribution inadvertently may have been slighted. Of course, any errors, inadequacies, or infirm prose are my responsibility alone.

Contents

Contents

Illustrations

*(Unless otherwise credited, the photographs are
reproduced through the courtesy of
the Franklin D. Roosevelt Library,
Hyde Park, N.Y.)*

List of Participants

Winston S. Churchill, Prime Minister of the United Kingdom
Sir Alexander Cadogan, Permanent Under Secretary of State for Foreign
Affairs
General Sir John Dill, Chief of the Imperial General Staff
Admiral Sir Dudley Pound, Admiral of the Fleet, First Sea Lord, and
Chief of the Naval Staff
Air Vice-Marshal Sir Wilfred Freeman, Vice Chief of the Air Staff
Professor F. E. Lindemann (Lord Cherwell), Adviser to the Prime Min-
ister
Mr. J. M. Martin, Principal Private Secretary to the Prime Minister
Commander C. R. Thompson, Personal Assistant to the Prime Minister
Brigadier Vivian Dykes, Director of Plans, War Office
Captain B. B. Schofield, Director of Trade Division, Admiralty
Colonel L. C. Hollis, Military Assistant, Secretary to War Cabinet, Min-
istry of Defence
Lieutenant Colonel E. I. C. Jacob, Military Assistant, Secretary to the
War Cabinet, Ministry of Defence
Group Captain W. M. Yool, Staff Officer to the Chief of Air Staff
Captain A. R. S. Nutting, Military Assistant to the C.I.G.S.
Commander M. G. Goodenough, Plans Division, Admiralty
Paymaster-Captain R. V. Brockman, Secretary to the First Sea Lord
Captain R. P. Pim, Operations Division, Admiralty
Lieutenant Commander H. W. McMullan, Operations Division, Admiralty
Paymaster-Captain L. A. de C. Ritchie, Mr. H. V. Morton, Mr. Howard
Spring, Representatives of the Ministry of Information
Inspector W. H. Thompson, Personal bodyguard of the Prime Minister

Franklin D. Roosevelt, President of the United States

Harry Hopkins, Personal adviser to the President

Sumner Welles, Under Secretary of State.

Averell Harriman, Special representative of the President and Lend-Lease "expediter" in England

General George C. Marshall, Chief of Staff of the General Staff

Admiral Harold R. Stark, Chief of Naval Operations

General H. H. Arnold, Chief of the Army Air Corps

Vice-Admiral Ernest J. King, Commander in Chief, Atlantic Fleet

Major General James H. Burns, Executive Assistant to the Assistant Secretary of War

Rear Admiral Richmond K. Turner, Director of War Plans, Department of the Navy

Commander Forrest Sherman, Office of the Chief of Naval Operations

Lieutenant Colonel Charles W. Bundy, Assistant Director of the War Plans Division, War Department

Captain John R. Beardall, Naval Aide to the President

Captain Elliott Roosevelt, Junior Military Aide to the President

Lieutenant (j.g.) Franklin D. Roosevelt, Jr., Junior Naval Aide to the President

THE FIRST SUMMIT

Roosevelt and Churchill

at Placentia Bay 1941

I. Introduction

IN EARLY AUGUST, 1941, Washington, D.C., sweltered in 90-plus temperatures and awesome humidity. Residents who could flee the capital were using any excuse to do so. Congress was still in session, caught up in a bitter struggle over Selective Service renewal, but many members were out of town, having arranged weekend visits to more congenial climes. On a broiling Sunday, August 3, newspapers carried an announcement that President Franklin Delano Roosevelt was leaving on an excursion of his own. White House Press Secretary Stephen T. Early informed the news services Saturday morning that the President had decided to take his yacht, U.S.S. *Potomac*, on a cruise off the New England coast.[1]

Few reporters on the White House beat were surprised by Early's announcement. F.D.R. had been wanting to get away for a few days' rest for several months. Certainly the President deserved a respite from the steadily increasing demands upon him. Except for one weekend at Hyde Park in early June and a short outing along the Potomac River in July, Roosevelt rarely had been off the grounds of the White House since March. Rexford Tugwell has written that in this difficult period F.D.R. never "escaped from the wash," never was able "to think of the old accustomed things — his trees, his stamps, Warm Springs, and all the rest." [2]

Those who were close to the President realized that he was a tired and deeply frustrated man. Since passage of the Lend-Lease Act in March the administration's program had stalled and the country was caught in a tangle of crossed purposes. Lend-Lease was the embodiment of Roosevelt's cherished policy of "all aid short of war." He possessed great hopes for this program. The inspiration may have come from Winston Churchill, but the idea was his, and F.D.R. took what were for him extreme risks in jamming the legislation through a surly Congress. He seems to have thought for a time that Lend-Lease would be the ultimate action needed in aiding Great Britain.[3]

Yet, even before the program was fairly launched, President Roosevelt had to recognize that many Americans, including several of his most valued advisers, believed his faith in Lend-Lease misplaced. He soon was made aware that his good friends, the British, grateful for relief afforded by Lend-Lease, saw it as one giant step forward where they needed many more. Demands for more aid, for convoying, for additional U.S. merchant shipping, even for an American expeditionary force, poured in from London.[4] F.D.R.'s reaction for a time was to withdraw from direction of affairs. He used a series of colds and sinus infections to shut out importunate visitors bringing proposals for deeper American involvement. He kept fairly to himself, isolated in the roomy second-floor bedroom in the White House East Wing.[5] The key to this period of withdrawal was frustration. The President believed his forthright action in obtaining Lend-Lease had placed him far in advance of public opinion, that he had "temporarily exhausted his credit both with Congress and with the country." [6] He must now remain passive until the public caught up.

Presidential intimates often could not refrain from pleading for action. In May the "old Curmudgeon," Secretary of Commerce Harold L. Ickes, was despairing: "In every direction I find a growing discontent with the President's lack of leadership. He still has the country if he will take it and lead it. But he won't have it very much longer unless he does something. It won't be sufficient for him to make another speech and then go into a state of innocuous desuetude again." [7] Henry Morgenthau, Jr. confessed to his diary that the President and his sickly familiar, Harry Hopkins, appeared to be completely baffled. "They feel that something has to be done but don't know just what." Hopkins had told him, "he thinks the President is loath to get into this war, and he would rather follow public opinion than lead it." [8]

There was deep concern that Roosevelt had become so dependent

upon the vagaries of polls and pollsters that he could not act deci-
sively. F.D.R.'s inability to pull the nation along by the power of his
assertive confidence was a novel and fearsome occurrence, and his
advisers did not know what to make of it. Henry L. Stimson, recording a telephone conversation with the President on June 30, captured
the mood which pervaded the White House: "First [the President]
said he had some good news — that there was a Gallup Poll which
was coming out which was going to be very favorable, much more so
than the Gallup people had anticipated." Stimson was not impressed
and replied that he was "glad" but that he wished to remind the
President again "that all these polls omitted one factor which he
seemed himself rather to neglect — namely . . . the power of his
own leadership." As he had so often in past months, President Roosevelt replied defensively that he appreciated Stimson's argument
but he "had been feeling so mean" and he had no pep.[9]

Not until late July, with his vacation cruise imminent, did the President return to work "with a flare-up of his old gusto." [10] In cabinet
meeting on August 2, a discussion of the need for immediate dispatch of fighter planes to the Soviet Union elicited a forty-five-minute
lecture from the President which, if discomforting to Stimson who
looked "thoroughly miserable," was immensely heartening to all his
advisers.[11] Next day, finishing last-minute work before leaving the
White House, F.D.R. seemed not to have a worry in the world. An
imaginative *Time* feature, counting down the presidential departure,
was to observe: "Franklin Roosevelt patted his perspiring forehead
and glanced at his cluttered desk. There was the . . . old optimistic
cast in his eye. It was still possible to hope, in spite of all, that the
U.S. would not have to get in a shooting war . . . The heat was
melting the tar on Massachusetts Avenue. Mr. Roosevelt . . . fled
from the White House, fled from Washington. A week or ten days
on the yacht *Potomac*, out on salt water, would be fine, and, so far as
he could see, it was a good time to take a vacation." [12] If the prospect
of a brief vacation was all that was needed to restore the President's
normal ebullient confidence, his subordinates were encouraged.

Late Sunday morning the flag came down from the White House

staff, and the President, accompanied only by his physician, Admiral Ross T. McIntire, his military aide, General Edwin "Pa" Watson, and his naval aide, Captain John R. Beardall, drove up Pennsylvania Avenue to Union Station. The presidential party made its way across the almost-deserted lower concourse to a special train waiting to carry them to the New London, Connecticut, submarine base where *Potomac* was anchored.[13]

Promptly at 11:00 A.M. the train pulled out of Union Station. Roosevelt's assistants, wishing to start their boss' rest therapy at once, steered those reporters who were going as far as New London away from the President's specially equipped car. They refrained from discussing anything more serious than the weather, racing results, and the merits of gin rummy hands. Roosevelt spoke of nothing except the boat races he hoped to see, the fish he expected to jump on his hook, "and the wonderful rest and quiet away from people and telephones." [14] The train, speeding past watchful soldiers standing with fixed bayonets at every bridgehead, reached New London at 8:15 P.M. It backed to within a hundred yards of *Potomac's* gangway. After a ten-minute ceremonial meeting with the base commandant and Robert A. Hurley, the Governor of Connecticut, F.D.R. boarded the ship to the squeal of a bosun's pipe and snap of the presidential ensign being run up the mast. A few minutes later, in the afterglow of sunset, *Potomac* set a course down the Thames Channel to salt water.[15]

Newsmen covering the sailing were agreed that President Roosevelt had earned some relaxation. They detected nothing unusual about this latest of his vacation trips, though some, having summoned visions of lapping waves and sea breezes, were disgruntled that, for the first time, no newsmen were to accompany the President. Early had explained on Saturday that it was not possible to accommodate reporters on the escort ship, U.S.S. *Calypso* (a Coast Guard patrol vessel), and that the President had refused to requisition a destroyer escort as had been done for previous cruises. Early stressed that the cruise was to be on "a day-to-day basis." Railroad equipment would stand by to rush the President to Washington if the international situation suddenly worsened. For obvious reasons, he enjoined strict secrecy and insisted that "from the time the President boards the *Potomac* until the time he returns to shore the movement of the ship will be a confidential naval operation." The threat of submarines was not mentioned but it occurred to all. Secretary of the Navy Frank Knox, a former newspaperman, joined in an appeal for voluntary censorship. "I can assure you that it is a purely rest or vacation trip," Knox said, "and I ask the newspapers not to display any enterprise in attempting to follow him or speculate on his whereabouts. The man has been carrying a tremendous burden and we should let him have a week or ten days of complete rest." Reporters gave in, some returning to Washington, others trudging up to Swampscott, Massachusetts, where the schedule called for the President's disembarkation ten days later. After all, as a *New York Times* correspondent wrote sympathetically, "it was no more than the start of a vacation for a man who has . . . longed for some sea air." [16]

For twenty-four hours the President's activities followed the prescribed routine. After a leisurely cruise up the coast *Potomac* dropped anchor for the night at Harbor of Refuge, Point Judith, Rhode Island. Next morning, August 4, the ship proceeded to South Dartmouth, Massachusetts. At 10:00 A.M. Roosevelt took the wheel of a Chris-Craft speedboat and roared in to the dock of the local yacht club where several members of Danish and Norwegian royal families-in-exile were waiting for him. The Department of State had requested that the President invite these personages aboard the *Potomac* for a short tour.

F.D.R. generally was not fond of entertaining royal displaced persons, but took this occasion to satisfy State's persistent requests.[17] The little episode, sure to receive large play in the newspapers, contributed an extra touch of authenticity to the cruise, and so he dutifully escorted the royal visitors on a tour of the yacht. Besides, Roosevelt was immensely proud of his ship and was fond of pointing out the many innovations he had planned and had installed.[18]

Potomac was originally the Coast Guard offshore patrol vessel

Electra. She had been converted late in 1935 and used for the first time by President Roosevelt in the spring of 1936. The ship made the transition from smuggler-chaser to pleasure cruiser with ease and style. One hundred and sixty-five feet long, with a draft of nine feet and displacement of 450 tons, *Potomac* rated a top speed of fourteen knots and carried a complement of fifty officers and men. During the conversion a deckhouse had been added just forward of the fan-tail, which extended nearly half the ship's length. From atop it F.D.R. could fish with perfect ease and it contained a lounging-dining saloon and the President's stateroom. Also on the main deck, amidships, were fully equipped galleys. Below were accommoda-tions for six guests, the Secret Service contingent, and the crew. For the President's convenience a small, hand-operated elevator had been fitted into the after funnel, a dummy. One final addition was made in 1940. Fifty-caliber machine guns were mounted on the afterdeck and in the bows. They impressed the visitors more than any other feature.[19]

Tour completed, the President invited his guests to stay aboard for a brief run over to Buzzard's Bay, where the blues were reputed to be running. After desultory angling, conversation, and a light meal the *Potomac* returned to South Dartmouth in late afternoon. F.D.R. exercised a presidential prerogative by electing to transport the viva-cious young princesses, Astrid, Ragnhild, and Martha, back to the yacht club. Other members of the royal party returned via ship's boat.

The interlude spent with the Scandinavian royal exiles was promi-nently featured in early editions next morning. Such fluff almost al-ways received front-page display during the August doldrums, and the press inquired whether other newsworthy, if frivolous, items would be forthcoming.[20] Newspapermen, at Swampscott and in Washington, were becoming a little edgy about this presidential fish-ing trip. It was almost too relaxed, too unplanned for belief. They nervously discussed rumors, mere whispers as yet, that the President was engaged in some project of staggering importance and secrecy, for which his "pleasure cruise" was a brilliantly conceived cover. A

few of the stories even had Roosevelt meeting with Winston Churchill — but no one took seriously that particular whimsy.[21]

For once, fact "scooped" the inexhaustible tide of journalistic speculation. As soon as Roosevelt returned from the yacht club his tiny
task force set a course for Menemsha Bight, Vineyard Sound. To
this point the cruise had been according to advertisement; but if any
reporter had been on *Potomac* that evening as it dropped anchor he
would have realized that the President was involved in something
more than a fishing trip. Dancing on the dark waters of the sound
where Viking ships reputedly had rested 1000 years before, were the
lights of a flotilla of American warships. Towering above *Potomac*
and *Calypso* was the heavy cruiser, U.S.S. *Augusta*, flagship of the
Atlantic Fleet. Close by loomed U.S.S. *Tuscaloosa*, another heavy
cruiser. Also present were five destroyers, *Madison, Moffett, Samp-
son, Winslow,* and *McDougal,* comprising Destroyer Division Seventeen. Most startling of all, waving greetings from the decks of *Augusta* and *Tuscaloosa* were the principal officers of the United States
Armed Forces: General George C. Marshall, Admiral Harold R.
Stark, General Henry H. Arnold, and the Commander in Chief, Atlantic Fleet, Admiral Ernest J. King.

Had a fortunate reporter not entirely lost his wits from the shock,
he might have deduced that the impossible was taking place: the
President of the United States and his principal military advisers
were undertaking one of the best-kept, most startling secret adventures in modern history. F.D.R. was preparing to begin a journey
through dangerous seas to an epic conference with the Prime Minister of Great Britain, Winston Churchill. At this meeting between the
president of the most powerful "neutral" country in the world and
the leader of a belligerent nation there were larger fish to be caught
— or lost — than anyone had imagined when the President began
his cruise.

II. "Sail on, Oh Ship of State"

ESPITE APPEARANCES the meeting at Argentia had a long and complicated genesis. The desirability of conferences à *deux* was admitted by Roosevelt and Churchill very early in their relations, but war exigencies — which made understandings founded upon personal contact increasingly urgent — stood in the way. In the dark months of 1940–41 Prime Minister Churchill found himself unable to leave his command post for any length of time. The President, also struggling with the burdens of office in a national emergency, faced other problems: his physical limitations and the potential consequences of a meeting with the leader of a belligerent nation.

In retrospect, such an encounter seems a natural result of the increasingly intimate wartime correspondence between Roosevelt and Churchill. The President had opened this exchange on September 11, 1939, by a congratulatory letter to Churchill on his reappointment as First Lord of the Admiralty. F.D.R. invited the English leader to "keep in touch personally with anything you want to know about." Churchill responded with alacrity.[1] In this way began a momentous correspondence, amounting in the next six years to some 1500 messages. After Churchill became Prime Minister in May, 1940, the correspondence became an indispensable channel between the two leaders and their governments.[2] Both men found personal diplomacy congenial. It avoided the misunderstandings and obfuscation they believed plagued traditional diplomacy. Many decisions, some of the most critical nature, derived from communications between Roosevelt and the "Former Naval Person," the title Churchill adopted after he became Prime Minister.

The two leaders, both religiously convinced of the power of personality, soon became impatient with even this novel expedient, and their thoughts turned to settlement of outstanding difficulties vis-à-vis. Roosevelt was particularly dependent upon personal administration; when a crisis arose his first reaction was to summon close aides to a White House conference.[3] When all else failed he could exert the fantastic charm and personal magnetism which almost never failed. Both he and Churchill had tremendous confidence in their powers of persuasion, and each apparently assumed the other was susceptible to them.

Several times in 1940 each man privately expressed desire for a meeting, moved largely by growing fascination and curiosity. Roosevelt undertook the first important step at the dawn of the New Year, 1941. He had been shocked and disturbed by a letter from Churchill, dated December 8, 1940, which candidly described Great Britain's position as the second year of war proceeded. Churchill's note revealed the desperate British plight as could no report from resident American missions. This message led to a period of withdrawal while F.D.R. thought out its implications, and was the stimulus for his "arsenal of democracy" speech and for the idea of lend-lease; it also set his mind on a personal meeting with the Prime Minister.[4]

Churchill had written that the danger of Great Britain's "being destroyed by a swift, overwhelming blow" had "for the time being" receded; but new danger lay in the German effort to cut the island's supply lines. There was a steady attrition of the merchant marine, and the Prime Minister warned that "unless we can establish our ability to feed this island, to import the munitions of all kinds which we need . . . we may fall by the way and the time needed by the United States to complete her defensive preparations may not be forthcoming." He appealed to America to help its sister democracy in the hour of peril. Giving voice to England's financial desperation, the Prime Minister requested the "gift, loan, or supply" of American warships, all merchant vessels the United States could spare, increased munitions, and, most important, extreme leniency in terms of payment. His cable placed the survival of the United Kingdom in American hands.[5]

Roosevelt mulled over the plea for several weeks. How could he get across to the Prime Minister the possibilities of American aid and the difficulties which circumscribed any response? Around Christmas, in the course of a talk with Harry Hopkins, the President remarked, "You know — a lot of this could be settled if Churchill and I could just sit down together for a while."

"What's stopping you?" demanded Hopkins.

F.D.R. said he could not arrange a meeting just then, because "they have no ambassador over here — we have none over there."

Hopkins immediately proposed a way of surmounting that problem. With the "gleam of high adventure" in his eyes, he said, "How about me going over, Mr. President?"[6]

At first Roosevelt would have nothing to do with the idea. He needed, he said, Hopkins' assistance in preparing the approaching State of the Union address, arrangements for the third Inaugural, and in devising strategy for the unavoidable battle in Congress over lend-lease. Captivated by the notion of meeting Churchill and getting a firsthand view of England, Hopkins persisted, enlisting the support of Missy LeHand, the President's personal secretary, and Justice Felix Frankfurter. For a time F.D.R. stood against all the pressure his aide could bring. Anxiety over Hopkins' always precarious health, and, probably, concern about possible consequences of a meeting of the ultra-liberal Hopkins and Churchill, the personification of the English aristocrat to many Americans, caused him to hold back.[7]

Then, suddenly, mysteriously, Roosevelt mastered these scruples and decided that Hopkins should go to England. On January 3, Early called to congratulate Hopkins on his trip — which the President had just announced at his weekly press conference. Robert E. Sherwood, Hopkins' biographer, intimates this was the first "Harry the Hop" knew of his boss' change of heart.[8] To forestall another reversal, Hopkins left immediately, traveling by Pan American clipper to Lisbon and thence to England aboard British Overseas Airways.

The chief purpose of Hopkins' mission was exploration — of Churchill's reaction to a meeting, and of the doughty English leader. Selection of Hopkins as his emissary assured the President that the matter would remain confidential and that his instructions would be followed to the letter. Someone may have suggested that the differences between Hopkins and Churchill might be put to good use; wondering how he would get along with the strong-willed English statesman, Roosevelt may have reasoned that if his quick-tempered, prickly aide hit it off with Churchill, then he himself would have little difficulty. Hopkins also realized that he must establish satisfactory relations with Prime Minister Churchill or waste his trip.

For years Harry Hopkins had been making himself useful to the President. Equally nimble at backstairs intrigue and poker night tomfoolery, the former social worker shifted smoothly between service as a sounding board for "the boss'" ideas, a shield against criticism of the President (and sometimes a magnet attracting away abuse), and the role of errand boy and court jester.[9] The ties between F.D.R. and Harry Hopkins were volatile and complex. Hopkins was no rustic Svengali, nor an *éminence grise;* he rarely showed ambitions or desires distinguishable from those of Roosevelt. Marquis Childs once wrote,

> Should the President on a dull day suggest casually to his friend and confidant, Harry L. Hopkins, that the national welfare would be served if Mr. Hopkins were to jump off the Washington Monument, the appointed hour would find Mr. Hopkins poised for the plunge. Whether with or without parachute would depend on what the President seemed to have in mind. Mr. Hopkins would know about that, for he had made a career of understanding, sensing, divining, often guessing — and usually guessing right — what is in Franklin Roosevelt's mind.[10]

The President found such absolute loyalty indispensable, even though Hopkins' presence at his side caused political difficulties. Outsiders found Roosevelt's attachment to Hopkins inexplicable. During a private interview in January, 1941, the Republican standard-bearer in 1940, Wendell Willkie, asked the President directly, "Why do you keep Hopkins so close to you? You surely must realize that people distrust him and they resent his influence." Roosevelt replied, "I can understand that you wonder why I need that half-man around me. But — someday you may be sitting here where I am now as President of the United States. And when you are, you'll be looking at that door over there and knowing that practically everybody who walks through it wants something out of you. You'll learn what a lonely job this is, and you'll discover the need for somebody like Harry Hopkins who asks for nothing except to serve you." [11]

Hopkins had several defects, some of which the President exploited. He was hardly self-effacing and was jealous of his position to an unhealthy degree, often preventing men or their ideas from reaching the President if they did not first come to him. He was an opportunist; he would eagerly sacrifice principle for action or the appearance of action; he looked to the immediate rather than the long-term effects of decisions. As well, Hopkins shared his master's contempt for established lines of authority. The tempting epithet, "yes-man," does apply to Hopkins, although it is a one-dimensional description of his relations with the President. Certainly, Hopkins could not be relied upon to offer balanced judgments of F.D.R.'s notions, and that fault became increasingly important. In contrast Hopkins did possess the virtue of midwestern bluntness — a valuable and rare quality in Roosevelt's entourage.

In the critical year before Pearl Harbor Hopkins' influence with the President did much for the national welfare. Even men so antithetical to him in personality as Stimson and Marshall paid tribute to his contributions. Stimson admitted to his diary that, contrary to an earlier judgment, "the more I think of it, the more I think it is a godsend that he should be at the White House . . . Hopkins . . . is a man that I have grown to appreciate and to respect more and more the more I see him. In this talk I had the first opportunity of talking with any responsible man in the Administration virtually who knew exactly what we are going to do in the situation that I see and what everybody ought to see if they'd look." [12] Crucial was Hopkins' ability to adjust to changed circumstances, to shift from concentration upon domestic reform to the complexities of world politics. He may have adopted a simplistic view of international affairs; still, he got results. Roosevelt termed him "the perfect Ambassador for my purposes. He doesn't even know the meaning of the word 'protocol.' When he sees a piece of red tape, he just pulls out those old garden shears of his and snips it." [13] Roosevelt was sending his assistant to England to propose one of the most startling instances of red tape-snipping in modern history.

Hopkins was to be, nonetheless, on his best behavior. The President's enthusiasm for a meeting with Churchill, conveyed to his aide during several talks before departure, made clear the project was highest priority. He told Morgenthau, "I have just got to see Churchill myself in order to explain things to him." [14] F.D.R. revealed his eagerness in a letter to Harold L. Ickes the day before Hopkins departed. He mentioned a desire to talk with Lord Halifax (the new British Ambassador soon to arrive) about "a more general meeting," but that, unwilling to wait, he was "sending over to London Harry Hopkins for two or three weeks so that he can talk to Churchill like an Iowa farmer." [15] This simile expressed the essence of Hopkins' success as presidential adviser, errand boy, and general factotum.

When Hopkins arrived, the Prime Minister was able to exert all his formidable charm since he had no bothersome opinions regarding Roosevelt's aide. When he learned that "Harry Hopkins" was coming to England, Churchill is said to have asked, "Who?" His Parliamentary Private Secretary, Brendan Bracken, had met Hopkins some years before, was aware of his position in Roosevelt's administration, and briefed the Prime Minister. Immediately grasping the significance of the visit, Churchill "ordered the unrolling of any red carpets that might have survived the Blitz." On learning of Hopkins' suspicion "of anyone who might presume to challenge Roosevelt's position of pre-eminence among world statesmen," Churchill, on the day of Hopkins' arrival, delivered a speech (ostensibly in honor of Halifax's sailing) which rejoiced at Roosevelt's reelection and praised the President in language sufficiently fulsome to mollify even Hopkins.[16]

Roosevelt's envoy reached England too exhausted to notice carpet colors or to remark upon the warmth of his reception. Bracken was waiting when the plane touched down at Poole. He waited in growing puzzlement for Hopkins to debark. After the other passengers were already in the terminal, Bracken boarded the plane and found Hopkins "still sitting, looking sick and shrunken and too tired even to unfasten his safety belt." [17] He recovered, aided by friendly ministrations on every side and by a good night's rest — something he had not enjoyed since the trip began because of his terror of flying.

Herschel V. Johnson, Counsellor of the United States Embassy, met the Hopkins party at the railroad station and escorted the weary envoy to Claridge's, the ultra-posh West End hotel at which the Embassy had reserved a suite. Over dinner a reviving Hopkins discussed with Johnson the situation in England. The Counsellor, warm advocate of aid to Britain, was encouraged by Hopkins' appreciation of the urgency of all-out American support. In contrast to many American visitors Hopkins desired only "to find out if they were asking for *enough* to see them through." He gave Johnson the first real assurance that victory had arrived.[18]

Next day, January 7, Hopkins met the Prime Minister and, contrary to predictions, the "Iowa farmer" and the English aristocrat immediately became friends. The first meeting took place at a private luncheon at No. 10 Downing Street. Hopkins had been instructed to express to Churchill President Roosevelt's desire to meet him "to talk over the problem of the defeat of Germany." [19] Before he could deliver this message Churchill announced exactly the same wish. At once they started to work out details. In the course of a three-hour conversation they set a tentative date of March or April; one or both suggested Bermuda or Newfoundland as the best site. Nothing was said about subjects for discussion at the meeting. The two men ranged over many issues, not least of which, presumably, were Britain's desperate position and the likely American response. Hopkins was unable to make definite commitments, but told Churchill of the President's ideas about lend-lease and attempted to convey his boss' determination "that at all costs and by all means he will carry you through, no matter what happens to him." [20] It is doubtful, however, that he included a faithful rendering of that statement in the jubilant cable to Roosevelt describing the Prime Minister's receptivity to the idea of a summit conference.

The first meeting, and the many subsequent ones during Hopkins' twice-extended stay, made it clear that he and Churchill were able to work together. Of course, the principal concern was whether the President and Prime Minister would get along. After meeting Churchill, Hopkins believed this was possible, although aware of dangers in bringing two such gigantic egos into proximity. The President and Prime Minsiter in his opinion were completely different, but "they possessed to a superlative degree the ability to provoke loyalty, enthusiasm, devotion, even a kind of adoration — and also the ability to provoke." [21] Hopkins told Edward R. Murrow in an off-the-record interview: "I suppose you could say that I've come here to be a catalytic agent between two prima donnas." [22] Discovery that the presence of a catalyst in such a meeting might prevent any violent reaction, Hopkins felt, justified his mission.

There were additional benefits. From the January visit came an important new channel of communication — between Hopkins and the Prime Minister. The two got along famously. Churchill invited his newfound ally and friend to Chequers for several of his weekend soirees; together they toured military installations and war plants. The Prime Minister cabled Roosevelt how pleased he had been to make friends with Hopkins "who has been a great comfort and encouragement to everyone he has met. One can easily see why he is so close to you." [23] Hearing of the rapport between his friend and Churchill, F.D.R. was so pleased that he bragged about his astuteness in sending Hopkins during a cabinet meeting.

> The President started off by handing himself large bouquets for having sent Harry Hopkins to London. I do not know how much it was hindsight. . . . Apparently the first thing that Churchill asks for when he gets awake in the morning is Harry Hopkins, and Harry is the last one whom he sees at night.[24]

Secretary of Interior Ickes, recorder of this presidential statement, was not among Hopkins' greatest admirers and could not refrain from adding: "Probably a good deal of this is true and the attachment of Churchill to Harry Hopkins may be entirely genuine. However, I suspect that if, as his personal representative, the President should send to London a man with the bubonic plague, Churchill would, nevertheless, see a good deal of him." [25]

Roosevelt's envoy was equally taken with the Prime Minister. In late January he sent back an interim report: "The people here are amazing from Churchill on down and if courage alone can win — the result will be inevitable. But they need our help desperately and I am sure you will permit nothing to stand in the way. Some of the ministers and underlings are a bit trying but no more than some I have seen." He continued: "Churchill is the *gov't* in every sense of the word — he controls the grand strategy and often the details — labor trusts him — the army, navy, and air force are behind him to a man. The politicians and upper crust pretend to like him." The report ended with reconfirmation of the necessity for a Roosevelt-Churchill conference: "I cannot emphasize too strongly that he is the one and only person over here with whom you need to have a full meeting of minds." [26]

According to Hopkins, Churchill desired to see the President "the sooner the better." Reporting that he had explained about Roosevelt's difficulty in leaving the country until the Lend-Lease Act was passed, Hopkins nevertheless urged on February 2 that he "was convinced this meeting between you and Churchill is essential — and soon — for the battering continues and Hitler does not wait for Congress." [27] During Hopkins' six-week stay, the British policy of giving high-level American visitors carte blanche to inspect military and industrial facilities and to discuss (and assimilate) British strategy paid off handsomely. Just before he left London, Hopkins cabled final impressions to the President. He stressed that previous telegrams "have in no ways overstated the need" for massive aid and referred to his concern that these messages had proved "an altogether inadequate way of expressing the determination of Britain to defend itself and to finally win this war, or to accenting in your own mind the urgent military and naval necessities here." [28] If Hopkins had not been convinced of the necessity for intervention, the mission to England converted him. He went home determined to spread the Word.

It appeared the President had little need for Hopkins' evangelism. In private conversation he admitted a personal commitment to the struggle against Axis tyranny. When in January Wendell Willkie visited England with Roosevelt's blessing, the President penned a brief note to Churchill, expressing better than any other statement his sympathy with England's trial. In his own hand and from memory, Roosevelt inscribed: "Dear Churchill, Wendell Willkie will give you this . . . I think this verse applies to your people as it does to us. 'Sail on, Oh Ship of State/ Sail on Oh Union strong and great/ Humanity with all its fears/ With all the hope of future years/ Is hanging breathless on thy fate.'" [29] The practical Churchill probably thought how much more valuable would have been a declaration of war, or even an additional ten destroyers; the romantic Churchill cabled the President that he "was deeply moved by the verse of Longfellow's," and that he intended to have it framed "as a souvenir of these tremendous days, and as a mark of our friendly relations which have been built up telegraphically but also telepathically under all the stresses." [30]

Until the two leaders could meet, the medium for telegraphic and "telepathic" communications was Harry Hopkins. To strengthen his sensitivity to the Prime Minister and to complete the numerous tours, Hopkins stayed much longer than planned. By the end of January, however, he was ready to return. In truth he was homesick. On January 30, the night of F.D.R.'s annual birthday celebration with the Cuff Links Gang, Hopkins wistfully cabled how much he wished he could be with the President, "but at about 1 A.M. as you are setting down to dinner with the old friends I too will raise my glass and wish you long life and good health." [31] A few days later, having accomplished the major purpose of their meeting, Hopkins and Churchill bid each other au revoir, and Roosevelt's assistant undertook the wearisome journey back to Washington.

*

1

The meeting Hopkins and his two great friends so desired was delayed. Despite good intentions, the lend-lease debate lasted longer than expected and Roosevelt had to recognize that an extended absence from Washington was not possible until the appropriations bill had been approved and arrangements for allocation of aid worked out. F.D.R. signed the Lend-Lease Act on March 11, and then he pressed for agreement on time and place for the meeting. Now Churchill was compelled to request postponement: British intervention in Greece and the drawn-out agony of withdrawal as panzer divisions rolled through the Balkans demanded that Churchill, a Prime Minister who could not refrain from generalship, not leave England. The debacle of Crete followed in May, causing such political and military turmoil that Churchill once more was unable to get away.[32]

President Roosevelt acquiesced in the second and then third deferment. It may be that he was beginning to understand the problems of bringing off his ambitious project. One may speculate that his carefully planned cruise through the Bahamas in March originally was intended as cover for a meeting with the Prime Minister.[33] If so, F.D.R. should have been thankful Churchill could not attend then and there. The *Potomac*, caught in gale-force winds, at one point almost capsized. The tight quarters, which caused added friction between several of Roosevelt's combative advisers, made evident that more elaborate arrangements were required if a Roosevelt-Churchill conference were to proceed smoothly.[34] There were other drawbacks to a meeting in the Caribbean. Mustering place and crossroads for Allied shipping, it had attracted Nazi agents and some German submarines. This fact and the dense populations of those islands with adequate harbors militated against a secret meeting. Besides, the Prime Minister would encounter considerable danger in reaching a Caribbean rendezvous. He would be forced to make the crossing by air, since the perils in a diagonal traverse of U-boat-infested convoy routes were far too great. Flying had its own dangers. Churchill must pass awkwardly near to German-held territory, and the specter of the Luftwaffe intercepting and shooting down his plane was frighteningly real. Were Churchill called back to London because of some urgent development, he must return by air, and the Germans, forewarned, might prepare a disturbing reception off Bordeaux or Brest.[35]

For physical, political, and symbolic reasons it was necessary that Churchill undertake the larger part of the journey, that the Old World come, as it were, cap-in-hand to the New. F.D.R. could not go to England. Politically it would be suicidal; and the chance, even the one in a million chance, that a churning torpedo, machine-gun bullet or shrapnel from a stray bomb might cut him down made such a journey inconceivable. Roosevelt also quickly concluded that a meeting with the Prime Minister in the United States was out. Such a visit could not be kept secret and, therefore, the Germans would be primed for the return voyage. There would be violent reaction from isolationists and, likely, a campaign of speculation about the purposes of the visit which would cancel out its beneficial effects.[36]

The President considered the possibility of visiting Ottawa (a visit by him to the Canadian capital had been in the works for some time and was public knowledge), being met by a cruiser at Quebec, and sailing, without newsmen, "ostensibly to survey the defenses of the lower St. Lawrence." This plan had several good points and, Roosevelt admitted, one large defect. It would be "difficult" to explain beforehand why Mackenzie King was not to accompany the President on his tour of inspection and afterward why he had not been invited to participate in the conferences. As Roosevelt, referring to Prime Minister King, later, said: "I really couldn't take him." [37] Still, the visit-to-Canada ploy had much to recommend it.

2

The issues of secrecy and timing took on greater importance as Roosevelt's expectations for the conference evolved. His eagerness to meet with Churchill remained primary but, as usual, his reasoning was complicated. He certainly did not ignore the powerful effects upon morale of a dramatization of Anglo-American solidarity.

For some time after the passage of Lend-Lease President Roosevelt seemed of two minds about the project. He was still convinced of the need for private talks with Churchill, but the malaise which gripped F.D.R. during this period blocked energetic planning. Hopes that Lend-Lease offered a rationale for United States policy satisfying to advocates and opponents of intervention alike, that "all aid short of war" would unite his countrymen, were quickly dashed. The nation was drifting toward disaster; the President recognized the danger but, apparently, was unable to seize the rudder and to call for sufficient motive power to avert a calamity.

F.D.R. had a singular perception of the *mésalliance* between the Presidency and public opinion. While possessing unshakable faith in the abstractions of the democratic process, he demonstrated rather less confidence in the electorate's ability to arrive at mature, considered judgments in practice. Roosevelt was often disturbingly paternalistic, assuming that the role of the President was that of a kindly but firm teacher, giving his pupils precepts for right action. The previous eight years had shown F.D.R. to be without peer as a pedagogue and practitioner of the arts of political persuasion as well as a master magician and actor.[38]

The chief ingredient in the President's success was the aura of confidence he exuded — confidence in himself and in the strength and resourcefulness of the American people. In crisis after crisis, the infectious smile, that ebullient wave, the gift of phrasing lofty sentiments in breezy, unaffected language captivated the nation and revived belief in the bright promise of the future. Even bitter enemies of the New Deal were caught by the mesmeric appeal of the "snake charmer" in the White House. Roy Howard, head of the Scripps–Howard newspaper empire, admitted as much in March, 1941: "Roosevelt has shown an ability to muster mass support such as has been seldom seen in this country," he wrote Alf Landon. "Bryan used to be able to hypnotize them with his oratory but they wouldn't stay put. When Roosevelt hypnotizes them, they seem to stay right in the trance until he's ready to let them out of it." [39]

One American disagreed entirely with Howard's assessment of the President's hold over the popular mind. That man was Franklin

Roosevelt. No other conclusion explains the President's actions in spring and summer, 1941. He apparently thought the magic touch no longer worked, that he faced "a new ball game" in which the brand of aggressive, exuberant leadership that had scored so impressively in the struggle against economic depression was not effective. [40] Whether he was correct is in dispute; Roosevelt's earlier feats of leadership rested upon public receptivity to bold action. "Do something" had been the cry in 1933, and F.D.R. had responded to the universal clamor. No comparable mandate, not even a state of tolerant apathy seemed to exist in this foreboding time of international crisis.[41]

Roosevelt was an assiduous student of public opinion polls and he gained from his study confirmation of his own "hunches" about the futility and foolhardiness of his taking a consistently advanced position. The American people were enmeshed in contradictions. Overwhelmingly desirous of British victory and favoring material contributions to that end, the vast majority of Americans wanted, nevertheless, at all costs to stay out of the conflict. When William Allen White, that American-as-apple-pie newspaper editor, wrote from Emporia, Kansas — "I am one of those in the 75 percent of Americans who, for a year, have been ringing up in the Gallup Poll as favoring the President's foreign policy. I am also one of the 95 percent who have been ringing up in the Gallup Poll for this same period as wishing to avoid war" — Roosevelt was compelled to accept his logic.[42] In the absence of the raw material of consensus, F.D.R. believed frank, assertive leadership would be self-defeating. Its indiscriminate application would cause the fearful beast of public opinion to lash out, shattering present support for the President's policy of gradualism, rejecting his leadership and, possibly, resulting in his impeachment and removal from office.[43]

Roosevelt also believed that the bold stand regarding Lend-Lease had moved him far in advance of majority thinking.[44] The task before him, as it had been in 1937 when he had turned to full involvement with foreign affairs, was education. Recalling the President's state of mind, Samuel I. Rosenman has written that his boss "knew that we could do what we had to do only if Americans realized that

we had to do it — only if they recognized the urgency of the day." [45]
In 1941 Roosevelt found tutorship a frustrating, often onerous, assignment. Classroom discipline had broken down; it was difficult to
gain the attention of the students; most disturbing, troublemakers
who claimed to represent the press denounced his lectures as fabri-
cations and distortions of the truth. In a letter to Mrs. Ogden Mills
Reid, wife of the publisher of the New York *Herald Tribune,* Roosevelt described certain of the limitations under which he labored.
Mrs. Reid had claimed that "the thinking among Americans is a long
way ahead of Congress. They are strong at the core, they can stand
strong stuff." [46] She urged that the President tell the country frankly
of the dangers it faced and of the sacrifices it must accept. Roosevelt
agreed with the first conclusion, but to Mrs. Reid's demand for blunt
speaking he responded,

> The government has followed a steady course but it must be re-
> membered that the government cannot change its "editorial" policy
> overnight. The people write our editorials, the Congress reads and
> acts and passes the job on to the Executive branch . . . The process
> requires time — a much longer time than it takes to set up the type
> that fills a column . . .

Mrs. Reid had commented that she presently favored universal
military service, although she had been a lifelong pacifist. F.D.R.
replied, "From what extremes do the pendulums swing for us as individuals. Governments, such as ours, cannot swing so far or so
quickly. They can only move in keeping with the thought and will of
the great majority of our people." When the President ventured an
opinion and was "criticized and charged with spreading war hys-
teria," he had to conclude that rapid movement simply was not possible.[47]

Franklin Roosevelt certainly chafed under the restrictions this passive role placed upon him. It may be that as he carried forward
plans for the meeting with Churchill, he began to grasp its potential
for easing those restrictions. It seemed a marvelous pedagogical device, and such opportunities for him to act out and expound upon
some incident had been nonexistent in recent months. James Mac-

Gregor Burns has written: "The lack of an overt act deprived the President of the weapon he needed — the chance to dramatize a *situation*, to interpret an *event*. He needed such an opportunity to arouse the people and, even more, to galvanize Congress." [48] What effects might not the bombshell of a Roosevelt-Churchill conference, prefaced by some stirring call for unity in the confrontation between good and evil, have upon attitudes at home and in Great Britain? If the targets were chosen properly, the charge shaped to explode in the desired direction, the detonation perfectly timed, it might be of immeasurable value. Perhaps a secret meeting of the democracies' two great leaders was *the* event for which he longed.

Others saw different advantages to accrue. Secretary of War Stimson reported a conversation with William Herridge, who "was very anxious to have a dramatic stage-up between Roosevelt and Churchill which will show that there is no possibility of division of policy between them." [49] Ickes wrote in June that it might be "the psychological time" for calling the meeting in Washington of the "parliament of democracies" suggested earlier in the year by Frank Knox. Roosevelt's reply to this idea reveals that his thoughts about a meeting with Churchill had begun to jell. He told Ickes he doubted whether any "restatement" of goals by such a diverse group "would be as effective from the standpoint you have in mind [its effect upon morale] as the statements of the heads of those important countries now bearing the brunt of resistance against Hitlerism." After all, the big nations had the guns; and a meeting such as Ickes was proposing would include large numbers of representatives of small nations "and would probably give rise to a certain amount of confusion and muddying of issues." [50] F.D.R. was determined to retain control of any meeting called for purposes of shaping opinion. In his view, such an affair would be successful only if it met his necessary criteria: secrecy, drama, proper timing, and of course, really important actors. If properly handled, all could be present in the meeting with Churchill.

❋

3

F.D.R. left no explanation of his reasons for pushing forward with the conference. Indeed, sole evidence of his continued interest in the project between mid-March and mid-July rests on secret conversations be held with Vice-Admiral Ernest J. King, at that time Commander in Chief of the Atlantic Fleet. Their tête-à-têtes in April–June had all the hallmarks of a spy thriller. Admiral King, temporarily in Washington, received a telephone call on April 18 from one of the President's secretaries. She informed him the President wished to see him at Hyde Park the next afternoon. When King arrived, F.D.R., "driving his specially-built Ford himself, took him through his Christmas-tree nursery and up the hill to his secluded stone cottage." Roosevelt wanted to be certain they had privacy. Presumably he checked doors and windows for eavesdroppers before waving the bemused King toward a comfortable, floral print-covered chair and telling him of his desire for a "carefully concealed meeting" with the Prime Minister of Great Britain "about the middle of May." The reason he gave Admiral King was simple. Mentioning his and Churchill's frequent communications, F.D.R. complained that "those friendly relations were not the equivalent of a heart-to-heart talk." [51]

The President wished advice on the best site for the meeting from the standpoints of secrecy, accessibility, and security. Roosevelt said his first thought had been to go to Ottawa to return the recent visit of the Canadian Prime Minister and, afterward, to proceed by rail and cruiser to meet Churchill at Argentia, Newfoundland. The United States Navy was building an air station there on the shores of Placentia Bay and, thus, naval air protection would be added to the guns of a screen of American and British warships. [52]

King found flaws in this plan. The first concerned the President's idea of traveling by rail to some port on Canada's east coast. For reasons of security possible points of embarkation narrowed to those few Canadian ports with rail connections south of the St. Lawrence River. King brought up the further difficulty of the unpredictable ice conditions in this region, and F.D.R. and the Admiral chose Gaspé (Quebec) on the eastern side of the Gaspé Peninsula "as the most likely port at which the President could quietly board a cruiser" for the voyage to Newfoundland. King stressed the need for more knowledge of ice conditions, and "as the President readily understood the problem" he ordered King to check this question and other points.[53]

To prevent speculation about his interest in such matters as river ice, F.D.R. devised a complicated stratagem. When ready to discuss the project, Roosevelt would inform Admiral King by calling him on the telephone and making "a prearranged cryptic remark about ice." The call, with its mumbo-jumbo message, came at the end of April during the Admiral's next visit to the Navy Department. King hurried to the White House. Lack of time plus the difficulty of keeping secret a twenty-four-hour rail trip, he reported, made the plan impracticable. Under the circumstances the proposed date for the meeting would have to be set back.[54]

Hiding his disappointment, F.D.R. said he had half-conceived a different, bolder plan for traveling to Argentia entirely by sea. He would not elaborate the details, but he did promise his co-conspirator information "in a month or two." The President again invoked strict secrecy, asking that King not divulge their conversations to anyone, including his superior, Admiral Harold R. Stark.[55]

Roosevelt did little more in tandem with anyone, including Churchill, to advance the project until mid-July. He kept his own counsel and spent much time perfecting a ruse to conceal his movements to and from the meeting. The need for absolute secrecy so preoccupied him that he put off other matters until the last minute. There were no exchanges of views on agenda or the size, composition, and functions of accompanying staffs. Not even the essentials of "when" and "where" were given final confirmation. Of course, Roosevelt and Churchill, the central figures in the conspiracy, were agreed that initiative for all these decisions must repose with the President.

III. Final Preparations

WITH HOPKINS once more acting as intermediary, in late July F.D.R. and Churchill came to agreement on a date and place. Roosevelt got his way on the conference site. He always had preferred Newfoundland and believed a rendezvous at Bermuda to be impractical "on account of the long and rather dangerous replaning hop from there to England in case Churchill had to hurry back." [1] Besides, President Roosevelt assumed the Prime Minister would jump at a chance to test his sea legs aboard some great warship. Newfoundland merged perfectly with F.D.R.'s scheme for eluding journalistic bloodhounds.

Hopkins was instructed to arrange exact dates with the Prime Minister, whom he was dispatched to see in mid-July. This second trip by Hopkins was as sudden as his first. Quite possibly the President had promised to send back his aide when the time came for final preparations. At any rate, on Friday, July 11, he called Hopkins in for a long talk and informed him of his imminent departure for London.[2] Roosevelt cabled the new United States Ambassador, John G. Winant, that evening: "Hopkins goes to England very soon for a short visit. Please tell Former Naval Person." [3] This time Churchill knew who Harry Hopkins was and why he was coming. Winant, who was close to Hopkins but knew nothing of the visit's purpose, replied that the Prime Minister "was delighted to hear Harry was coming," adding, "so am I." [4]

"Very soon" to an impatient President Roosevelt — who believed all omens were favorable for the meeting — meant the same day. Saturday, July 12, was one of the more hectic days in Hopkins' career. Most of it he spent "boning up" on problems the British were sure to raise. Early Saturday he breakfasted with Sidney Hillman, with whom he discussed production difficulties. He lunched with Sumner Welles, who reviewed diplomatic matters at issue between Great Britain and the United States. The afternoon sped by in a flurry of conferences on shipping and supply problems. Roosevelt's confidant ended an exhausting day at the British Embassy as dinner guest of Lord Halifax. Early next morning he boarded a B-17 being ferried to England.[5]

Hopkins carried only the briefest of instructions on issues to be treated at the conference. In notes of his final talks with the President were three items: "Economic or territorial deals — NO; Harriman not policy; No talk about war." [6] Of these the second point referred not to the conference but to an awkward situation that had arisen between Ambassador Winant and Averell Harriman, Lend-Lease "expediter" in London. Although they were close friends, Winant had been deeply injured by Harriman's intimacy with British officials, especially Churchill. London bypassed the Embassy because Harriman, as Lend-Lease representative, could deliver the goods.[7]

The first and third items on Hopkins' memo dealt with issues relevant to an agenda. "Economic or territorial deals — NO" spoke for itself. Roosevelt desired that the British (and implicitly the Russians) make no promises concerning economic or territorial adjustments, for propaganda or any other motive.[8] F.D.R. agreed with Woodrow Wilson's view that such questions must await resolution at a peace conference, removed from the feverish atmosphere of wartime.[9] He expressed these feelings directly while Hopkins was en route, a clear indication of his anxiety that the Prime Minister appreciate his position. On July 14 Winant received a cable for transmission to No. 10 Downing Street. The message referred to rumors concerning British negotiations with certain governments-in-exile about territorial adjustments.[10] Also in question was a proposed Anglo-Soviet treaty of alliance, which was rumored to have secret articles providing for postwar boundary and political arrangements. The cable requested explanation of these supposed activities. Winant soon replied that he had delivered the message personally and ventured the opinion, "I know he feels as you do on this subject." He reported that Churchill had asked his Foreign Secretary, Anthony Eden, to draw up a statement covering all situations and that this was to go immediately to Washington.[11] Nothing was heard, however, until the two leaders met at Argentia. At that time the reasons for British procrastination became evident.

The third point — no talk about war — was both patently clear and impossible. It was another manifestation of the President's schizophrenic outlook regarding United States participation in the war. No one, not his chief advisers, not Churchill, not even Hopkins, claimed to know President Roosevelt's ultimate intentions. Most assumed that the sequential steps of the past two years would lead, sooner or later, to full intervention, and that F.D.R. was making ready the country for that last stride. Many years later Arthur Krock said he was convinced: "Since his [the President's] belief was the American people would not stand for open preparation for war, he would have to deceive them about it and do the best he could along that line but denying it." [12] Observers were assuming F.D.R.'s policy was rational; as Hamilton Fish Armstrong commented to the President in June, "I have watched with admiration in these last weeks the gradual development of your program of aid to Britain. I think I understand your ultimate objective and your cogent reasons for wishing to proceed step by step, leaving the final decision to an overt act by the enemies of the United States or to the development of an even greater public demand here." [13] Krock, Armstrong, and the others who held this opinion may have been in error. Roosevelt was never notably guided by logic, and there is considerable evidence that he continued to hold the belief that victory was possible without direct intervention by the United States.[14]

He was unready and unwilling to face this central question, especially if it were posed by Prime Minister Churchill. Believing the most serious threat to mutual understanding was the issue of American intervention, F.D.R. desired to abolish this issue by ignoring it. For various reasons, not least of which was the domestic political situation, he had determined that Churchill and his lieutenants be made to promise not to raise the subject. Hopkins received the assignment of persuading the Prime Minister.

There was little chance Churchill would give in on this point. American intervention had become the Prime Minister's guiding principle. At the time of Dunkirk he had promised England that the New World in all its power and might would come to the rescue of the Old.[15] Much of the amazing British spirit of determination rested on faith that someday soon the Yanks were coming. In recent months, with no sign out of the West, trust in American nobility had flagged.

From outside, it was believed the constant air attacks, the military reverses of spring and early summer, with other frustrations, were battering at the English people's will to resist.[16] In Great Britain war weariness was attributed to another cause: the failure of the United States to come into the war. One of Joseph Davies' English correspondents admitted as much in early August:

> For many months past we have been hoping and anticipating the entry of the United States into the war. Now I fear it is a case of "hope deferred maketh the heart sick." I am sorry to say that there has been a tendency during the last few weeks to depreciate the assistance and help which we receive from Washington. A month or two ago any allusion at a public meeting to the Lease and Lend Act and to the material benefits which you so kindly and generously shower upon us was cheered to the echo. But only a few days ago a Member of Parliament told me that he had tried deliberately to evoke cheers for the United States with little or no response, but that when he alluded to Russia there was an immediate reaction which almost took the roof off the building.[17]

The growing skepticism among his countrymen was a major factor in forcing Churchill to reiterate the logical inevitability of United States intervention. Significantly, after Hopkins' arrival, the Prime Minister asserted in the House of Commons that America was "advancing with rising wrath and conviction to the very verge of war." [18] His subordinates took America over the verge in a number

of well-timed speeches. For example, Lord Beaverbrook, the puck-
ish Minister of Supply, spelled out five reasons why the United
States must and would enter the conflict in a signed article in *American Magazine.*[19] Domestic problems being what they were, the
British government was not about to let pass any opportunity to restore morale (and to realize Churchill's vision of a victorious Anglo-
American coalition) merely to spare President Roosevelt's sensibili-
ties.[20]

The President was to remain adamant, for he had a stronger motive than indecision for avoidance of the subject. Justified or not,
F.D.R. feared congressional reaction to a meeting with Churchill.[21]
He wanted to be free to state without contradiction from his leak-
prone entourage that American intervention had not been at issue.
He believed even at this late date that Congress might impeach him
if it could unearth evidence he had assumed war powers which the
Constitution accorded to the legislative branch. Even if Roosevelt
had confided this fear to the Prime Minister it would have had little
effect. For all his pride in being half-American and ostensibly understanding of the American system of government, Churchill was a
parliamentarian. Problems resulting from tension between legislative and executive power in the United States escaped him.[22] Roosevelt's anxiety about Congress would not, as Harry Hopkins foresaw,
restrain the Prime Minister from moving to the all-important question at the first and any opportunity. The effect of a direct clash on
this issue could not be predicted, but the potential for grief was
large.[23]

1

Hopkins' mission to England in July was much changed in tone
and approach from the one some six months earlier. Now the British
welcomed him as a friend, an advocate of all-out United States aid
without regard to consequences. By this second trip the Englishman-
in-the-street identified "Mr. Hurry-upkins" with Lend-Lease, the
American action with greatest meaning to the United Kingdom.

Roosevelt's envoy reached England on July 18, having flown via

Gander, Newfoundland, in a B-17. Although he was exhausted, Hopkins went at once to see the Prime Minister. He reported a meeting in the very near future was now definite. He had received final confirmation.[24] In his memoirs Churchill described with studied naïveté this corroboration of the oft-attempted conference. "One afternoon in late July," he innocently confided to readers, "Harry Hopkins came into the garden of Downing Street and we sat together in the sunshine. Presently he said that the President would like very much to have a meeting with me in some lonely bay or other." The Prime Minister claimed he replied casually he would like nothing better and was confident the War Cabinet would give its permission.[25]

A "final" date and place was soon fixed. Churchill agreed to come to Placentia Bay, Newfoundland, and set the time of his arrival for Friday, August 8, or Saturday, August 9.[26] The United Kingdom delegation would, of course, be transported by the most modern British battleship available. The Prime Minister gave first thought to *King George V*, first and most famous of the class bearing its name; but after consultation he asked for the battle-tested *Prince of Wales*.[27] This was an agonizing decision. Use of either warship as a transport, the most powerful one ever, seriously weakened England's battleship strength in the Northern Approaches. However, *Prince of Wales* was just completing refit after its clash with *Bismarck*, and delaying its return to service by a fortnight was much the lesser of two evils.

Once transportation had been arranged, Churchill had to select a staff to accompany him. As natural, the size and importance of the supporting delegations ascended. While the project remained in discussion the two principals had tended to view it as a dramatic, entirely personal encounter. Presence of a powerful naval armada would provide a perfect backdrop. High officers of the British and United States governments, whose participation would detract from the solitary splendor of a Roosevelt-Churchill meeting "in some lonely bay or other," would not be needed.[28]

The President favored an intimate meeting, but Churchill exhibited second thoughts once the conference became imminent. Probably he reasoned that a wiser if less dramatic method of exerting maximum pressure for his confessed aim — to bring the United States into the war — demanded a large group of advisers and experts.

At first the Prime Minister limited his entourage to military and naval authorities. He may have thought the testimony of men experienced in this strange new kind of warfare would sway President Roosevelt. At the least, they would put across the British point of view to their American counterparts whom F.D.R. undoubtedly would now bring. Churchill cabled on July 25 that he had secured permission from his War Cabinet.[29] (He also had informed the Dominions' Prime Ministers that he was soon to meet with the President of the United States. This was not merely courtesy, because Churchill "hoped that from the meeting some momentous agreement might be reached which would require ratification by the Dominions."[30]) He notified the President that he intended to bring an array of military and naval expertise, including the First Sea Lord, Admiral Sir Dudley Pound; Chief of the Imperial General Staff, Field Marshal Sir John Dill; and Air Vice-Marshal Wilfred Freeman. Two other officers, Lord Ismay, the Prime Minister's most trusted professional adviser, and Air Chief Marshal Portal, were to be left behind to "mind the shop."[31]

Hopkins supported the idea of bringing in military men. "The problems of supply and other matters so important that I earnestly hope you can bring Marshall and Arnold with you," he wrote the President on July 26.[32] It would also, he thought, "be useful for Marshall to learn something of the British Army point of view."[33] This argument, pointing to the urgency of consultation and understanding between the chief military figures of the two nations, was difficult to refute.

Some days later Churchill informed Washington he was again expanding the British delegation. Perhaps because of pressure from the joint chiefs he added representatives of Defence and Admiralty planning staffs. Corresponding pressure from the Foreign Office led to last-minute inclusion of a professional diplomat, Sir Alexander Cadogan, Permanent Under Secretary of State for Foreign Affairs. The Foreign Office breathed easier, for Cadogan's presence made certain there would be systematic examination of certain issues at Argentia. Whether such matters as policy toward Japan, response to the German threat in the Mediterranean, and Anglo-American policy vis-à-vis the Soviet Union would have had full discussion at a meeting of Roosevelt and Churchill alone is impossible to say.

These additions found graceful acceptance in the White House. The President made only one objection, which was minor but characteristic. The British Admiralty on July 27 made a recommendation that Loon Bay, on the west coast of Newfoundland, be the site of the meeting. For some reason, suddenly, serious objection to Argentia had been raised. Writing about this afterward the President stated: "My Naval advisers and I told the British Admiralty we much preferred Argentia Harbor . . . especially as that was the new base recently placed in commission . . . and already fitted with radio and manned by a number of planes, minesweepers, etc. The British Admiralty acceded to this choice." [34] Roosevelt's insistence upon Argentia was transparent. He wanted to extract every benefit from the meeting; and he would not surrender such a choice one as conferring with the Prime Minister under a protective shield of United States warships, shore-based artillery, and combat aircraft.

The decision to bring brass and gold braid and Churchill's injection of a diplomat into the proceedings did cause F.D.R. anxious moments. He was not much concerned about the diminution in dramatic effect that their presence presaged. That could be compensated for, and he appreciated the advantage of diplomatic and military conversations under his and Churchill's supervision. Anxiety derived from the strain which enlargement of the meeting placed on his elaborate precautions to ensure absolute secrecy. Prolonged absence of top advisers from their duties, while the President was away from Washington, would surely lead to speculation.

F.D.R.'s efforts to minimize this threat were unexpectedly successful. The first principle of his "security system" was restriction of information concerning the conference to as few people as possible. The President carried this rule to startling lengths. General George C. Marshall and Admiral Harold R. Stark were not informed until just three or four days before departure, and Roosevelt forbade them to let General Henry H. Arnold, Chief of the Air Corps, into the secret until zero hour plus one. Nor could Marshall and Stark tell the handful of subordinates picked to accompany them.[35]

This iron rule of silence extended to President Roosevelt's official family. Neither Secretary of War, Henry L. Stimson, nor Secretary of the Navy, Frank Knox, had any idea a Roosevelt-Churchill meeting was being arranged. The august Secretary of State, Cordell Hull, had known of the exploratory messages between the White House and London in the spring, but he had been ill and was recuperating at White Sulphur Springs during July and he was not told anything was afoot until his return to Washington on August 5. The White House staff also was kept in the dark about the real purpose of the boss' fishing trip.[36]

As noted, the President's second security principle was to inform those he had selected to accompany him as late as conceivably possible. Admiral King was in on the secret from the beginning, although he was not told of the route. Marshall and Stark learned of the project when called to the White House on the afternoon of July 30.[37] Breaking the news, F.D.R. cautioned his chiefs to devise logical covers for their absences—a tall order under the circumstances. Their hurriedly constructed stories would not withstand determined investigation but for several days no one, not even their civil superiors, thought to question them. The President's "mania" for secrecy was observed — at high cost in preparation by the U.S. military and naval authorities for meeting their British opposites.

Fortunately, Roosevelt selected Under Secretary Sumner Welles, a friend and adviser, to represent the Department of State. Welles' knowledge of foreign affairs and intimate involvement with questions of postwar policy made him a perfect choice. Besides, he was one of the few State Department officials of any rank whose abilities and judgment the President trusted. Welles was a fellow Grotonian, a Harvard man, and this established an "old school tie" relationship which proved extremely strong. Some years younger than the President, Welles had been a page boy in F.D.R.'s wedding, and they possessed numerous family and social ties.

According to the press, which held Welles in puzzled awe, the Under Secretary had been born with a silver spoon in his mouth and was swaddled in striped pants. Welles was the quintessential diplomat. *Time* said, "He has a firm hold on every one of the diplomatic virtues: he is absolutely precise, imperturbable, accurate, honest, sophisticated, thorough, cultured, traveled, financially established." Certainly Welles presented a formidable appearance. He was six feet three inches tall, always dressed impeccably in Savile Row suits, and had a resonant, precise voice which recalled the deep tones of Basil Rathbone. Reporters were fond of such labels for him as "glacially toplofty" and "a tall glass of distilled ice water"; however, Welles was not merely "an intelligent Tory" as Robert Bendiner once claimed. His brilliance served not a class but rather the nation and, insofar as cold calculation allowed, the cause of international peace and cooperation.[38]

Welles entered diplomatic service in 1921. Having decided the most rapid route to high position was the ill-attended Bureau for Latin American Affairs — then considered a career dead end — he parleyed quickly won expertise into a meteoric rise in the Department. Welles resigned in 1925 because of policy differences with President Coolidge. He served as an unofficial adviser to Roosevelt before the latter assumed office and soon thereafter returned to the Department, once more with responsibility for Latin America. In 1937 F.D.R. had Welles appointed Under Secretary of State. As his duties and interests expanded, Welles was increasingly used by the President as counselor and confidant. This easy access to the White House by a subordinate first antagonized and finally alienated Cordell Hull. By 1940 the strained relations between Hull and Welles were common gossip, and the Secretary was threatening to resign "because the President very obviously seeks Sumner Welles' advice in preference to his own." Careerists said that though Welles was "an exceedingly able man — a brilliant fellow," he was shockingly disloyal and disrespectful to his Chief. This willingness to ignore "channels" did not sit well with Hull or many State officials; however, the President was apt to regard any violation of the bureaucratic canon as a virtue. He continued to deal with Welles and to bypass his Secretary of State — as was demonstrated by the secret invitation to the Under Secretary to go to Argentia. Even later than Marshall and Stark, Welles learned of the long-awaited meeting with Churchill and that he was to go. He knew Roosevelt's ardor for a meeting, but the news still came as a surprise. Welles did a remarkable job of arranging things in the Department and of preparing for the conference. As Acting Secretary in Hull's absence he found it difficult to get away. He did not accompany the President's party, but in company with Averell Harriman flew up to Newfoundland on August 8, arriving just a half day before Prime Minister Churchill.[39]

Welles somehow found time to set down a rough draft of a declaration of war and peace aims. At some time before his departure, President Roosevelt indicated a desire for such a statement so that the approaching meeting would "hold out hope to the enslaved peoples of the world." Welles prepared a document which combined the President's ideas with principles derived from studies of the Department of State.[40]

Other than this one matter (which might prove all-encompassing) and the points Harry Hopkins transmitted to Churchill, setting down guidelines for diplomatic discussions relied upon educated guesswork. For differing reasons Roosevelt and Churchill both preferred a flexible agenda. Each expected conversations to range, if informally, over "pertinent" subjects. Prime Minister Churchill was to write of his expectation that "a conference between us would proclaim the ever closer association of Britain and the United States, would cause our enemies concern, make Japan ponder, and cheer our friends." Hardly a specific list, this statement did refer to certain obvious questions: American intervention in the Atlantic, aid to Russia, "the increasing menace" of Japan.[41]

Two matters, clearly, were high on the mental agenda of both leaders. Japan headed the list, and not far behind came the new situation occasioned by Hitler's attack against the Soviet Union. The Russian bear's success in defending itself, and Roosevelt and Churchill's opinions regarding its chances, conditioned every issue, present and future, raised at Argentia. Disposition of Lend-Lease aid, the thrust of diplomatic approaches to Russia, and the strategic consequences of this new development in Eurasia required full discussion. Still, because of almost complete lack of knowledge about Russian military strength, American and British leaders had little on which to base these crucial decisions. In making arrangements, Roosevelt and Churchill seem tacitly to have postponed the Russian question in hope that events would light up the blackness.

2

Harry Hopkins was not content to shunt aside the Soviet Union. He knew discussions at Argentia would be *in vacuo* "without some real knowledge of the situation and the prospects on the Russian front." In an audacious display of "personal diplomacy" Hopkins proposed to answer these questions by going himself to Moscow and bearding Premier Joseph Stalin in his lair.[42]

It is unclear who first suggested this idea; probably Hopkins was responsible. Recollections of Churchill, Winant, and Harriman all support this conclusion.[43] Hopkins had a penchant for direct solutions to problems that baffled his more complex superiors. Whoever suggested the mission, it received unreserved backing from Churchill and Roosevelt. At the beginning of his second English stay Hopkins inquired of the Prime Minister if it were possible to fly to Moscow and return within a week. When he learned the R.A.F. Coastal Command had opened an air route to Archangel, the President's envoy confided to Churchill his plan to see Stalin. The Prime Minister was unenthusiastic. He agreed that information regarding conditions in Russia would be valuable, and "that Stalin might agree to provide some part of it to the personal representative of the President." But the journey would be dangerous and exhausting. Churchill was reluctant to see Hopkins make further demands on his health.[44] There was a further reason for the P.M.'s hesitancy. Going to Moscow could prevent Hopkins from making the Atlantic crossing on *Prince of Wales* and might result in his missing all or part of the conference with President Roosevelt. Churchill had come to value Hopkins' friendship and advice too highly to permit that. He only dropped this objection when it became known that Hopkins could get back from Moscow in good time for the Argentia meeting.[45]

Excited by the prospect, Hopkins brushed aside objections. On Friday evening, July 25, he and Winant drafted a cable to Roosevelt asking permission for the adventure. "I am wondering whether you would think it important and useful for me to go to Moscow," Hopkins inquired cautiously. "Air transportation good," he claimed, praying F.D.R. would not look into the rigors of an Arctic flight to Russia. He urged that everything possible be done to maintain a Russian front: "If Stalin could in any way be influenced at this critical time I think it would be worth doing by a direct communication from you through a personal envoy . . . Stalin would then know we mean business on a long term supply job." [46] Implicit were the benefits the trip would bring to the Argentia discussions. Hopkins concluded with a footnote that he planned to leave England for the United States no later than Wednesday, July 30, if F.D.R. thought the Moscow trip inadvisable. Next evening the President's decision reached London. It was favorable. "Welles and I highly approve Moscow trip and assume you would go in a few days." [47] F.D.R. also was anxious that Hopkins get back in time to be at the meeting with Churchill.

With a presidential OK the next step was to request permission from the Soviet government; and no one could predict the result. The Communists proved practical, as permission came immediately.[48] Stalin evidently was better informed than had been Churchill of the place Hopkins occupied in President Roosevelt's circle.

American and British leaders showed equal awareness of the mission's advantages. Sumner Welles was most optimistic, and in his capacity as Acting Secretary of State did everything he could to ensure success. He drafted the message which the President sent to Hopkins for presentation to Premier Stalin. This note made clear the importance attached to the trip: "I am sending Mr. Hopkins to Moscow in order that he may discuss with you personally . . . the vitally important question of how the assistance which the United States is able to furnish the Soviet Union in its magnificent resistance against the treacherous aggression of Hitlerite Germany may be made available most expeditiously and most effectively." The message informed Stalin that Hopkins would communicate directly to the President the views expressed to him, and ended with the strong request: "I ask that you treat him with the same confidence as you would if you were talking with me personally." [49]

Winant received the assignment of locating Ivan Maisky, the Soviet Ambassador, to get a visa for Hopkins. He had a difficult time tracking the Ambassador, who had become sufficiently anglicized to participate in that hallowed British institution, the country weekend. When brought to earth Maisky scribbled a visa in his own handwriting and Winant returned the passport to Hopkins as his train was pulling out of Paddington Station.[50]

While these arrangements were in process Hopkins discussed with Churchill and his advisers the integration of British requirements into the "Victory Production Program" then being drawn up in Washington. Differences about grand strategy and economic and military calculations, which formed another topic for the agenda, were uncovered by these talks. In particular, the recent trip of Averell Harriman to the Middle East had reinforced American doubts about policy in that region.[51] Hopkins asked that the British try to understand the American attitude, for "we in the United States just simply do not understand your problems in the Middle East, and the interests of the Moslem world, and the interrelationship of your problems in Egypt and India." He claimed this was due to insufficient information, for "the President himself has never been given a comprehensive explanation of the Middle East campaign." [52] The Prime Minister attempted to correct this error by calling a meeting of the Admiralty Liaison Conference to which Hopkins and Harriman were invited. Churchill gave an exhaustive review of the military situation, the most revealing of any in the period before Argentia. Its summation dealt with the importance of the Mediterranean and the role American forces might play there:

> We could not prevent the harbor at Gibraltar being denied to us at any time, if the Germans chose to go down through Spain. Indeed they might press on through Morocco to Dakar. We certainly had not the resources to transport and operate several divisions in that area to oppose them, but this might be a fruitful area for operations by the United States if they wished to intervene with a military force. He had not, at any time, asked of the United States if they wished to provide soldiers, and at present there was certainly not the shipping which could transport them in large numbers. Later on, when the great ship-building programs had got into their stride, the situation might be different and it might be found that North and West Africa and Norway . . . would prove suitable theatres for United States forces to conduct operations.[53]

Churchill's words stayed with Hopkins who transmitted a summary of the address to the President. In addition, he and the Prime Minister arranged that Harriman leave "at once" to report "on all matters which we have discussed here in the last week." Hopkins thought it "essential" that the President "have a background of this before going to Canada." [54]

Hopkins then went off to Chequers for what was left of the weekend. He informed his host early Sunday of the go-ahead for the trip to Moscow. He decided to go on with a promised broadcast over the BBC, having cabled Roosevelt: "Will not upset the diplomatic applecart, so have the State Department keep their shirts on." [55] That Sunday at Chequers compared with Hopkins' last frantic day in Washington. Churchill decided Hopkins should leave that night for Invergordon on the east coast of Scotland and made all arrangements. After lunch, during which both men expressed pessimism about Russian chances, the President's envoy retired to his chilly bedroom to put final touches on his address.[56]

The popular war correspondent, Quentin Reynolds, had come to Chequers to help with the speech. He wrote a first draft which Hopkins rejected with words to the effect: "My God . . . You've got me declaring war against the Nazis." [57] Hopkins toned down the speech, but it remained a revealing statement of his convictions. "I arrived here from America one week ago on business," . . . he announced. "I did not come from America alone — I came in a bomber plane, and with me were twenty other bombers made in America. These airplanes tonight may be dropping bombs on Brest, on Hamburg, on Berlin." He described President Roosevelt's determination to help destroy "the ruthless power of that sinful psychopath of Berlin." Of his latest visit to England he said: "The President asked me to come over here. My instructions from him were these. 'Find out if the material we are sending to Britain is arriving. Find out if it is what Britain wants. Let me know if there is anything more that Britain needs.' " [58]

The above, including the hint about convoying, echoed President Roosevelt's feelings. The final portion, a litany of hope and promise extolling the mounting American assistance, was all Hopkins. He intoned,

> We in America may be three thousand miles away. But today the Atlantic is merely a channel. A bridge of friendship spans it; a bridge of sympathy and admiration extends from Washington to London . . . Your Prime Minister has asked us for the tools. I promise you they are coming; an endless assembly belt stretches from our western coast to this Island, and to the Middle East; that nothing will be allowed to interfere with the full efficiency of this supply line . . . President Roosevelt promised that he would take steps to ensure the delivery of goods consigned to Britain. Our President does not give his word lightly. People of Britain — people of the British Commonwealth of Nations — *you are not fighting alone*.[59]

If Hopkins' concluding statement represented Roosevelt's views, Prime Minister Churchill could look forward to a satisfactory conference. But by that time the Prime Minister may have realized that his friend Harry's rhetoric sometimes outdistanced facts. The facts dictated a confrontation on all the issues touched on in the long months of preparation for Argentia — and more.

Hopkins' mission to England in July took the conference to the brink of fulfillment. To the onlooker, movements of the principals in the next few days gave no hint. Hopkins' trip to Moscow, the announcement of an inspection trip by Prime Minister Churchill over the August Bank Holiday, F.D.R.'s upcoming cruise off New England all had no seeming connection.

IV. Down to the Sea in Ships

HARRY HOPKINS was first off the mark. Late Monday evening, July 28, an ungainly PBY flying boat, with Hopkins aboard, wallowed aloft from Cromarty Firth off Invergordon, Scotland, and headed eastward. Once again Hopkins was standing in for President Roosevelt, this time in consultations with Joseph Stalin, the dictator of Soviet Russia. The information he was to bring back from Moscow in an important sense transformed the Roosevelt-Churchill meeting into a three-power conference.[1]

Shortly after Roosevelt's aide delivered his BBC speech, he left the Prime Minister's country home for Scotland. Anxious that Stalin believe the British were giving all possible assistance to Russia, Churchill stopped Hopkins on the smooth green lawn outside Chequers to describe "in minutest detail" the efforts Great Britain was making and plans to get supplies to the Soviet Union. When Hopkins asked if he could repeat any of this confidential information to Stalin, the Prime Minister replied: "Tell him, tell him. Tell him that Britain has but one ambition . . . today, but one desire — to crush Hitler. Tell him that he can depend on us . . ."[2] The old Bolshevik-hater carefully restricted the promise of cooperation to the present emergency, but he left no doubt of British determination to help the Soviets and to make Hopkins his as well as President Roosevelt's representative.

Accompanying Hopkins were General Joseph T. McNarney and Lieutenant J. R. Alison, a pilot assigned to familiarize the Russians with the performance of the P-40 fighter. Bad weather conditions over the Arctic first caused postponement of the flight; but London was so anxious that Hopkins return in time to catch the *Prince of*

Wales that the pilot was ordered to ignore adverse weather. Partly because of that order, the flight was extremely rough. There had been no time to fit the passengers with proper flying equipment. They had to endure twenty-four hours of flying in freezing temperatures with only hardtack rations. For most of the trip Hopkins sat on a machine gunner's stool in a blister near the tail. Canvas stretchers were available to be used as bunks, but Hopkins suffered severely from the Arctic cold and got almost no sleep.[3]

On reaching Archangel the Americans underwent the further ordeal of a lengthy reception. Ambassador Laurence Steinhardt reported that the welcome accorded Hopkins by the Soviet government and the unusual coverage of his arrival by the Soviet press indicated that "extreme attention" was being given to the visit.[4] The airplane taking the party to Moscow was not to leave until 4:00 A.M., and a weary Hopkins hoped to catch a nap in a warm, vibration-free bed; however, he was pressed into accepting an invitation to dinner on the yacht of the local naval commander. The dinner fulfilled in every respect the stereotyped Russian official banquet: caviar, game, and tuns of vodka. Hopkins got to sleep at 1:30 Wednesday morning.[5]

The mission shortly was flying over the vast expanses of European Russia. During this four-hour trip "Hopkins began to be reassured as to the future of the Soviet Union. He looked down upon the hundreds of miles of solid forest and he thought that Hitler with all the panzer divisions in the Wehrmacht could never hope to break through country like this."[6] He was to meet few Americans in Russia who shared this opinion.

Steinhardt and another outsized Russian welcoming committee met Hopkins at the Moscow airport. The Ambassador took the President's personal representative directly to the Embassy and put him to bed, but Hopkins refused to rest. He was too excited about the Russian situation and prospects for United States military aid. Steinhardt was certainly interested in the latter subject, for little information about Washington's plans had reached him. Perhaps his pronounced distaste for the Russian Communist dictatorship had weakened his position. Hopkins was to state: "It was personally clear that Stalin had no confidence in our Ambassador or in any of our officials in Moscow." [7] His bias against diplomats was hard to overcome.

Back in Washington, President Roosevelt also was fond of blaming the State Department and its passion for "red tape" for the confusion which characterized U.S.-Soviet relations. F.D.R. had demonstrated sympathy for the Soviet Union from the outbreak of the Russo-German conflict. At his press conference on June 24 he said, "Of course we are going to give all the aid we possibly can to Russia. We have not yet received any specific list of things, and of course people must realize that you can't just go around to Mr. Garfinckel's and fill the order." [8] He pointed out that Great Britain had first claim upon American production. Within the next few days the administration did take steps to provide limited aid. Some $40 million in Soviet assets were "unfrozen" and the President announced he would not apply the provisions of the Neutrality Act to Russia. These were, as Raymond Dawson has shown, "gestures of good will" which did not commit the United States to a specific course of action. [9]

Roosevelt adopted a "wait and see" attitude because of his own uncertainty about the wisest course and because most of his advisers were convinced that Russia was doomed to quick, crushing defeat. [10] He also had to be careful of the deep antagonism of the public (and of many Department of State officials) toward "godless Russia." The long years of calculated insults and Marxist chauvinism, the refusal of Moscow to look beyond the short-term benefits of its appeasement of Germany had not been banished by the events of June 23, 1941. [11] Roosevelt understood his countrymen's distaste for Soviet opportunism, but he was inclined to look at the situation pragmatically, as a potentially tremendous accretion of strength to the struggle against Hitler. "Now comes the Russian diversion," he wrote Admiral Leahy on June 26. "If it is more than just that it will mean the liberation of Europe from Nazi domination — and at the same time I do not think we need worry about any possibility of Russian domination." [12] The significant point was that F.D.R., for some reason, refused to accept the judgment of his military advisers regarding the inevitability of a swift German victory. He began to claim confidently that the Russians would at least survive the summer and, therefore, they should be given "every possible encouragement" to continue resistance.[13]

On June 30 the Soviet Ambassador to Washington, Constantine Oumansky, submitted his government's first general request for American aid. This request was broken down — after several painful discussions — into a detailed list of demands totalling over $1,800,000,000. Oumansky's statement put emphasis upon Russia's urgent need for aircraft (3000 bombers and 3000 pursuit planes), antiaircraft guns, aviation fuel, and lubricants. Under Secretary Welles received this list sympathetically but could offer no encouragement that anything more than a symbolic response would be forthcoming. He did not feel free to inform Oumansky that a large part of the material on the list was not available even for United States forces.[14]

The President did ask the War and Navy Departments to report on which items could be given to the Soviets before October 1 — so that they could be used before the Russian winter halted large-scale operations. The President's intervention resulted in the eventual emergence of a "comprehensive list" of $21,940,000 in supplies. The Russians' plea for ordnance and aircraft had been completely ignored.[15] F.D.R. was decidedly unhappy with this "runaround" since he desired that the bulk of immediate aid be equipment which would go directly to the battlefront, bolstering Russian morale by its presence. At cabinet meeting on August 2 the President complained: "I am sick and tired of hearing that they are going to get this and they are going to get that . . . Whatever we are going to give them, it has to get over there by the first of October, and the only answer I want to hear is that it is under way." Specifically, he demanded that Stimson arrange to send some 190 fighters and 5 British and 5 U.S. bombers. The Secretary of War was to "get the planes right off with a bang next week."[16] This was a token response but important as demonstrating the administration's commitment to the Russian front. "American aid was to serve as tangible evidence to the Kremlin of America's unstinting cooperation with the Soviet Union. This, the White House hoped, would allay Soviet suspicions about the West and keep the Russians in the Allied alliance," Ronald Lukas has commented. He adds that the policy "made the American Air Force the sacrificial lamb on the altar of Soviet good will," although nobody but Marshall's hard-pressed staff knew how great a blow to the national defense was each plane given the Soviets.[17] When there was not enough to go around, priorities were necessary. That fact was known early in the game and Hopkins took with him to Moscow a proposal for a three-power supply conference to work out priorities.

First he required information about Russia's military capabilities. He asked Steinhardt bluntly whether the situation was as ominous as U.S. and British experts claimed. To Hopkins' surprise Steinhardt replied that Russia would not be easy to conquer. He described the tremendous obstacles facing foreigners who attempted to break down the walls of official suspicion and to obtain a clear picture of the battlefront. Hopkins said grimly that an assault on these barriers was the major purpose of his mission. Then he and Steinhardt went out on the balcony of the Embassy and watched Moscow's seventh major air raid.[18]

The Ambassador's ill-concealed skepticism changed to amazement as he watched hitherto locked doors swing open before Roosevelt's diminutive envoy. Thursday afternoon, after a sightseeing tour of Moscow (during which he noted how "insignificant" was the damage caused by German bombers the previous evening), Hopkins went to the Kremlin for his first meeting with Premier Stalin.[19] Promptly at 6:00 P.M. he was shown into Stalin's office, an immense room, simply furnished, "but with every modern, up-to-the-minute office facility." The walls were covered with maps, the finest Hopkins had ever seen. When the American entered, Stalin was seated behind a huge desk on which there were five or six telephones and a battery of push buttons. Though surprised by the Premier's small stature and severe dress, Hopkins thought him "simple, modest and democratic." There was no doubt, however, that Stalin was "top man, running the show," though for the American envoy the velvet glove only was displayed.[20] Hopkins presented President Roosevelt's introductory message. He explained through an interpreter that his mission was not diplomatic "in the sense that I did not propose any formal understanding of any kind or character." He conveyed the sentiments of the President and the Prime Minister with regard to support for Russia. Stalin replied in a most genial manner. He expressed belief that the policies of the Soviet Union, the United States, and Great Britain, in contrast to the immoral actions of Nazi Germany, coincided in their acceptance of "certain moral standards" for international society.[21]

Hopkins steered the discussion toward "practical" matters. He informed Stalin that the U.S. and U.K. needed answers to two questions: "What would Russia most require that the United States could deliver immediately and . . . what would be Russia's requirements on the basis of a long war?" Inclusion of the second question proved President Roosevelt did not subscribe to the well-nigh universal pessimism about Russian chances; his faith was justified, Hopkins believed, by Stalin's next remarks. After he had listed immediate Russian needs, the dictator turned to long-term requirements. He gave priority to high-octane aviation fuel, aluminum, and certain other raw materials. "Give us anti-aircraft guns and the aluminum and we can fight for three or four years," was his response to Hopkins' quizzical look. With a pose of great candor, he reviewed the numbers and quality of Russian equipment. When Hopkins expressed interest in having further discussions regarding the supply situation — with the Premier or with other officials — Stalin said, "You are our guest; you have but to command." He himself would be available each evening from six to seven and meetings would be arranged immediately with representatives of the Red Army. It should be noted that Hopkins' subsequent discussions with Russian military leaders did not duplicate the open atmosphere of his meeting with Stalin. These men "did not dare to utter a word on any topic beyond the prescribed agenda," he stated in his report. Still, the talks were useful, for Hopkins was able to add to his bag of impressions regarding the Soviet system and military situation.[22]

Hopkins spent the second day of his visit in meetings with the English Ambassador, Stafford Cripps, and with the Commissar for Foreign Affairs, V. M. Molotov. The interview with Cripps was uncomfortable for both men. They were totally dissimilar. The British diplomat, tall, thin, ascetic, "seemed to look disapprovingly at those who did not live their lives on the same cold, passionless level as his own." [23] Cripps was convinced that Russian resistance was a mirage. "The Germans will go through Russia like a hot knife through butter," he had informed London not long before.[24] For a number of reasons his position in Churchill's government was degenerating, and he and Hopkins limited their talk to the forthcoming Anglo-American conference "in its relation to Russia." They decided it would be wise, at the conclusion of that meeting, for Roosevelt and Churchill to dispatch a joint message to Premier Stalin. Cripps wrote a memorandum based on their discussions which Hopkins took back with him to Argentia.[25]

The meeting with Molotov dealt mainly with the Far East. Hopkins told the Bolshevik diplomat, whom he considered "the professorial, studious type," that in the event of further Japanese aggression the temper of the American people and the disposition of the President was to make no threat "which would not be followed by action if necessary." America was concerned for the security of the North Pacific and would not look with "complacency" upon a Japanese adventure in Siberia. Molotov guardedly responded that the Soviet government appreciated President Roosevelt's concern. He admitted the attitude of the newly formed Japanese government toward his country was "uncertain" despite the understandings established by the Matsuoka conversations and the Japanese-Soviet Neutrality Pact.[26]

Molotov then made a statement which had a most familiar ring. The "one thing" he thought would restrain Japan was a "warning" by the United States. He trusted that such a warning, though directed primarily to the South Pacific, "would include a statement that the United States would come to the assistance of the Soviet Union in the event of its being attacked by Japan." Hopkins' reply was noncommittal. He had no power to commit his country to such a step, and he was well aware of the President's negative attitude toward the proposal.[27]

The high point of the mission was a three-hour talk between Stalin and Hopkins during the evening of July 31. The two men, alone except for an interpreter, explored issues of the war and of Soviet-American relations. Notably, their interpreter was Maxim Litvinov, proponent of collective security in the mid-thirties. He had been plucked from the ash heap of discarded Soviet diplomats and dusted off for the occasion. Through him Stalin gave Hopkins a detailed précis of the military situation. The Red Army, he claimed, possessed "a few more" divisions than the Germans, and about one-third of these units had not yet been committed to the struggle. "Germany underestimated the strength of the Russian army," Stalin boasted, "and have not now enough troops on the whole front to carry on a successful war and at the same time guard their extended lines of communications." The Nazis had found that "moving mechanized forces through Russia was very different from moving them over the boulevards of Belgium and France." [28] Stalin provided an enormous amount of information regarding Soviet armored and air forces. This was intelligence for which American and British military attachés had pleaded for many months.

The Premier stressed that he did not underestimate the Germans. "So far as men, supplies, food, and fuel are concerned, the German Army is capable of taking part in a winter campaign in Russia"; but it would be difficult for the Nazis to mount an offensive after the first of September and impossible after October 1. He expressed "great confidence" that the battleline during the winter would stretch in front of Moscow, Kiev, and Leningrad, "probably not more than 100 kilometers away from where it now is." Hopkins was impressed, although he was careful to note: "no information given above was confirmed by any other source." [29] He himself was persuaded.

When the flow of information slacked off, the American envoy stated (in pursuance of his instructions from Roosevelt and Churchill) that the American and British governments "were willing to do everything that they possibly could during the succeeding weeks to send material to Russia." However, those supplies "must obviously be already manufactured." Stalin must understand that they probably would not reach the front lines before the date for coming of bad weather he had mentioned. Further, supply problems could be solved only if the United States had "complete knowledge" about the status of the battle, about Russian weaponry, "as well as full knowledge of raw materials and factory capacity." He had noted Stalin's evasiveness on this last point. Lend-Lease aid in "heavy munitions" would not be transferred to the Eastern front "unless and until a conference had been held between our three Governments at which the relative strategic interests of each front . . . was fully and jointly explored." And, of course, a supply conference could not reasonably take place "until we knew the outcome of the battle now in progress." Stalin brushed aside this clumsy statement to say he would welcome a proposal for a meeting to settle supply priorities.[30]

The talk ended with an exchange of views on matters of broad diplomatic importance. Stalin spoke "bluntly" of the desirability of America's entry into the war. Expressing "great thanks" to President Roosevelt for his interest in Russia's struggle, he requested that Hopkins transmit a full report of his remarks. He then said,

Hitler's greatest weakness was found in the vast numbers of oppressed people who hated Hitler and the immoral ways of his Government . . . These people and countless other millions in nations still unconquered could have received the kind of encouragement and moral strength they needed to resist Hitler from only one source, and that was the United States . . . The world influence of the President and Government of the United States was enormous. (Contrary-wise . . . the morale of the German Army and the German people . . . would be demoralized by an announcement that the United States is going to enter the war against Hitler.) . . . It was inevitable that we should finally come to grips with Hitler on some battlefield. The might of Germany was so great that, even though Russia might defend herself, it would be very difficult for Britain and Russia combined to crush the German military machine . . . The one thing that could defeat Hitler, and perhaps without ever firing a shot, would be the announcement that the United States was going to war with Germany.[31]

Stalin assumed the American people "would insist on their armies coming to grips with German soldiers." He wanted President Roosevelt to understand that he would welcome United States forces "on any part of the Russian front under the complete command of the American army." Hopkins said only that his mission related "entirely" to matters of supply. The question of U.S. entry into the war "would be decided largely by Hitler himself and his encroachment upon our fundamental interests." [32] Nonetheless, his opinion of the Russian leader rose even higher as he listened to Stalin's shrewdly phrased appeal, with its emphasis upon the moral leadership of Franklin Roosevelt.

This marathon session was Hopkins' final contact with Premier Stalin. Their conversations had been remarkably productive; it was clear that his mission had succeeded beyond all expectations. He had received more information about the U.S.S.R.'s military strength and its prospects "than had ever been vouchsafed to any outsider." [33] The Iowan's achievement was so stunning that Ambassador Steinhardt, reporting to the President and Acting Secretary Welles on August 1, could not conceal his astonishment. He wrote that Stalin and Hopkins "discussed with a frankness unparalleled in my knowledge . . . the subject of his mission and the Soviet position." [34] The only possible explanation was Hopkins' standing with the President.

F.D.R.'s aide, though close to exhaustion, was well satisfied. He had come to Russia a strong advocate of aid; he would return home with persuasive evidence that such aid would not be thrown away. He talked of this with Western correspondents the evening before his departure. Appearing "pale and tired, with one thin leg dangling over the other as he slumped in his chair," Hopkins' voice often died away to "an inaudible mumble" as he spoke; but the import of his words came across quite clearly. "My short visit here," he said, "has given me even more confidence that Hitler is going to lose." [35] Next morning, in a final cable to the President, he was still more positive. Hopkins stated that he was bringing back a full report and personal messages from Stalin. "I would like to tell you now, however," Hopkins announced jubilantly, "that I feel ever so confident about this front. The morale of the population is exceptionally good. There is unbounded determination to win." [36] This cocksureness came entirely from the confidential talks with Stalin. Hopkins saw nothing of the actual battle and would not have learned anything if he had been allowed to visit the front. His judgment was impressionistic and subjective; but the two men who were to be most influenced by his confidence tended to think in similar terms.

Hopkins left Moscow for the return flight to England and thence to Argentia on August 1. In his baggage were ninety pages of notes and a goodly supply of caviar and vodka. Hopkins was to have need of the satisfaction he felt about the mission as sustenance on the return journey. The flight to England was rougher than the outgoing one, because the sluggish PBY had to buck strong head winds. The pilot had wanted to wait at Archangel for clearing skies, but Hopkins insisted on an immediate departure. "He knew, although he would not say, that if they delayed another day he might miss the battleship *Prince of Wales* which was to carry Churchill to the Atlantic Conference." [37] Hopkins' haste almost resulted in his missing everything. Through an oversight he left behind in Moscow his precious medicine satchel, and he was made desperately ill by lack of the pills which kept his ravaged body functioning. Knowledge that preparations for the Newfoundland meeting were reaching completion may have made the flight more easily endured.

1

The President and Churchill, indeed, were putting final touches to their respective plans while Hopkins' airplane labored westward. The first act of Roosevelt's charade has been described. Prime Minister Churchill's scheme was far less elaborate, although the secret was guarded closely in England. Churchill could better control the press because of wartime censorship, and he did not fear to bring a considerable number of people into the conspiracy. A much larger group was to accompany him; but, though the Prime Minister "delighted" in the "security" that surrounded his trip out of the country, he was not the enthusiastic plotter F.D.R. had shown himself to be.[38]

Churchill did respect his friend's wishes about keeping the time and place of the meeting hushed up. Only those for whom this knowledge was absolutely necessary received it.

If English preparations were not as dramatic or as conspirational, mystery did cloak the Prime Minister's movements in the week before departure. Churchill would be vulnerable to German attack for over two weeks. The possibility of such an encounter caused F.D.R. to lose his sense of perspective; Churchill adopted a more casual attitude. His most difficult problem was the covering operation for the movements of his subordinates. He had to assemble a staff from among men engaged in direction of the war and their absence had to be shielded for a much longer time. Also, as the "prime" minister of a parliamentary coalition government, Churchill was involved on a day-to-day basis in debate in the House of Commons.

In contrast with F.D.R.'s well publicized fishing trip the British followed a policy of no comment, no explanation. Until the hour of departure the Prime Minister pursued a normal schedule. To meet with Roosevelt on August 9 the *Prince of Wales* had to sail by August 4 at the latest. The journey from London to Scapa Flow involved yet another day.[39]

On Tuesday, July 29, Churchill gave an important speech before Parliament on the much-disputed issue of war production. Next day he returned to the Commons for debate, which focused on the responsibilities of his close friend and adviser on scientific matters, Lord Cherwell.[40] Also on July 30 he presided over the ceremonial signing of the pact between Poland and the Soviet Union. The Prime Minister then traveled, as had been announced, from London to Chequers, where, it was generally assumed, he wished to enjoy a long weekend away from the pressures of the war and the current parliamentary crisis. Before leaving, he engaged in one piece of deception, having a photograph taken of himself outside No. 10 Downing Street buying a flag from a beaming woman. The picture was for publication on Flag Day which was celebrated on August 10 in Great Britain.[41] Newspapers did not carry the Prime Minister's itinerary, for that would be a direct invitation to German bombers to churn up the formal lawns around the great Tudor mansion.

Left behind to arrange final details of the journey were several of Churchill's most trusted advisers. Portal and Ismay were to carry on the war; Eden, the zealous and "apparently tireless" chief of the Foreign Office, was to keep watch over Britain's world-spanning diplomatic interests and would assist Clement Attlee in speaking for the government in the House of Commons. In charge of "local arrangements," making sure that no one missed the train and that security was observed, was Brendan Bracken, the red-haired extrovert who had been Churchill's Parliamentary Private Secretary and who, in mid-July, had taken the hazardous post of Minister of Information.[42] Bracken became excited about the meeting's potential influence upon British morale and prevailed upon the Prime Minister to allow two or three writers to accompany him and to make a "historical record" of the event. One observer believed Bracken worked up the idea because "he hoped to pull off a coup that would bring him credit instead of the kicks in the pants which every former Minister of Information had been receiving." [43] Churchill said he had promised President Roosevelt that no reporters would be brought to Argentia, since none were to be allowed to accompany the President and one-sided coverage would result in a journalistic hue and cry in the United States. Bracken proposed to get around this agreement by sending men who could not be easily identified as reporters. In retrospect, his assumption that "writers" might be acceptable while "journalists" would be banned was "amusingly naïve"; it was, however, plausible and Churchill approved his young friend's liberal interpretation of the "no reporters" rule.[44] Bracken's colleague in the Ministry, Francis Williams, was asked to find suitable candidates. He finally came up with the names of Howard Spring, author of such popular novels as *Oh Absalom,* a man "who had started life as a newspaper reporter," and H. V. Morton, widely known writer of travel books, who also had newspaper experience.[45] The two writers were duly called to the Ministry of Information's headquarters in Bloomsbury on August 2 and asked if they were interested in a three-week trip outside of England. They were given no explanation of the purpose or destination. Both accepted, with only the slim clue that dinner jackets would be *de rigueur* as evidence that the journey was to be unusually important. "It was like the opening of a good Buchan spy novel," H. V. Morton said.[46]

Few in the Prime Minister's entourage knew more. For instance, Captain B. B. Schofield, Director of the Trade Division, Admiralty, was ordered in late July to gather up all data relating to shipping protection, British convoy organization, and tonnage losses, and to prepare himself for a three-week voyage. "It was all very mysterious," Schofield has written, "but I knew better than to ask questions." [47] At noon, August 3, the most ticklish part of the operation took place. Many of the thirty-five people in the delegation came down to the Admiralty, their presence there on a Sunday morning a red flag to the alert onlooker. A line of cars drew up and various staff officers, secretaries, and cipher clerks jammed into them. As the automobiles crept forward, a messenger came out with a large geographical globe, another revealing clue. Once the Prime Minister's prized sphere had been tenderly placed into a taxi, the motley caravan drove off.[48]

Its destination was Marylebone Station, where a special train, twelve coaches with dining cars, sleepers, day compartments, and guard's vans, was standing at No. 4 platform. The engine bore the name of "Sansovino," and Lieutenant Colonel E. I. C. Jacob, Secretary to the Defence Council, felt that "augured well" for the expedition.[49] Those such as Schofield, Jacob, and Colonel L. C. Hollis, who had come directly to the station, watched later arrivals board the train and peered into compartments to see which of their colleagues had been invited. They spied Captain H. V. Brockman, Sir Dudley Pound's secretary, of whom Schofield asked the whereabouts of the First Sea Lord. "Joining later," Brockman enigmatically replied. He pointed out a sleeping-car attendant who had berth assignments.[50] The absence of all the service chiefs was noted, along with the fact that no women were present. Indeed, "Jo" Hollis lost several sixpences because he made a foolhardy wager the Prime Minister would take Mrs. Churchill.[51]

Precisely at 12:30 P.M. the train pulled out of the station and headed north. An hour later it stopped at "a little wayside station,"

Wendover. Looking out, the staff saw the Prime Minister, in a navy blue yachting uniform, standing on the platform. With him were Pound, Dill, Freeman, Cadogan, and Lord Cherwell. Churchill climbed on board "in terrific form," shouting orders that the train start immediately.[52] He had found waiting for the journey to begin almost unbearable. Being forced to dawdle at Checquers was the only blemish upon the promise of the day. His impatience and enthusiasm "grew more and more intense — actually boyish" as the hour for departure neared. The party was to leave for Wendover at 1:15, but Churchill insisted on starting at 1:05. He appeared supremely happy, "grinning at all and flashing his most bewitching smile on even unknown persons." [53] Of course, he had to wait once more at Wendover Station; the other members of his party were not permitted to relax until the Prime Minister was safely aboard and the train was in motion.

Lunch was served immediately, "all the food in the world having been collected." The P.M. sat with Pound, Dill, and Cadogan. Afterward, the staff was invited to his car to be introduced. Now garbed in his favorite siren suit, Churchill "looked extremely pleased with life." He announced that the group was bound for Scapa Flow, "where we were to board H.M.S. *Prince of Wales* and in her we were to sail to Argentia in Newfoundland where the Prime Minister was to meet the President of the United States and his Chief Staff Officers." [54] For many of the company this was the first confirmation of their destination. About four o'clock Churchill retired for his customary nap and his guests drifted back to their compartments or joined in casual conversation with neighbors.

Jacob and Brigadier Vivian Dykes, Director of Plans in the War Office (known affectionately as "Dumbie"), struck up a conversation with Howard Spring, the author. Spring had a unique contribution for the growing file of stories about the rush with which the mission had been arranged. He lived in Cornwall and had received a telephone call inquiring whether he could pack a bag and come up to London for a trip. As he explained his dilemma, "he had not liked to refuse although, as luck would have it, his teeth were at that moment

in the hands of the dentist being repaired, with the result that he had
to set sail without any." [55] Jacob admitted that this did not impede
Spring's conversation "but made it a bit hard at mealtimes." The talk
ranged over the bad times in Ireland after the First World War,
imaginary bridge hands, to the prospects for a successful conference
with the Americans. The topic of food came up frequently, for the
fare was of a kind and variety such as the company rarely enjoyed.
"Travelling in this kind of train seems to be one long meal," Jacob
sighed contentedly on Sunday night. [56]

The noise of the speeding train was lulling and most of the party
either drowsed over cards or retired early. Their destination was
Thurso, the railhead closest to Scapa Flow on the wild north coast of
Scotland, an overnight journey even for the London, Norfolk, and
Eastern Railroad's crack streamliners. After his nap the Prime Minister devoted several hours to his work, sitting under a shaded reading lamp, "surrounded by dispatch cases and boxes of papers, his
glasses down on his nose, while two secretaries sat opposite with
notebooks on their knees." [57] He was not in the least fatigued and
invited his senior officers to stay with him after dinner. The mood of
this group grew lighter as the evening progressed. Churchill
downed his usual pint of champagne "and a bit more." The tenor of
the conversation suggests that some of the others attempted to match
him glass for glass. The Prime Minister drank a great deal, but as he
boasted: "I have taken more out of alcohol than alcohol has taken
out of me." He asked Lord Cherwell, a fine mathematician, to work
out how much champagne he had drunk, at the rate of a pint a day
for his entire adult life. The answer pleased him immensely. But
then, one interested spectator has written, "he turned to the professor again and asked him how many railroad coaches it would require
to stow and carry all that champagne." When Cherwell decided that
one end of the Prime Minister's compartment would be sufficient,
Churchill "was very put out and disappointed, feeling himself a very
uninteresting imbiber at best . . ." When Sir John Dill asked how
many yards of cigars he had smoked, the Prime Minister "wouldn't
get into it," perhaps fearing another blow to his image of himself as a
lusty Elizabethan. [58]

By morning the train was speeding through bleak Scottish high-lands, treeless, completely undistinguished "except for an occasional lonely loch." It was raining and gloomy at 9:30 when the party reached Thurso. Their baggage was soon unloaded and at 10:00 the group set off for Scrabster, from whence they were to travel to Scapa Flow. The tiny harbor of Scrabster was too shallow for destroyers to come alongside the quay, and the party boarded lighters which took them out to the warships. Churchill and the Chiefs of Staff em-barked in H.M.S. *Oribi*, and the others were taken aboard H.M.S. *Croome*. Although the sky continued to be overcast, there was a smooth sea and the sleek destroyers made twenty-five knots on the passage to the Orkneys. Passing through the double boom guarding the southern entrance to Scapa and edging around Flotta Island, the British delegation saw the ships of the Home Fleet in the distance. Churchill looked first at *King George V* and then turned to its sister, *Prince of Wales*. At that distance he was unable to recognize the slight figure standing on *Prince of Wales'* foredeck, but he knew Harry Hopkins had returned from Moscow and was on board.[59]

Hopkins had been subjected to a terrible ordeal on the flight back. His plane, bouncing and tossing in gale-force winds, was fired on off the Murman Coast and took twenty-four hours to reach Scapa Flow. He was so ill when given into the custody of Admiral Sir John Tovey, Commander in Chief of the Home Fleet, that this worthy feared his charge would die before morning. Physicians were sum-moned and the President's personal envoy was put to bed.[60] Ambas-sador Winant, who came up to Scapa for a discussion of the Russian trip and other matters, found Hopkins under heavy sedation. He had to return to London without any long talks.

Winant was able to confirm that Hopkins had returned alive. Be-fore seeing his friend, he cabled to Welles for President Roosevelt that Harry had arrived safely and was on board *Prince of Wales*. He did not mention how "utterly worn out" was Hopkins, not wishing to alarm the President; instead, he said that Hopkins was tired but all right, that "he did a real job," and that the doctors had promised to keep him in bed for a few days.[61]

No doctor, no mere admiral, could prevent Hopkins from coming on deck to greet the Prime Minister. One story had him perching on a live torpedo while Churchill was crossing from *Oribi;* it must be apocryphal, for *Prince of Wales* had no torpedo tubes. The Prime Minister, catching sight of his American friend, strode forward eagerly. Hopkins thought Churchill looked "brutally well" and active for a man in his late sixties. Taking Hopkins' hand, the Prime Minister said simply, "My boy, I'm glad to see you." [62] He observed the American's pale, drawn appearance and insisted that he get some rest before the sailing. There would be plenty of time later for bringing each other up to date.

Churchill left almost at once for *King George V* for a luncheon with Admiral Tovey. His aides were shown to their quarters. Most then spent the remainder of the afternoon wandering through the huge battleship while waiting for their gear (which was coming across on the much slower lighters) to arrive. Sailing time was 4:00 P.M., but the baggage did not arrive until a few minutes after the hour. Eventually the party's "kit" was swung on board, along with such miscellany as ninety grouse for President Roosevelt, several large map cases, and Professor Lindemann's small globe (the Prime Minister's bulky one having been accidently left behind).[63] Just before *Prince of Wales* weighed anchor the Prime Minister dispatched a last message to President Roosevelt. He reported, "Harry Hopkins returned dead-beat from Russia but is lively again now" — his personal diagnosis. "We are just off," he informed the President. "It is twenty-seven years ago today that Huns began their last war. We must make a good job of it this time. Twice ought to be enough." [64] To his colleagues, as they watched the great naval base fall back into the mist, the Prime Minister said only, "I hope we shall have an interesting and enjoyable voyage . . . And one not entirely without profit." [65]

H. V. Morton knew nothing of the great stakes to be gained or lost at Argentia. He thought only of Churchill's gamble in making the journey and he was unable to banish the memory of another ocean-borne mission — "the only one in recent history compared to this: when Kitchener left for Russia during the last war in H.M.S. *Hamp-*

shire, and met death off the coast of Hoy." [66] Several among Churchill's entourage had similar thoughts. The Prime Minister had ignored their protests, had merely laughed when they said, "Hitler would give fifty divisions to capture the British Prime Minister — or kill him." [67]

2

From the moment Roosevelt's little fleet steamed out of Vineyard Sound, nineteen hours after the British contingent cleared Scapa Flow, *Augusta* received continuous information from Naval Operations regarding Nazi surface, air, and U-boat activity. A close check was kept as well on the sea lanes between Maine and Newfoundland. [68]

Roosevelt's anxiety during this first day was balanced by his amusement with American officers who had been rushed to the rendezvous in Vineyard Sound. The whirlwind of events had been almost too incredible for them to accept, as their bemused faces revealed. Two days earlier most had been at their desks in Washington. General Arnold was on an inspection tour through the southeastern states, when, enroute from Baton Rouge to Ellington A.F.B. on July 31, he received the following telegram from General Marshall: "Return to Washington — arriving not later than 10:00 P.M., Saturday, August 2nd." He was given no explanation for cancellation of the trip, and after his return was unable to learn the reasons for the flap. All Marshall would tell him was that heavy uniforms were required for departure the next day for an unnamed destination. Arnold decided he had best take his Sam Browne belt as sartorial insurance. [69] The Chief of Staff, Marshall, could not tell his wife more, although "she surmised from the clothing he packed and the inordinate security precautions . . . that he was going northward with the President." [70] Without orders, officers involved gathered together data on strategy, production, and material priorities which would be needed, as Arnold observed, "regardless of where we went." [71]

Over the weekend Washington insiders noticed that Marshall,

Stark, and other high-ranking officers had disappeared from view. The first theory to mind, tacitly encouraged, credited them with following President Roosevelt's example and fleeing the capital for a few days. One rumor had Marshall and Arnold flying to the West Coast on an inspection junket. Secretary of War Stimson, in the dark, at first accepted this explanation. He grumbled to his diary on August 4: "When I got back here this morning I found that Marshall was away on an inspection tour to be gone until Friday, and also Bundy [War Plans Office Director], and also Arnold of the Air Corps . . . so I had to do a lot of shooting around myself with subordinates to help me, the Heads of the Departments being in so many cases absent." [72] The President put Marshall and Stark in an awkward position by forbidding them even to tell their superiors.

When Stimson dictated this his "Heads" had begun their journey. At 12:00 noon on the third, Marshall and Arnold met General James Burns and Colonel Charles W. Bundy at Washington airport for the flight to New York. Admiral Stark, Rear Admiral Richmond K. Turner, and Commander Forrest Sherman were waiting at the 125th Street docks. The party boarded a destroyer leader which threaded its way down the North River past Hell Gate and out the East River to College Point where *Augusta* and *Tuscaloosa* were anchored. Marshall and Stark transferred to *Augusta*, Arnold and the others to *Tuscaloosa*. Admiral King's flagship led the now sizable complement of naval vessels out of New York Harbor to a berth for the night at Smithstown Cove. [73]

Next morning they moved on north. The complexities of shipboard life both confused and fascinated the Army officers. As senior officer on *Tuscaloosa* General Arnold ranked the admiral's cabin, with a special orderly and a cabin boy. He did not know what to do with all this attention. The situation topside was equally baffling. Standing on the bridge later in the morning, Arnold was intrigued by the multiplicity of varicolored streamers that waved from different ships. Sherman explained they were signal flags and at Arnold's request translated the flag code. "Suddenly, from the *Augusta* appeared more flags than I have ever seen on a ship at any one time in

my life — two or three halyards of them. 'Forrest,' I exclaimed, 'will
you kindly tell me just what . . . all that business is?' Sherman hesitated and at last said reluctantly, 'That's Admiral King asking the
Captain of the *Tuscaloosa* just what the hell he thinks he's doing
. . .' " [74] Arnold also found out that Sherman and the naval contingent knew no more than he about the purpose of the trip.

Late in the afternoon, when the ships reached Vineyard Sound,
everybody's questions were answered. Marshall and Stark called a
meeting aboard *Augusta*. When the entire group had assembled
(and Admiral King, who became furious when he discovered people
aboard his ship without his personal permission, had been pacified),
the C.N.O. and Chief of Staff announced the party was to meet the
President and to proceed with him to Newfoundland for a "Bremer
Pass" [sic] conference with Prime Minister Churchill and staff. [75]
There was only a short time for contemplation of this information.
The naval flotilla stood off Martha's Vineyard for some hours before
Roosevelt's little fleet steamed into the sound. Due to the lateness of
the hour and F.D.R.'s proclivity for retiring early there was no visiting between the two contingents that night. Early next morning
Roosevelt and his staff transferred to *Augusta*. As soon as necessary
stores and luggage were loaded, the big cruiser and its sister ship,
shepherded by destroyers, put to sea. Heading east past Nantucket
Shoals lightship until they were far outside shallow waters (in which
mines might be laid), the squadron was 280 miles out by Tuesday
morning. Wartime precautions were put into effect when the President came on board. When an anti-mine paravane fouled, Admiral
King refused to allow *Augusta* to lay to even for the short time
needed to repair it. [76]

Once Roosevelt was on the way to Newfoundland the *Potomac*
undertook a further mission — under strict orders from its absent
chief. To maintain the fiction of a presidential pleasure cruise, at
least until the Prime Minister was safely across the Atlantic, Roosevelt directed that the yacht proceed as if he were still on board. He
received great pleasure from this little subterfuge. "At this point," he
later wrote, "fits in the delightful story of what happened to U S.S.

Potomac and her little escorting ship." [77] She returned to Buzzard's Bay and in the late afternoon of August 6 entered the Cape Cod Canal. Lieutenant Commander George A. Leahy, Jr. dressed some of the crew in civilian clothes (one wore white ducks and flaunted a long cigarette holder) and had them lounge on *Potomac's* sundeck where they waved gaily to passersby. Even the Secret Service seems to have been taken in. Its head, Colonel Starling, swore that he knew the President's whereabouts at all times, but F.D.R. doubted this as Secret Service operatives guarded the yacht all during its slow trip through the Canal.[78] To lend further credence to the ruse periodic communiqués were dispatched from *Potomac*. These stated in general terms that "all on board" were enjoying themselves.[79]

Far out in the Atlantic the U.S. warships sped on at a steady twenty-one knots. Roosevelt, his aides, and advisers relaxed — reading, thinking, listening to the radio. A Presidential mess was established on *Augusta*, although F.D.R. technically was King's guest because the cruiser flew the flag of C in C, Atlantic Fleet. *Augusta* was well suited to be a presidential transport and Roosevelt was to use her for that purpose all through the war.

Augusta was of the *Northampton* class and had been launched in February, 1930. She displaced 9,050 tons, was 569 feet long, and carried a crew of 795 maximum. Rated top speed in this class of heavy cruiser was 32.7 knots. As a pawn in the U.S.-British rivalry over definition of "cruiser," *Augusta* carried armament which spoke for the position of American admirals — 9 8-inch guns, 8 5-inch antiaircraft guns, and assorted weapons of smaller caliber. *Northampton* class vessels carried four planes in hangars amidships. Three of these ships, *Augusta, Chicago,* and *Quincy,* had been fitted as flagships and extra accommodations had been included. *Augusta* had served in the Pacific until April, 1941, when Admiral King had requested her as flagship of the Atlantic Fleet. *Tuscaloosa,* though of the later *Minneapolis* class of heavy cruisers, had similar dimensions, speed, and ordnance.[80] These heavy cruisers, built during the moratorium on battleship construction, were roomy, comfortable, and the quarters of the commanding officer were actually luxurious. Arnold was amazed and, from the tone of his diary, somewhat shocked by the opulence. "Admirals are wonderful fellows," he noted. "They travel . . . deluxe, a bath (with Roman bath tub), portholes that sailors look thru while one performs such acts as he must, a large bedroom with a double bed, and a sitting room. An orderly and a room steward. Push buttons and bells everywhere. I am enjoying the luxury while I can." [81]

The President, to all appearances, was equally pleased with the accommodations. He devoted considerable time to answering the "most urgent" of the radiotelegrams which came through Naval Operations communications.[82] He also kept close watch over press speculation about his whereabouts, and he even made additional efforts while at sea to maintain the fiction of an innocent fishing trip. One may speculate that his thoughts turned repeatedly to Winston Churchill. He took along to Argentia jealousy of Churchill's reputation for eloquence; and he was concerned about whether the English statesman's "reactionary imperialist attitudes" would cause difficulty.[83] Characteristically, he said nothing about these anxieties to his subordinates. These men were also thinking of the approaching meeting with British leaders. It is likely, however, that Marshall and Stark were as much interested in the personal traits of their distinguished shipmate, the President. For both this was a unique opportunity to get to know President Roosevelt. Although Stark had been a friend of F.D.R.'s since the First World War, he knew as little as anyone else of the President's "heavily forested interior." [84] Roosevelt allowed very few to get close to him. His easy informality served to obscure his thoughts and the emotions behind the thoughts.[85] Observation of F.D.R. in these days before Argentia did not offer much encouragement that he was prepared to fight for the national interests of the United States. During the voyage he refused to give thorough attention to those problems certain to arise at the conference. On the evening of August 6 King gave a dinner, an impressive meal, at which he, Roosevelt, Stark, Marshall, McIntire, Watson, and Beardall talked. Downing clam chowder, roast leg of lamb with mint jelly, a large selection of vegetables, and steamed plum pudding, the company discussed almost every imaginable topic save the one of what was to be the American position at Argentia.[86]

The President's thoughts were clearly fixed on the personal aspects of his meeting with Churchill. His advisers became more and more concerned about conversations with British military and naval authorities. Arnold had visited England earlier in the year and had been impressed by "the thoroughness with which the British prepare for such conferences." He feared the Americans were "going into this one cold." [87] On learning the purpose of the trip, he decided to attempt to have Marshall, Stark, and the President accept a minimum American program for discussion at all levels. He hoped they would accede to three principles he considered crucial: development of the United States Army, Navy, and Air Force to meet the present international situation; "as a policy, give to the British, the Chinese, and other foreign governments only such items as they could use effectively, after first meeting our own requirements"; no commitments until United States authorities had opportunity to study the proposals and requests "with all their ramifications" made by the British. At some time during the voyage, Arnold later claimed, these principles (which would limit drastically any military or naval conversations) were accepted by Marshall, Stark, and finally by President Roosevelt.[88] The President's fondness for Arnold was his admiration of the Air Corps Chief's "passionate devotion to air power and . . . eagerness to shoot for previously undreamed of achievements in the air" undoubtedly influenced his decision.[89]

The morning of August 7 found Roosevelt's "task force" approaching the coast of Newfoundland. In these shallow waters mines once more became a threat and *Augusta's* anti-mine paravanes were rigged at 4.00 A.M. "God, what a noise, vibrations and clattering and hammering," one of the passengers groaned. "How can one sleep?" [90] Admiral King, the original for the "steel-eyed, hard-bitten" naval officer stereotype, cared not a whit. At 6:45 the flotilla, which had been joined by the old *Arizona*, dowager empress of the battleship fleet, and several destroyers during the night, passed Cape Saint Mary Light, an indication the Americans were but a few hours from their destination. Finally, at 9:24, *Augusta* dropped anchor in Berth No. 2, Ship Harbor, Placentia Bay, Newfoundland.

Roosevelt must have gazed at the busy scene with great interest, fixing in his mind the appearance and atmosphere of the site he had selected. Until the Destroyer-Bases Deal had brought Argentia into the United States defense orbit, few Americans had heard of the harbor, a small dimple in that large indentation in Newfoundland's southern coast which bore the equally obscure name of Placentia Bay. Such ignorance was understandable. Argentia was isolated, possessing little value for settlement or exploitation. Its last brief claim to importance in world affairs had come some two hundred years earlier. France, then engaged in a great struggle with Great Britain for control of the New World, had established a strategic naval position, euphemistically named "Plaisance," on a promontory at the head of the bay.[91] For a time Plaisance represented France's bid for hegemony over the Western Atlantic. Then a British squadron destroyed the little base and Argentia slipped into oblivion.

The Americans who had come to construct another naval base on this site found a barren, desolate land geographically similar to Alaska. Behind the low hills which rimmed the bay, the terrain, dotted with stumpy pine trees and underbrush, was carved by deep ravines. Many of these contained fast running streams, which offered superb trout fishing for those hardy enough to brave the eternal damp and chill which wrapped southern Newfoundland.

In August, 1941, Argentia's slate-dark waters were crowded with shipping. Besides the two cruisers, *Augusta* and *Tuscaloosa*, the ancient *Arkansas*, and the frisking destroyer division, the anchorage contained American ships of all types and sizes. Sailors and officers of the neutrality patrol destroyers, *Salinas, Belknap, Rhind*, and *Mayrant*, rushed to rails nearest the cruiser in hopes of confirming with their own eyes the odd rumor that the President of the United States was on board the Atlantic Fleet flagship. They knew something unusual was going on, because on August 5 a signal from "*Comtaskforce 1*" (King's title on this mission) had ordered that a large space in the inner harbor be reserved and that this area be picketed continuously after dawn, Thursday, August 7. A special patrol by air over Placentia Bay and its southern approaches was requested and had begun on Wednesday.[92] There had to be a good reason for these elaborate precautions.

The executive officer of the *Mayrant*, Ensign Franklin D. Roosevelt, Jr., was anxious to learn the truth of the rumor that his father was visiting Argentia. The President's third son found to his surprise and pleasure that the stories were true. The *Mayrant's* presence was supposedly a fortuitous circumstance. F.D.R. had not made a prior request for either Franklin, Jr. or his second son, Elliott. Admiral King probably was responsible for Roosevelt's reunion with his naval son. Certainly, Franklin, Jr. was taken by surprise. "All I knew was that the *Mayrant* was ordered off convoy duty . . . last week," his brother Elliott quoted him as saying. "They told us we were to patrol as part of the screen force guarding the entrance to the harbor. Then this morning they said I should report to the Commander-in-Chief aboard the *Augusta* . . . I was trying to figure what the hell I had done so terrible that Admiral King would want to haul me on the carpet." His uneasiness vanished when he discovered the "Commander-in-Chief" to be his father.[93]

Roosevelt intervened directly to have his son Elliott, an Army Air Corps officer stationed at Gander Bay, brought to the conference. Immediately after arrival he asked Arnold if Elliott could be aboard *Augusta* by the next day. General Arnold promised to make arrangements.[94] Elliott soon received an order to fly down to the naval air station at Argentia. Supposing nothing unusual was in store, he was "amazed and puzzled" when his Grumman aircraft "cleared the mountain spur overlooking the harbor at Argentia — the bay was filled with warships and a lot of them big too." He did not guess what was transpiring until he was piped over the side of *Augusta* and caught sight of the familiar figure of "Pa" Watson.[95] F.D.R. was happy to see his sons, both of whom had been away for months, and he pressed them into service. He borrowed what he mockingly called "the gold spinach," i.e. *aiguillettes,* and commissioned Franklin, Jr. and Elliott as junior aides for the occasion.[96]

Apart from this family reunion there was little to do but wait. During the forenoon of his initial day at Argentia Roosevelt engaged in some casual fishing, first from *Augusta's* forecastle and then from a ship's boat. He caught one large fish, which no one was able to identify, and directed that it go to the Smithsonian Institution.[97] The remainder of his catch was smaller, mainly dogfish and halibut. Abandoning this activity, F.D.R. cruised along the shoreline, interested particularly in the waterfront and in progress on the development of the new base. It was apparent that construction of the naval air station was far from complete; but submarine nets and sound detectors were in operation, contributing to the protection of Argentia's visitors.

Returning to *Augusta,* Roosevelt held a conference with his military and naval advisers. There had been a brief meeting that morning on the problem of supplying aircraft to the Soviet Union. F.D.R. had received an urgent message from Washington and had asked his advisers to prepare a reply. They decided that current production would permit a "token gift" only — seventy fighter planes during September, October, and November, and five B-25's a month for that quarter. With encouragement from the President they increased Air Force strength in the Philippines to one group of P-40's and one group of B-17's. Arnold commented: "That was a distinct change in policy." Previously Roosevelt had resisted such a provocative act.[98]

During the afternoon there was another conference. At first only service personnel took part. They took this opportunity to discuss in general terms the coming conferences with the British. The officers believed the British should receive only such items of war as could be sent without jeopardizing the defense of the United States, since "if and when we entered . . . the people of the United States would want action, not excuses, and we, the leaders, would be holding the sack." [99]

Such conclusions, however, were tentative until Roosevelt confirmed them. After he joined the discussion he did no such thing — that is, if his advisers dared present their views. Roosevelt was concerned with practical, immediate matters. He brought up the issue of convoying. Making clear that he had recognized American responsibility for safe delivery of cargoes, he is supposed to have said: "It was too late to start shooting after an attack had been made by submarines; the responsibility for safety applied to a whole convoy and not to just any part of it." To emphasize what at least was partial surrender to convoying, he drew on a map a line extending from east of the Azores to east of Iceland "and outlined the duties and responsibilities of the Navy up to that line." [100] Here was a momentous act. Roosevelt was extending the "western hemisphere" far outside its accepted geographical limits, easing British difficulties in the North Atlantic and, importantly, stretching American strategic interests to cover the Azores. F.D.R. had decided on this step earlier, on July 15 when he sent with Hopkins a similarly marked map torn from an issue of *National Geographic;* but he desired that public announcement follow the joint American-British conversations at Argentia.[101] The postponement was a shrewd concession, one might guess, to the desirability that the conference show some results.

In his usual oblique manner Roosevelt turned to the central question — the United States position vis-à-vis the war. He reviewed things his subordinates should expect the British to request: increased tonnage from the Maritime Commission, tanks from the Army, planes from the Air Corps. Primarily for political reasons, he expressed a desire to have the Marine contingent on Iceland relieved by soldiers. Then he turned to the morning's decision on sending planes to Russia and approved it.[102] Roosevelt was happy to be able to give the Soviets proof that he at least believed in their staying powers. He told his son Elliott earlier in the day, "I know already how much faith the P.M. has in Russia's ability to stay in the war," and then he snapped his fingers to indicate the British leader had none. Elliott asked if his father possessed more faith in the Russians. The President answered, "Harry Hopkins has more. He's able to convince me." [103]

Roosevelt emphasized the need for strengthening the Philippines in view of the possibility of further Japanese aggression. At this time he held out a promise of a strong American response if this took place, saying, "he would turn a deaf ear if Japan went into Thailand, but not if they went into the Dutch East Indies." [104] All this, particularly the last statement, was enlightening; but the Army and Navy officers must have felt disappointment at their Commander in Chief's remarks. His statements reaffirmed the policy of material and moral aid to the British, and no guidance should this policy prove insufficient.

Perhaps from unwillingness to suffer further lecturing from his Chief of Staff, General Marshall, or from the gentle but equally firm Stark, perhaps because he wished to learn the views of the younger Army and Navy representatives, Roosevelt asked only Arnold, Burns, Turner, Sherman, and Bundy to stay for dinner Thursday night. In any case, Marshall and Stark returned to *Tuscaloosa*.[105]

The tempo of preparation for Churchill's arrival increased the next day. Marshall, Stark, and their staffs stayed out of the President's way. Aboard *Tuscaloosa* they could work on an agenda for the talks — without Roosevelt's intervention. Marshall, Arnold, General Harms (Commandant of the Army Air Corps' operation in Newfoundland), and Elliott Roosevelt took a break from this work to fly up to Gander and St. John for a brief aerial tour. A similar sense of adventure led Stark and King to requisition a Navy patrol plane for an investigation of the Avalon Peninsula, which King once had recommended over Argentia for the naval base.[106]

Just as the explorers were returning, a four-engine flying boat came in with Sumner Welles and Averell Harriman. Welles had many matters of diplomatic importance to discuss with the President, who had been receiving only the most critical messages from the State Department. Harriman, Lend-Lease chief in England, had flown back just in time to accompany Welles to Argentia. F.D.R. plied him with questions about Churchill, Hopkins, and the situation in Great Britain. In all, Welles and Harriman had three hours with Roosevelt before the Prime Minister arrived. They came aboard *Augusta* at 4:36 P.M., were the President's guests at dinner, and left the ship at 7:50 P.M.[107]

These conferences, few in number and brief in duration, represented the total time Roosevelt's diplomatic, military, and naval advisers spent in consultation with their chief. It was a slipshod way to prepare for such a meeting, but, as shown, the participation of other officials was a last-minute concession. The principals, Roosevelt and Churchill, had always seen the meeting as a dramatic confrontation in a congenial, private setting. On the eve of the conference the personal encounter remained the most important aspect, at least to Roosevelt. The expansion of the original aim is nonetheless notable. In a remarkably short time the "professionals" had succeeded in transforming the meeting into an important conference.

3

The five-day voyage had afforded the British an excellent opportunity to review their diplomatic and military program; but, of course, efforts to force unity upon Churchill's group were largely unnecessary. Almost two years' experience with the kinds of questions to come up at Argentia and the Prime Minister's large control over military and economic affairs, as well as diplomacy, ensured that the British delegations would speak with one voice.

Churchill did worry about the personal side of the meeting. He was asking the same questions about President Roosevelt the President was asking about him. Hopkins later wrote: "As we sailed from Scotland Churchill spoke of Roosevelt as if he had never met him, as of course he hadn't in any such circumstances as these. What sort of man was Roosevelt? What actually did he think of this and that? And always: Tell me more about Roosevelt." [108] The Prime Minister's attitude toward F.D.R. was a blend of curiosity and some feeling akin to awe. Hopkins later commented to friends, "You'd have thought Winston was being carried up into heaven to meet God." [109] Awareness that the future of his beloved Empire depended upon the American President lent natural solemnity to the situation. As a product of the English system of government Churchill was aware of Roosevelt's superior rank as a Chief of State. He always treated the President with some of the deference due a reigning monarch.[110]

With Hopkins this trip across the Atlantic cemented a close friendship. Because of the enforced leisure Hopkins and other passengers were treated to an unusual sight — Winston Churchill at play. He immediately gave indications of determination to enjoy shipboard routine. Once *Prince of Wales* reached the open sea, he went below to his quarters, the Admiral's roomy stateroom located over the stern. Heavy vibration from the battleship's mighty screws soon drove him to another cabin near the bridge, but not even the inconvenience of transferring his things roiled Churchill's disposition. Colonel Ian Jacob, Secretary to the Defence Council, noted with amazement that the "old man" did not a bit of work during the evening and was "in a thoroughly good temper." After dinner he invited the company in to watch a motion picture, *Pimpernel Smith,* a tongue-in-cheek spy film which featured Leslie Howard. The Prime Minister was attentive throughout and "quite obviously" enjoyed the performance.[111]

Sometime after midnight *Prince of Wales* ran into heavy seas which caused much heaving and rolling. By morning most of the party "were not feeling too happy," though the Prime Minister seemed to glory in the turbulent weather. The ocean became so rough that *Prince of Wales* had to choose between slowing down or dropping its destroyer escort. Admiral Pound ordered the destroyers, which had been taking a heavy beating, to turn back. Two flying boats patrolled overhead until late afternoon but after they departed the great battleship plunged on alone.[112]

For a time a strong northwest wind came straight at the ship, blowing the spray off the wave tops and making the quarter- and maindecks untenable. Churchill compensated by exploring the battleship, going through all the compartments several times daily and swinging up and down ladders to the bridge. He got his exercise in this way and also a thorough look at the ship. The 35,000-ton battleship was not at its best for the Prime Minister's inspection. Repairs of the wounds suffered in the engagement with *Bismarck* (during which *Prince of Wales* had forty casualties and took a direct hit on the bridge) had been completed hurriedly for the meeting.[113] There had not been time to remove all the dents, shell holes, and patches of scorched paint. But the party found a happy, well-disciplined ship and evidences of recent battle action heightened the pleasure of traveling on her. Of course, no one knew this voyage was to be the high mark of the great ship's life. Four months later *Prince of Wales* sank, with heavy loss of life, under a rain of Japanese bombs and torpedoes. They were aware that danger was present in the North Atlantic. Captain Leach received several reports of U-boats in the path, and he ordered "zig-zags and wide diversions" to Churchill's keen disappointment.[114]

Tuesday established the routine for the remainder of the voyage. Churchill slept late, and the rest of the group followed suit. All meals were at "movable hours" and "people come in and out to and from their work as it suits them." The Chiefs of Staff met at 10:30 A.M. in the Warrant Officer's Mess. During this first session, Jacob commented, "they seemed in quite good shape, but no more inclined to rattle through their business than they are on land." *Prince of Wales* naturally was observing strict radio silence. No one could send messages; but cables from London pursued the delegation across the Atlantic. A number of "Abbey" telegrams arrived, "mostly filled with political stuff which did not get a very good reception." Churchill ignored these for close perusal of the morning news summaries. He seemed "quite content" to forget about the march of events and simply to enjoy himself. He spent a large part of Tuesday morning in the "miniature war room" which Captain R. P. Pim, Operations Division, Admiralty, had constructed. In this were boards on which the positions of all convoys and known enemy vessels were displayed, along with maps detailing the latest military information.[115]

After lunch Pound, Dill, Freeman, and their assistants disbanded in favor of naps. They resumed at 4:00 over tea. The Prime Minister walked into the room a few minutes later. He inquired what the Chiefs of Staff were doing and said wryly, "It did him good to see them working." [116] He then joined Hopkins at the other end of the room for a session of backgammon in front of the wireless. Several times during the voyage the two matched wits at backgammon for shilling-a-game stakes. Hopkins was astonished that the Prime Min-

ister "can play backgammon and discuss British and American politics, the war, Vichy France, Pierre Laval (and you should hear him
on Laval), the movies, books, personalities, and speculate on what the
winter will bring to Russia — all this and not miss a move in backgammon." [117] An inveterate gambler, Hopkins apparently came out
ahead. He commented discreetly: "The Prime Minister's backgammon is not of the best . . . He approaches the game with great zest,
doubling and redoubling freely." [118] The American offered to teach
Churchill gin rummy, the cutthroat card game then popular in the
United States, but his great friend refused to learn. He was, however, willing to try almost any other diversion. He even settled down
with C. S. Forester's best seller, *Captain Horatio Hornblower* — a
gift from one of his ministers — and found this glorification of English sea power "vastly entertaining." [119]

In the evenings the company usually gathered to watch a motion
picture. Although the quality of the films varied greatly, the Prime
Minister's presence made each showing a gala. Author Howard
Spring described one of these affairs:

> The double scuttles of the ship are closed — the inner ones black —
> and the curtains are drawn across them. The long mess-room is bril-
> liantly lit. On four or five rows of chairs such officers as are not on duty
> are sipping their after-dinner drinks, wearing the stiff winged collars
> and black bows of the ceremonial evening hour. In front, the screen
> has been put up. All is warm and bright and a little sophisticated as
> the mess-servants of the Royal Marines, in their white jackets, move
> here and there. Then an imperceptible tremor, or a sudden slight cant
> of the room, reminds you of the reality beyond this appearance. Out-
> side this shell of white-painted steel the long rollers of the Atlantic
> are racing by . . . So they sit and wait, and at nine o'clock Mr.
> Churchill comes in with Sir John Dill and Sir Dudley Pound and
> other notables, wearing dinner-jackets, smoking pipes and cigars.
> Everybody rises till Mr. Churchill sinks into a deep leather chair in the
> front row. He is chewing an extinct cigar. The performance at once
> begins.[120]

Tuesday night the fare was *Citizen X*, for which Churchill displayed
"great enthusiasm," and a short film of Hopkins' arrival in Moscow.

Colonel Jacob said: "It depicted him getting out of his aeroplane and being greeted by some Russian with a beard, rather an amusing contrast to . . . *Citizen X,* which I believe has had to be taken off in London because of its anti-Russian bias." [121] *The Devil and Miss Jones* was shown on Wednesday, a "rock-bottom" Western picture, *High Sierra,* Thursday night. On Friday evening, however, the Prime Minister's favorite, *Lady Hamilton,* with Vivian Leigh and Laurence Olivier, was presented. In his diary Sir Alexander Cadogan wrote: "Film Lady Hamilton after dinner . . . P.M., seeing it for the fifth time, still deeply moved." [122] When the cannon fire of Trafalgar died away and the image of Nelson's noble, moribund face had dimmed, there was a long, emotional silence. The Prime Minister at last turned to the audience and said, "I thought this would be of particular interest to you, many of whom have recently been under the fire of the enemy's guns on an occasion of equal historical importance. Good Night." [123] No one can repudiate his sense of history on this occasion.

Not all the voyage was devoted to backgammon, exercise, and moviegoing. The Prime Minister and Hopkins discussed every detail of the Moscow mission. Churchill listened raptly as Hopkins described the meetings with Stalin and his experiences in the Communist capital.[124] He accepted the American's optimistic evaluation of Russia's military potential. The interlude also gave them opportunity to estimate the effects of this information upon the approaching discussions. Both were agreed that great changes must be made in supply arrangements. Churchill acceded in principle to diversion to Russia of munitions already consigned to the United Kingdom. On one point he and his old enemies were agreed. He emphasized to Hopkins, as had Commissar Molotov, the necessity for a firm warning to Japan. Another matter apparently discussed raises puzzling questions. Robert E. Sherwood includes in his description of the voyage the statement: "They discussed the phraseology of the Atlantic Charter which the Prime Minister was to present to the President." [125] If Hopkins brought up the desire of F.D.R. for a joint declaration of war and peace aims at this time, Roosevelt again had indulged in his compulsion to keep his left hand ignorant of what the right was doing. As we shall see, Sumner Welles had only just learned of the President's interest in such a declaration and as *Prince of Wales* steamed west was frantically composing a rough draft.

Although radio silence forbade the sending of messages, Churchill could receive them and construct replies. He piled up an enormous backlog of orders and memoranda to be transmitted as soon as *Prince of Wales* could resume transmisson. One message was dispatched because of the urgent supply situation and, perhaps, for other reasons. On August 7, Churchill invited the powerful Minister of Supply, Lord Beaverbrook, to participate in the conference. "If you feel like coming, which I should greatly welcome, aim at afternoon eleventh or morning twelfth, but please do not run needless risks. It may be advisable for you to stay on this [American] side." [126] Before leaving, the English leader had prepared for such an eventuality. He had placed the "Beaver" in charge of upholding British needs in the new situation created by the decision to aid Russia. Even before talking with Hopkins the Prime Minister "dreaded the loss of what we had expected and so direly needed." [127] A Canadian by birth, Beaverbrook was especially committed to the Imperial tie and he would be a tenacious defender of the "Britain first" policy; also he might prove useful if the Americans raised embarrassing questions about the system of imperial preference.

Hopkins used part of the leisure time to catch up on correspondence. His letters varied from bread-and-butter notes, or a tender missive to his daughter Diana, to a terse summary of Russian experiences written to Brendan Bracken. To Lord Ismay, Hopkins wrote that he wished there had been time to tell about the trip to Moscow. He deprecated the rigors of the journey "although the caviar and smoked salmon were almost too much." Hopkins ironically was worried lest he sin against that temple of the *haut monde*—Claridge's Hotel. He wrote Winant that he had left without paying his bill at the famous hotel, and begged the Ambassador to take care of the matter and also to tip Hopkins' valet and waiter a couple of pounds apiece.[128]

During the voyage the entire company followed with great interest developments in England concerning their whereabouts. Their cover story (or lack of one) proved remarkably durable, despite a number of items suggesting that Prime Minister Churchill was involved in more than an extended weekend or inspection trip. London papers on August 1 carried reports that Churchill would make a full report on the production issue "shortly." It was noted without comment that he had not appeared in the House on either the first or second of August. The *Times* carried a story August 4 that "Hurry-Upkins" had returned to London and was expected to see the Prime Minister and Eden soon. Without comment the *Times* reported that Averell Harriman, "defense expediter," had left August 2 for a brief visit to the United States.[129]

After repeated statements that Churchill would take part in debate on the conduct of the war, London dailies reported that Eden was to speak for the government. No one linked the concurrent absences of President Roosevelt and the Prime Minister. As late as August 8 the English press accepted stories about F.D.R.'s vacation cruise. Either voluntary censorship was effective or the best way to avoid suspicion is to take no action to ensure secrecy.

The first break in this wall originated on the Continent. The British monitored a report on German radio August 4, giving its source as Lisbon, that Churchill was en route to a meeting with the American President.[130] There had been leakage or clever guesswork about the P.M.'s plans. Although the government was able to keep this rumor from spreading, the ministers in charge feared others might develop and endanger their chief. According to records in the archives of the Department of State, Churchill had left behind a statement to be given out if speculation got out of hand. "The Prime Minister," this release explained, "accepted an invitation to meet President Roosevelt for a discussion of the general course of the war, the methods of United States aid to Britain and matters of common interest. The Prime Minister is accompanied by the First Sea Lord, the Chief of the Imperial General Staff, and the Permanent Under Secretary of State for Foreign Affairs. The meeting is taking place on board ship somewhere in the Atlantic. No further statement can be made at this stage as to the matters discussed at this meeting or the date of the Prime Minister's return to this country." Through Winant the British government cabled Washington for approval before issuing the statement. Eden proposed to release it August 6 if it proved necessary.[131]

The Secretary of State replied almost immediately that the President thought any statement "highly inadvisable" at this time. Facing collapse of his plans F.D.R. urged: "In my judgment all that need be said is that Prime Minister is on short vacation. References to accompanying officials especially bad. Any statement now is direct invitation to Germans to attack him and his party going and returning. When in doubt say nothing." [132] Eden and his colleagues bowed to Roosevelt's wishes.

They continued to fear a leak. Clement Attlee, pro tem chairman of the War Cabinet, cabled to Churchill his anxiety that Germany's gigantic battleship *Tirpitz* might intercept *Prince of Wales*. He urgently requested guidance. The Prime Minister broke radio silence to soothe Attlee. "I don't see much harm in leakage. If asked a direct question [in the House] questioner should be asked not to put his question; but if he persists the answer should be, 'I cannot undertake to deal with rumors.'" Concerning a possible sortie by *Tirpitz* Churchill mourned, "I fear there will be no such luck." [133] The Prime Minister assured Attlee that Roosevelt undoubtedly would provide escort for the British contingent on the return journey.

Whether that first German radio broadcast was inspired guesswork or a conclusion based on solid information may never be known. The fact that German U-boats and bombers did not attack *Prince of Wales* perhaps is negative evidence that Hitler was unaware of what was transpiring. *Der Führer* may have held back from fear of repercussions in the United States. Lending some weight to this idea is the official German reaction to rumors of a Roosevelt-Churchill meeting. The American Chargé d'Affaires in Berlin, Leland B. Morris, reported that the Foreign Office had announced such a meeting "would be a matter of relative indifference for the course of affairs." Problems facing the two statesmen "could not be disposed of by a personal meeting," the German statement asserted scornfully.[134]

As the British party neared the rendezvous, the relaxed atmosphere on board gave way to tension. No one actually knew what the morrow would bring. Both sides had great hopes, but lack of prior knowledge about each other's intentions, and, more worrisome, the potential for misunderstandings and personality clashes in such an environment made the last few hours anxious ones for all concerned. Even Hopkins admitted he was "slightly jittery" because,

> What would come of the conference I . . . didn't know. And there was no one able to tell me. Churchill didn't know. I'm sure that the President didn't know. Each man is single-hearted in his desire to see Hitler crushed; that was the common ground they'd meet on. But what means they'd adopt, if any, to hasten that highly desirable end, neither knew. What they'd be able to tell the world neither knew.[135]

Everyone was wondering about his opposite number. Did the two delegations in fact speak the same language? How many of the Americans still yearned secretly to twist the British lion's tail? How deeply did the United States representatives understand the rising desperation which lay beneath England's brave front?

When *Prince of Wales* had crossed into the Roosevelt-proclaimed "western hemisphere," Canadian destroyers took up screening positions and escorted the battleship to its destination. At about half-past seven Saturday morning (ship time), as the British were approaching the entrance to Placentia Bay, a large American destroyer came alongside and transferred a pilot. Under his direction *Prince of Wales* slowly moved through heavy morning mist toward the head of the bay. There was a surge of activity on board, "everything being got ship-shape for entering the harbour." [136] The Marine detachment and band fell in on the quarterdeck and the rest of the company took their places for the welcoming ceremonies. When all was ready and *Prince of Wales* had come within a mile or so of the United States warships in the anchorage, the battleship made a sudden turn to starboard and to everyone's surprise headed out to sea. The explanation soon reverberated over the loudspeaker. There had been a mixup about the time, due to the time zones, and *Prince of Wales* had arrived an hour and a half early. The Prime Minister was furious and banged about the main deck, "hunting a target for his wrath." [137] However, nothing could be done except steam in a great circle in the outer reaches of the bay until the appointed hour and then go through the whole process once more.

The second time there was no slipup. At 9:00 precisely on August 9 *Prince of Wales* slowed to come about to its berth in the dark waters off Argentia. As it had steamed up the desolate inlet the summer mist had prevented British and American parties from catching full glimpses of one another. Then, dramatically, the mist broke to reveal a dazzling panorama. The camouflaged British warship, a White Ensign stirring over its stern, found itself in the midst of many other armed ships, of all sizes and shapes, all displaying the Stars and Stripes, their decks lined with cheering seamen. Overhead droned American patrol planes. On the deck of the British battleship their pilots could discern a pudgy figure in some kind of naval uniform. A United States heavy cruiser just a short distance away bore on its quarterdeck another figure, sitting patiently in a wheelchair.[138]

V. The Meeting Begins

Two hours elapsed before Roosevelt and Churchill met. There were frantic last-minute preparations on both ships. Every detail of the ceremonies of greeting had to be perfect, so that a display of pageantry and martial airs provided the proper note of warmth and color for the conference's opening. Captain Beardall and Admiral King's Chief of Staff crossed to *Prince of Wales* for the customary boarding call. Beardall was to inform the Prime Minister of F.D.R.'s wishes regarding their first meeting, social engagements, and formal discussions.[1] This visit eased the preconference tension. British officers had wondered if the United States considered Placentia Bay American territory. They were pleased that the launch bringing the two naval officers bore the Stars and Stripes. Since naval custom required display of an ensign only in a foreign harbor, the Americans viewed their ninety-nine year lease of Argentia as temporary.[2]

Beardall presented a presidential invitation for Churchill to visit *Augusta* and to remain for lunch. The principal British advisers were invited also. There was hurried attention to uniforms, epaulettes, and other details. In the midst of these preparations Harry Hopkins, forgotten for the moment, transferred to *Augusta*. While *Prince of Wales* was moving through morning mist to her mooring, he had paced the bridge in bathrobe and slippers. On spying the distinctive silhouettes of new American destroyers and then the bulk of *Augusta*, Hopkins rushed to his cabin to pack. Disdaining the assistance of his "batman" he threw clothes, medicines, and papers from his Russian mission into several travel-worn valises, bade a quick au revoir to his hosts and hurried off.[3]

"How are you, Harry?" said the President as Hopkins clambered onto *Augusta's* maindeck. "Are you all right? You look a little tired." Hopkins' first words were, "The Russians are confident," and, flatly, so was he. He said he was "all right" though glad to be home. "I said that I wanted most to give him my report," Hopkins later recalled. "I added that I hoped that he'd spend as much time with Churchill as possible." The President nodded absently. He and the other men aboard were too excited about meeting Churchill to concentrate on facts and figures.[4]

At once Hopkins settled into his role as intermediary. The President confided to him a wish first expressed to Beardall. "I have just talked to the President," Hopkins wrote the Prime Minister, "and he is very anxious, after dinner tonight, to invite in the balance of the staff and wants to ask you to talk very informally to them about your general appreciation of the war, and indeed to say anything that you would be disposed to say to a group as large as will be present. I imagine there will be twenty-five people altogether. The President, of course, does not want anything formal about it." Hopkins knew Churchill would be delighted with an opportunity to preach one of his famous sermons. The suggestion may have come from Hopkins, and it is not unlikely that the idea was suggested to Hopkins by his reticent friend during their voyage.[5]

Meanwhile, on Saturday morning important amenities had to be observed. At 11:00 A.M. Churchill stepped into the admiral's barge for the short journey to *Augusta*. Dressed in the semi-naval blue uniform of Warden of the Cinque Ports, surrounded by his resplendently garbed Chiefs of Staff, and followed by a second boatload of British officers, he sat quietly as the final gap separating him and President Roosevelt narrowed. No one can say what passed through that versatile mind. There was much certainly for the Prime Minister to consider as the dark Newfoundland waters slid by — a potential clash of personalities, the tactics of his appeal for American entry in the war, the threat of Japan, future military operations. Possibly, his remarkable ability to concentrate on any given moment allowed him to throw off these serious matters and take in the details of the

American warship and the appearance of the men waiting on its quarterdeck.

Perhaps he noticed the unwarlike glitter and polish of *Augusta,* as did other British observers. The contrast between British and American ships more than anything else struck H. V. Morton, who witnessed the ceremonies: "The *Prince of Wales* was camouflaged; her guns protruded from their turrets like rigid pythons. The American ships were uncamouflaged and shone in peacetime grey. We had been in action, and our brass was either painted or tarnished and our decks were not what they would have been in other days. The American ships were spotless. We admired the beautiful steps of their pinnaces, the gleaming brass, the pine-white woodwork, as those craft lay tossing in our grim shadow." [6]

The seriousness of the occasion seemed even to repress Churchill's usual exuberance as, deliberately, he mounted *Augusta's* gangway. As he set foot on deck a United States Marine band struck up "God Save the King." Full honors were rendered, with sideboys and a Marine color guard splendidly outfitted in dress blues.[7] The grouped officers and statesmen stood at attention for the British and then American national anthems. President Roosevelt, in a light brown Palm Beach suit, waited in the midst of his advisers under an awning just below the bridge. Supporting him at his left elbow was his son, Elliott. The last notes of "The Star-Spangled Banner" died away. Winston Churchill, his stocky figure the center of interest, stepped forward and, bringing a letter from his pocket, presented it with a slight bow to the tall man whom he faced.[8]

These movements were icily formal. As the representative of King George VI, Churchill was delivering credentials to President Roosevelt, his monarch's equal as a chief of state. George VI, who had been F.D.R.'s guest two years before, had written an informal note, dated August 3, highly appropriate for the meeting. "My dear President Roosevelt," it began. "This is just a note to bring you my best wishes, and to say how glad I am that you have an opportunity at last of getting to know my Prime Minister. I am sure you will agree that he is a very remarkable man, and I have no doubt that your meeting will prove of great benefit to our two countries in the pursuit of our common goal." [9] The formal part of the welcoming ceremonies ended with presentation of this message. The frozen tableau on *Augusta*'s deck broke up in smiles and handshakes. American and British staffs flowed together in mutual introduction. Soon Churchill had produced his cigar case and was smoking a long Havana; the President brought out his beloved cigarette holder. Roosevelt invited his guest on a tour of the cruiser and the Prime Minister willingly accepted. As the two leaders moved away, their staffs dispersed to the first round of conversations.

Some of the British and American officers earlier had slipped off to *Augusta*'s wardroom for coffee, the strongest potable available on a United States warship. There was general chatter while further introductions were made. General Arnold was especially useful, because he had met all the British officers present during his recent visit to England. The officers automatically paired off — army, air, and navy talking together — until, shortly after twelve o'clock, they were summoned into Admiral King's cabin for a buffet luncheon. One of the British remembered this as a "very good fork lunch," a convivial gathering, but, unfortunately, again "entirely dry." [10] There is evidence that Roosevelt and Churchill's meal was equally convivial and less arid.

Only one incident disrupted this atmosphere of fellowship and harmony. The President learned Churchill had stolen a march on him by bringing several journalists and photographers to the meeting. This act violated the understanding regarding exclusion of reporters which Roosevelt had requested. Two writers, H. V. Morton and Howard Spring, were present in the guise of Ministry of Information officials. Harry Hopkins informed the President of this deception immediately on boarding *Augusta*. Roosevelt was furious. Elliot Roosevelt later wrote that his father "had made an agreement with Churchill that there should be no newspaper coverage . . . either by reporter or cameramen. After that, in carrying out his part of the bargain, he enjoyed himself thoroughly, giving the press the slip . . . But when Churchill arrived . . . he arrived complete with press retinue . . . It was the first time that Churchill surprised Father in this way. It was not the last." [11] The President, angered by Churchill's nonchalant abrogation of his elaborate scheme for secrecy, claimed that "if the exclusive right to the story was in the hands of British writers the Press of America would tear him to pieces." He moved immediately to repair the breach: Morton and Spring were not to write anything immediately; they were forbidden to board any of the American ships; they were not to attempt to interview the President or any American representatives. [12] General Arnold dispatched a plane to Gander Bay for Army Air Corps photographers. The American press would be provided with a pictorial record of the proceedings.

Another piece of English strategy was not so easily dealt with. The greater size of the British contingent, of all ranks, became apparent at the welcoming ceremonies. Churchill's staff totaled twenty-one; the President's party, including his two sons and Harry Hopkins, came only to fifteen. This is striking when one recalls that the United States was the host nation. An American participant said bitterly: "In contrast to the small party Roosevelt brought along . . . Churchill — well, he didn't have everybody from A to Z, but he had everybody from Beaverbrook to Yool." [13] This British advantage proved unimportant because the meetings developed into tête-à-têtes rather than formal conferences.

The two leaders set this pattern with their first meeting. At their private luncheon in Roosevelt's cabin they discussed organizational arrangements and little else. Almost certainly this first talk, with Hopkins as pilot, stayed in noncontroversial channels. Here and throughout the conference Roosevelt and Churchill were like two fencers, circling, attempting to discover the other's best moves, the vulnerable points of each. [14] The duel was bloodless except for one brief exchange when Churchill unintentionally pinked F.D.R.'s self-esteem. The P.M. commented carelessly how pleased he was finally to meet the President in person after their long exchange of letters and telephone conversations. The cabin temperature plunged momentarily, for the two men had met previously and F.D.R. remembered the occasion well if Churchill did not.[15] On an official junket in 1918 he had been introduced to the already famous Winston Churchill at a dinner in Gray's Inn; it galled that the Prime Minister had not been sufficiently impressed to file a mental note on the encounter. Nothing was said at Argentia or later but F.D.R. never completely forgave Churchill his failure to recognize nascent greatness in Assistant Secretary of the Navy Franklin Roosevelt.[16]

Roosevelt and Churchill agreed that meetings should be functional in character. Military and naval officers would confer with their opposites, diplomat with diplomat, President with Prime Minister. This idea of separation by function prevailed — with rather less than satisfactory results. The conference was singularly confused ("short and disorganized," recalled one participant) with messages being delivered to the wrong people, meetings called on the spur of the moment, and, in general, chaos prevailing. Colonel Jacob later explained: "A group of ships is about the worst setting for a conference you can imagine. One ship — yes, but several definitely — no. Quite often the person you wanted to talk to quitted a ship just as you arrived on board, and as there was a limit to the number of launches etc., and as all departures and arrivals were a matter of ceremony, communications were very unsatisfactory." [17]

A second principle of organization was that there should be no coordination between the various groups. Except for the general session Saturday night this rule of separation was maintained. Roosevelt and Churchill were the sole links; and, evidently, they were not interested in keeping their subordinates informed.[18] Even the most urgent matter, the agenda, was governed by these agreements. Roosevelt and Churchill touched on topics for discussion at their luncheon; but the heavy spadework was left to the diplomats meeting elsewhere in the ship.

1

Once they had sampled Admiral King's varied buffet Welles and Cadogan retired to one of *Augusta's* comfortable staterooms. Their conversation ranks with Churchill's speech Saturday night in impor-

tance. It was the first of several valuable discussions between the
two men, conversations which provided unity for the conference,
knitting the shorter talks of Roosevelt and Churchill.[19] This first
meeting brought out the main points on each side. It also demonstrated the attitudes of these two diplomats and friends. Welles and
Cadogan were similar in background, training, and outlook. Both
were reputed to be cold and aloof men. Churchill's bodyguard said
of Cadogan that he was "the coldest [man] I ever encountered — a
real oyster." [20] *Time* once labeled Sumner Welles one of the very
few men in America who could carry a swagger stick — with all that
implied.[21] Perhaps these traits created a bond. Welles and Cadogan
talked of personal feelings and anxieties, not merely national policy.

The meeting began with Welles giving his counterpart a copy of a
letter from the Premier and dictator of Portugal, Dr. Antonio Salazar, replying to an earlier missive from President Roosevelt. Welles
felt this a matter "which might well be discussed between the President and the Prime Minister not only on the military and naval issues
involved but also more specifically from the standpoint of foreign
policy." [22]

Both the British and Americans feared a German seizure of the
Portuguese Azores as a preliminary to an attack on the American
mainland, and negotiations long had been underway for a defensive
occupation by British or American forces. Salazar resisted the suggestion strenuously, objecting to slurs upon Portugal's independence
and sovereignty on the part of American officials; but he had, in the
letter which Welles now handed to Cadogan, vaguely indicated that
in case of a German attack, American assistance, perhaps with Brazilian cooperation, would be accepted. Such a "gesture" as inclusion of
token Brazilian forces, Welles thought, "would have a tremendously
helpful effect upon Portuguese opinion and do much to mitigate
. . . German propaganda in Portugal." [23] Of course, final decision
on *Operation Indigo* (unfortunate punning designation for the
Azores operation) rested with Roosevelt and Churchill.

Welles introduced the next item with some trepidation. "I knew
that our two governments were in agreement that one of the major

issues that we should now discuss at the meeting between the President and the Prime Minister," he stated carefully, "was the . . . Far Eastern situation." This matter, the most important diplomatic problem of Argentia, is dealt with fully elsewhere; but the range of British-American difficulties over policy toward Japan was provocatively limned by this first discussion. Welles began with a review of negotiations of the past four months between Hull and Admiral Kichisaburo Nomura — now suspended because of Hull's illness and the fact that they had reached impasse. Welles remarked that in a recent interview with Nomura he had expressed the opinion that talks served "no further useful purpose." Japan had embarked on a policy of aggression "diametrically opposed" to the policies its representatives espoused in the conversations.[24] As background he referred to Roosevelt's proposal of July 24 for neutralization of Indochina and told Cadogan this proposal now embraced Thailand.

The British diplomat was fully cognizant of these developments. He asked if there had been any reply to the President's proposal. There had been just before Welles left for Newfoundland. On August 6 the Japanese Minister brought two notes to the Department. Hull, back at his desk, displayed a new firmness, informing Minister Wakasugi that Japanese ambitions, now revealed in stark ugliness, made further negotiations impossible. Hull was not yet prepared to stop talking; but "he was in no hurry whatever to consider the messages handed him or even to read them." Before leaving, Welles also had talked with Wakasugi. He related to Cadogan the details of that conversation and of Japanese counterproposals.[25]

Welles then spoke, as one member of an international fraternity to another, of his personal views regarding the Far Eastern crisis. The time had come, he said, when the United States must reach "a very definite decision" as to that troubled region. Recent establishment of a total economic embargo had shown the period of "extreme patience" on the part of America was at an end. "The Government of Japan further realized . . . that if Japan pursued her present policy of conquest, a conflict between Japan and the United States — whether it came sooner or whether it came later — was inevitable."

It was clear that the Japanese counterproposals contained many features which were wholly unacceptable. Nonetheless, Welles believed it wiser "to utilize this counter proposal as a means of protracting the conversations . . . in order to put off a showdown (if such was inevitable) until the time that such a showdown was from our standpoint more propitious." [26] He was revealing the springs of the President's attitude toward Japan and, at the same time, expressing the contradictions of that policy.

By the Argentia conference American leaders seem resigned to conflict — sooner or later — with Japan.[27] Hull was the exception, apparently, since he was determined not to overlook any means of giving aid to the "moderates" in Japan. He believed "that by dealing with [Japan] as tactfully as possible that peace crowd might win out over there." [28] But whether or not this policy was successful, Hull and others desired to postpone a showdown to shore up American military and naval power. The alternative, a stand against the Japanese in hope of convincing them that further aggression would result in war, was never seriously considered.

Welles emphasized that should the course he was recommending be adopted there would not be "the slightest relaxation" of "any of the economic or financial measures of sanctions which it [the United States] had proclaimed nor the slightest changes in any of the military or naval steps taken by the United States." This generality would not raise British hopes for American reinforcement in the Far East; it did embody certain specific diplomatic acts. By direction of the President, Welles urged that even such a desperate move as Japanese occupation of Thailand not be a *casus belli* for Great Britain. The War and Navy Departments (and by default makers of foreign policy) were convinced the chief object for the time being should be avoidance of war with Japan "inasmuch as war . . . at this time would not only tie up the major portion of, if not the entire, American fleet but would also likewise create a very serious strain upon our military establishment and upon our production activities at the very moment when these should be concentrated upon the Atlantic." [29] Not for the first time was the United States outstripping its British ally in the strategy of "Europe First."

Far Eastern policy went first on the agenda. Welles "trusted" that the British government would take the view of this question he had described, namely, "the dragging out of conversations . . . without the slightest relaxation of the military and economic measures" and without "the slightest commitment" that the United States would accept the Japanese counterproposal.[30] He thought this negotiation poker would not provoke further Japanese aggression.

Whatever his own feelings, Cadogan was too seasoned a diplomat to let them guide his answer. He realized the American wished to make him a transmitter and interpreter of the policy of caution. Cadogan expressed agreement with the Under Secretary's statements, but left no impression of commitment to the American position. Although stating his belief that Churchill "would likewise be inclined thereto," he throttled Welles' hopes. "Mr. Churchill," he explained, "had recently apparently come to believe that Japan had reached the point where she was willing to take on at the same time the Soviet Union, Germany, the Netherlands East Indies, Great Britain, the Dominions and the United States." This willful exaggeration was in hope of frightening Roosevelt into action. The Prime Minister felt only the "stiffest warning" from the United States would have any effect. Only the previous week the British government had made a formal commitment to the Dutch regarding defense of the Netherlands East Indies. Cadogan described this pledge:

> The Prime Minister had been unwilling to make any such commitments because he was not assured of the position which the United States would take in the event that Japan attacked the Netherlands East Indies and that Great Britain then went to the latter's assistance. The Foreign Office had pointed out to the Prime Minister that the United States Executive could not make any such commitment without the consent of Congress and that such prior assent by the Congress was not conceivable. Finally and reluctantly the Prime Minister had authorized the . . . following commitment to the Dutch Government, namely, that if Japan attacked the Netherlands East Indies, the Netherlands Government, fully aware of the resources which Great Britain had in the Far East, could expect Great Britain to give all possible assistance . . . within the limits of its available resources.[31]

His elucidation of Churchill's decision to enter an arrangement with the Dutch demonstrated the dependence of Great Britain — in truth, of all countries with interests in the Pacific — on the United States. The British commitment, circumscribed by double admission of its feebleness, deposited protection of the Indies and of the entire Pacific in the lap of America.

Welles was anxious to determine the boundaries of this pledge before the President took up Far Eastern problems. He inquired whether the Netherlands government "clearly understood" that Great Britain would assist "only . . . with the resources which she had available at Singapore and at other nearby places." The Americans did not want Britain to weaken its forces in the Atlantic merely to throw them into a hopeless cause in the Far East! Cadogan assured him the Dutch understood "precisely that" and, further, his government was not committed "insofar as time or quantity of assistance." [32] Pressure from the Dominions had been the precipitating reason for the commitment; it formed one basis of Churchill's desire for a strong pledge from the United States. When the embargo issue arose, the Australian government had demanded that Churchill obtain from the President "a commitment that in the event that Japan attacked the Netherlands East Indies and that Great Britain then went to the latter's assistance . . . the President would agree that he would request of the Congress authority necessary . . . for the United States to assist the British, the Dominions and the Netherlands East Indies forces to resist Japanese aggression." [33] It had not been possible to act upon the Australian request before the imposition of sanctions against Japan. Increasingly worried by the fuzziness of Washington's position, Australia's Prime Minister, Robert G. Menzies, made a further effort to get a flat commitment from the United States. He cabled Churchill and the Dominions' Ministers on July 30 that "if the Americans feel in their hearts that in the event of warlike retaliation by Japan they could not remain aloof from the conflict, surely they can be made to see that a plain indication by them to Japan at this stage would probably avoid war. I recognize the traditional reluctance of the United States to enter into outside commitments in advance, but where the commitment seems inevitable, there is everything to be gained by promptly accepting it, and everything to be lost by delay."[34] Churchill must have been delighted, for he entirely agreed with Menzies' argument and it provided him with an excellent excuse for proposing such an ultimatum. The Prime Minister, of necessity, had bowed to this demand, Cadogan stressed, and found it necessary to raise the question with F.D.R.[35]

Welles made a diplomatic reply. He was "unable to indicate" what would be Roosevelt's decision were this proposal made to him. In his own judgment, however, any such commitment was undesirable. The suggested agreement implied "the bringing of pressure on the Congress by the President . . . to undertake a declaration of war." Patiently, Welles explained that the determining factor in any decision would be public opinion. American opinion was mounting "very sharply and very rapidly" against Japan's aggression; but it was not yet ready to support steps toward war. He believed that American involvement in hostilities would come if Japan continued its course. He also believed that "any such agreement on the part of the President . . . would have no practical effect but if it became known would have a reaction on American public opinion altogether counter to that which the British and American governments . . . would desire." To dilute this bitter draft Welles admitted the matter was one "which the President would have to determine himself."[36]

2

With probable relief the diplomats turned from the Orient to a perplexing but less divisive problem closer to home, the "old question" of Vichy France. After the fall of France the United States undertook to open a window into the darkness of occupied Europe by relations with the French regime which ensconced itself at the spa of Vichy.[37] This was a reasonable act because the Vichy government was the constitutional successor to the defunct Third Republic. What now seems questionable is the continuation of the "Vichy gamble" in face of large evidence of its failure. There were many

reasons, including concern for disposition of the still powerful
French fleet, why F.D.R. continued a policy which steadily became
more unpopular in the United States. "What was paramount in Roosevelt's mind was the security of the British and French fleets," Sumner Welles once commented. "With the major part of our own navy
necessarily concentrated in the Pacific, continued Anglo-American
supremacy was his primary concern. Were Hitler to obtain the bulk
of the French fleet, that supremacy would be lost."[38] The American
presence at Vichy was to stiffen the resolve of Marshal Pétain and
the shifting coterie around him not to surrender that fleet.[39] Roosevelt, as a devout Mahanist, perhaps overestimated its importance;
certainly he miscalculated Hitler's desire for the French navy.

F.D.R.'s faith in sea power also supported the second aim of policy
toward Vichy. The President was supremely aware of North and
West Africa's importance for operations against the Americas. Con-
versely, the region was an obvious "launching pad" for attack on
Hitler's *Festung Europa*. The French naval base at Dakar was the
first rung up the ladder to Europe, but its seizure was out during the
conceivable future.[40] For multiple reasons American activity focused on the Vichy-ruled province of North Africa.

Until the United States entered the European war its attitude
toward this region was defensive — to prevent German seizure.
Simple in principle, the policy was complex in execution. Vichy's
version of musical chairs, with power shifting from anti-Germans to
moderates to collaborators and back, was not easily followed by
Washington or by the American Ambassador, Admiral William D.
Leahy. Especially confusing was the relation between Vichy and its
High Commissioner for North Africa, the World War I hero and
military commander during the Third Republic's death agony, Maxime Weygand. The Roosevelt administration believed that Weygand sympathized with the anti-Axis coalition. It attempted to
strengthen his position in hope that if Vichy did capitulate entirely to
Hitler, North Africa (and perhaps the French West African possessions) would stand by themselves.

To carry forward the North African policy Roosevelt used a favorite method, the dispatch of a personal representative.[41] Robert Murphy, a career diplomat who held the official position of Counselor of the Embassy at Vichy, undertook, in December, 1940, the first of many missions to French Africa. As he recalls this assignment, he was urgently summoned to Washington and taken for an interview with Roosevelt,

> [who] believed that North Africa was the most likely place where French troops might be brought back into the war against Nazi Germany. Spread out on his desk was a large map showing all of French North and West Africa, and the President told me he had given much thought about how to help French officers who were operating in the relatively independent conditions prevailing in Africa. The President then said that he wanted me to return to Vichy and work unostentatiously to get permission to make a thorough inspection tour of French Africa and to report my findings to him. The French African policy of the United States government thus became the President's personal policy. He initiated it, he kept it going, and he resisted pressures against it. [42]

The conclusions Murphy reached as a result of this tour — his judgment of Weygand and his advocacy of economic aid to the civil population of North Africa — became the basis of American policy.

Thus, by May, 1941, Roosevelt's attitude with regard to Vichy was well defined. He proposed that the United States and Great Britain recognize that Vichy was "in a German cage" but still issued orders to Weygand, Syria, and Indochina; that pressure be put on Vichy, because it had ordered French possessions to resist British occupation, to issue orders for them to resist German occupation as well; that food be shipped to North Africa as an effective and humanitarian means of balking Germany; that Germany be kept out of the North African ports as long as possible.[43]

In the weeks before the Argentia conference the North African situation was in flux, partly because of the above policies. Darlan, an advocate of collaboration, perhaps even of military alliance with Germany, was appeasing Japan — as Hull and others at State thought he secretly had been toadying to the Nazis. Hull was much disturbed, telling Welles over the phone from White Sulphur Springs: "Our people will have to watch mighty closely or wake up some morning with a despatch from Vichy to Weygand about joint German defense of North Africa." [44] From Murphy at Algiers came a worried report vindicating the American (and his) course and claiming that the tide at Vichy was "running rapidly in the direction of concessions to the Germans in French Africa." Weygand was becoming convinced that Vichy danced to German music. "Under such circumstances," Murphy cabled, "if the General can be brought to believe that the African trump . . . can be played with a chance of winning, he will feel justified in taking responsibility." [45]

The consensus was the crisis would occur soon. On August 5 the English press carried a report that Darlan had received authority over North Africa, with Weygand taking orders from him.[46] This was disaster — if true. Actually there had been an administrative shuffle with Darlan becoming Minister of Foreign Affairs and Weygand, as High Commissioner, formally his subordinate. This act was followed on the eve of the Newfoundland meeting by Weygand's summons to Vichy for top-level consultations.[47]

The British were little perturbed by these developments, for they never had been convinced Weygand possessed either the freedom or determination to act that was attributed to him by the Roosevelt administration. They opposed the Vichy regime. But British hostility to Vichy, manifested in petty and serious hindrance of American policy, was largely sterile. Its principal expression and one of the largest obstructions to support of Weygand was the economic blockade.[48] London's actions made many Americans believe that the British were their own worst enemy. Secretary of War Stimson, in a note to his diary, said of a meeting of the "secret three": "Hull was full of his troubles with British stupidity and British lack of tact and it does seem that something ought to be done to keep them from cutting their own throats." [49] While not objecting formally to United States relations with Vichy, the British government opposed such measures as supplying foodstuffs to North Africa and metropolitan France.

The British press, apparently with official backing, caused Roosevelt embarrassment by showing that German infiltration of North Africa in violation of the armistice was well under way. On February 19 the British government accepted a report that "a German delegation, including specialists in preparing airfields and submarine bases, had taken over the French Air Force in Morocco." [50] They supposedly were disguised as tourists. Murphy had to interrupt his discussions with Weygand to check out this story. On arrival in Rabat, he learned that one lone German armed with a tourist visa issued in Paris had appeared. The French resident general had promptly shipped the visitor back and had ordered that similar visas should be canceled. Rumors more difficult to deal with were repeated British pronouncements that Weygand was planning independent action, that he was "a David preparing to slay the German Goliath." [51]

Welles' comments to Cadogan indicated discomfort with the embarrassing, contradictory statements regarding Vichy in general and North Africa in particular. In his judgment the course of the United States in the past year had been "of great practical value." He claimed the personal influence of the President and of Admiral Leahy had contributed to defeat "of the plans and intrigues of Laval, Darlan and company." He was exaggerating the value of the American presence at Vichy; but Cadogan admitted that F.D.R.'s actions "had resulted in a continuing and close contact with the French authorities in North Africa . . . and for the existence of a situation there today which meant that every kind of resistance by the local authorities was being interposed against German infiltration and actual domination." Hitler intended the occupation of Spain, Portugal, and strategic points on the Atlantic Coast of Africa "at some time not very remote." [52] French resistance to or delay of the Nazi advance would provide valuable time.

Cadogan's agreement allowed the American diplomat to spring a trap. If Cadogan's statement represented the views of the Foreign Office, he pointed out, it was not the opinion "of other individuals and departments of the British Government." He went on to complain that "every time the United States announced any step in the policy which it had been pursuing there was either bitter criticism on the part of the Ministry of Economic Warfare . . . or on the part of a very considerable portion of the British press. If the British Government believed . . . the policy . . . was wise and to their advantage, I felt that the least that we could ask was that there be avoided a constant carping criticism." Cadogan tried to explain that these occurrences and the badgering of Brazil by British agencies arose from lack of coordination rather than from design. He confessed that absence of direction (with which Welles certainly was familiar) hampered the Foreign Office; he promised to do "what he could" to correct the problem.[53] Welles was not mollified, for he believed the highest individuals in the British government — excluding Cadogan — approved this obstructionism. The two men laid the matter to rest and turned to one final item, a joint declaration of war and peace. It was one matter on which Welles and Cadogan were in complete agreement.

Their marathon session had lasted the whole of Saturday afternoon. Its two participants had touched almost all those questions which later arose — the Azores, Vichy and French North Africa, the Far East, and component points (the "no deals" message and the Lend-Lease Agreement) in the Atlantic Charter. They had done an admirable job. Discussion remained exploratory and conditional, for final decision on every subject lay with the President and Prime Minister. No one could foresee their conclusions. Welles could not be certain whether his confident statement of American intentions would be supported, modified, or discarded. Eating one's words was a steady diet for those who served Franklin Roosevelt.

3

While Welles and Cadogan labored deep within *Augusta*, the business and fun of this unique conference went forward. After a three-and-one-half hour visit Churchill returned to *Prince of Wales* at 2:30 P.M. Most of his staff had gone back an hour before, having made arrangements for a later meeting.[54] Some returned to their cabins only long enough to shed dress uniforms for more comfortable garb and then joined a bull session in Arnold's quarters on *Tuscaloosa*. Another rule, that of informality, had been established. Whether this atmosphere or the effect of his first meeting with Roosevelt influenced the Prime Minister is not known. Churchill did violate a hallowed naval custom when he returned to *Prince of Wales*. Later, pictures showed him stepping onto the quarterdeck of the battleship puffing vigorously on a frazzled cigar, a surprising transgression for one of his experience with matters naval.[55]

All day there was shuttling back and forth between American ships, *Prince of Wales,* and the English and Canadian destroyers, traffic not limited to participants in scheduled meetings. Officers and sailors of the three nations were eager to find out how others were getting on. In many respects Americans, British, and Canadians were alike — sharing a common profession, language, traditions. Their interrogations, because of contrasting situations and decidedly uncommon recent experiences, were dissimilar. Americans wanted to know about the war, how it had been to engage a flesh-and-blood enemy. Fuzzy-cheeked American sailors listened in awe as equally youthful Britishers pointed to dents and scars in *Prince of Wales* caused by *Bismarck's* sixteen-inch shells. One jagged shell hole just off the officers' mess (possibly left unrepaired by intent during the battleship's refitting) was a popular attraction. English sailors asked repeatedly whether the "scuttlebutt" was correct about no rationing or food shortages in the United States; they wanted to hear what it was like not to be in a struggle for survival. Doubters among them were convinced by the incredible lavishness of everything on U.S. ships. Even the advertisements in wardroom magazines shouted a staggering affluence.[56] More important, these revealed the depth of America's unconcern about the war. British officers drew that precise conclusion from perusal of American periodicals. "The Ward Room is flooded with American magazines . . ." Colonel Jacob noted. "There is a wide assortment, including *Time, The Saturday Evening Post, Collier's Weekly, Life,* etc. There are papers on Hollywood, on baseball, and on Bible prophecy. They make one quite sick, and I have not found a single reasonable article on the war from the British point of view." [57] Group Captain [now Air Vice-Marshal] W. M. Yool was even more explicit. "The general impression one got in talking to the Americans was that they were still very remote from the war and quite a long way from joining in as yet," he has remarked. "This impression is reinforced by looking through a host of American magazines which were showered upon us and from which one gathers that the main preoccupations of the Americans consist of, 1) the elimination of B.O.; 2) keeping the bowels open; and 3) lying on a beach with a blonde." [58]

The prosperous Americans deluged their new friends with food, candy, and cigarettes; in some cases generosity was not disingenuous. As with Lend-Lease, the Americans hoped to get something back. But in contrast to F.D.R.'s proudest achievement, these open-handed sailors desired an immediate return on their investment. Negotiations hinged on a small but universally known difference in British and U.S. naval regulations. The British rose to the occasion and good English liquor was dispensed to thirsty visitors. [59]

The President's party was exempted from this particular regulation and F.D.R. impressed several British guests during the conferences with the strength of his Martinis, which he brewed from dry gin and a potent Argentine vermouth. Nonetheless, on Saturday afternoon F.D.R. dispatched a personal, unconditional contribution to the English and Canadian warships. Harry Hopkins had told him of the reduced rations, lack of tobacco and sweets in the British services, and the President had brought along something in compensation. To *Prince of Wales,* H.M.S. *Ripley,* H.M.C.S. *Restigouche,* and H.M.C.S. *Assiniboine* went nineteen hundred and fifty gift boxes, each containing cigarettes, fresh fruit, and cheese. Fifteen hundred were sent to the great battleship, one hundred and fifty to each destroyer. Each box included a card of greeting which read: "The Commander-in-Chief, United States Navy, Sends Greetings and Best Wishes, Franklin D. Roosevelt, President of the United States." [60] The Prime Minister was on deck when the packages were delivered to *Prince of Wales* and "showed great interest and appreciation in their distribution." Churchill was "persuaded" to pose for photographs with American Marines unloading the parcels. Thompson, his bodyguard, recalls that the Prime Minister did the persuading: "Right off he called for a number of the Americans to gather round him and a picture was taken of this happy group. The gesture was appreciated all over and the picture was the envy of the Marines' comrades back on the *Augusta*." [61]

Dinner on Saturday evening was in honor of Churchill and his staff. This was an important occasion, more than a time for display of fine manners, gourmandizing, polite conversation, and both sides realized it. Churchill, who retired for a brief nap after his pleasant exertion on the quarterdeck, tossed about and slept only fitfully because of the "terrible tension" which pervaded the ship. He hardly spoke a word during the familiar — and usually enjoyable — metamorphosis from garish dressing gown-clad citizen to starched and immaculately outfitted statesman.[62] Similar manifestation of excitement and anxiety cropped up on *Augusta* and *Tuscaloosa,* as the Americans prepared for this first (and as it turned out only) formal dinner.

Accompanying Churchill as he boarded the President's cruiser on the stroke of 7:00 were Sir Alexander Cadogan, Admiral Pound, General Dill, Air Vice-Marshal Freeman, and Lord Cherwell. Present to welcome them were the President, Hopkins, Welles, Stark, Marshall, King, and Harriman. In another of the mixups which developed, Arnold had not received an invitation. He recounted later that night that he "was sitting at dinner on *Tuscaloosa* when a bombshell exploded. Twice during P.M. a messenger came in and tried to deliver a message to me. He took me to be General Marshall. I told him the Chief of Staff was not aboard." Soon another message arrived that if Marshall were aboard he was expected on *Augusta* at 6:45 P.M. for dinner. Arnold insisted that General Marshall was not present; the same thing happened twice more. Just at 6:45, as Roosevelt's other guests were arriving, a message arrived: "The name Arnold should be substituted for Marshall." Groaning, "What a position for a guy to be in," Arnold arose from the table on *Tuscaloosa* and walked into Roosevelt's stateroom on *Augusta* five minutes later. "That Captain's gig never traveled so fast in its life," he later recalled. The dinner was going full blast when he came in, and King assured him somewhat maliciously that his absence had gone unnoticed.[63]

The British were outnumbered — even before Arnold's tardy entry — but on their side was the redoubtable mind and eloquent tongue of Churchill. Conversation flowed as the company enjoyed its meal in the glow of heavy silver, flickering candles and the sheen of the cabin's inlaid paneling. *Augusta's* chef had outdone himself with a typically American yet versatile banquet. Dinner began with almonds (which someone in Roosevelt's party fancied since they appeared on every menu during the cruise), vegetable puree, and hors d'oeuvres. The entrée was broiled spring chicken, almost extinct in meat-starved England, along with buttered sweet peas, spinach omelet, candied sweet potatoes, mushroom gravy, hot rolls, and currant jelly. Sliced tomato salad, assorted cheeses, and crackers followed. For dessert Roosevelt's guests could choose among chocolate ice cream, cookies, or cupcakes. In place of liqueurs they were offered coffee, tea, mints, or ginger and, of course, the heady wine of Churchill's oratory.[64]

Conversation stayed mostly on general matters. There were brief speeches by the President and the Prime Minister, Pound, Dill, and Freeman. The two leaders were deferred to but, probably, the company was eager to hear Hopkins on his trip behind the Kremlin's wall. Hopkins had presented his full report to F.D.R. that afternoon and Churchill heard the story during the ocean journey; others, however, wished to learn how talkative the Russian leaders had been to "Harry the Hop." They realized that his conclusions about the Russian front, because of his influence with Roosevelt and Churchill, would guide Anglo-American support of the Soviet Union. The decision to aid Russia had been taken, but how much aid — and how soon — depended largely on Hopkins' recommendations.[65]

His remarks enthralled his listeners. For the first time there were solid facts about the military situation in the U.S.S.R. Some questions Roosevelt's aide could not answer, for neither he nor Russian leaders could predict the future. Discussion of Soviet problems led to Japan. Molotov's remarks to Hopkins had shown that the Russians were deeply worried. They realized the temptation for Japan to invade Siberia. Molotov desired a strongly-worded warning that the United States, in event of Japanese aggression, would come to the Soviet Union's aid.[66] Notably, the wording of this request was similar to that of Churchill's.

Also a topic of conversation at dinner was a joint declaration "laying down certain broad principles which should guide our policies along the same road." [67] The idea had been canvassed by Welles and Cadogan. The astute Cadogan did not fail to inform his chief that Roosevelt seemed determined to have some statement on war aims. (A moot point is whether Hopkins and Churchill discussed the idea during the voyage to Argentia.) The Prime Minister "leaped at this chance to identify the policies of the two nations even more closely." [68]

4

Thorough discussion of these questions was left until the next day. After dessert the tables were cleared and the company settled back for an informal talk by Churchill on the war. Members of the President's retinue who had not attended the dinner and senior officers from *Augusta* and other American warships witnessed Churchill's performance. His talk was the highlight of the first day and one of the most important events of the conference, a Churchillian tour de force, among his best performances ever. A master of swift, brilliant generalizations and poetic imagery, the Prime Minister was highly entertaining. Churchill pulled out all the stops in a superb appeal to emotion. Even Elliott Roosevelt, violently Anglophobic, was impressed: "Churchill rared back in his chair . . . slewed his cigar around from cheek to cheek, and always at a jaunty angle, his hands slashed the air expressively, his eyes flashed. He held the floor that evening and he talked. Nor were the rest of us silent because we were bored. He held us enthralled even when we were inclined to disagree with him." [69] Stranger still to Elliott than his reaction to the old bulldog's speech was the role of his father. The F.D.R. everyone knew dominated every gathering, always assumed the lead; yet his son and others noticed that the President listened, silent, intent, as Churchill, ranging widely, held the audience.[70]

Despite the remarkable control over his auditors thus shown, Churchill's peroration did not lead to the dialogue or to the commitment for which he had planned. Warned by Hopkins, Roosevelt was armed against the Englishman's rhetoric. The Prime Minister would not sway him to open advocacy of American intervention. Neither would words — no matter how brilliant — move Welles and Harriman. The President's purpose, it appears, was twofold. He was curious about his guest's fabled oratory.[71] He was putting Churchill to another test — to be graded by Roosevelt the consummate politician and public speaker. His aide's paeans had reinforced this curiosity. Also involved was the desire for information and an insight to Churchill's thinking.

One may speculate that F.D.R. possessed another motive for asking the Prime Minister to speak before this assembly of high American officials, a group which included the chiefs of the military and naval establishments. The speech was thoroughly safe. The President did not want Churchill to move Marshall, Stark, and Arnold to support entry. Stark and Marshall, at least, already favored such a course, with certain important conditions; they and others had to be reminded periodically that the Congress alone could make a decision for war.[72] They were infected with war virus already, and F.D.R. did not much fear a spreading of the disease.[73]

Roosevelt saw (and Churchill came to appreciate) that the war fever the British leader was propagating differed from that of F.D.R.'s advisers. The Prime Minister was pressing for participation in a "limited" war, a conflict by attrition, by blows at the periphery of the Axis empire; above all with minimum expenditure of British and American blood.[74] The war which Marshall and company foresaw was hardly as beautiful or as frugal. Theirs was a doctrine of total war that rejected "stopgap" measures such as strategic bombing. They advocated a massive assault on Hitler's *Festung Europa* and willingness to accept hundreds of thousands, perhaps millions, of casualties as the price of victory.

Roosevelt was confident the decision for war would remain in his hands. He was concerned about the type of warfare that would result from American intervention, if it came. He had been unable to shake his advisers' faith and he deeply feared the implications of total war.[75] Perhaps he hoped that Churchill, on the strength of his supposed expertise in modern warfare, would serve as a Jenner and inoculate the American leaders with a limited-war serum.

The Prime Minister's talk did have that intent. He presented a "masterly review" of the world crisis and described England's and the British Empire's military position. He went into detail about the Middle East, arguing that the Germans should be attacked where there existed even or fairly equal terms.[76] It had been shown on many occasions, most recently during the Admiralty liaison conference of July 24 which Hopkins attended, that American planners opposed reinforcement of the Middle East. Some were advocating total withdrawal because of belief that the devious English were using American aid to further their imperial ambitions.[77] Turning to the Far East, Churchill reiterated his conviction that a joint warning to Japan was necessary to avert war. He particularly stressed the strategic advantages of Singapore as the focus of Allied reinforcement.

Churchill shifted next to an argument for which the President had been waiting — the strategy and resources the British believed were needed for victory. He said that "this was a mechanized war, not a war of 1917–18 where doughboys in the mud and trenches fought it out to a conclusion. This was a mobile war, in the air, on the land, at sea." He downgraded the importance of immense land armies and called for the production and dispatch of swarms of heavy bombers "to bring home to the Germans the horrors of war just as the Germans have brought it home to the British." [78] In sum, the Prime Minister proposed blockade, subversion, and, most important, strategic bombing, as the means to victory.

He then urged that when all "this disturbed condition in Europe was over" the United States and Great Britain take the lead in creating a new League of Nations to maintain order throughout the world and to prevent "recurrence of any such terrible tragedies as we were now witnessing." [79] On this noble and high-principled note Churchill concluded his address.

There apparently was no mention in these remarks of American entry into the war. Since no exact transcription of his "informal talk" exists, it is impossible to say just how he dealt with this most delicate of subjects. Elliott Roosevelt has written that Churchill did ask bluntly an American declaration of war. "It's your only chance," he had the Prime Minister exclaim. "You've *got* to come in beside us! If you don't declare war, declare war, I say, without waiting for them to strike the first blow, they'll strike it after we've gone under, and their first blow will be their last as well!" [80] It is unlikely Churchill took such a position in the face of F.D.R.'s expressed wish for silence. To have done so the first evening of the conference would have been unwise, even dangerously foolish, for there were several days remaining to convince the President. A more reasonable rendition comes from a member of the United States military delegation, Colonel C. W. Bundy, who noted: "By inference Churchill advocated early American action to join Britain and Russia." [81]

Roosevelt certainly followed the drift of the Prime Minister's remarks. If the British leader hoped the President would follow his guest's spirit of adventure and pledge his determination to bring the United States into the war, he was disappointed. Roosevelt made no reply, either to the Prime Minister's implied request or to the specific statements. In view of his habit of retiring early, he may have been too sleepy to respond. The hour was late. Churchill, Cadogan, Dill, and the other English guests left *Augusta* at 11.45 P.M. The Americans returned to their quarters on *Tuscaloosa* a few minutes later. [82]

The first day of the Argentia meeting had been filled with drama and hope. Harmony had prevailed. Roosevelt and Churchill had met and not found any serious obstacles to cooperation. The episode of the smuggled journalists rankled, but Roosevelt had taken immediate steps to remedy that British gaucherie. If suggestions for intervention irritated the President, he did not show displeasure. He perhaps recognized the impossibility of asking Churchill to remain mute on this matter.

Harry Hopkins certainly went to bed Saturday night a satisfied if exhausted man. He had proven a successful "marriage broker." Now that the two leaders had come together, it was necessary to keep the engagement off any rocks which the morrow might reveal.

VI. United in Purpose

SUNDAY DAWNED CLEAR and pleasantly warm, unusual weather for southern Newfoundland. "A really lovely morning," observed Colonel Jacob, "just like a summer's day on the west of Scotland." [1] A soft breeze stirred the hundreds of brightly-colored flags and pennants overhead, the sun shone from behind thin clouds. There was "a beautiful shimmering grey look" on the waters of the bay, and the rocky hills all around Argentia were clad in deep, lush green. The setting conspired to dramatize the fact of Anglo-American unity. [2]

Sunday morning beheld the emotional summit of the meeting. The President and his staff were Churchill's guests at a combined church service on *Prince of Wales*. Every care was taken to ensure the success of this occasion. The Prime Minister personally had supervised a dress rehearsal of the ceremony on August 8, as the British warships plunged through heavy seas toward Argentia. He desired that every detail be perfect, that nothing detract from the affirmation of the common traditions and goals of the two English-speaking nations. For example, Captain Leach addressed the ship's company over the loudspeaker to call for a "special effort by every man" during the divine services. "They were to raise steam in an extra boiler so as to give the hymns full value." [3] The President was equally determined. Each member of his staff was "requested" to attend the service "by command of the President." Lest someone forget, written invitations were delivered to all at one o'clock Sunday morning. [4]

The leading destroyer, U.S.S. *McDougal*, its bow level with *Augusta's* main deck and *Prince of Wales'* stern carried Roosevelt to the great British warship. The President was hatless and wore a blue double-breasted suit. Holding a cane in his right hand and aided by Elliott on his left, he crossed a narrow gangway from *Augusta* to the destroyer, there to receive the salute of a Marine honor guard and band. *McDougal* then made a "Chinese landing" (bow to stern) on *Prince of Wales*. F.D.R. walked slowly along a starboard gangway to the deck, where he was received aboard with full honors. Fifteen hundred or more men, including approximately two hundred and fifty United States sailors and marines, stood at rigid attention for the two national anthems.

Roosevelt walked the length of the ship to his place of honor on the quarterdeck. The Prime Minister, dressed today in the uniform of the Royal Yacht Squadron, watched stolidly although he may have been as surprised and moved by this display of courage as were several of his aides. Captain Yool recalls that "many of us in England had thought that the President was unable to walk at all . . . One got the impression of great courage and strength of character as he slowly approached the assembled company. It was obvious to everybody that he was making a tremendous effort and that he was determined to walk along that deck even if it killed him." [5] This may have been the longest walk F.D.R. had ever attempted since being stricken with polio.

The President and Prime Minister were seated side-by-side in the center of a hollow square, with their Chiefs of Staff behind and serried ranks of British and American sailors on two sides. In accordance with English practice, the Marine Band marched aft, took position in front of a contingent of grim-looking Petty Officers, and wheeled to face the pulpit, signaling the beginning of divine services. All was solemn and quiet as two chaplains, English and American, stepped forward and opened hymnals. It was a stirring moment. Churchill was to write,

> None who took part in it will forget the spectacle presented that sunlit morning on the crowded quarterdeck — the symbolism of the Union Jack and the Stars and Stripes draped side by side on the pulpit; the American and British chaplains sharing in the reading of the pray-

ers; the highest naval, military, and air officers of Britain and the United States grouped together behind the President and me; the close-packed ranks of British and American sailors, completely intermingled, sharing the same books and joining fervently together in the prayers and hymns familiar to both.[6]

Unity veritably flowed from the occasion, but the Prime Minister determined to add to the surfeit. Following Royal Navy custom, Captain Leach read the lesson. The verse, Joshua 1: 1–9, seemed aimed directly at the President: "There shall not any man be able to stand before thee all the days of thy life; as I was with Moses, so I will be with thee: I will not fail thee, nor forsake thee. Be strong and of good courage . . ."[7] The hymns, which Churchill selected, and various of the prayers were suggestive of the duty of the United States to join its beleaguered sister democracy. "For Those in Peril On The Sea," traditional anthem of seafarers, reminded the congregation of common dangers which British and American sailors were facing. Then came the rousing hymn, "Onward Christian Soldiers," with its simple appeal for volunteers "marching as to war . . . with the cross of Jesus going on before." The chaplains offered prayers for President Roosevelt, for the King, for all in authority, for those in the invaded countries that they might have strength to hold on "till the day of deliverance." They prayed for all who had suffered by reason of the war and for the victory of right and truth. "Stablish our hearts, O God, in the day of battle, and strengthen our resolve, that we fight . . . till all enmity and oppression be done away, and the peoples of the world be set free from fear to serve one another."[8] Invocations of a noble crusade directed to a mixed bag of crusaders! The final hymn was "O God, Our Help in Ages Past," which, Churchill later recalled, "Macaulay reminds us the Ironsides had chanted as they bore John Hampden's body to the grave."[9] The historian-politician Churchill could trace the present struggle to the great English battle for parliamentary supremacy, an interesting manifestation, perhaps, of the Whig interpretation of history.

The effect of this service, two great men communing in an isolated retreat, was overpowering. F.D.R. described the events of Sunday

morning as the "keynote" of the entire meeting.[10] Elliott Roosevelt
has reported his father said, "If nothing else had happened while we
were here, that would have cemented us. 'Onward, Christian Soldiers.' We *are*, and we *will* go on, with God's help." [11] Undoubtedly, the President was affected — one would have to have been a
much colder man than Franklin Roosevelt to have shrugged off such
an experience.

Churchill's response is a matter of record. He described the
church service as "a deeply moving expression of the unity of faith of
our two peoples." [12] His journalistic shadow, Morton, has written
that the Prime Minister "was affected emotionally . . . His hand-
kerchief stole from his pocket." By early evening Churchill was mus-
ing: "The same language, the same hymns, and, more or less, the
same ideals . . . I have an idea that something really big may be
happening — something really big." [13] If he won nothing else from
the Americans, Churchill had this proof of Anglo-American understanding; and he could claim true understanding results inevitably in
commitment.

The British and American sailors, "so alike . . . that they might
have been brothers," probably attached less meaning to the service.
It was another opportunity to swap experiences, complaints, and to
make more substantial trades. And it was a glorious opportunity for
shutterbugs. During and after the service Roosevelt and Churchill
were surrounded by photographers, some professionals recording the
occasion for posterity, the majority clicking Brownies and Leicas
from the deck and after turret. The President and Prime Minister
willingly cooperated, remaining in their chairs, chatting, for half an
hour or so after the chaplains had given the benediction and the
service ended. The photographic melee continued while the presidential party was being shown around the huge battleship. Roosevelt had a wheelchair tour of *Prince of Wales,* "taking much interest
in the working of the armament, particularly the antiaircraft batter-
ies." For his special pleasure an exhibition of one of the quadruple
turrets training its massive fourteen-inch guns was laid on.[14]
F.D.R.'s scrutiny of the battleship's antiaircraft defenses was more

practical, for they were its sole, tragically inadequate protection four
months later.

Almost immediately, reality replaced these pleasant diversions.
Those hard-working diplomats, Welles and Cadogan, bypassed the
tour to exchange information on two most urgent subjects — policy
toward Japan and the proposed joint declaration. Before they went
in to the Prime Minister's luncheon Cadogan said that "in accordance with the conversation at the President's dinner last night" he
had drawn up tentative drafts concerning "parallel and simultaneous
declarations" by the United States and Great Britain.[15] This first
draft of a joint statement on war and peace aims finds analysis later;
the suggested message to Japan, which formed the basis for discussion of Anglo-American policy in the Far East, as presented to
Welles, read,

> Draft of Parallel Communications to the Japanese Government
> Declaration by the United States Government that:
> 1. Any further encroachment by Japan in the Southwestern Pacific
>   would produce a situation in which the United States Government
>   would be compelled to take countermeasures even though these
>   might lead to war between the United States and Japan.
> 2. If any third power becomes the object of aggression by Japan in
>   consequence of such countermeasures or of their support of them,
>   the President would have the intention to seek authority from Con-
>   gress to give aid to such power.

Parallel declarations by the British and Netherlands governments
were included. Cadogan commented that the Soviet regime should
be informed of any action. "It will be for consideration whether they
should be pressed to make a parallel declaration."[16] This last remark must have sounded impractical, even to Cadogan, in view of
Russia's preoccupation.

1

The British proposal for an ultimatum, for that was the substance
of this document, was the culmination of several months of diplomacy and events which outdistanced diplomatic endeavor. Future

policy regarding Japan was the most urgent and, as it developed, the most important issue dealt with at the meeting. Japanese ambitions, seemingly insatiable, threatened in mid-summer to engulf the Far East in war. The great question was the position of the United States if a conflict erupted.

Before the conference at Argentia, the leading role of the United States in the Pacific had been admitted by all anti-Axis nations with interests in that area. America took the lead both in search for a settlement (through the talks between Hull and Kichisaburo Nomura, the Japanese Ambassador in Washington) and in actions to block any Japanese advance. Great Britain, speaking for the Commonwealth, the Netherlands government, and perhaps also the Soviet Union, recognized the hard fact of American primacy, for only it had the power to restrain Japan. So Churchill was anxious that the United States align itself with the other powers in an anti-Japanese entente.

American policy before Argentia was not reassuring. It had featured alternate use of carrot and stick, a confession of Washington's indecision. Ambassador Grew had expressed one approach when he argued that "the risks of not taking positive measures to maintain our future security in the Far East . . . are likely to be much greater than the risk of taking positive measures as Japan's southward advance proceeds." In his view, "we shall avoid war with Japan if Japan once becomes convinced that we mean business." [17] Yet Grew was not always an advocate of firmness, and others, especially the Secretary of State, insisted that negotiation and compromise offered the only hope for a peaceful settlement in the Far East.

Confusion about Japanese intentions also influenced American policy. In a letter to Harold Ickes on July 1 the President said: "The Japs are having a real drag-down and knock-out fight and have been for the past week — trying to decide which way they are going — attack Russia, attack the South Seas . . . or whether they will sit on the fence and be more friendly with us." [18] The Nazi invasion of Russia revived speculation that Japan might turn north, a move some high American officials would have welcomed.[19]

The Russo-German conflict had tremendous effect in Japan. It forced the dominant faction, already committed to imperialism, to choose the direction of advance. On July 2 civil and military leaders met in the Emperor's presence. They made fateful decisions. Japan would establish the Greater East Asia Co-Prosperity Sphere, "no matter what international developments take place." The China Incident must be ended and, to accomplish that, Japan had to advance into "the Southern Regions." Although talks with the Americans should continue, all agreed that "in case the diplomatic negotiations break down, preparations for a war with England and America will . . . be carried forward." [20]

Washington and London learned of the July 2 decisions through "Magic," the technique being used to break certain Japanese codes. This knowledge enabled the American government to foresee the advance into Indochina and trace its execution. It forced consideration of possible responses, and eventually resulted in action.[21]

On July 10 Welles, Acting Secretary in Hull's absence, told Lord Halifax the President authorized him to say that if Japan took "any overt step" to conquer additional territory various economic sanctions would go into effect. Envisaged was a massive embargo on trade with Japan. Discussion began immediately between Washington and London as to the best way of effecting the restraints. These talks continued while Japan was stepping up its demands on French Indochina. By July 12 the Japanese request for bases, under threat of invasion, was known. Three days later the State Department had the details — eight strategically located air bases and two great ports at Camranh and Saigon.

In spite of repeated appeals from Great Britain the United States did almost nothing. Admiral Leahy received instructions to try to persuade Vichy "to procrastinate as far as possible"; but this proved futile.[22] As a substitute for military resistance the Roosevelt administration adopted economic countermeasures. Notably, Hull called from White Sulphur Springs to support "concrete measures . . . to impose economic, financial, and other restrictions." [23] The cabinet discussed an embargo on July 18; all the members favored a move of some kind but were undecided about how far it should extend. State, nonetheless, prepared orders to freeze Japanese assets, to prohibit imports of silk, and to restrict export of oil to "normal" quantities. These acts were not put into effect for another week. The President was not sure which course to adopt, and he was getting contradictory advice. "The Navy favored prudence; the Treasury wanted freezing; the State Department did not object to freezing, but was not clear as to what would follow; the British government seemed ready for anything; and the Secretary of State . . . was telephoning that he thought it best to leave the decision to those on the ground." [24] Perhaps a Washington *Star* editorial cartoon of June 5, 1941, best expressed the confusion within the administration with regard to embargoes. The cartoon depicted a Washington service station with Secretary of Interior Ickes leaning against a gas tank and saying, "Sorry, no gas today"; a car with a Japanese driver pulling in, Hull filling the gas tank; and a caricatured Under Secretary Welles inquiring, "Any oil, sir, today?" [25]

On July 24, F.D.R. informed the cabinet that he was ordering all-inclusive freezing of Japanese assets, an effective method of shutting off trade with Japan. He summoned Admiral Nomura and warned him that if Japan attempted to seize oil supplies in the Netherlands East Indies, "the Dutch would, without the shadow of a doubt, resist; the British would immediately come to their assistance, war would result between Japan, the British, and the Dutch, and in view of our own policy of assisting Great Britain, an exceedingly serious situation would immediately result." [26] Having brandished what was for him a large stick, Roosevelt put it aside, proposing that the neutralization of Indochina — after Japanese forces were withdrawn — would ease tension. He seems to have had little hope for this idea, although he raised it in all seriousness.

The embargo went into effect on July 26, and it opened a new phase in American policy. Herbert Feis has written that it forced Japan "to choose between making terms with us or making war against us." [27] Did this mean that the Roosevelt administration accepted the inevitability of war with Japan? Perhaps. But the British could not be certain, the Dutch were not convinced, and it appears Roosevelt himself was undecided. Great Britain and the Netherlands instituted parallel embargoes; they also pressed for a public statement by the United States, declaring its intent to defend their territories against Japanese aggression.[28]

Washington failed to clarify the larger question of policy. In the interval between the embargo and Roosevelt's meeting with Churchill the U.S. made a day-to-day response to Japanese moves. The embargo shook Japan's leaders, but they did not reverse course. "They were soon to rush full speed ahead," Herbert Feis has observed, "lest they would not have enough oil to reach those distant ports which were marked on the Imperial chart."[29] In early August attention focused on Thailand and on the proposal to neutralize Indochina.

The President cabled Churchill his suggestion that Indochina be declared off-limits to each side "something like Switzerland." He had as yet received no answer, and "when it comes it will probably be unfavorable." The Japanese response arrived on August 6, after F.D.R. had departed Washington.[30] Welles brought it along to Argentia. He also gave the President late information about Japanese designs on Thailand. Thai and British fears had been expressed weeks earlier, and the Prime Minister of Thailand had requested that America publicly state its determination to oppose Japanese pressure on his nation.[31] Although Hull believed that "if we don't watch out a possible move toward the Burma Road will be made," he balked at a strong stand. "That doesn't mean we have to take the lead," he said.[32] On August 4 Welles presented the American position to Minister Wakasugi. His statement was made immediately before leaving for Argentia. Welles said that Japan's recent actions forced the United States government to conclude Japan "finally and definitely" had adopted a program of expansion through use of force. This could only lead to disaster, for it would result, "whether it came tomorrow, or next month, or next year, or even later," in armed hostilities.[33] The Under Secretary left unspoken America's course in such an event; that he felt compelled to do so explains the draft warning Sir Alexander Cadogan presented to him six days later.

2

Welles experienced profound dismay on reading this document. It meant neither his frank conversation with Cadogan the previous afternoon nor the President's lack of response to Churchill's appeal Saturday night had had noticeable effect. The British draft called for action repeatedly emphasized as being impossible. To halt the course of Japanese ambitions it would have the United States take countermeasures as irrevocable as military force. It would commit the President to ask from Congress power to give aid — unspecified but obvious — to powers resisting Japan. In plain language that was a demand for a declaration of war. The Roosevelt administration was caught. In return for British and Dutch loyalty in supporting the embargo it must now consider guarantees of protection.

British intransigence undoubtedly dulled Welles' appreciation of the luncheon at which he was one of the guests of honor. The Prime Minister had provided a feast for the presidential party — now his guests on British territory, the officer's wardroom. This rather plain but spacious room was on the same level as the quarterdeck and obviated any difficulty about moving the President up and down ladders. Churchill, Roosevelt, Hopkins, Harriman, Welles, Cadogan, and the military and naval chiefs sat down to a banquet which contradicted Great Britain's dietary insufficiencies. Nor for Churchill did traditional English fare suffice. The luncheon menu, under his personal crest, listed a combination of French and English delicacies: smoked salmon and caviar as hors d'oeuvres, turtle soup, roast grouse with *coup Jeanne d'Arc* as the main course, dessert, coffee, and an assortment of wines and liqueurs.[34] Conscious that he was entertaining a head of state, Churchill had planned the meal with care. Duff Cooper had bagged the grouse in Scotland at the Prime Minister's order; another dozen brace had been frozen and brought along as a gift for the President.[35] Churchill had almost despaired of finding turtle soup — it was not high on England's import priorities — when his bodyguard, C. R. Thompson, uncovered several dusty cans in a Regent Street shop.[36] During the meal a Royal Marine band provided "mood music," ranging from marches (The United

States Marine Hymn and The Middy), a "valse" by Strauss, to selections from *La Bohème* and *The Student Prince*.[37]

Conversation around the huge table was informal, the kind of talk Roosevelt and Churchill enjoyed and at which both excelled. For a space the pressures of leadership were put aside. The Prime Minister proposed a toast to Roosevelt. F.D.R. responded by toasting the King. "There was a great scraping back of chairs and shuffling of feet and a moment of silence while the glasses were lifted up and . . . the wine sipped." [38] Respect had been done to requirements of ceremony and the company settled back to enjoy the meal. Harry Hopkins even relaxed so much as to venture a risqué joke.[39] Perhaps at this time Admiral King laid to rest fears that the German battleship, *Tirpitz,* would attempt to intercept *Prince of Wales.* British reconnaissance had reported through U.S. Naval Operations that *Tirpitz* was moored in the inner dockyard at Kiel and thus offered no threat to the Prime Minister and his party during their voyage home.[40]

The company assuredly discussed weighty matters, but one must depend on inference to identify them. Probably the British steered conversation away from the Far East. The draft statement Welles had received prior to the luncheon required time for digestion. Pressing for a reaction might prove embarrassing; and, besides, Churchill intended to speak to the President privately.

After lunch F.D.R. and the Prime Minister adjourned to an anteroom where the members of Churchill's staff were brought in to be introduced to the President. Colonel Jacob, recording his impressions, said Roosevelt looked much better, "less care-worn," than he had expected. "His face was fine, strong . . . particularly when seen in profile and he has a very genial smile." Sumner Welles, Jacob wrote, "looks exactly as if he had stepped out of a film; he is the kind of man you always see in the films as the business lawyer." [41] The President talked briefly to the staff and to a number of officers from *Prince of Wales.* As a parallel occasion to Churchill's speech of the previous evening, there was no comparison. His remarks were superficial.[42] Churchill then took his guest aside for a private chat. Its major topic everyone understood to be Japan.

F.D.R. left *Prince of Wales* at 3:00 P.M. The ship's company assembled on the forecastle to give three cheers as *McDougal* edged away. The President grinned broadly and waved toward the bridge. The Prime Minister waved back. Then, as the motion pictures testify, "he suddenly looked down at his feet where a little black and white kitten was rubbing itself against his leg. He . . . stooped down and picked up the little animal, and it became part of his . . . salute . . . to the President. . . ." [43] Such gestures belied Churchill's real concern about the way in which the conference was going. As Welles was leaving to accompany the President to his flagship, the Prime Minister stopped him and said that he had given Roosevelt copies of documents earlier presented to the Under Secretary. In Welles' words, "He impressed upon me his belief that some declaration of the kind he had drafted with respect to Japan was in his opinion in the highest degree important." Churchill did not believe "there was much hope left" unless the United States declared its intent to oppose — with force if necessary — any Japanese move to the south. If such a move occurred, peace between the United Kingdom and Japan appeared hopeless. "Japan immediately would be in a position through the use of her large number of cruisers to seize or destroy all of the British merchant shipping in the Indian Ocean and in the Pacific, and to cut the lifelines between the British Dominions and the British Isles unless the United States herself entered the war." The Prime Minister insisted that only a declaration of the nature described would restrain Japan. "If this were not done, the blow to the British Government might be decisive." [44] That Churchill delivered this exhortation to Welles is revealing of his talk with F.D.R. Why make these points to a subordinate, unless the effort to persuade the President had failed?

The remainder of Sunday afternoon passed in "strategy sessions" and the pursuit of other kinds of activities on both sides. F.D.R. summoned Welles for a brief discussion of the British declaration of war and peace aims. They probably discussed the Prime Minister's inflexibility about Japan and explored responses for Monday's joint meetings. Sometime in the interim, certainly, Roosevelt became convinced that a U.S. declaration of some kind was unavoidable, that the British government and Churchill had based their position and prestige in the Far East on a forceful statement by the American government. Churchill conferred on the identical subject, and somehow found time to send off more instructions and recommendations to Attlee and the others left in charge at London. Conversations between military and naval representatives, which had begun after the luncheon, continued. Notably, large numbers of American officers found their way to *Prince of Wales* around the cocktail hour. Indeed, "all the afternoon parties of officers and ratings from the American ships kept coming over and being entertained and shown around." Colonel Jacob complained at the clamor and noise thus generated. "Life on board in these circumstances is most unrestful," he said. "It is apparently impossible for any visitor to slip on and off without having to be given the appropriate honours, and if you are on the Quarter Deck you find yourself continually having to stand to attention while someone is being piped on board or piped away or, if the people are very important, while guards are presenting arms and bands playing." [45]

The Prime Minister was guilty of adding to the afternoon's confusion by leaving the ship for a time. He decided abruptly to take advantage of the weather to get some exercise. He had been so busy shuttling between *Prince of Wales* and *Augusta* that there had been no time for investigation of the low hills which surrounded the harbor. Dressed in an "easy tourist suit," the Prime Minister, accompanied by Cadogan, "the Prof," Harriman, Spring, Morton, J. M. Martin, and his bodyguard-valet, went in a ship's boat to a small shingly beach. From there the party explored the rocks and small wooded hills running down to the shore. Churchill appeared cheerful, even lighthearted. One of his companions was amazed by the P.M.'s ability to dismiss the "crushing disappointments and reverses" of the past year, to let his deep burdens "sink into the deep oceans we had traversed." [46] He kept up a continuous stream of humorous comments upon the trip, the food, and, perhaps, indulged in some gentle but expert character assassination of the Americans he had met. "His heart was growing lighter," speculated Thompson. "He was seeing some way out." Churchill's good humor survived a sudden rain shower which blew up shortly after four o'clock and drenched the party before its members found shelter. "He merely cupped his hand over his cigar and went on talking and pointing and puffing." [47] After a bit, the rain let up and the men returned to *Prince of Wales,* rather the worse for wear, but clearly having enjoyed the outing.[48]

Others of the British delegation visited the *Augusta.* It was arranged that the First Sea Lord should see the President at 5:00 P.M. and that General Dill and Air Vice-Marshal Freeman — together, following British practice — would talk with him at 6:00. Dill and Freeman found that Marshall, Arnold, and Burns were present, standing both literally and figuratively behind F.D.R. Talk focused on production of tanks and heavy bombers and on the strategic importance of Liberia, the Azores, Cape Verdes, Canaries, Azores, Dakar, Dakar, the Azores. Churchill came in at this point and eagerly jumped into the discussion. He had been invited to dinner, and though the military was "still talking priorities and their all around effect" the President ordered them out at 7:00.[49]

Roosevelt's dinner Sunday evening was a smaller occasion, a gathering of the two leaders' official families. Present besides the President and Prime Minister were Cherwell, Thompson, Martin, McIntire, Watson, Beardall, Elliott and Franklin, Jr., and Harry Hopkins. Simultaneously, Admiral King entertained the naval members of the two staffs in his quarters. As one American phrased it, "the brass and braid had departed," and dinner Sunday night provided F.D.R. with "much more of an opportunity to get to know Churchill." [50] The only description of the affair is by Elliott Roosevelt. If one applies considerable skepticism, his account offers a colorful interpretation of what *might* have taken place in *Augusta's* master cabin. Contrasting Sunday evening with the previous night, Elliott wrote,

> Last night Churchill had talked without interruption, except for questions. Tonight there were other men's thoughts being tossed into the kettle, and [it] correspondingly began to bubble up and — once or twice — nearly over. You sensed that two men accustomed to leadership had sparred, had felt each other out, and were now readying

themselves for outright challenge . . . Churchill still arrogated the conversational lead, still dominated the after-dinner hours. But the difference was beginning to be felt.[51]

Roosevelt's son sets up this change as background for an open, highly-charged quarrel between his father and Churchill about colonialism and the British Empire.

"Father started it all," writes Elliott, "by bringing up imperial preference. 'Of course,' he remarked, with a sly sort of assurance, 'of course, after the war, one of the preconditions of any lasting peace will have to be the greatest possible freedom of trade.'

"He paused. The P.M.'s head was lowered; he was watching Father steadily, from under one eyebrow.

" 'No artificial barriers,' Father pursued. 'As few favored economic agreements as possible. Opportunities for expansion. Markets open for healthy competition.' His eye wandered innocently around the room . . .

"Churchill's neck reddened and he crouched forward. 'Mr. President, England does not propose for a moment to lose its favored position among the British Dominions . . .'

" 'You see,' said Father slowly, 'it is along in here somewhere that there is likely to be some disagreement between you, Winston, and me. I am firmly of the belief that if we are to arrive at a stable peace it must involve the development of backward countries. Backward peoples . . . I can't believe that we can fight a war against fascist slavery, and at the same time not work to free people all over the world from a backward colonial policy.'

"Around the room, all of us were leaning forward attentively. Hopkins was grinning. Commander Thompson, Churchill's aide, was looking glum and alarmed. The P.M. himself was beginning to look apoplectic. Roosevelt ignored the danger signals.

" 'The peace,' he concluded, 'cannot include any continued despotism. The structure of the peace demands and will get equality of peoples.' With that said, he allowed Churchill hurriedly to change the subject." [52]

The Prime Minister's commitment to Empire was a central tenet of his public and private life. His views, unfortunately, were based on outdated ideas and, one must say, emotions. Indeed, his understanding of imperial conditions seems not to have progressed beyond the experiences of young adulthood. Lord Moran has written that Churchill's India remained the vast, magical land he had known as a subaltern with the 4th Hussars. "The P.M. looked with pride on the story of our Indian Empire — Henry Lawrence and Clive and Dalhousie were men after his own heart." Moran has also observed that the President, looking at British India, "saw only a subject people in the grip of a conqueror, a lamentable example of British imperialism." [53] F.D.R. found it impossible to understand Churchill's faith in England's imperial destiny. "He doesn't see things as you and I do," the President once confessed to Rexford Tugwell. "He is amazingly unreformed. He wants this war to result, as others have, in another extension of the Empire. And he wants us to back him up." [54] Roosevelt believed — and frankly told Churchill on at least two occasions — that the United States could not and would not underwrite colonialism or contribute to repression of popular movements looking toward independence and self-government. Such aspirations were, after all, expressions of the principle of self-determination.

Despite Elliott Roosevelt's testimony, it is doubtful whether a direct and bitter clash occurred in Roosevelt's quarters that Sunday night. F.D.R. also believed colonial systems were doomed, because they were anachronistic in a world which was heeding the call for social justice. He was by no means a zealot, and he adopted a largely passive attitude at Argentia and through the war. The issue of British colonies was, after all, legally a matter of concern only to the United Kingdom and Commonwealth. Roosevelt refused to transgress upon these prerogatives, except to offer well-intentioned suggestions. When his wife, immediately after his return to Washington, sent along a report violently critical of Great Britain's India policy and asked for the President's reaction, F.D.R. replied, "I can have no thoughts about India." [55] When later confronted by nationalist leaders who waved the Atlantic Charter's promise of self-determination, Roosevelt usually pointed to the United States' record in the Philippines and "assured African and Asian leaders that their freedom would come just as surely and just as completely." [56] Words not deeds defined his position.

The President did hope his English friend would come to accept the inevitable. He further desired evidence of Churchill's acceptance of the fact in the form of guarantees of Indian independence. This action was on a practical basis. Reflecting widespread American belief that political tensions in India were seriously impeding the war effort, F.D.R. argued that if India were promised independence, the Indian populace would cooperate fully in the war.[57] However, even if he were to accept this argument (which he emphatically did not), Churchill dared not antagonize the imperial diehards within the Conservative Party led by Lord Beaverbrook and L. S. Amery, Secretary of State for India.

There was, literally, no common ground for discussion of this issue by the two men. The Churchill who asserted, "Don't forget that when we win, as we shall, we shall not tolerate any separation of . . . any French colony from France," hardly could be expected to be less adamant with regard to British possessions.[58] Had the President really phrased his dislike of imperialism as his son claimed, threatening to withdraw American aid if England continued "to ride roughshod over colonial peoples," open conflict, probably disrupting the conference, could not have been averted. Clearly, he did no such thing. Disagreement — whatever form it assumed — did color discussion of other matters. Sunday night witnessed the dissolution of much of that unity and harmony confirmed earlier in the day. How much of the morning's glow had evaporated is not clear. Churchill and party did not leave *Augusta* until past midnight, and the contrasting habits of the two leaders may also have had effect. F.D.R. tended to get grumpy if kept up too late.

VII. Hypothethical Questions

WHILE THE TWO LEADERS pondered the outlines of the future, another sort of confabulation was going on. In informal sessions Saturday and Sunday, in general conferences on Monday and Tuesday, and at odd times during the four days at Argentia, the military leaders of the two nations met together. These meetings emphasized the uniqueness of an encounter between a "neutral" President and the Prime Minister of a belligerent power. In addition, they revealed wide differences between American and British attitudes and strategy.

The staffs looked to these conferences with ambivalence. They were eager to meet the men with whom, quite probably, they were to work for the next few years; they were also fearful that personal antipathy or, worse, evidence of incapacity would make prosecution of a coalition war, at best a difficult affair, a total disaster. With the exception of General Arnold, whose visit to England in March had acquainted him with the British Chiefs and their principal subordinates, none of the military and naval leaders had met while in their present positions. Marshall knew Sir John Dill as the man who occupied the British post comparable to his own. He had been reading cables signed C.I.G.S. for many months and thus had a general idea of Dill's outlook — but notions were insufficient. Admirals Stark and Pound were similarly ignorant. Arnold, Freeman, and certainly the other officers present — Bundy, Burns, Sherman, Turner, Jacob, Yool, Goodenough, Schofield, Dykes, Nutting — were not widely known because of their preoccupation with planning and logistics. Perhaps the principal gain from the conference for these men was the personal contact it afforded. "It is always much easier to deal by

126   *The First Summit*

telegram and letter with someone whom you have met than with a stranger," one participant said, and Arnold believed the "chance to get acquainted" was worthwhile, even if nothing else occurred.[1]

A start on acquaintanceship was made. The Chiefs of Staff were required to participate in the welcoming ceremonies. Their subordinates ducked into *Augusta's* wardroom and, with due apologies from the Americans, sat down to coffee and cookies. One U.S. officer stated: "The American Navy visits the British Navy in order to get a drink, and the British Navy visits the American Navy in order to get something to eat." [2] Arnold and Freeman fought free of the crush on the main deck after a few minutes, found a vacant corner, and launched into a discussion of bomber production schedules. Shortly after twelve o'clock both staffs filed into Admiral King's suite for what one British officer remembered as "a very good fork lunch." British and American staffs then divided roughly by function and arranged informal conferences for the afternoon. At all of these meetings items for an agenda were suggested, though apparently there was little or no coordination between the groups.

The First Sea Lord, Pound, accompanied by Schofield and Goodenough, "went into a huddle" with Admirals Stark, King, and Turner in King's cabin.[3] The forcefulness of Admiral King made a deep impression upon the British. Schofield commented on his "grim and sour" look, and another of his colleagues termed King "rough, ruthless, and unbending . . . anti-British, and particularly anti-Royal Navy." [4] The C in C, Atlantic Fleet considered himself an observer and took almost no part in discussions; however, the British could guess from the tightness of his deep-scored, craggy face when British naval requirements were mentioned where his sympathies lay.[5]

Stark was of another sort. Longtime friend of President Roosevelt, he had been appointed Chief of Naval Operations in 1939 over several of his seniors. He was physically unprepossessing, bespectacled and scholarly in appearance. Jacob described him as "a little white-haired man with bright eyes and a hooked nose." [6] Many thought Stark an able officer but unduly responsive to the President's views. Roosevelt called him by his nickname, "Betty," and their intimacy, whatever its drawbacks, gave Stark easy entry to the White House. It was said that he lacked strength, was timid and "unusually cautious"; but colleagues respected his ability and until Pearl Harbor the President followed his advice more often than not.[7] At Argentia Stark was at times overshadowed by Richmond K. Turner, head of the Navy planning office. Turner struck one British observer as the "dominating personality" among the U.S. naval people. Tall, with iron-gray hair, rimless glasses dominating his lined, humorless face, Turner was a man of strong character and pronounced opinions who found compromise extremely difficult. Jacob judged that Stark had "a much more engaging personality and generally seems to talk sound sense," but that probably he was "under Admiral Turner's thumb."[8] The British revised their plans accordingly.

Admiral Stark's experience had been almost entirely in staff work. Sir Dudley Pound, the British Chief of Naval Staff, had commanded a battleship, the *Colossus*, at Jutland. Pound had been First Sea Lord since spring, 1939. Distinguished in appearance, imperturbable, he was deeply conscious of Royal Navy traditions. Churchill admired Pound as a representative of the breed of naval officer he had known and worked with thirty years earlier. Unfortunately, at sixty-four, Pound was beginning to show his age. Clement Attlee remembered him as being "very old" and "very deaf," and believed that "towards the end he was getting a bit of a passenger."[9] In fact, Pound's lameness and somnolence were symptoms of the grave illness (a brain tumor which was not discovered until much later) which afflicted him. The disease was by no means incapacitating. As Forrest Pogue states, though "inclined to doze through dreary stretches of some of the meetings, he instantly came to life when he thought his fleet was threatened."[10] He was a methodical person, one who believed in following the script exactly; the Americans, like their British compatriots, often themselves fought drowsiness while listening to Pound drone through staff papers.

There was no problem Saturday afternoon. The naval leaders chatted briefly. Pound then produced a paper "reviewing the political and military situation throughout the world" which had been prepared by the British Chiefs of Staff. Just as Arnold feared, the British came primed with charts, graphs, and piles of background studies. They had drafted a document, the "Review of General Strategy," dated July 31, 1941, which they hoped to make the basis for all military discussion. The Americans had no proposals aside from an offer to talk about Lend-Lease distribution. They did no more on Saturday than glance over the British document. Its description of sources and stocks of raw materials needed did bring a humorous response from the C.N.O. One point which referred to the possible shortage of rubber and tin should Malaya fall to the Japanese caused Stark to say, "Tins, why the greatest problem in our country is how to get rid of the darned things." [11] He was more serious with regard to the shortage of escort vessels for Atlantic convoys, and discussion focused on this problem. The British had to admit that despite the fifty overage destroyers from the Destroyer-Basis Deal, they still required some 380 ships to assure protection of the convoys. "Admiral Stark was most cooperative and promised all the help possible," Schofield recalls, "but Admiral King looked pretty glum throughout the proceedings. I think he felt Stark was being a bit too forthcoming for a non-belligerent!" [12]

Other Americans were less generous. At Arnold's invitation, Marshall, Dill, Freeman, "Jo" Hollis, and Jacob shifted to *Tuscaloosa* for a talk. When the group had found seats in Arnold's comfortably furnished cabin, Marshall asked the two senior British officers if they cared "to give their views about the present war situation." [13] They briefly restated the arguments contained in their strategy estimate, placing special emphasis upon equipment needs. The size of the British requests was stunning. Freeman asked for 6000 more heavy bombers than the United States planned to produce and called for a total strength of 10,000 combat aircraft. "The thing scares me — it is so big and I know they cannot meet it," Arnold exclaimed, as he tried to recapture Freeman's analysis later that night. "British production of Heavy Bombers 500 a month. U.S. production of Heavy Bombers 500 a month. We can't do it as easily as that. 2000 pilots a month. Where will they come from?" He concluded mournfully it was "wishful" thinking.[14]

Marshall refused to express an opinion on general strategy. He did reply indirectly by describing the growing pains which plagued the United States Army. He pointed out that everything being supplied to Great Britain was at the expense of American forces. Jacob noted sympathetically: "He mentioned the difficulty they had in sending modern equipment to their outlying possessions; in fact, his remarks might have been made almost word for word by one of our own Chiefs of Staff two years ago when we were being pressed to send things to France, and to equip all the small nations, at a time when we had nothing even for ourselves." [15] Marshall was to return to this theme at almost every meeting.

The American Chief of Staff impressed the British despite his pessimistic words. Marshall and Dill warmed to each other immediately. They had much in common. Both had spent the great part of their careers in staff positions; both had made brigadier in the First World War (although Marshall's appointment had reverted when peace came); and there was just a year's difference in ages. Forrest Pogue has written that "in his sincerity, frankness, and self-discipline Dill in many ways resembled Marshall." The main difference between the two was to be uncovered by events. Along with manifest integrity, there was "a strong touch of the stereotyped New England Yankee" in Marshall's reserve, his orderly habits and innate conservatism.[16] "It was perfectly apparent you had a very, very strong man as Chief of Staff," was the estimate of Colonel C. W. Bundy, assistant to the Secretary of War.[17] Marshall was so good at his job that he became indispensable to President Roosevelt. At the Arcadia conference in December, 1941, Lord Moran commented: "Marshall remains the key to the situation. The P.M. has a feeling that in his quiet, unprovocative way he means business, and that if we are too obstinate he might take a strong line. And neither the P.M. nor the President can contemplate going forward without Marshall." [18]

In contrast, the C.I.G.S. possessed great personal charm but appeared to lack self-confidence and determination. One should qualify Moran's indictment: "What he lacks is the he-man stuff," for Dill's constant battles with the Prime Minister would have exhausted any save the strongest of men.[19] Churchill put forward one wild scheme after another for Dill to oppose; the constant battles with his Prime Minister combined with anxiety over the illness of his wife, who had become totally paralyzed in 1940, to sap his strength. Fortuitously, Dill came to Washington after a forced resignation and he and Marshall built on the friendship established at Argentia. Their relationship was one of the most important of the war.[20]

Arnold and Freeman, the third pair of Chiefs of Staff, hit it off immediately. The junior member of the American Chiefs (as head of the Army Air Corps, Arnold was Marshall's subordinate) was already acquainted with most members of the British delegation. He had not known Freeman previously; but the two airmen soon discovered their views closely coincided. The thickset, white-haired American and Freeman, a dark, handsome man who possessed a subtle sense of humor, became close friends. At Argentia they were almost inseparable, neither taking much part in the general discussions.[21]

The meeting in Arnold's cabin broke up at 3:30 P.M. and Marshall, Dill, and their staffs left. Going to an adjoining cabin, two of the Britishers, Jacob and Hollis, continued a conversation begun during the meeting with Bundy. They were curious about the extent of American strategic planning. Finally, Bundy, who was involved in such preparation as had taken place, showed them "a draft of a Paper . . . drawn up for the President, setting out their idea of the phases of American participation in the war." This document, an early version of the Victory Program of September, 1941, was gratifying in that it proved the Americans were aware of the necessity for careful planning. However, Jacob and Hollis noticed that it directly contradicted British views regarding the strategy of ultimate victory. That cast a pall, and after sharing a cup of tea with Bundy the two British officers suffered through the rigamarole of being piped off the United States cruiser and onto *Prince of Wales*.[22] Immersed in the boarding ceremonies also were Freeman, Averell Harriman, General Burns, and Arnold. These worthies were in search of a relaxing drink and followed Jacob and Hollis into the battleship's wardroom where a considerable crowd had gathered. The Prime Minister came in as the Americans were leaving, and yet another review of the afternoon's discussions had to be undertaken.[23]

No agenda had been accepted prior to the conference and no preliminary dispatches regarding questions to be discussed had been exchanged. However, the talks on Saturday afternoon made it clear that the British wished to discuss grand strategy, while Marshall and his colleagues were prepared only to deal with problems of supply and production. By tacit agreement an informal agenda which included these two matters was confirmed. A third topic was discussion between Roosevelt and Churchill of military aspects of diplomatic decisions. The Americans felt they were on shaky ground, for their instructions were negative, precluding "even the shadow" of any new commitment. Marshall recalled "the British would have liked to have gone much further. They were at this business every day — all day . . . We were in the position of mobilizing and equipping an Army. Just how this was to be handled on our side largely remained to be determined. Therefore we were not prepared to give them any fixed advice." [24] But how could spokesmen for the United States convince the British that the state of American armed forces made elaborate discussion of coalition strategy completely unrealistic? What could be done to get across to the British Chiefs the restrictions and lack of direction under which the U.S. military labored? President Roosevelt had dragooned them into the meeting with almost no warning. The suddenness of his decision, though surprising, was not an unusual occurence, for American leaders had come to expect the unexpected from him.

1

F.D.R. seems to have wanted his military advisers along for moral encouragement and as points for America in his and Churchill's game of oneupmanship. That they might make strategic decisions apparently did not cross his mind. It had occurred to his advisers, and they may have had an inkling of the Prime Minister's purpose in adding military assistants to the guest list. American spokesmen, especially Marshall and Stark, were well aware of F.D.R.'s aversion to thinking about involvement in the war.[25] They surmised that he had excluded the topic from the agenda; and they were perhaps surprised that Pound, Dill, and Freeman argued so boldly for intervention. The President had given no indication that the subject would come up.

Tangled lines of communication were no new development for the Americans. From the beginning of concern about the fate of the democracies there existed a difference between Roosevelt and his advisers over military affairs. To the military and naval chiefs belonged the defense of the United States. The Constitution, Article II, Section 2, provided that they were to carry out these duties under their Commander in Chief. A directive for the War Plans Division of the General Staff stated that civil authorities were to determine the "what" of national policy and professional soldiers the "how." [26] Such neat statements frustrated those who served a President such as Franklin Roosevelt. What were the professionals to do if there were no principles? Or, what if principles were contradictory? America's military development was in just such a tangle at the time of the Argentia meeting. The confusion had two causes: the responsibility of military leaders to press for priority of United States forces and a balanced army; and, second, Roosevelt's inability to accept the logic of his program of all-out aid to Great Britain.[27]

F.D.R. reacted to his duties as Commander in Chief in unexpected ways. Guiding his actions was hatred of modern war.[28] Until the moment Japanese bombs fell on Pearl Harbor, it seems irrefutable that Roosevelt desired to avoid large-scale participation of U.S. forces. "I have said before, but shall say it again and again and again . . ." he notably promised American mothers during the 1940 campaign.[29] As danger to America grew, his determination to help the Allies produced a second aim — aid to those nations fighting Nazi Germany. The President thought of these two goals as complementary. Material support of countries resisting aggression, he reasoned, would prevent American involvement, a tidy solution which appealed to Roosevelt because it relied on a favorite assumption — faith in America's industrial machine.[30] To F.D.R. "arsenal of democracy" was a splendid description.

His military advisers did not accept these credos. They saw them not as complementary, but as dangerous contradictions which could leave America defenseless. Aid to the democracies ultimately would drag the United States into the war, with insufficient production to ensure victory unless the country early went on a war footing. Further, the British Empire had not the human resources to achieve victory; American boys would have to fight.

For a long time neither the President nor his advisers appreciated the seriousness of their disagreement. When it became plain, due to plans for huge ground armies, Roosevelt shifted the argument. In the three years before Pearl Harbor he embraced an alternative course — strategic air power. When, in early July, F.D.R. shook off his lethargy to confirm arrangements for the conference with Churchill, he asked Secretaries Stimson and Knox for a complete statement of the resources necessary to win the war. This investigation became the Victory Program of September, 1941, an amazing achievement, for the President "was inviting the two Secretaries to evolve a strategy for the United States and to translate it into industrial terms while the policy of which that strategy was to be the instrument was still undecided." [31] Three elements were lacking: the time and circumstances of American entry, names of all the enemies, and the degree of participation.

Military planners had to ignore the first point on which Roosevelt could not provide guidance. They had to assume that the United States on entry would face all the Axis powers. After this, Roosevelt's views diverged from those of his advisers. They were aware of and deplored his predilection for air-sea power and the strategy of limited war. A striking comment on administrative control under Roosevelt is that military leaders felt able to construct a program which put emphasis on ground forces, while the President was advocating an entirely different policy.[32] Roosevelt long had possessed some knowledge of air power and it had occupied an important position in his dissertation on grand strategy a year earlier.[33] He confessed to Rexford Tugwell that he was "tormented" by the failure of American military men to comprehend strategy in an air age. "The airplane, he was certain, changed everything." [34] In the spring and summer of 1941 the President became a strong if temporary convert — largely because of British missionary zeal.

A powerful, independent role for air power was central in English strategic thought. The circumstances in which Great Britain found itself after the fall of France made strategic bombing seem the best method to obtain Germany's defeat. Unable to begin an invasion of the Continent, unwilling even to face the prospect, many Englishmen saw air power as an ideal, indeed, the only, solution.[35]

A most influential exponent of air power was the Prime Minister. By temperament and by experience Churchill was sympathetic to a doctrine which promised maximum effect for a small expenditure of men and resources. "The Navy can lose us the war," he stated in September, 1940, "but only the Air Force can win it. Therefore our supreme effort must be to gain overwhelming mastery in the air. The Fighters are our salvation, but the Bombers alone provide the means of victory. We must . . . develop the power to carry an ever-increasing volume of explosives to Germany, so as to pulverize the entire industry and scientific structure on which the war-effort and economic life of the enemy depends." [36] The Prime Minister was to cling to this view, couched in differing language, for most of the war. He lost no opportunity to press it on Roosevelt.

The British discovered a true believer in the American camp in the person of General H. H. Arnold. On his "unofficial" visit to England in early 1941, Arnold was impressed by his English colleagues' confidence in strategic bombing. "My discussions in England with Portal, Churchill, and the others," he reported, "left me with the impression that by air alone we might bring Germany so completely to her knees that it might be unnecessary for the ground forces to make a landing . . . Air power and air power alone could carry the war home to Central Germany, break down her morale, and take away from her the things essential to combat." Arnold concluded sententiously: "Modern war had completely changed the old concepts." [37] Returning home, he found his superior, Marshall, unconvinced; but Arnold succeeded in spreading the gospel at a higher level. Secretary Stimson, a moderate air power enthusiast, recorded that Arnold's account of his trip at a White House conference "was the best yet," and that Roosevelt had reacted favorably.[38]

Even the Department of State dredged up support for the policy. In late February it received a document from an unnamed but apparently authentic source in Germany claiming that the economic situation was "desperate" and the economy might collapse if damage were in the right places. An official at State said: "If authentic (and I have no real doubt of it because of the manner of its acquisition) it will point to policy. First to acquaint the British so they can direct their air attacks with increased and more discerning accuracy, and second, to get them just as many long-range bombers as possible and as quickly as possible." The Department had the former German Chancellor, Heinrich Brüning, verify the document, and then presumably it went to the White House.[39]

Marshall's anxiety about the President's intent is negative evidence of F.D.R.'s conversion. If, indeed, he had read the ABC-1 report, Roosevelt seemed to contemplate broad changes in the plan. He approved ABC-2, the report on air collaboration, which set out a strategy of overwhelming, sustained air offensives against Germany. "It is abundantly evident that there is a close conceptual relationship between Mr. Churchill's direct expressions of opinion to President Roosevelt and this ABC-2 agreement," Trumbull Higgins has written.[40] Marshall worried "a good deal" about changes by the President "in plans for possible eventualities involving expeditionary forces across the seas." He could not be sure how powerful might become Roosevelt's attachment to air power.[41]

What was clear was that F.D.R. would like any policy obviating American participation in a land invasion of Europe. Churchill as well as American leaders realized this. He attempted to make the naval setting at Argentia a climactic episode in the struggle for air versus ground supremacy. The Prime Minister told his Chiefs of Staff early in July that "all concentration should be given to the Air Force as the war would be won by bombing." [42] He cabled the President in similar vein on July 25. He had been considering "our" war plans for 1942 and 1943, and proposed that after securing bases it was necessary to plan "on the largest scale" the forces for victory. "In broad outline we must aim first at intensifying the blockade and propaganda," Churchill asserted. "Then, we must subject Germany and Italy to a ceaseless and ever growing air bombardment. These measures may themselves produce an internal convulsion or collapse." If this did not occur, "plans ought also to be made for coming to the aid of the conquered populations by landing armies of liberation when the opportunity is ripe." [43] The key in this statement seemingly in favor of land invasion is the phrase, "armies of liberation"; Churchill saw the function of ground forces as occupation, not invasion.

If the President had shown this message to his military advisers, they would have been better prepared for proposals by the British at Argentia. There is no evidence he did so. Perhaps Roosevelt thought it best to have Churchill and the British officers administer their "serum" personally. The Prime Minister's confidence in strategic bombing intrigued Roosevelt, and he hoped it would so affect Marshall, Stark, and their staffs.

2

The first test came during Churchill's remarks on Saturday evening after the President's dinner. Although the Prime Minister's statements disturbed the American Chiefs they were pleased to have been invited. They took care not to embarrass their host, then or later. Colonel Bundy's notes on the address, written from memory a week later, reveal that caution applied as well to secret memoranda. Churchill's aims, according to this summary, were strong reinforcement of the Middle East, a joint warning to Japan, some fifty ships transferred out of the Western Atlantic for antisubmarine operations nearer Britain, and to "revive" the idea of a league to enforce peace. Bundy noted that the Prime Minister offered "strong opinions" about modern warfare, that he believed much fewer numbers of troops would be used in the Western theater than in 1918.[44] Arnold made more extensive comments on this last subject. Churchill said, "This was a mechanized war, not a war of 1917–18 where doughboys in the mud and trenches fought it out to a conclusion. This was a mobile war, in the air, on the land and at sea." [45] Churchill was not indulging in flights of fancy for the occasion; his views were well documented. A month before, Pierrepont Moffat had reported from Quebec that the Prime Minister was telling assistants "that when the British landed troops in Europe they would go as policemen." [46]

The details of the British program were revealed on Sunday. Hoping to treat strategy while the Americans presumably remained under the Prime Minister's oratorical spell, the British Chiefs suggested at lunch "a short meeting with the American Chiefs of Staff at which to hand over the strategy paper." [47] This effort went by the board, for Marshall and Stark decided to return to their quarters. Before they departed, Colonel Hollis presented them with three copies of the "Review of General Strategy." An accompanying letter requested that major points of criticism be given Hollis the same day so the British would be able to respond to them on Monday. Hollis formally asked for a general meeting for Monday morning. Marshall and Stark accepted the sheaf of papers, agreed to a time for the conference Monday, but refused further comment.[48] Arnold believed "a foulup in communications" prevented a full meeting Sunday afternoon; but then his reaction to the British prospectus was: "a sound paper in some respects from my point of view." [49] More plausibly, the Americans were at a loss how to respond to the document. The Army representatives, excepting Arnold, were angry that questions apparently laid to rest by the ABC-1 Conversations (U.S.-British-Canadian staff discussions regarding military cooperation in the event of American entry into the war) had been revived; Stark and his staff probably welcomed their resurrection. At any rate, American hesitation meant a second day was allowed to pass without formal discussion between them and the British spokesmen. Colonel Jacob complained,

> The day has been almost wasted from the point of view of joint discussion. We have been here two days and have not yet succeeded in getting the opposite sets of Chiefs of Staff together round a table. We have thus given away the strength of our position, which lies in the

fact that our three Chiefs of Staff present a united front on the strate-
gical questions, while it is quite clear that theirs do not. We have
played into their hands by allowing the discussions to proceed in separate compartments. Perhaps we shall have better luck tomorrow.[50]

The "Review of General Strategy" did represent the coming back
to life of many notions assumed dead and buried. It attacked the
problem of how to win the war in two stages: survival and victorious
offensive. It began calmly that "the vital consideration is to ensure
the security of the United Kingdom and of our sea communications,
while we build up and deploy the forces necessary for the offensive
described in Part 2." The British Chiefs made certain statements
about the strategy of the holding phase. German entrance into
Spain would make Gibraltar untenable "and force occupation of the
Canaries"; perhaps bases in French Morocco and French West Africa; "the United Kingdom would have no forces available for the
African tasks"; loss of the Middle East would be "disastrous," and its
retention depended largely on American assistance; "security of the
Singapore base was essential for Far East operation." [51]

Of course, "intervention of the United States would revolutionize
the whole situation." The British Chiefs felt no need to dissimulate
as Churchill had. They argued for immediate and full American
entry. "At sea the situation would be immediately relieved, and this
should be reflected in reduced shipping losses. Even if Japan intervened, the balance of advantage would still be with us. American
forces might be able to prevent enemy penetration in Morocco and
West Africa, and could take over potential commitments in the Atlantic Islands." They said blandly: "It is clear, however, that if intervention is to come, the longer it is delayed the greater will be the
leeway to be made up in every direction." [52]

The British Chiefs then demonstrated the ability to extrapolate
future victory from a desperate present, and gave an "extremely
hopeful" analysis. "We must first destroy the foundation upon which
the German war machine rests — the economy which feeds it, the
morale which sustains it, the supplies which nourish it . . . and the

hopes of victory which inspire it." How do this? Blockade, bombing, subversion. If the heavy bomber received top priority, its weight in combination with other methods would assure victory, "if these methods are applied on a vast scale, the whole structure upon which the German forces are based . . . will be destroyed, and . . . the armed forces of Germany would suffer such a radical decline in fighting value and mobility that a direct attack would once more become possible." Grudging recognition of possible need for land invasion led to an appeal for acceptance of strategic bombing. "When that time will come," the report avowed, ". . . will depend largely on how well we are able, with American assistance, to keep to our program of Air Force expansion and to obtain and protect the necessary shipping. It may be that the methods described above will by themselves be enough to make Germany sue for peace . . . We must, however, be prepared to accelerate victory by landing forces on the Continent to . . . strike into Germany itself." Invasion armies would be forces in the Churchillian sense, occupying and exploiting territory already wrested from German control by bombing and partisan uprisings.[53]

The Americans united in insisting that American production requirements receive priority.[54] Yet even this was difficult to maintain. Marshall and his colleagues may have gotten "a clear indication" of expected requests from Churchill's speech. The demands, when they began spilling out of attaché cases Sunday afternoon, were still numbing. Arnold talked with Air Vice-Marshal Freeman about the British bomber proposal. He learned to his dismay where those 10,000 planes were to be found. "His program now is clear. Britain has built it around our entire production . . . O.P.M. figures have at last confused almost everyone," Arnold said.[55] Freeman's explanation emphasized the need for a program. The British had gotten some "very optimistic" figures from American officials and had accepted them without question. "If we had given the British what those hastily arrived-at statistics called for," Arnold complained, "they would have received one hundred percent of all planes produced in the United States." Freeman was "very much disappointed," for he had believed all those B-17's and B-24's were already sitting in hangars.[56]

There was a meeting about the convoy question and a skirmish in late afternoon over assignment of American aid. Elliott Roosevelt recalled,

> Britain's advocates were again hard at it, trying to convince us to divert more and more and more Lend-Lease supplies to the United Kingdom and less and less and less to the Soviet Union . . . In these conversations Marshall and King and Arnold continued insistent that there was logic in giving the Soviets all the help that could be spared . . . Admiral Pound, General Dill, Air Chief Marshal [sic] Freeman — these three rang every change on the argument that the stockpiles, in the long run, would prove of more value to the overall Allied war effort. They hammered at the idea that war material to the Soviets was destined just to be war material captured by the Nazis, that American self-interest dictated a channeling of the bulk of supplies into England.[57]

Elliott's neat dramatization of American sympathy for Russia contrasted with British opposition is shot through with holes from premise to conclusions. The Soviet Union was not receiving Lend-Lease at the time. His description of British greed is patently false. The Prime Minister had turned over his own supplies to Russia.[58] Basis for discussion was an analysis of Russian production of selected items, probably furnished by Hopkins. It purported to show the Soviets turned out 2500 planes and 24,000 tanks per month. Comparing these staggering figures with U.S. totals, Arnold joked: "I think that we should ask them for help." [59] The conferees agreed that only token aid should go to the Russians at present. A meeting could be arranged later (after more was known about the results of the great German offensive then moving to its climax) to deal with long-term assistance. The meeting adjourned — without specific decisions having been reached — at 7:00 P.M. when the stewards began setting up for the President's dinner.[60]

❖

3

In a parallel conference on convoying, solid progress was made. During the Argentia meeting American and British representatives succeeded in working out measures coordinating naval activities in the Atlantic. In fact, the one indisputable dividend of the meeting was agreement for United States escort of shipping in the Western Atlantic. One authority has written: "Among the naval authorities it was recognized that the question of convoy escort, which had been hanging fire for many months and to which Mr. Churchill again called attention, was most urgent. Discussions of this issue resulted in one of the few definite decisions arrived at during the meeting; arrangements were completed for American escort of British as well as American merchant shipping as far as Iceland." [61]

Inside and out of the administration there had been powerful pressure for convoying — and for public announcement of it. By late May, 1941, a slight but increasing majority of Americans apparently favored convoys.[62] Roosevelt agreed, but seemed to fear that the public opinion polls might be erroneous. As early as January 17, 1941, the President had asked that the Navy "should be prepared to convoy shipping in the Atlantic and continue to patrol the east coast." [63] Most of his advisers saw convoying as a way in which America could give direct aid to England without serious risk of war. The struggle against German air, surface, and submarine attacks had to be won. To some leaders convoying offered a palliative for British demands. Their reasoning was: "Upon the assumption . . . that the United States will enter the present war sooner or later, it appears . . . highly desirable that the entry be made sufficiently soon to avoid either the loss of the British Isles or a material change in the attitude of the British Government directed toward appeasement . . . It must be recognized that the Army can, at the present time, accomplish extremely limited military support . . . and from this point of view it is highly desirable that we withhold active participation as long as possible." [64] Army planners were willing to have the Navy take strong measures. The Navy was glad to take on this task.

On April 15 there had been a discussion at the White House of the "neutrality patrol." Roosevelt was concerned whether convoying "should be ordered secretly or by proclamation," not by its wisdom or necessity. Secretaries Morgenthau, Stimson, and Knox urged frank announcement. F.D.R. wished "more advice and more time for consideration," and Hopkins was anxious about possible results "whose gravity he felt the President did not recognize." [65] The Secretary of State advocated caution. Breckinridge Long, Hull's assistant, opined that although convoying was not an act of war it would invite German attacks. This argument probably impressed Hull. (Long thought so.) "He is not apt to be specifically committal, but . . . I am sure he held the same opinion. He went to the President's conference and I understand he and the President were of the same mind — and that others were not." [66]

Carrying out the policy, despite its increasing public acceptance, proceeded by fits and starts. The planning office of the Chief of Naval Operations had been drawing up operational plans since December, 1940. After the ABC-1 talks plans were discussed with the President; in April he postponed approval.

The matter lay dormant until after F.D.R.'s May 27 speech. When preparations were made for United States' occupation of Iceland, convoy escort was studied once more, plans exhumed for naval escort to and from Iceland. "As these convoys would traverse the Northern Atlantic as far east as Longitude 26° West, such convoys escorted by the U.S. Navy would follow the same . . . routes from Newfoundland to Iceland as the British convoys. The inclusion of such British shipping in American-escorted convoys . . . had been envisaged since September, 1940, and had been called for in the ABC-1 report. . . . The Joint Army and Navy Plans — Rainbow No. 5 — . . . had provided that this part of the staff agreement would be made effective, on Presidential direction, as a Hemispheric Defense measure short of war." [67] Protection of flag shipping between the United States and its outposts was logical. Extending protection to vessels of foreign registry, however, was politically charged. Events nonetheless proved it inevitable.

In absence of evidence of Roosevelt's attitude, his Secretary of

State's reaction may be taken to demonstrate the political calculations. On May 12, Hull talked with Breckinridge Long about convoying. Claiming he "had to carry the brunt of policy recently because of the President's illness," the old Tennessean confessed he was under pressure to initiate convoying. He believed that at present it was "inadvisable" to approach the question directly. "There was not a unanimity of opinion in the country, and . . . it was better to have as large a percentage of opinion as possible." It would be wiser to extend the "patrolling system"; if properly carried out, these measures could be expanded "without serious opposition" and gradually might develop into something stronger. The Secretary asked Long, "Did you ever see a tadpole turn into a frog?" His assistant appreciated the simile, noting that night in his diary: "So that is about the state of our convoy policy." [68]

The British Admiralty suggested in June that the United States do full convoy escort. It asked that the Navy assume responsibility for the western half of the Atlantic.[69] Admiral Ghormley, naval liaison to the Admiralty, replied under instruction that plans for this eventuality were being drawn up but "there is no present intention of the United States Government to execute any such measure." [70] Insertion of the word "government" was intentional. Anglo-American discussions of detailed arrangements for U.S. convoy escort duty went on from mid-June until Argentia.

Roosevelt approved convoy escort at the end of June. The "mere presence" of Axis vessels and aircraft between the United States and Iceland was to be proof of hostile intent.[71] But again there was Roosevelt's sensitivity to public opinion. American newspapers had printed exaggerated accounts of patrol activities in the Atlantic. Senator Burton K. Wheeler, a leader of the isolationist bloc, introduced a resolution on June 30 demanding "thorough and complete investigation" of reports that the Navy was convoying.[72] Knox on July 2 denied categorically that naval vessels had encountered German ships while on Atlantic patrol. It was "absolutely untrue" that the Navy was convoying ships bound to and from the United Kingdom.

The isolationist group in Congress forced Knox and Stark to ap-

pear before a closed session of the Naval Affairs Committee.[73] They
gave nothing away but the publicity caused another of those painful
reassessments in the White House. Navy planners modified their
proposal. Navy Hemisphere Plan No. 4 (W.P.L.-51) replaced
W.P.L.-50 on July 11; Allied or neutral shipping could join American-escorted convoys only if "specific directives" were forthcoming.
Tasks assigned the Navy were limited. Axis vessels or aircraft were
only to be shadowed and their movements reported. In practice,
however, a provision "in utmost secrecy" nullified these restrictions.
The Chief of Staff was to arrange for one or more American or Ice-
landic flag vessels to depart — eastbound from Halifax or westbound
from 26° West longitude — "at intervals not greater than those at
which British convoys depart." The document admitted that "the
practical result would be the sailing of regular British convoys and
United States flag vessels in company." [74] Subordinates were copy-
ing Roosevelt's penchant for deviousness.

F.D.R. still hesitated. The order went into effect on July 25, as
Stark had predicted; but without the provision for "ships of any nationality" to join American-escorted convoys.[75] When the naval
heads of the United States and Great Britain assembled at Argentia
W.P.L.-51 was floating somewhere in the void.

At the remote Newfoundland rendezvous, far from the paralyzing
accusations of isolationists, Roosevelt approved United States protection of all shipping in the Western Atlantic.[76] Maintaining sea
communications was "repeatedly emphasized" in talks between the
sailors and between them and their civil superiors. Solution of this
problem had to precede all others. Aid to the Soviet Union was
limited by Allied ability to protect convoys to Archangel or find ships
for the Persian Gulf and Vladivostok routes. Defense of the British
Isles, of the Mediterranean and the Middle East, relied on the seas.
The situation was a classic example of seapower. Stark gave final
approval to W.P.L.-51 on August 10; his instructions were dispatched from Argentia on August 13 to take effect on September 16,
1941.[77]

In the meantime the Atlantic Fleet undertook escort duty on the

Iceland route. American warships shepherded convoys from Halifax-Newfoundland to a position south of Iceland where the Royal Navy took charge. Although left unsaid, this arrangement provided protection of British and neutral vessels. Samuel Eliot Morison has written: "We were, theoretically, escorting our own and the Icelanders' ships to and from Iceland; but the little clause, 'including any other shipping of any other nationality which may join,' allowed others to come along if they chose; and many, of course, did so choose." [78]

A major step in winning the battle of the Atlantic, this course meant the beginning of undeclared hostilities with Germany. U-boat commanders would find it impossible to maintain Hitler's proud appellation, "supermen," in distinguishing between the national origins of threatening warships. Some dark, foggy night a German torpedo would cut into an American destroyer's hull. The British understandably looked forward to such an occurrence.

4

Sunday night was given over to dinner parties. The First Sea Lord dined with Stark and King. Dill was the host for a larger gathering in the after cabin of *Prince of Wales*. He, Freeman, and Cadogan welcomed Marshall, Arnold, Burns, and Welles as they came aboard, damp from a barge ride through heavy fog and drizzle. Captain Leach was also present at this affair. During the meal he consented to describe his ship's part in the pursuit of *Bismarck*. The *Prince of Wales* had been berthed in Scapa Flow and men from the shipyards were still working in her gun turrets when the word came to put to sea. Leach himself was away fishing but returned before the battleship sailed. He had little to say about the battle, noting only "the carnage, wounded and dead, was so bad that he withdrew from action." [79] Captain Leach was the only man on the bridge not killed or wounded.

According to available testimony, this colloquy was exceptional. The British were surprised and depressed by American lack of interest either in the *Bismarck* action or the naval war. "Streams of U.S. officers have been coming over again today," Jacob wrote on Monday night, "and it is very interesting to see their outlook. From what I have heard there has not been a single enquiry from any one of them about the ship, its capabilities and equipment, or its part in the 'Bismarck' action. They do not appear in the least interested in the progress of the naval war. It is of course possible that they think . . . that questions might be embarrassing, but the fact remains that they seem to be much more concerned in getting a few drinks and in having a good time . . ." [80] Argentia demonstrated to the British how detached was America from the war. Not just the advertisements in wardroom magazines but the comments and attitudes of most American officers drove this lesson home. "My own impression, recorded at the time," W. M. Yool relates, "was that the Americans were still very remote from the war and as yet a long way from any desire to join in." [81]

The British took seriously their duty of talking up United States entry into the war. As noted, they also attempted to uncover such plans as the Yanks had developed for fighting the war once in. Jacob and "Dumbie" Dykes were ordered or took it upon themselves to pump Colonel Bundy further about the "Victory Program" he had described Saturday. Bundy said American planners were "tentatively aiming" at an army of four million men. The two Britishers were horrified by such "wasteful use of manpower and manufacturing capacity." They told Bundy, "It hardly seemed conceivable that large scale land fighting could take place on the Continent of America, and shipping limitations would make it quite impossible for large forces to be transferred quickly to other theaters." [82] Those observations came straight from the British strategic estimate; and they were to be repeated in other cabins by other Britishers throughout Sunday evening. However, when Churchill called his Chiefs of Staff in for a short consultation at 9:30 Monday morning they had to admit that the Americans had refused to respond. Hopefully, the formal meeting would be different.

The first full staff conference got underway at 11:00 A.M. Monday on *Prince of Wales*. Attending were Pound, Dill, Freeman, Hollis, and Jacob for the United Kingdom; Stark, Marshall, King, Arnold, Turner, Sherman, and Bundy for the United States. Pound presided and gave brief opening remarks. He said it was the wish of the British Chiefs that he read, paragraph by paragraph, their strategy review. He hoped they might "in due course" receive the "comments and views" of the Chief of Naval Operations and Chief of Staff "on the subjects discussed therein." Stark, the principal American spokesman on this occasion, rose to remind Pound that "this meeting was for discussion only and that considered comments on the British paper would be sent later after thorough study." [83] Such careful study, he remarked, seemed necessary "in view of the apparent fact that the General Review is, in several particulars, at marked variance with the agreements reached in the ABC Conversations." United States military authorities believed ABC-1 was satisfactory, and "that it ought to continue to serve as the basic guide for the Military effort of both the United States and the British Commonwealth." [84] He agreed, however, there was no harm in going over the paper.

Methodical analysis gave way before intemperate interjections by both sides, however. The usually calm Marshall was emphatic in questioning the "manner and method" of British operations; "plans for the Middle East must be studied to determine the extent of the development ultimately to be required and its relation to what can practically be expected from the United States." [85] The Americans had no intention of bailing out Great Britain. Marshall clearly preferred that the British abandon or downgrade their effort because the Russian front was much more important.

For Russia he urged coordination of aid "if she continued to hold out." Russian demands were bound to be very great and the "loss and wastage of material" in the Middle East could not be borne for long. He mentioned that he was able to send only fifteen tanks to the Philippines, and the relative effect of sending 200 planes to Russia compared with the same number to the Dutch East Indies or Philippines.[86] "The priority battle was a fact," Marshall commented at the Monday meeting. Stark supported his colleague. He also believed there should be a complete reevaluation by the British of their priorities. Stark mentioned "the extent to which material sent to the

Philippines gave direct aid and support to Singapore and Australia." [87]

Marshall blamed British selfishness for the current equipment situation in the Philippines. He took as an example the lack of antiaircraft guns in the United States and its territories. Freeman replied with an accusation of his own. Diversion of aircraft, because of pressure from "American political sources," already had wreaked havoc with British plans. He was referring to Roosevelt's recent intervention to demonstrate American willingness to assist the Soviet Union.[88]

A distinctive situation arose at the conference because Churchill had modified certain views over the preceding weeks. Opposition to massive reinforcement of the Middle East had caused him to say that "nothing that might happen in Malaya could amount to a fifth part of the loss of Egypt, the Suez Canal, and the Middle East." [89] The apparent explanation for this change was Hitler's attack on the Soviet Union. "The British, for their part," the U.S. Army historians Matloff and Snell assert, "relieved by the German attack on the U.S.S.R. . . . ceased to dwell on the oft-repeated demand for American naval forces in the Southwest Pacific and began to urge an early entry of the United States into the war against Germany and the desirability of American collaboration in the Mediterranean." [90] American naval authorities were sympathetic toward this shift. Stark indicated he attached little importance to the Far East. As quoted by Colonel Jacob, he said: "We can afford to see it all 'go West' without bothering ourselves unduly." Stark and Turner also recognized the strategic importance of the Indian Ocean and the Near East. Their "chief concern" was that "as little as possible of the U.S. Fleet should be drawn into the Far East," and they gave the impression they believed that the war could be won by winning the Battle of the Atlantic. Marshall's remarks proved "the American Army and Navy authorities have not got together and thought out a joint policy." Along with many military men he possessed emotional ties to the Philippines. He advocated reinforcement of the Far East "so as to constitute a serious check to Japanese southward expansion." Singapore he considered an important strongpoint but the

Middle East was a minor element in United States Army Planning.[91]

The Americans responded only to about half the items. Stark slapped indirectly at British policy by pointing out paragraph 20 of the Review "might be interpreted to give heavy bombers priority" over protection of shipping routes.[92] British arguments in favor of strategic bombing had not impressed either Marshall or Stark. Both stressed the "bad effect" assignment of first priority to bomber production had on their services' development. "As far as we can judge," commented one British officer in disgust, "they each had an exaggerated idea of its effect. They clearly regard the air as something subsidiary to their own particular concerns, and do not appreciate the importance of acting offensively against Germany." [93] Further evidence of this skeptical attitude came when discussion turned to aircraft production. Pound expressed appreciation for planes supplied by the United States. Catalinas (PBY's) assigned to Coastal Command had performed superbly, but he said it was a rude shock to learn that "practically none were to be delivered in the next few months." More Catalinas were essential because of the "probability" that Coastal Command would not get any more Liberators. "This probability was the result of representations made by Mr. Hopkins to have the Liberators taken out of the Coastal Command and used to bomb Germany." Here the Admiral dumbfounded his American listeners. They objected to this interference by Roosevelt's aide which clearly demonstrated the President's support of strategic bombing. Stark, King, and Turner "all expressed their view that the Northwest Approaches are a critical area, and their disagreement with Mr. Hopkins' proposal." Stark strongly opposed any attempt by the United States to "dictate" British use of material. This appears a complete reversal of roles, but London gladly would have accepted Hopkins' proposal — had it included increased deliveries of bombers. These sentiments and the fervor with which they were conveyed relieved the British Chiefs. Freeman admitted London was feeling the weight of "strong American pressures to use all 4-engined bombers to bomb Germany," but so far all Liberators received had been assigned to the Northwest Approaches.[94]

Next arose proposed operations against the Azores, Cape Verdes, and Canary Islands. Obviously, coordination was necessary in the aftermath of discussions by the President and Prime Minister. Pound said a British force would be ready in September to seize the Canaries; but in event Germany did not move into Spain shortly he doubted the practicality of such an operation during the winter months.[95] Marshall opposed invasion of these islands and said the President had told him "definitely" that "a peaceful movement into the Azores has become more possible. Salazar . . . was now disposed to accept, on his invitation, British or American protection." Dill stressed that British preparations for the Canaries meant that America must take responsibility for the Portuguese archipelagoes. "He expressed his belief that it would not be necessary to occupy the Azores and Cape Verdes if the Canaries were held, since the Azores and Cape Verdes would be 'masked' by the Canaries." Aware of Roosevelt's feelings, Admiral Turner replied that it would be better — strategically and politically — for the United States to go ahead with Operation Indigo "if it could be done peacefully." [96]

The U.S. Chiefs never betrayed eagerness for *Operation Indigo*, which meant primarily more logistical problems. They thought it another of those half-baked ideas which the President was prone to suggest. Marshall labeled Roosevelt's habit of tossing out new operations "his cigarette holder gesture." [97] The Army, in the throes of massive expansion, had not yet recovered from the blows dealt its training program by occupation of Iceland. Marshall explained the difficulties, the draft situation, limiting draftees' service to the Western Hemisphere, regular personnel serving three-year enlistments, dispatch of 10,000 men to Iceland. The British grasped, perhaps for the first time, the hazards under which their American colleagues labored.[98]

The conferees took up the question of Dakar. Pound ordered his assistant, Colonel Hollis, to provide the Chief of Naval Operations with a copy of the latest British study of the West African stronghold's defenses. General Dill stated that "25,000 men and two regiments of tanks could take Dakar, that the defense forces included 50,000 men, largely Senegalese, with no tanks and relatively little equipment." [99] He did not suggest from whence these forces might come, and the Americans had information — from such respected sources that even President Roosevelt accepted its authenticity — that Dakar would be a tougher nut to crack than the British supposed.[100] It was tacitly recognized that lack of resources prevented any serious consideration of an operation against Dakar whatever the Germans might do.

Discussion of paragraphs ten–fifteen of the "Strategy Review" brought out more evidence of American distaste for the Middle East. The British Chiefs stated they would go ahead with transfer of certain forces to the Far East, and they accepted the American refusal to make parallel additions to U.S. naval strength in the Pacific. Stark did make several concessions to British plans for joint operations in the Atlantic. One of these promised that, in event of American entry into the war, United States naval units would shift to Gibraltar. This would free Britain's Force "H" for duty in the Far East.[101] These decisions doomed the great battleship on which they were made, for to carry them out *Prince of Wales* was dispatched to Malaya in November, 1941.

Another point of Far Eastern strategy was the proper response of the United States and United Kingdom should Japan attack the Soviet Union. The British could not decide whether to declare war on Japan in such a contingency "because the U.S. was unresolved as to its own action if the British did go to Russia's aid." [102] It was one more hypothetical question left unanswered. Admiral Stark later commented: "I have done my utmost to get a decision — it can't be had now either here or in London — I make no forecast." [103]

All these matters took up so much time that it became clear reading and discussion of the entire paper could not be accomplished. The result was that the last section, which contained "broad ideas of how to set about winning the war," was not dealt with at all. Admiral Pound read the subheadings of the remaining parts, and Stark again promised that "after careful study" he and Marshall would provide a full commentary. The meeting adjourned without provision for holding another.[104]

Monday afternoon passed in smaller meetings, Marshall with Dill, Freeman with Arnold, and numerous chance encounters usually in vicinity of *Prince of Wales'* wardroom. They amounted to one more review of now familiar problems. Freeman once again argued for priority of British requirements in planes, tanks, and other equipment. "My God, what a list," Arnold exclaimed as he reread it Monday night. The Americans' replies were unchanged. "No promises — just see what can be done." [105] Queries about personal reactions to the "Strategy Review" brought careful answers (the degree of caution depended on service affiliation) that it demanded serious study. British officers did not have the heart to pursue that lead. The C.I.G.S. went over to see Marshall at 4:00; even for these two sympathetic spirits the conversation was awkward. Marshall kept strictly to production issues; indeed, he appeared uninterested in strategy. "It would do General Marshall, Admiral Stark, and Admiral Turner a power of good if they could come over and spend a month in England," privately complained a frustrated British spokesman. [106]

On Monday evening F.D.R. and Churchill dined together, but military and naval leaders refrained this once from the task of furthering Anglo-American understanding. After a buffet supper, Americans quartered on *Tuscaloosa* settled down to watch Spencer Tracy and Robert Montgomery outfox and outfight Frenchmen and hostile Indians in *Northwest Passage*. They were again disappointed, for the order to darken ship came with one-fourth of the final reel to be shown. "Bed at 11:00. What a day," was Arnold's summation. [107] The British held "guest night" in the wardroom, and entertained between fifteen and twenty officers from U.S. and Canadian warships in the harbor. It went off well despite the fact that, as one of the hosts observed, "our guests were an extraordinarily mixed collection." [108] There was singing of traditional sea chanteys, a goodly amount of drinking, and in the latter stages impassioned jazz and ragtime piano played by a young American lieutenant.

That another formal meeting of the Chiefs of Staff took place appears to have been by accident. There was another communications lapse, and until mid-Tuesday morning the Americans had no idea a meeting was desired. Pound asked his colleagues to come to his cabin at 10:00 A.M. Captain Schofield was designated runner to inform the United States Chiefs a final conference was requested for 11:30. The First Sea Lord then limped off in search of Captain Leach and spent over an hour with him discussing the course to be followed on the homeward voyage and other nautical details. His staff ascribed Pound's erratic behavior to excitement at bestriding a warship's deck. "Going back to sea has quite gone to the 'Whale's' head," said Colonel Jacob.[109]

Schofield could not track down all the American leaders. He found Stark but not Marshall or Arnold. The latter recalled he began the morning in blissful ignorance of any more meetings with the British. For want of something better to do, he asked Bundy "if he wanted to go over to *Augusta* to see if General Marshall had any last minute instructions." Bundy said, "Yes." Sherman wanted to go also, and at 9:00 the three men boarded the *Augusta.* They found the Chief of Staff in his cabin. Stark, Sherman, and Harry Hopkins came in at 9:45. The group talked about the British bomber program, during which Marshall approved Arnold's recommendations. After a time Stark rose, explaining, "I have to be aboard *Prince of Wales* at 11:30 to continue discussion re Far East." Thinking that the C.N.O. was referring to a talk with Royal Navy delegates, Marshall said, "I will go over with you and say goodbye to Dill." [110] Some of the others decided to say "adios" to Freeman, Dykes, and the rest. The Americans went over separately. Arnold reached the battleship at 10:45. It was boiling with activity. Lord Beaverbrook's arrival, last-minute arrangements for visits to the President, and departure preparations had created "a scene of absolute chaos." [111] While picking his way through loose gear, Arnold met the Prime Minister and was invited into his cabin for a glass of port. Churchill asked if the American airman planned to attend the Chiefs of Staff meeting. When he learned Arnold knew nothing of any meeting, the Prime Minister insisted he was expected and personally escorted him to the First Sea Lord's cabin. Churchill was furious. He returned, muttering, to his cabin, when Hollis assured him the meeting was being arranged. It was a close thing. Bugle peals overhead announced the arrival of the C.N.O. and Turner just at 11:30 and Marshall did not come in until a few minutes later.[112]

The meeting necessarily was brief — the British were to depart in late afternoon — but in several respects it was productive.[113] All were present who attended the first conference, with the exception of Colonel Bundy. Over sherry the Chiefs recapitulated their private discussions of the status of ABC-1. British delegates asked again what the United States intended if it entered the war. They received no answer. As a result, most of the time was devoted to "reviewing the situation with respect to material assistance rendered by the United States." [114] At their conversation Tuesday morning Roosevelt and Churchill laid down guidelines for the division of military aid between the United Kingdom and U.S.S.R. These confirmed arrangements proposed by Hopkins and anticipated later agreements — the Victory Program and decisions of the Moscow Supply Conference. As an American contribution to the task of coordinating aid requests, Stark read a proposal which was to have tremendous future importance, a plan to make the Joint Board the agency with highest responsibility for distribution of material. Out of this evolved the Combined Chiefs of Staff.[115] These comments ended the staff talks. The two delegations made hasty farewells, and the Americans transferred to *Augusta*. A short time later they gathered to wave goodbye to their new friends and prospective colleagues as *Prince of Wales* steamed out of the anchorage and turned east.

VIII. The Third Climacteric

T HE ISOLATION in which the meeting was transacted made it difficult for those present to maintain a sense of perspective. Engaged in the exciting task of reforming the world, Roosevelt and Churchill forgot at times that events elsewhere promised to out-run many decisions taken in the tranquility of Argentia. Much information was supplied to the conferees regarding German and Japanese machinations, the course of policy in Vichy, Madrid, and Lisbon, fluctuating public support at home; but not enough was known or reported to ensure that decisions related to the actual situation. Sometimes, it seemed as if the President and Prime Minister believed events were frozen until they had completed deliberations. In fact, great acts and daily routines proceeded without the slightest pause. In F.D.R.'s absence Lord Halifax informed the White House that the Duke and Duchess of Windsor gladly accepted the President's invitation to tea after his return to Washington. In the Prime Minister's absence his brother, Major John Spencer Churchill, acted as proxy godfather at the christening of the first son of A. G. Malan, great fighter ace and hero of the Battle of Britain. Other British fliers were landing battered Wellingtons, Blenheims, and American-made B-24's after bombing strikes against Berlin, Essen, Hanover, and other German industrial centers. Across the Atlantic pickets marched defiantly outside the huge shipyards in Kearny, N. J. Although entangled in the climactic stage of its private war over the draft extension bill, Congress paused to approve a number of defense construction bills, one of which was a supplementary appropriation of $13 million for the expansion of Argentia naval air station. Monday was a normal day.[1]

The morning news summary showed that confusion about the battle in Russia was still great. The German High Command stated Soviet resistance was crumbling and that *Panzergruppen,* driving disorganized Russian units before them deep in the southern Ukraine, were about to reach the Black Sea. Communiqués from Moscow disputed the Nazis' claims, announcing "there was nothing of importance to report from any part of the battle front." The situation was critical if German claims were true. Should their forces turn the southern flank of the wobbly front Russia had erected in mid-July the end might be near. A quick victory in the East would allow regrouping of Nazi forces for the feared drive across the Iberian Peninsula to the Atlantic and perhaps beyond.

It appeared that one check to a movement in this direction, Vichy's striving for an independent position, was being removed. Reports of the current policy debate at Vichy were worrisome. Some observers interpreted Marshal Pétain's radio broadcast on August 10 as directed to the United States as much as to his own people. He had warned that interference in French affairs would have extremely serious consequences.[2] Ambassador Leahy wrote Sunday that Pétain's regime was taking the position that "the principles which govern Mr. Roosevelt and his collaborators and those which Marshal Pétain wishes to apply to reconstruct the country are incompatible." He had been told it would be "intolerable" for France to embrace "a universal political conception" (parliamentary democracy) which had been proven an "anachronism" in the New Europe.[3] The cabinet meeting on North African policy set for Saturday had been postponed until Monday. When it was held the outcome likely would confirm the primacy of Admiral Darlan and his "collaborationist" schemes.

To all indications Japan's leaders were also poised upon the brink of fateful decisions. Magic informed the U.S. government of the agreement worked out in the Imperial Conference of July 2 to carry forward the movement to the south even if war with America and Britain ensued. But did this rule out any possibility of a Japanese-American settlement? What was the timetable of Japan's advance and could anything be done to postpone its being put into execution? Did the July 2 decision mean Japan was abjuring the tempting prospect held out by Berlin of an easy conquest of Siberia? The last of these questions was answered in early August. The Chief of Staff of the Japanese Army received trustworthy information that Germany would not knock out the Soviet Union in 1941 and that a long war was likely. This intelligence caused Army leaders to accept the view of the Foreign Ministry that "so long as the Soviet Union maintains neutrality and does not pose a menace to the Far East" Japan should respect the Neutrality Pact.[4] Answers to the other questions were not to be obtained even in Tokyo.

The Japanese proceeded with the occupation of French Indochina and launched an aggressive campaign for concessions from Thailand. On August 1 President Roosevelt had extended his neutralization proposal to cover Thailand. Japan's reply, presented to Hull on August 6, was a rejection linked to an expression of interest in further negotiations should the United States offer concessions.[5] Two days later an important Japanese official answered the President *en clair:* Japan was being subjected to military, economic, and political encirclement by the "ABCD" powers, and the situation was becoming intolerable.[6] This accusation resulted from a speech by Foreign Secretary Eden in the House of Commons. Eden had warned that Japanese meddling in Thailand would have "grave consequences," quite possibly war.[7] Notably, Secretary of State Hull would say only that the United States had "increasing concern" about events in the Pacific. Lord Halifax tried in a talk with Hull Saturday afternoon the same tack that Churchill was taking with the President. He inquired about the amount of aid America might give "in case Singapore or the Dutch East Indies should be attacked." The Secretary of State's response was evasive as usual. Hull said should Japan maintain its aggressive course the United States and the United Kingdom "should naturally have a conference at once." [8]

Two facts of which the British Ambassador was ignorant reinforced Hull's habitual distaste for commitments. The first development was a possible breakthrough in worsening relations between

Japan and the United States. The previous day, August 8, Ambassador Nomura had delivered a proposal that Prince Konoye meet with President Roosevelt in a "supreme effort" for an understanding.[9] It is now known that Konoye was staking everything on this desperate gamble to avoid a conflict with the United States. When he brought up the idea on August 4 Navy leaders had given their support; but Tojo, the Minister of War, had imposed an ominous condition upon Army approval: if a meeting with the American President could not be arranged or if it proved a failure, Konoye must promise not to resign but to lead the nation into war. The Prime Minister acceded.[10] He sent off the proposal to Nomura and also had Foreign Minister Teijiro Toyoda get Ambassador Grew's reaction. The American diplomat, a veteran of almost ten years in Japan, was enthusiastic. He wrote up a lengthy report of the interview with Toyoda, had it verified by the Foreign Minister, and insisted that it be encoded immediately and dispatched to Washington.[11] Unfortunately, Hull did not heed Grew's recommendation. The Secretary of State brushed over the proposal when Nomura raised it on August 8. He thought the idea a waste of effort if not a cover for some Japanese skulduggery. He was fearful also that the President might destroy all that had been achieved (or could be still) in Hull-Nomura conversations.[12] Hull could not reply on his own anyway. The President must decide such an important matter. Even if Hull knew how to reach F.D.R., he was unwilling to forward the proposal for presidential consideration when not he but imprudent men such as the British Prime Minister and Harry Hopkins would be consulted. He had no way of knowing what impulsive actions were being foisted upon the President. He refused to speculate about a conference and told reporters only "the President had made no mention of such a meeting when they conferred by telephone the day before Mr. Roosevelt sailed." [13] No one in the Department of State knew what was going on or where Under Secretary Welles had gone, and Hull would not explain. Breckinridge Long surmised by the Secretary's irritable remarks regarding the "intimate association" of Welles with the President that the Under Secretary was at the "probable conference" with Churchill.[14] Other cabinet members did not know that much. Stimson's diary entry for August 7 read: "The mysterious absence of the President and the Chief of Staff and the Chief of Naval Operations still continues and speculation is very rife." Only on August 11 did the Secretary of War admit that a meeting such as was being trumpeted by the newspapers was a strong probability.[15]

American newspapermen were surprisingly slow to catch on. Over the weekend suspicions that Roosevelt and Churchill were meeting changed into virtual certainty. The German-sponsored radio broadcast from Lisbon on August 6 was monitored in the United States and given wide circulation. Reporters began to look skeptically at the peculiar lack of information about Prime Minister Churchill's itinerary, the abnormally vague language of the press releases concerning the President's cruise, and the unpublicized disappearance of high officials from both Washington and London. No one put together all the pieces until Richard Rendell, Washington correspondent for the Chicago *Times,* asked the British Embassy if the Duke of Kent, who was to visit the capital in mid-month, would speak at a National Press Club luncheon. He was told the Duke's schedule was filled and the Embassy spokesman with whom he talked hinted this was so because "an important personage" was shortly to visit the United States. The press immediately concluded that the unnamed dignitary was Churchill, and although Rendell soon learned the British Embassy had been referring to the Duke of Windsor, his inquiry set wheels spinning.[16] Reactions by administration figures opened the way for additional speculation. Hull, Stimson, and the rest refused to answer or pleaded ignorance. The clincher came when Steve Early was given numerous opportunities to knock down the story and refused to seize them.[17] Of course, Early knew no more than his inquisitioners but he could not convince anyone of this. He was in a tight spot, not sure whether to laugh off the questions or say nothing. If he denied all and subsequent developments proved him a liar, he stood to lose the respect of the Washington press corps. Yet admission that a Roosevelt-Churchill meeting was conceivable might have disastrous results.

Back at Argentia the President gave no sign that he regretted not having informed subordinates of his plans. They would have been spared some mental turmoil and public embarrassment; but that was a small price for the added insurance of secrecy. Roosevelt was delighted at the remarkable durability of his and the Prime Minister's cover stories. He had no intention of sending confirmation of the meeting until all shreds of doubt were dispelled by reporters' detective work. F.D.R. may have shared the reports of official Washington's befuddlement with the Prime Minister at their Monday meetings. He did not, however, disclose all the information received since Sunday night.

1

The dialogue between President and Prime Minister resumed at 11:00 A.M. Monday when Churchill and Cadogan boarded *Augusta* to find F.D.R., Welles, and Hopkins awaiting them in the main cabin.[18] The meeting lasted only a brief time but dealt with crucial matters. It formed an interesting study in tactics. Reading his great friend's temperament impressively, Churchill applied his own version of the carrot and stick ploy, giving Roosevelt a breather before pressing forward on policy toward Japan.

The conferees first took up the Portuguese situation. Roosevelt read aloud the letter from Prime Minister Salazar. Cadogan had informed his master of this development and the British had worked out their position. It was agreed that Salazar's letter was "highly satisfactory" and made possible arrangments for occupation of the Azores to assure that Germany would not seize the islands. Although the Portuguese statement was good news, it placed Churchill in an awkward position. Arithmetic dictated that his country had not the ability "conveniently to carry out [its] commitment . . . to the Portuguese Government to assist in the defense of the Azores." He prefaced this admission with description of a "highly secret operation" to seize the Canary Islands, a necessary step and one which, unfortunately, precluded British participation in the Azores campaign.[19] Designated *Operation Pilgrim*, this movement was to begin after the September full moon. Churchill and his government were reluctant to renege on the centuries-old (1373) British-Portuguese alliance. The Prime Minister stressed his determination to act even though this step would "almost inevitably" cause a Spanish attack "and that such attack would render untenable . . . the harbor of Gibraltar." By the time of the Argentia conference the British judged the Spanish situation was "going from bad to worse." Hitler would undertake occupation of Spain and Portugal "with the subsequent penetration of North Africa" if there were a Soviet collapse or even a winter stalemate. Such a development would isolate Gibraltar anyway, and control of the Canaries was of "utmost importance" in protecting the South Atlantic convoy routes.[20]

A larger view of *Operation Pilgrim,* understood by both F.D.R. and Churchill, saw it as a precautionary move, "as an alternative to the occupation of Dakar, which was the key to the situation in West Africa and the crucial base for protection of the shipping coming from the Cape of Good Hope."[21] They anticipated that Admiral Darlan, who seemed currently in control in Vichy's clamorous game of musical chairs, would acquiesce in a German demand for submarine facilities at Dakar. The British and U.S. fleets were incapable of taking the West African base against probable French resistance; thus, "only the occupation of the Canary Islands and eventually the Cape Verde Islands could give assurance of adequate protection of the Atlantic trade routes." At Argentia this "whole nexus of questions" seemed so pressing that Churchill insisted on forcible occupation of these islands even before Germany advanced down the Peninsula.[22] To the Prime Minister's relief Roosevelt concurred.

Renunciation of the commitment to Portugal was not unexpected and Roosevelt accepted it with equanimity. He probably was relieved the British had taken themselves out of the picture. The Azores occupation would look better, he thought, if it were solely American. He informed the Prime Minister of the lengths to which United States planning had progressed. The ABC-1 discussions had envisaged a preventive occupation. Joint discussion had met postponement, but American planners had gone ahead at Roosevelt's order. Because of lack of troops and the amphibious character of the project the Navy bore chief responsibility.

Through the spring Ambassador Bert Fish sent reports on Portuguese military strength in the Azores and reinforcement of the garrisons.[23] American leaders did not trust Salazar's stated willingness to allow a preventive occupation. There was concern that an expeditionary force might appear off the islands and encounter battle-hardened German divisions. Failure would have been intolerable — to Roosevelt as well as to the United States Marines.

The proposal by a Marine staff committee to the Chief of Naval Operations was to prevent any repulse. It called for seizure first of San Miguel, Fayal, and Terceira and extension of control to remaining islands. This plan required a total of 29,060 men in the landing force; twenty squadrons of aircraft, carrier-embarked; and naval fire support by two battleships, eight heavy or light cruisers, and two squadrons of the new destroyers. No date was set for *Indigo 2;* the planners assumed it would be carried out shortly, and cut orders for the transports to rendezvous at New York.[24]

Churchill agreed upon his return to London to have his government inform Portugal of its inability to assist in defense of the Azores. To sweeten this draft Whitehall was to tell Salazar that the United Kingdom "therefore desired him to request the United States offer such assistance." Roosevelt said that "immediately" after he received such a request he would dispatch the necessary forces. He also would invoke the understanding with President Vargas for a token Brazilian contingent to join the expedition.[25]

American action of this kind ruled out "in the near future at least" assumption of responsibility for the Cape Verdes. Churchill promised breezily that Britain would take on the project, if guaranteed that America eventually would assume the role of protector as it had in Iceland. He attempted to ease fears of an open confrontation with Germany during *Operation Indigo* — saying that "during the time that the United States was landing . . . forces in the Azores, the British Navy would maintain a large force between the Azores and the mainland of Portugal . . . to render impossible the sending of any German expeditionary forces should Portugal at that time be already occupied by Germany." [26]

Roosevelt hence was willing, even eager, to work out plans in the Atlantic to meet a hypothetical emergency — a German thrust to the south and/or an appeal for protection by Portugal — while danger in the Far East evoked no such response. This fact did not escape the British. Once agreement had been reached regarding action in the Atlantic, Churchill said he wished next to discuss the Far East.[27]

He desired discussion to proceed on the draft memorandum presented to the President and Welles the previous day. There was to be no more pussyfooting. Roosevelt put off the moment of truth. He distributed copies of the two statements handed to Secretary Hull by the Japanese Ambassador on August 6, Japan's reply to the oil embargo and proposal for neutralization of Indochina.[28] The Prime Minister read them carefully and then remarked that "the implication was that Japan, having already occupied Indochina, said she would move no further provided the United States would abandon . . . economic and financial sanctions and take no further military or naval defensive measures and further agree to concessions to Japan, including the opportunity for Japan to strangle the Chinese government." He concluded that all these conditions were "particularly unacceptable." [29] This tangled, angry response was received in silence, an indication of its basic truth and also, perhaps, of the difficulty Roosevelt had in forming a suitable reply. He did answer tangentially. He was anxious there be no confusion about *British* intentions in the Pacific and wondered if it would be desirable "in his proposed statement to the Japanese Ambassador" to make reference to British policy.[30] This query must have baffled Churchill. For the first time F.D.R. had revealed he was bowing to British desires and would make a declaration on the Far Eastern situation; but in the same breath he mentioned problems with regard to Great Britain's position. The President, realizing his audience's puzzlement, explained: "He thought it would be advantageous for him to be in a position at that time to state that he had been informed by the British government that Great Britain had no aggressive intentions

whatever upon Thailand." Churchill "heartily" concurred, probably
hoping it would stimulate the President to move to the important
point — what was to comprise the American statement. Welles suggested that the President say that Great Britain "supported wholeheartedly" the neutralization of Indochina and Thailand. The Prime
Minister favored this course, believing it had an element of "face-
saving" for the Japanese and yet would constitute "a flat United States
warning to Japan" of the consequences of further aggression.[31]

At some time, one notes by these comments, the discussion turned
from the wisdom of a presidential warning to how to phrase the
declaration. A condemnation of Japanese aggression against the
Russian maritime provinces? Welles liked this idea and spoke for
firmness. The "real issue," he argued, was Japan's conquests "in the
entire Pacific region." One might suspect that he was attempting the
hoary diplomatic maneuver of weakening a policy declaration by expanding its application; but that would constitute too harsh a judgment. The countries under his version of the statement were China,
Russia, and British and Dutch dependencies — not Thailand or Indochina. Welles said the declaration would be more advanta-
geously based on broad policy rather than any opposition to Japanese movements.[32] He may have had in mind Roosevelt's earlier
decision to resist Japanese invasion of the Indies but not Thailand.
The President gave quick approval to the suggestion. He wrote in:
"There must not be further encroachment in the North," then sat
back satisfied.[33] Churchill enthusiastically accepted this modification.

After agreement on the need and scope of the presidential statement, the conferees dealt with its substance. F.D.R. conceded much
to the British view; but words not deeds comprised his attitude. "He
felt very strongly that every effort should be made to prevent the
outbreak of war with Japan." [34] How did the warning fit this campaign? Either Roosevelt believed appeasement the wisest course or
that a firm stand would prevent war with Japan. His statement did
not make clear which; of course, Churchill hoped the latter was the
basis for American action.

The President said he would inform the Secretary of State of his whereabouts and ask him to tell the Japanese Ambassador that F.D.R. was to return from an undisclosed location the next Saturday or Sunday (August 16 or 17) and desired to see him "immediately upon his return." [35] Next came the words for which Churchill had been waiting. In this interview with Nomura Roosevelt promised to satisfy the first of the proposed steps contained in the British draft. He intended to proffer another carrot as well. If Japan made specific rather than contingent the commitment (in the first paragraph of the August 6 message) that it "will not further station troops in the Southwestern Pacific area, except French Indochina, and the Japanese troops now stationed in French Indochina will be withdrawn," the United States would resume conversations and "explore the possibilities inherent in the various proposals made by Japan for the reaching of a friendly understanding." [36] Churchill contented himself with saying of the August 6 note: "These were smoothly worded offers by which Japan would take all she could for the present and give nothing for the future." [37] He said nothing about the offer to revive American-Japanese negotiations.

F.D.R. continued, describing his "mighty swat" at the Japanese warlords. Should Japan fail to disavow its aggressive plans and engage in more expansionist acts, "various steps would have to be taken by the United States notwithstanding the President's realization that the taking of such further measures might result in war between the United States and Japan." [38] A strong stand.

Still, the President linked the warning with a vista of long negotiations and the belief that hostilities would not occur during these talks. He was following his star — flexibility, the need of alternate courses. The statement suggested that Roosevelt was speaking on his own and not as a maker of policy; e.g. the phrase, "in his belief." Considering F.D.R.'s control of foreign affairs, this statement has little weight. Another reservation was the lack of reference to part two of the British proposal — that in event of a Japanese attack on any associated nation the President would "seek authority from Congress to give aid to such power." Roosevelt refused to discuss the

clauses. It was not in his power at present he confessed — a curious
reading of presidential responsibility. The promise to ask such authority was one small step from a declaration of war. His interpretation of public and congressional opinion and his own inclinations
forbade such a step.[39] A last qualification was abandonment by
Churchill of desire for a joint statement, which lay revealed in the
speech Saturday night and in the draft proposal. He accepted a uni-
lateral American warning as better than no warning.

This proclamation appeared to confirm the demise of President
Roosevelt's desire to "baby along" the Japanese, but the British then,
and some historians later, suspected that the President's promise
masked a continuing effort to mollycoddle, even appease Japan.
Roosevelt did say that "by adopting this course any further move of
aggression on the part of Japan which might result in war could be
held off for at least thirty days." Churchill welcomed the President's
obiter dictum.[40] The Prime Minister had a contradictory attitude,
desiring American commitment to the Empire's side in a fast approaching conflict with Japan but fearing its effects. Roosevelt was
not alone in indecision about Far Eastern policy. But the Prime
Minister considered a warning, whatever its results, essential.

Policy toward Japan had been determined. It remained for Welles
and Cadogan, after consultation with their superiors, to coordinate
the language. In a glow of confidence that this was now possible,
Churchill returned to *Prince of Wales* at 12:56 P.M.[41] The most important meeting of the entire conference had taken exactly two
hours.

Churchill delayed his departure briefly to take his personal bodyguard cum valet in to meet President Roosevelt. Mutual concern for
their masters' safety had brought together Thompson and Michael F.
Reilly, head of the Secret Service detachment. Discovering that
Thompson had not met the President, Reilly dragged him off to the
presidential suite. They arrived just as Churchill was taking his
leave. The Prime Minister claimed the right to introduce his bodyguard. After Churchill performed this duty and left, President
Roosevelt asked, "How is he standing up under it, Thompson? How

is he really?" He seemed reassured to hear that the Prime Minister had deep reserves of energy and was able to replenish his strength because of his habit of regular naps. Before dismissing Thompson, Roosevelt asked curiously: "Is he hard to handle?" "Yes, sir," admitted the ex-Scotland Yard officer. "He's reckless and self-willed. Restraint of any kind is unendurable." "Well, take care of him," President Roosevelt said. "He's about the greatest man in the world. In fact he may very likely be *the* greatest." [42] These words were carried back to *Prince of Wales* without delay.

2

Roosevelt and Churchill gave over Monday afternoon to routine and relaxation. The President busied himself with correspondence and executive instruments sent up from Washington for his signature. He diverged briefly from routine business to write a note to King George VI, replying to the message from the British monarch which Churchill had delivered Saturday morning. The King and F.D.R. had corresponded infrequently but in an informal, cordial tone since the royal visit to Washington and Hyde Park several years before. Roosevelt wrote that he had enjoyed "three delightful and useful days" with Prime Minister Churchill and the British Chiefs of Staff. "It has been a privilege to come to know Mr. Churchill in this way and I am very confident that our minds travel together, and that our talks are bearing practical fruit for both nations." After expressing a wish that the King could have witnessed Sunday's memorable church services on the deck of *Prince of Wales,* F.D.R. closed with the assertion: "We . . . wish we could be of more help — but we are daily gaining in confidence in the outcome." [43] The "we" in this peroration might have been royal or plural; interpreted in either sense Roosevelt was not making any large commitment.

In mid-afternoon the President received the Governor-General of Newfoundland, Sir Humphrey Walwyn, for a short interview. He then returned to his chores, which he had to complete quickly. The Navy plane which had brought Welles, Harriman, and the mail to Argentia was to fly back late Monday afternoon. When the stack of official papers was depleted, the President had himself wheeled into Harry Hopkins' cabin for a chat and probably a fatherly lecture about the dangers of overtaxing one's strength. Hopkins, the person to whom belonged most credit for arranging the conference, had become extremely ill soon after arrival at Argentia and was on the verge of total exhaustion but refused to accept the obvious prescription of complete rest. He had invested too much in this meeting of his two great friends to forego the pleasure of seeing them together and observing the growth of mutual respect and understanding between them; besides, some cloud of suspicion might threaten to stunt their friendship and he must be present in his role of sunshine maker. In spite of anxious protests from friends in both camps, Hopkins managed to attend the most important meetings and all of the dinners.[44] F.D.R. was shocked when he learned of this, but he could understand his friend's satisfaction at overcoming physical and psychological obstacles to finish the task.

In the privacy of his quarters Churchill was drafting cables to his Foreign Secretary and to his Lord Privy Seal, Clement Attlee. The note to Eden contained a full account of the morning's decisions with regard to Japan. He reviewed the President's neutralization proposal and said he would cable the text of the Japanese reply "as soon as more urgent messages have been dealt with." Roosevelt intended, Churchill wrote, to "thus procure a moratorium of, say, thirty days in which we may improve our position in Singapore area and the Japanese will have to stand still." He admitted that negotiations appeared hopeless but "President considers that a month gained will be valuable." [45] Churchill had tried to make F.D.R. understand that the Japanese would double-cross him. He had failed, and it was necessary to accept the U.S. decision to resume conversations.

Churchill sent along the preliminary text of the warning. "I think this is entirely good," he said, and recommended that Great Britain and the Netherlands government associate themselves with it. His reasoning is enlightening. Either Japan would refuse the conditions by the President "or alternatively they will go on with their military action while lying about it diplomatically." In any case the American commitment could come into play "with great force, and the full effect of parallel declarations could be realized." Churchill supported Welles' reluctance to inform the Chinese fully "what we are doing for them." He did urge that the Dominions be informed of the forthcoming statement "and made to see that it is a very great advance towards the gripping of Japanese aggression by united forces." [46] It would also, he hoped, relieve Australian pressure for a strong stand in the South Pacific. To Attlee the Prime Minister restated these conclusions. He claimed F.D.R. intended to use as a draft the declaration he had written. [47]

In the middle of Monday afternoon, Churchill launched another expedition to explore and climb the low bluffs overlooking Argentia harbor. "First a whaleboat was lowered and manned by British sailors, who rowed it about to the companionway. Then down the steps scuttled the P.M., clad in a one-piece jumper with short sleeves and trousers cut off above the knees." [48] One may surmise this was a tropical version of Churchill's siren suit. He jumped from the boat as soon as it nosed onto the beach and charged up a high bluff immediately beyond. "Once there he peeked over the brink and noticed a number of his party stretched comfortably out on the sand . . . Promptly Mr. C. gathered up a handful of rocks and amused himself by scattering his dismayed followers with a few well-aimed tosses. High jinks in high places," wrote Elliott Roosevelt, a witness to the invasion. Churchill even indulged in wading about in the surf off the gravelly beach. [49]

Several of *Prince of Wales'* officers, along with Paymaster Captain Ritchie and A. R. S. Nutting, commandeered a cutter for an afternoon of fishing. They groped their way back about 5:30, thoroughly soaked and without even one dogfish to show. Argentia's fish population was no better disposed toward its legal owners than toward President Roosevelt and American interlopers. An expedition to forage for additions to the battleship's larder (and for delicacies to take home) had no more success. Paymaster Commander Wheeler and H. V. Morton scouted the small town of Argentia. They were unable to purchase the provisions they found at the well-stocked "general store," because of U.S. Navy currency regulations. The two men settled for a meal of fried ham (heaped on slabs of homemade bread thickly spread with butter) at a café near the edge of the settlement. Their bite-by-bite description of this feast had to be repeated several times to envious colleagues taking their ease in the battleship's wardroom.[50]

There was no relaxation for Welles and Cadogan. Welles went to *Prince of Wales* in early afternoon without having talked to the President, and he and the British diplomat compared notes on the morning discussions. They talked about informing the Chinese of the action the United States "in the person of the President" planned to take. Welles manifested that patronizing, paternalistic attitude American leaders were to hold toward China through the war. While he believed "very definitely" that the Chinese government should know "of what was being done in her interest," he feared that if they learned immediately of the warning the Chungking regime would "for its own interests" make its knowledge public. If publicity resulted . . . the extreme militaristic element in Tokyo and that portion of the Tokyo press which was controlled by Germany would . . . inflame sentiment in Japan to such an extent as to make any possibility remote, as it might be anyhow, of achieving results through negotiation with Japan." Cadogan agreed, but did not look forward to stalling the Chinese Ambassador after return to London. He reminded Welles how "terribly persistent" the Chinese were and sighed that their leading representative in England, Ambassador Wellington Koo, "would undoubtedly press him day in and day out for the substance of discussions at Argentia relevant to China." Without going into detail Cadogan proposed to tell the Ambassador that the two governments had agreed "that every step should be taken that was practicable at this time for China."[51] He did not appear confident this would satisfy the persistent Mr. Koo.

❧

3

The third day of the meeting closed on a calm note. Monday evening Churchill once again graced the President's table, carrying out the developing pattern of smaller, more intimate meetings. He boarded *Augusta* alone at 7:00 P.M. to dine with Roosevelt, Hopkins, and the President's sons.[52] It had been thought that Beaverbrook, who had flown into Newfoundland earlier in the day and was expected before nightfall, would attend. However, news arrived that "the Beaver" was rained in at Gander Lake and could not reach Argentia before Tuesday morning.

The major diplomatic matters before the two leaders had been settled, apparently to their mutual satisfaction. This meal offered each an opportunity for sincerity and frankness, even for the ripening of friendship within well-defined limits. Hopkins was in his element, acting as a foil for errant darts. Not that there were many for him to deflect. From all accounts the evening was tranquil. Elliott asserts that "still on the Englishman's mind" was the desire for an American declaration of war "forthwith." [53] He admits Churchill did not press the matter.

Perhaps the timing of Roosevelt's announcement of stronger U.S. naval measures — in essence, convoying — met with discussion. The President's advisers had been pressing for full and frank public revelation. At Argentia he said he did not think announcement of the full implications of this policy was wise. The speech should wait until American "patrol" activities were in effect and the U.S. Navy had assumed protection of *all* merchant shipping.[54] He promised to speak out sometime in September.

Elliott Roosevelt does claim that one flash of summer lightning flared in the President's cabin. Late in the evening the topic of imperialism heated the atmosphere. An anxiously pacing, gesturing Churchill supposedly halted before F.D.R., waved a "stubby forefinger" beneath Roosevelt's patrician nose and exclaimed: "Mr. President, I believe you are trying to do away with the British Empire. Every idea you entertain about the structure of the post-war world

demonstrates it." [55] Churchill's outburst was caused by the complicated and at times acrimonious discussions over the joint declaration
of war and peace aims which had been going on since Saturday afternoon. Roosevelt's response to the accusation, if he made one, is
lost. Certainly the conflict was unresolved when the dinner party
concluded at 11:30 P.M.

Bow view of H.M.S. *Prince of Wales* taken a month after the *Bismarck* engagement

U.S.S. *Augusta*, the heavy cruiser which served as President Roosevelt's flagship at the Atlantic Conference

U.S.S. *Tuscaloosa*, the sister ship of *Augusta* which transported F.D.R.'s military advisers to the meeting

The Prime Minister, members of his staff, and Harry Hopkins

e deck of *Prince of Wales* during the voyage to Argentia

Admiral Sir Dudley Pound, General Sir John Dill, the Prime Minister, and Air Vice-Marshal Wilfred Freeman meet in *Prince of Wales'* wardroom to concert strategy

Prime Minister Churchill presents King George VI's letter to the
President

BUCKINGHAM PALACE

3rd August, 1941.

My dear President Roosevelt,

This is just a line to bring you my best
wishes, and to say how glad I am that you have an
opportunity at last of getting to know my Prime
Minister. I am sure you will agree that he is a
very remarkable man, and I have no doubt that your
meeting will prove of great benefit to our two
countries in the pursuit of our common goal.

Believe me

Yours very sincerely

George R.I.

The President
of the United States of America.

King George VI's note introducing his Prime Minister to F.D.R., a
fellow head of state

United States and British military and naval leaders. From left: Air Vice-Marshal Freeman, General Arnold, Admiral Stark, Admiral Pound, Admiral King, General Marshall, General Dill, and Rear Admiral Turner

President Roosevelt crosses the gangway from U.S

cDougal to *Prince of Wales* for divine services

Churchill welcomes the President as the latter comes on board *Prince of Wales* Sunday morning

Divine services on *Prince of Wales*. This photograph was taken from the forward turret

British and American voices join with those of the President and the
Prime Minister during divine services

F.D.R. and Churchill in a pensive moment after the end of the church
service

WHITE TWENTY THREE X IN THREE PARTS X PART
ONE X FOR STEVE EARLY X

I am sending important statement to be given out by White House without comment on Thursday at 0900 A.M., E.S.T. You may inform Press and Radio in confidence late Wednesday night to stand by for a release the next morning —

Please on receipt of the statement take it to Secretary of State in great confidence and read it to him for his information —

There is no further news of any kind — All well

Roosevelt X

FROM: AUGUSTA
TO: OPNAV WASHINGTON

President Roosevelt's instructions to White House Press Secretary Steve Early regarding arrangements for announcement of the conference

- 5 -

or air armaments continue to be employed by nations

which threaten, or may threaten, aggression outside

of their frontiers, they believe, pending the establish-

ment of a wider and more permanent system of general

security, that the disarmament of such nations is

essential. They will likewise aid and encourage all

other practicable measures which will lighten for

peace-loving peoples the crushing burden of armaments.

Franklin D Roosevelt
Winston S. Churchill

End quote,

Roosevelt

END PART THREE AND END
WHITE TWENTY THREE

The final page of the Atlantic Charter. This typewritten draft, prepared for radio transmission and signed by the President for himself and Churchill, is the only written version of the Charter in existence

The President and the Prime Minister say goodbye on board *Augusta* Tuesday afternoon

Churchill turns for a final salute as he leaves *Augusta* at the end of the conference

The Prime Minister gazes back at
Augusta as *Prince of Wales* begins
the voyage home

The U.S.S. *Potomac*, with F.D.R. on board, off Deer Island, Maine, following the conference

President Roosevelt leaves Union Station, Washington, D.C., with Secretary of State Cordell Hull, August 17, 1941

Prime Minister Churchill is met by Lady Churchill upon his return to London

IX. *The Atlantic Charter*

THAT THE ATLANTIC CHARTER proved the longest-lived result of their meeting at Argentia amazed Roosevelt and Churchill. Its chief rationale was propaganda; yet the joint declaration on war and peace aims turned up like a copper penny throughout the war — alternately embarrassing and pleasing its designers.

Planning for some such statement had been going on for a long time in England and especially in the United States. Statements about war aims and the structures of peace were congenial to Roosevelt and his advisers on foreign policy — as such pronouncements have been to most Americans over the years. On many matters F.D.R. bypassed his Department of State; in regard to postwar planning he gave the inhabitants of "foggy bottom" great if not sole responsibility, and he listened to their recommendations.

Long before America became involved in the war Roosevelt felt that "if any good could come out of the Second World War, it would be the opportunity afforded the Americans and the British to bring order out of the resulting chaos and, in particular, to disarm all those powers who in his belief had been the primary cause of so many of the wars of the preceding century."[1] These words, put in his mouth by Sumner Welles, do not have the compelling ring of Wilson's "make the world safe for democracy"; but the purpose was the same.

Roosevelt's views on international affairs might justifiably be termed unsophisticated; and on some problems he had no views at all. However, he held to his opinions with tenacity. He was not and did not claim to be an original thinker, but he possessed in abundance the gift of using men and ideas to his own advantage and of giving clear expression to the vague ideas of others.

The President's views on foreign affairs early conformed to the "family tradition." From Theodore Roosevelt, he inherited faith in a strong navy. As one disgruntled editor had written in 1913, after F.D.R. delivered a bellicose speech on naval expansion: "After reading his manifesto about a powerful navy, one finds no difficulty in recognizing the kinship of Franklin D. Roosevelt . . . to the commander at Armageddon." [2] Both men, furthermore, believed that the United States must take a large part in world affairs.

Attachment to "internationalism" was one of Roosevelt's convictions, but there was confusion as to the best means of achieving the goal. According to Louis Wehle, the President believed that "war must still be the touchstone of policy in foreign affairs. At thirty Roosevelt was a worshiping Wilsonian. Into middle age he espoused a world order under a union of nations; but unlike Wilson, the evangelist, while pursuing peace, he never neglected military preparedness." [3] There was to be much Wilsonian idealism in the Atlantic Charter, as there was much of Wilson in the moral outlook of Roosevelt; but he came to advocate what he believed were "realistic" methods of achieving world order. Such reasoning was the basis for his scoffing in 1928 at the Kellogg-Briand Pact, and for his attempt in the 1930's to substitute national power for platitudes. One finds it ironic that this point of view culminated in the Atlantic Charter.

Oddly existing with this "realistic approach" were principles from his Wilsonian heritage. F.D.R. said to Adolf A. Berle, Jr. in June, 1941: "Don't forget that the elimination of costly armaments is still the keystone — for the security of all the little nations and for economic solvency. Don't forget what I discovered — that over ninety percent of all national deficits from 1921 to 1939 were caused by payments for past, present, and future wars;" [4] and in 1942 he told Mackenzie King that the "main emphasis" in the peace settlement should be on "the complete disarmament of Germany, the constant and thorough inspection of their industry, coupled with an international police force, particularly an aviation bombardment force." [5] Indeed, forcible disarmament of all nations must be contemplated.

Sumner Welles, not one to criticize the President, had to admit F.D.R.'s attitude toward small powers was "unduly impatient."

He maintained stubbornly that they should be satisfied if the English-speaking powers were able to assure them security from aggression, and in return should be willing to spend their national revenues upon education and upon raising living standards rather than upon armaments for which they would have no further need. He brushed aside all references to national pride, or to the age-old international hatreds of Eastern Europe. He dismissed as of little account the argument that no responsible government of a small country could be compelled to liquidate the military establishment upon which it believed the safety of the nation depended, unless the self-appointed policemen were prepared to occupy that country by force. He occasionally spoke of his project for an Anglo-American policing of the world as being "realistic." He could enumerate in considerable detail the various advantages that the peoples of the smaller countries would derive from such a policy of realism.[6]

Although for domestic economic reasons, early in his first administration, he had "torpedoed" the London Economic Conference, Roosevelt soon demonstrated his attachment to liberal trade policy. He succeeded in having enacted into law the reciprocal trade ideas of his Secretary of State, Cordell Hull. From that time he was an advocate — in theory, and sometimes in practice — of free, equal trade for all nations, but his advocacy varied with circumstances.

Then perhaps the most important of Roosevelt's principles as the United States moved closer to war was another Wilsonian ideal — conveyed by the jaw-breaking phrase "no predetermination."[7] The President was joined by other top-ranking American leaders in the desire that there be no "advance agreements" regarding frontiers or related questions. Belief that territorial agreements and "other political bargains" should await a universal peace conference merged nicely with F.D.R.'s desire to preserve flexibility in foreign affairs; it was, however, "a part of the entire fabric of wartime diplomacy," as Raymond Dawson correctly points out.[8]

The President did not suffer from lack of advice about the proper course for the United States. Naturally, suggestions increased in volume and in urgency as American involvement became a stronger possibility. For example, on October 29, 1940, the famous English novelist, H. G. Wells, proffered a statement of war aims. Disturbed about his government's failure to offer more than "vague and uncon-vincing promises," he turned to Roosevelt. "There is something bet-ter to be done for which there exists a number of precedents . . . from *Magna Carta* onward and that is to make a clear restatement in modern terms in view of modern conditions of the natural *Rights of Man*." [9] Hadley Cantril, a member of the Princeton Institute of Public Opinion Research, had been providing the White House with résumés of the Institute's surveys. On March 20, 1941, he wrote: "When listening to the President's speech the other night I was then, as I have been so frequently, somewhat disappointed that he did not spell out . . . the personal effects of a Nazi victory or the whole Nazi ideology. Wouldn't it be sensible if sometime he could elabo-rate with profuse illustrations what he means by the four freedoms? . . . I am convinced that the great majority of people in this coun-try have no idea how their own self-interest would be involved in any radical departure from the democratic way of life." [10]

Recommendations circulated within the administration. When told by Grenville Clark that "it is pretty hard to get the average American willing to go into the war until he sees what the next step is after the war," Secretary of War Stimson agreed, but complained about the real trouble — that no one had time to think about these matters.[11]

An elaborate commentary on postwar policy issued from a meet-ing of high administration officials in early May, 1941. The memo-randum recording the gist of this discussion not only rationalizes the role of the United States in the postwar world but also calls for a conference between the President and Prime Minister Churchill. The views therein, if not formally those of Roosevelt, represent the thinking of the inner circle.[12]

Certainly the introductory sentence of the memorandum con-formed to F.D.R.'s view of the postwar situation: "The years ahead are divisible into three periods, the period of war, the period of post-war transition, the period of the new world order." Only the last two were discussed by the group. As a first principle they agreed that the United States "should and would take much more responsibility in the coming peace than in the peace which is now past." Later conversation showed they assumed America would claim a dominant position after the war. The group scrutinized the interwar period "with a view to past error and future promise." One speaker argued that a return to the Versailles Treaty, by men who had learned from its tragic mistakes, might result in a satisfactory peace settlement. Although there was disagreement about his contention, all accepted the necessity of Anglo-American domination. It was suggested that many of the League's failures "could be traced to the failure of the Tripartite Treaty to come into effect; because of the absence of this instrument of order during the transition period, France began a lone search for security which distorted the future of the League." To avoid any such development after the current war close cooperation between the United States and the United Kingdom was essential.

Someone observed that the "avoidance of quarrrels" — an obvious reference to the difficulties over trade policy — was crucial. It was true that England's postwar financial position would push her toward currency controls and even more exclusive trading systems, and that "the story of British attitudes on raw materials in the 1920's and particularly in the 1930's . . . warns us of present dangers." America presently held a strong hand, "but it is important to come to agreements while Great Britain is willing to deal." The situation demanded "an immediate opening of conversations leading to the establishment of common institutions." One speaker noted that the democracies were given an opportunity to "grow" a League of Nations rather than to "make" one. A suggested agenda for such discussion included plans for immediate and joint action, and for postwar cooperation throughout the world. The issue of access to raw materials also belonged on the agenda. These questions could not be postponed much longer; and in fact some participants indicated impatience with the current rate at which the "fusion" of American and British interests was taking place. Some believed that immediate union was needed, and that it should be "open-ended" for adherence by nations presently under the Nazi yoke. At least, provision for the merger of America and England was essential.[13]

The group called for a "statement of our alternative to Hitler's new order, a definition of the New Order of the Ages proclaimed on the Great Seal of the United States," which would answer these questions and generate the "dynamic" for the task ahead. One speaker suggested a revision of Wilson's Fourteen Points, a "formulation" which could serve as both peace aim and war instrument. Such a double-barreled statement, he believed, "would have real propaganda value for bringing peace." For the President's benefit the secretary of the meeting wrote, "The need for a vigorous lead was repeated over and over . . . Without outspoken leadership, we are in the position of fighting something with nothing." [14] Obviously, the propaganda effect of a statement of war aims, and the steps presumably to follow, had highest priority.

Proposals of this kind in part duplicated activities already being carried on within high-ceilinged offices in the antiquated State-War-Navy Building next to the White House. Study of postwar problems in the Department of State had begun in December, 1939, with a committee "on problems of peace and reconstruction." Sumner Welles was largely responsible, although the Secretary approved. The committee acquired the title of Advisory Committee on Problems of Foreign Relations. Welles assumed the chairmanship. There were three subcommittees to consider respectively, political problems (including organization of peace), limitation and reduction of armaments, and economic questions. They met without agenda, minutes, or preparatory studies; and they functioned in this form for less than a year. [15]

The group dealing with economic problems continued its studies longer than the other two. Secretary Hull offered enthusiastic support and gave elaborate suggestions. Problems of international trade were, he devoutly believed, the source of all other international difficulties. Breckinridge Long said of the Secretary's obsession with economic policy: "Of course *that* is Hull. That is his . . . *raison d'être* . . . His trade agreements . . . are the base on which rest his whole foreign activity. Without that base the structure falls." [16] He spelled out his ideas on economic policy in a radio address in May, 1941. "The main principles," he asserted, "are few and simple": 1., extreme nationalism "must not again be permitted to express itself in excessive trade restrictions"; 2., "non-discrimination in international commercial relations must be the rule"; 3., raw materials must be available to all nations; 4., international finance must "lend aid to the essential enterprises and the continuous development of all countries." [17]

Hull's principles seemed an amplification of the goals of the President. Roosevelt's Annual Message of January, 1941, had expressed his definition — for the first time — of the foundation for a secure future, the so-called Four Freedoms (freedom of speech, expression, and worship; freedom from want and from fear). Roosevelt said these aims were "no vision of a distant millenium," but the basis "for a kind of world attainable in our time and generation." [18] He knew such vague words would not move the American people. He must find a way to bring the words into focus, to stamp them in American hearts and identify them with the policy of assisting Great Britain.

Circumstances ensured that some kind of statement on war aims would arise at Argentia. That it would take the form of the Atlantic Charter was not at all certain. As noted, Roosevelt passionately desired to postpone territorial and general political questions until a peace conference. The Department of State had campaigned to commit the United Kingdom to a liberal postwar economic policy: Hull and his helpers wanted the British to abolish "imperial preference." American planners adopted the notion that security was indivisible, and they opted for a general international organization over tight regional groupings. Their attitude on economic policy reflected these beliefs. "In this the post-war planners simply picked up the story at the point of the U.S.-U.K. 1938 trade agreement," one historian has written. "And the State Department's *Postwar Foreign Policy Planning* quite correctly . . . pointed out that economic planning was much further advanced than political planning." [19] Pressure for economic liberalization was applied prior to the meeting at Argentia, and it continued long afterward.

There had been several efforts to force Britain to an agreement.[20]

Then some bright officer in the Department had proposed that the United States link postwar abolition of closed economic systems with the negotiation concerning Lend-Lease agreements. The Department followed this suggestion with notable sprightliness.

Exhausting discussions within the Department of State produced in late May a draft Lend-Lease Agreement which embodied this purpose. The crucial part of the proposed agreement was Article VII: The United Kingdom undertakes "to give its full support to the liberal international trade policies which the trade agreements program of the United States seeks to promote." It will cooperate in improving trade and financial relations with the United States and with third nations, especially in instances where difficulties exist "by reason of clearing, compensation, payment or similar agreements or arrangements entered into by the United Kingdom." [21]

Churchill learned of this plot when John Maynard Keynes came to the United States in May. William L. Langer and S. Everett Gleason have the discovery reversed, for they claim: "It is unlikely that the mere resurrection of economic issues which had been debated *ad nauseam* for many years would have resulted in anything more than the continued expression of high hopes and pious intentions, had it not been for the fact that Lord Keynes . . . shocked the State Department by his expressions of opinion that the postwar economic structure could only be one of closed economies." [22] But it is clear that State had been planning before his arrival. If Keynes' ideas "shocked" Hull, Welles, and the economic subcommittee, he was even more perturbed by the proposal the Americans presented to him.

The British economist had sent ahead a statement of Allied war aims "designed primarily to counter German propaganda." [23] This memorandum was highly disturbing to the free traders in Washington. Keynes stressed national measures such as broad social welfare programs. On arrival he lunched with F.D.R., but "could not get beyond the President's affable but non-committal front." [24] He found Department officials uncomfortably frank, insisting that Article VII of the proposed Lend-Lease Agreement was a *sine qua non*.

Keynes could not give in, both because of the attitude of his government and his own inflexible views. This meant that no instrument on Lend-Lease was signed. The Department of State displayed unusual firmness. Hull "punctuated" the expression of American determination by threatening to make liberal trade agreements with the Dominions.[25]

1

The early summer of 1941 was a trying period for the Churchill government. While the British suffered Nazi attacks, their "friends" bombarded them with memoranda. Churchill steadfastly refused to pronounce on postwar questions, which might divide British opinion.[26] Mackenzie King admitted that his fellow Prime Minister "was so concentrated on the war that he could not see that settling certain broad problems of the peace now would in effect help the actual war effort." [27]

British political parties, of course, had placed on the record general statements about war aims. As early as March, 1940, before Churchill took office, the government had established a committee to study problems in connection with peace, proposing an exchange of ideas with American planners; but Hull squelched the suggestion.[28]

Churchill in January, 1941, was pressed in the House of Commons for clarification of principles for which Great Britain was fighting. The Prime Minister irritably responded: "As I have said, when a good opportunity presents itself, I or other Ministers will certainly be on the look-out to turn that opportunity to the best advantage." [29]

Soon after, the Schuster Committee, reorganized under Clement Attlee, sent to the Department of State, and thence to Roosevelt, a short memo which may be called a semiofficial statement of the Churchill government's war aims. The document called for a New Deal for the English people and all nations. It recommended: 1., "positive lines of action" for outlawry of war; 2., maintenance of security; 3., greater economic equality; 4., production for human welfare; and, 5., social justice. With regard to the third point, it proposed that the United Kingdom offer "international solutions" to colonial problems and access to raw materials, "lowering of trade barriers which are essential if greater economic equality between nations is to be brought about." There was strong emphasis on measures primarily national. Bruce concluded: "If Britain declares her revolutionary intentions in no uncertain voice, her determination will be followed in the Dominions, and we shall have provided the closest bond of cooperation with President Roosevelt, namely an identity of ideas." [30]

The Prime Minister did come to recognize the need for some public statement, and an address at Mansion House, May 29, 1941, by Foreign Secretary Anthony Eden, was intended to pacify the critics. Eden's speech was a repetition of Keynesian views and his description of the postwar economic scene disturbed the State Department. Continental Europe he saw as emerging from the war "starving and bankrupt." Liberated countries and "maybe" others would require resources, and Eden suggested that the United Kingdom contribute.[31] Otherwise, the speech was vague. It endorsed Hull's point about creating international financial institutions; but as Leo Pasvolsky, Special Assistant and Chief, Division of Special Research, commented to the Secretary: "It is too bad that Mr. Eden does not similarly endorse the other four points of your program, especially points 1 and 2, relating to excessive trade barriers and non-discriminatory treatment." Hull's adviser preferred the ideas of the British Labour Party, which viewed the world as a single economic unit, over Eden's "rather cryptic phrases" about social security.[32]

For better or worse, American leaders thought Eden's speech "one of the authoritative indications of British war aims." [33] Until the Atlantic Conference, Churchill's regime took no further action although more statements were issued. The Roosevelt administration knew only that Churchill held sharply different views from their own on aspects of the postwar world. As Pasvolsky lamented in June, the "vagueness" of Churchill's statements and of other British pronouncements "argue strongly for joint exploration of postwar problems by representatives of the two governments and for vigorous effort to work out a more or less precise post-war program." [34] He was not alone in requesting some joint negotiation. Other voices, for a variety of reasons, were calling for a meeting, preferably at the highest level, of American and British leaders.

2

In spite of all that had been done, creation of the Atlantic Charter proved as complicated as the earlier debate about war aims. From whence came the decision to link the Roosevelt-Churchill meeting with a statement of ideals is not entirely clear. The joint declaration certainly was of American inspiration. Churchill has written that he hardly had set foot on *Augusta's* deck when the President brought up the notion of a declaration "laying down certain broad principles which should guide our policies along the same road." [35] As has been shown, F.D.R. had some such purpose in mind for several months, and expressed his desire for a statement at the luncheon of Saturday. Churchill gracefully acceded. The two leaders and their principal assistants, Welles and Cadogan, carried forward the project.

Preliminary work occurred in meetings between the two Under Secretaries. Churchill and Cadogan had not much time to consult about the President's suggestion before this first meeting. Cadogan was conversant with his superior's views. At the meeting Saturday afternoon Welles revealed he was privy to Roosevelt's position.

Welles had to raise an awkward question as a preliminary. He reminded Cadogan of the President's July 15 message to Churchill "expressing the opinion that the British Government should make no secret commitments to any of its Allies without knowledge . . . or without the agreement of the United States." There "as yet" had been no reply.[36]

Rumors about secret commitments by the United Kingdom to restore prewar frontiers to various of the occupied nations had been filtering back to Washington for many months. The Roosevelt administration had discreetly stated its opposition to such arrangements but there was no indication the warnings were being heeded. An attempt to link the agreements on strategy in the ABC-1 Report

with a commitment "that the United States and United Kingdom
furnish each other . . . full texts and particulars of any treaties, secret or otherwise . . . which may affect . . . the peace terms to be
agreed upon after the cessation of hostilities" was flatly rejected by
the British.[37] The issue might have continued as merely another
nagging hindrance to full cooperation had not the Soviet Union
pressed its diplomatic offensive for political concessions. Before the
outbreak of the Russo-German war the United States and Great Britain stood together in refusing to recognize Russia's rape of the Baltic
States and Poland. Even before June 23, however, Washington
feared that British economic aid to the Soviets was to be followed by
political sacrifices.[38] Lord Halifax had shown there were grounds
for concern when, in conversation with Acting Secretary Welles on
June 15, he confessed he was "rather cynical with regard to the Baltic States." Welles was appalled and pointed out there was not one
distinction morally between Russia's actions and Hitler's brutal conquests.[39] He and Roosevelt feared that Churchill's government
might decide it could not afford moral niceties.

The negotiations for an Anglo-Russian agreement on military cooperation and the efforts during July, under British sponsorship, to
arrange a treaty between Moscow and the Polish government-in-
exile offered a reason for Roosevelt's July 15 telegram opposing secret agreements. On July 21 Winant and Hopkins followed up the
message by visiting Eden at the Foreign Office and emphasizing the
President's stand. Eden assured the Americans that he was as eager
"as anybody" to keep his hands free of awkward commitments.[40] As
a statement of British intentions, it was open to several interpretations. All indications pointed to British rejection of Soviet demands;
but since this information was also phrased ambiguously Washington continued to worry.[41]

Cadogan said the question of secret treaties was one of the "main
matters" Churchill desired to discuss with President Roosevelt. He
had with him the texts of all agreements into which Britain had entered, and would be "very glad" to go over them. Cadogan gave the
"most specific and positive assurance" that his government had made

no commitments on frontiers or territorial readjustment — with one exception, an "oral statement" to Yugoslavia before the coup d'état. The British Minister at Belgrade had stated "that at the conclusion of the war the subject of the jurisdiction over Istria was a matter which might well come up for reconsideration." There had been no mention either of Goritza or Trieste. In their alliances with Poland and Czechoslovakia the British had made no decision as to boundaries. Great Britain, in the cases of Norway, the Netherlands, and Belgium, had committed itself only to their "reestablishment" as nations. The French alliance, whatever its present status, was similiar.[42]

These confidences "much heartened" Welles. He was not personally sympathetic to the Rooseveltian doctrine of "no predetermination" but, he did oppose political concessions at that time. He gave Cadogan a convincing explanation of the source of the policy. Cadogan would remember, he said, the damage during the First World War "by the sudden revelation of the series of agreements which Great Britain had previously entered into." Rumors that Churchill's regime had made similar secret agreements had created "disquiet and suspicion." Cadogan asserted that Churchill "had it very much in mind" and the two diplomats agreed to consider a statement "at an appropriate moment" on postwar commitments. The matter remained unsettled several weeks after the conference, and in September the Roosevelt administration was still demanding a British disavowal of secret treaties.[43]

The other source of the joint declaration — a satisfactory formula for postwar economic arrangements — formed the final topic of this Saturday conversation. Cadogan said he had received the text of the proposed Lend-Lease Agreement the day before he left London but asked for a copy to refresh his memory. This Welles gave him and also copies of Acheson's memorandum of conversations with Keynes, and Keynes' letter to Acheson the following day.[44]

After allowing Cadogan time to read these documents the Under Secretary said there was no need "to undertake a dissertation upon fundamental economics." Describing the conversations, he stated: "I felt sure from my conversations with Sir Alexander during the past few years that he and I saw eye to eye with regard to the freest possible economic interchange without discriminations, without exchange controls, without economic preference utilized for political purpose, and without all of the manifold economic barriers which had in my judgment been so clearly responsible for the present world collapse." Welles was disturbed that Keynes represented "some segment of British public opinion" which desired after the war to resume "exactly that kind of system which had proved so fatal during the past generation." A healthy world demanded not policies already proven disastrous but identity of purpose and a spirit of self-sacrifice. Welles believed the Lend-Lease Agreement provided such assurances. One of the factors "poisoning" British-American relations in the interwar period had been the British debt, and he assured Cadogan that the formula, as drafted, would prevent any recurrence of that issue. Welles avoided direct reference to Article VII, which called for abolition of all discriminatory trade arrangements.[45]

This lecture placed Cadogan in an awkward position. He said that he could offer only his own opinion with regard to the economic issue. "He himself found the formula exactly what was required." He wished Welles to know — off the record — that he had "bitterly opposed" the Ottawa Agreements and that, in his opinion, they had nearly proved fatal. "He saw no hope for the future unless our two countries agreed, no matter what the obstacles might later prove, to press for the resumption of liberal trade practices and for the abolition of discriminations at the earliest possible moment." The Prime Minister would speak with President Roosevelt about this subject, and Cadogan claimed not to know what Churchill's "considered judgment" might be.[46]

Each man immediately reported this conversation to his chief. One might construct imaginary but logical descriptions of these interviews. Roosevelt would have been delighted and relieved that the British accepted his proposal — even though there would be difficulties. The Prime Minister was less enthusiastic but willing to go along. If his campaign for American entry into the war failed, a pledge of Anglo-American solidarity (into which he could read various meanings) would help.

Both sides now gave attention to the declaration. Churchill may have received warning of the President's intent. Welles, however, in the few hours before leaving Washington, had drafted a statement drawn from his conversations with Roosevelt and Department studies. His draft — which has never come to light — focused probably on the political aims of F.D.R. and on liberal economic policies.[47]

This result of his frantic effort was not used at Argentia, probably because of another of Roosevelt's stratagems. The President feared an American proposal would challenge the British Empire, that it would attack colonialism and trade discrimination. Convinced that discussion on this basis would founder, F.D.R. arranged that the British furnish the working draft. He evidently instructed Hopkins to notify the Prime Minister.[48] The President then rested in knowledge that Churchill would come through with an inspiring if vague manifesto. It would be possible to insert American principles in this proposal.

It was ever British policy to make draft proposals, so Churchill went along. After listing some of the ideas the President could expect in the document on Saturday night, he retired to his cabin and put a draft declaration — which he may already have prepared — into polished form. Churchill has written of this effort: "Considering all the tales of my reactionary, Old-World outlook, and the pain this is said to have caused the President, I am glad it should be on record that the substance and spirit of what came to be called the 'Atlantic Charter' was in its first draft a British production cast in my own words." [49] This "production," given to the Americans Sunday morning, read as follows:

> The President of the United States of America and the Prime Minister, Mr. Churchill, representing His Majesty's Government in the United Kingdom, being met together to resolve and concert the means of providing for the safety of their respective countries in face of Nazi and German aggression and of the dangers to all peoples arising therefrom, deem it right to make known certain principles which they both

accept for guidance in the framing of their policy and on which they base their hopes for a better future for the world.

First, their countries seek no aggrandizement, political or other;

Second, they desire to see no territorial changes that do not accord with the freely expressed wishes of the peoples concerned;

Third, they respect the right of all peoples to choose the form of government under which they will live; they are only concerned to defend the rights of freedom of speech and of thought without which such choosing must be illusory;

Fourth, they will strive to bring about a fair and equitable distribution of essential produce not only within their territorial jurisdiction but between the nations of the world.

Fifth, they seek a peace which will not only cast down forever the Nazi tyranny but by effective international organization will afford to all States and peoples the means of dwelling in security within their own bounds and of traversing the seas and oceans without fear of lawless assault or need of getting burdensome armaments.[50]

Cadogan gave one copy to Welles after church services. Churchill presented a copy to Roosevelt when he proffered the suggested warning to Japan. Notably, Churchill's conversation with Welles, as the latter was leaving *Prince of Wales,* entirely concerned the Far Eastern situation.[51]

The President went over Churchill's creation with his assistant late Sunday afternoon. Neither was happy with the British draft, but it did form a basis for discussion. The first three points, if not clear, answered Roosevelt's desire of no secret territorial or political agreements. Point four, which contained a meaningless promise "to bring about a fair and equitable distribution of essential produce . . . between the nations of the world," brought a cry of outrage from Welles. Roosevelt's reaction is not recorded. He was disturbed by the last clause, since he did not believe — at that time — in international organization. Also, F.D.R. had no wish to throw such a bone to the isolationists at home. He told Welles to redraft the declaration.[52]

Welles' anxiety about British policy was confirmed Sunday night, at the informal dinner of Roosevelt, Churchill, and their personal staffs. He was not invited, but reports of the Prime Minister's statements must have set him working into the night on a redraft. According to Elliott Roosevelt, F.D.R. provoked Churchill into a full defense of the British Empire. This dialogue, even if untrustworthy, deserves full quotation.

"Father started it," his son wrote. "Of course," he remarked with a sly sort if assurance, "of course, after the war, one of the preconditions of any lasting peace will have to be the greatest possible freedom of trade." He paused. The P.M.'s head was lowered; he was watching Father steadily, from under one eyebrow. "No artificial barriers," Father pursued. "As few favored economic agreements as possible . . . Markets open for healthy competition . . ."

Churchill shifted in his armchair. "The British Empire trade agreements," he began heavily, "are —." Father broke in. "Yes. Those Empire trade agreements are a case in point. It's because of them that the people of India and Africa, of all the colonial Near East and Far East, are still as backward as they are."

Churchill's neck reddened and he crouched forward. "Mr. President, England does not propose for a moment to lose its favored position among the British Dominions. The trade that has made England great shall continue, and under conditions prescribed by England's ministers."

"You see," said Father slowly, "it is along in here somewhere that there is likely to be some disagreement between you, Winston, and me. I am firmly of the belief that if we are to arrive at a stable peace it must involve the development of backward peoples. . . . How can this be done? It can't be done, obviously, by eighteenth century methods . . ." The P.M. . . . was beginning to look apoplectic. "You mentioned India," he growled. "Yes. I can't believe that we can fight a war against fascist slavery, and at the same time not work to free people all over the world from a backward colonial policy" . . . "There can be no tampering with the Empire's economic agreements." "They're artificial . . ." "They're the foundation of our greatness."

"The peace," said Father firmly, "cannot include any continued despotism. The structure of the peace demands and will get equality

of peoples. Equality of peoples involves the utmost freedom of competitive trade. Will anyone suggest that Germany's attempt to dominate trade in central Europe was not a major contributing fact to
war?" [53]

Elliott brought the exchange to a close on this note. Churchill may
have made some such statement. Elsewhere, he accused the President of wanting to destroy the Empire.[54] One doubts, however, if
F.D.R. would have waved such a large red flag before the Prime
Minister. As already stated, he believed the things Elliott has him
say on this occasion; but rarely did he allow them to influence his
negotiations.

Welles was not entirely convinced of the President's loyalty to
anticolonialism and freedom of trade. The alternative draft which he
gave Roosevelt Monday morning was a way of committing the President as well as Churchill. It read,

> The President of the United States of America and the Prime Min-
> ister, Mr. Churchill, representing his Majesty's Government in the
> United Kingdom, being met together to consider and to resolve the
> steps which their Governments should take in order to provide for the
> safety of the respective countries in face of the policies of the world-
> wide domination and of military conquest upon which the Hitlerite
> Government of Germany and the other dictatorships associated there-
> with have embarked, deem it right and proper to make known certain
> principles which they both accept for guidance in the framing of their
> respective policies and on which they base their hopes for a better
> future for the world.
>
> First, their countries seek no aggrandizement, territorial or other;
>
> Second, they desire to see no territorial changes that do not accord
> with the freely expressed wishes of the peoples concerned;
>
> Third, they respect the right of all peoples to choose the form of
> government under which they will live;
>
> Fourth, they will strive to promote mutually advantageous economic
> relations between them through the elimination of any discrimination
> in either the United States of America or in the United Kingdom
> against the importation of any product originating in the other coun-

try; and they will endeavor to further the enjoyment by all peoples of access on equal terms to the markets and to the raw materials which are needed for their economic prosperity;

Fifth, they hope to see established a peace, after the final destruction of Nazi tyranny, which by effective international organization, will afford to all states and peoples the means of dwelling in security within their own boundaries, and the means of assurance that human beings may live out their lives in freedom from fear. They likewise hope to see established by such a peace safety for all peoples on the high seas and oceans, and the adoption of such measures as will prevent the continuation of expenditures for armaments other than those which are purely defensive.[55]

Comparison with the British draft reveals several revisions. The preamble was largely unchanged. Welles removed phrases looking to joint action: Churchill's phrase "concert and resolve" became "consider and resolve"; "the framing of their policy" became in Welles' version "the framing of their respective policies." He retained reference to "policies of world-wide domination and of military conquest," but Churchill's censure of the German people, as well as the Nazi regime, went out.

He believed the first three articles of the British draft "essential in their import and admirable in their clarity." He left them, except for the clause in article three which seemed an American guarantee of these rights — by entering the war. "It was more than doubtful," he later wrote, "that the American Congress would at that moment have approved a pledge by the government of the United States to 'defend the rights of freedom of speech and thought' when those rights were abrogated in every Axis country."[56] He was also fully aware that these rights were denied to all who lived under Soviet Russian authority.

Welles wielded his scissors on articles four and five. The assurances given in the fourth article meant "precisely nothing." A fair and equitable "world economic order" after the war demanded commitment, for which the joint declaration provided a vehicle. Welles believed those "fatal impediments to world trade," American high protectionism and British Ottawa Agreements, must disappear. He approached the fifth article with some doubt. He approved support of international organization; but lack of reference to any determination "to guide the world, as soon as conditions made it possible, down the road . . . to a true reduction and limitation of armaments" was disturbing.[57]

These defects were remedied, first, by a clause abolishing trade discrimination. Here was the American attitude toward preferential trade agreements. He amplified the last article to include Roosevelt's approach to disarmament and, as a fillip, inserted "freedom from fear." Some of these changes were in anticipation of the President's reaction.

Roosevelt suggested several further changes — a few important, some minor. Welles later claimed they "considered and discussed" every word; the President wished to ensure that nothing should work out to his embarrassment. F.D.R. eliminated most of Churchill's bellicose preamble. The joint declaration was to affirm an Anglo-American alliance, but only in principle. It must not, he considered, contain references to "immediate issues" such as American participation in the war.[58]

This attitude led to the pruning of the first part of Welles' fourth article. After the shenanigans of Sunday night Roosevelt realized that commitment to free trade between the United States and the British Commonwealth was too powerful a draft for Churchill. The reference to access to markets and raw materials remained. In his own handwriting Roosevelt inserted the words "without discrimination," a condensation of the first clause.[59] To the third article he added a hope for restoration of self-government "to those from whom it has been forcibly removed." Churchill's casual reference to "safety for all peoples in the high seas and oceans" was given the status of a separate article, and the language stiffened to conform with traditional American policy regarding freedom of the seas. The President excised all reference to international organization. In its place went a statement dealing with disarmament of aggressors.

Welles returned to *Tuscaloosa* and prepared another draft. He appreciated Roosevelt's firmness regarding economic policy, but he opposed the position, taken apparently out of cynicism, on international organization. The new draft contained seven articles, since the President had added one and divided the fifth point:

> The President . . . and the Prime Minister . . . being met together, deem it right to make known certain common principles in the national policies of their respective countries on which they base their hopes for a better future for the world.
>
> First, their countries seek no aggrandizement, territorial or other;
>
> Second, they desire to see no territorial changes that do not accord with the freely expressed wishes of the peoples concerned;
>
> Third, they respect the right of all peoples to choose the form of government under which they will live; and they wish to see self-government restored to those from whom it has been forcibly removed.
>
> Fourth, they will endeavor to further the enjoyment by all peoples, without discrimination and on equal terms, to the markets and to the raw materials of the world which are needed for their economic prosperity;
>
> Fifth, they hope to see established a peace, after the destruction of the Nazi tyranny, which will afford to all nations the means of dwelling in security within their own boundaries, and which will afford assurance to all peoples that they may live out their lives in freedom from fear and want.
>
> Sixth, they desire such a peace to establish for all safety on the high seas and oceans;
>
> Seventh, they believe that all of the nations of the world, for realistic as well as spiritual reasons, must come to the abandonment of the use of force. Because no future peace can be maintained if land, sea, or air armaments continue to be employed by nations which threaten, or may threaten, aggression outside of their frontiers, they believe that the disarmament of such nations is essential. They will likewise further all other practicable measures which will lighten for peace-loving peoples the crushing burden of armaments.[60]

Welles had exercised considerable freedom in transcribing the President's language but left intact the spirit of the changes.

In this, its third incarnation, the proposed declaration differed markedly from Churchill's original essay. Roosevelt and Welles could not be sure how the Prime Minister would react. The references to disarmament would not be objectionable, for they were satisfactorily vague and idealistic. Absence of any reference to international organization, they knew, would distress the Prime Minister. The redraft of article four was expected to do more than distress him.

The joint declaration came up between the two leaders late Monday morning. F.D.R., Churchill, Hopkins, Cadogan, and Welles met in the Admiral's cabin on *Augusta*. Roosevelt was dressed informally, in keeping with his efforts at peacemaking. The Prime Minister wore a dress uniform, as he did throughout the conference.

After more pressing diplomatic matters had been dealt with, Churchill asked that the company take up the proposed declaration. F.D.R. at first took this suggestion as meaning arrangements for its announcement. He said he thought the "best solution" was an "identic statement" in London and Washington on Thursday, August 14, announcing that "the Prime Minister and the President had met at sea, accompanied by the various members of their respective staffs; that these officers had discussed the question of aid under the terms of the Lend-Lease Act to nations resisting aggression, and that these military and naval conversations had in no way involved any future commitments between the two Governments, except as authorized under the terms of the Lend-Lease Act; that the Prime Minister and the President had between them discussed certain principles relating to a better future for the world and had agreed upon a joint declaration.[61] In reply, Churchill indicated that he cared not how and when they proclaimed the joint declaration; he was concerned about its contents and how it was received. He said he could not allow the announcement made as the President described it. The President considered this rank heresy.

The Prime Minister objected "very strongly" to the way in which the statement made clear there had been no commitments. Roosevelt replied the point was extremely important "inasmuch as a statement of that character would make it impossible for extreme isolationist leaders in the United States to allege that every kind of secret agreement had been entered into." Churchill was also concerned with public opinion. He feared the effect on the British people; and thought "any categorical statement of that character would prove deeply discouraging to the populations of the occupied countries and would have a very serious effect upon their morale." Might not the announcement, he wondered, "be worded in such a way to make it positive rather than negative, namely, that the members of the staffs of the Prime Minister and of the President had solely discussed questions relative to the furnishing of aid to countries resisting aggression under the terms of the Lend-Lease Act?" Once he grasped the meaning behind the Prime Minister's convoluted phrasing, Roosevelt agreed to have the announcement couched in this manner. If he were interrogated by those nasty isolationists, "he need merely reply" that nothing had been discussed or decided except matters referred to in the declaration. With this agreeable evasion confirmed the company turned to the declaration.[62]

Welles gave the President, Churchill, and Cadogan copies of the rewritten proclamation he had finished just prior to the meeting. Apparently, the Prime Minister began to read it aloud. There was no hesitation as he droned through the first three points. He did suggest insertion in point three of "sovereign rights and" before the words "self-government." This minor change found ready acceptance. On reading the fourth article his voice likely trailed off into silence. The article bore little resemblance to the one he had drafted Saturday evening. "He immediately inquired whether this was meant to apply to the terms of the Ottawa Agreements." Welles replied firmly, "Of course, it did." He launched into a lecture about attempts by the United States "for the better part of nine years" to remove "all of those artificial restrictions and controls . . . which had created such tragic havoc to world economy during the past generation." Welles understood the "immediate difficulties" this caused the Prime Minister; but the phrase "they will endeavor to further" did not require a "formal and immediate contractual obligation" on the part of the United Kingdom. Roosevelt supported his subordinate because of article four's propaganda value. He believed the point of great importance "as a measure of assurance to the German and Italian peoples that after the war they would receive equal economic opportunities." [63]

Churchill demonstrated impressive restraint. He pleaded his lack of authority — introducing his listeners to the constitutional complexities of the British Commonwealth. The government of the United Kingdom was unable to agree to the article without consulting the Dominions. The member nations were unlikely to accede to destruction of the Ottawa Agreements. And Churchill never intended to submit the outrageous fourth article to them. The wily Prime Minister was displaying what he believed a trump card. He could play this constitutional requirement against the President's desire for announcement of the Atlantic Charter immediately after the conference's end.[64]

Churchill claimed to be on the side of the angels in liberalization of trade. The issue, he said, was connected intimately with "his personal life history." He treated the Americans to a brief history of "the days at the outset of the century when Joseph Chamberlain first brought up the proposal for Empire preferences and the predominant part which this issue had played in the political history of Great Britain during the past forty years." He was "heartily in accord" with the principle of free trade. "As was well known," he had always opposed the Ottawa Agreements. Whatever Churchill's theoretical attitude, the dictates of British politics controlled his response.[65] Again he flashed that hole card. "It would be at least a week," he said, "before he could hope to obtain by telegraph the opinion of the Dominions with regard to this question." [66]

At this awkward moment Hopkins stepped in and resumed the role of intermediary. The President's aide was always willing to gloss over disagreements. "It was inconceivable," he stated, "that the issuance of the joint declaration should be held up by a matter of this kind." Hopkins proposed that Welles and Cadogan draft new phrasing "which would take care of these difficulties and prevent the delay of which Mr. Churchill spoke." This offhand rejection of long months of effort infuriated Welles, who thought further revision "would destroy completely" the fourth article. It was not a question of phrasing, he insisted, but vital principle. "If the British and the United States Governments could not agree to do everything within their power to further, after the termination of the present war, a restoration of free and liberal trade policies, they might as well throw in the sponge and realize that one of the greatest factors in creating the present tragic situation . . . was going to be permitted to continue unchecked." Without support by the President and Prime Minister a policy of "constructive sanity" would never see the light, Welles pleaded.[67]

Churchill and Cadogan both admitted the difficulty lay not merely with wording. The Prime Minister then put his cards on the table. "The Dominions would have to be consulted," he sighed. It was even possible the Commonwealth nations would turn down article four and "consequently the proposed joint declaration could only be used some time after news of the meeting . . . had been given out." To "ease the situation" he suggested insertion of a simple qualifying phrase, "with due regard for our present obligations." The maneuver had the predictable effect on F.D.R., who was more concerned with issuing a statement of some kind than with the Department's economic policy. Too softhearted to concede the point in front of Welles, F.D.R. suggested that Churchill "try and draft some phraseology which would make that situation easier."[68] The Prime Minister graciously acceded. It was arranged that Welles call on the English representatives later in the afternoon to go over Churchill's redraft.

With that crisis settled in his favor, the Prime Minister returned to reading the American draft. He expressed "entire accord" with the fifth and sixth articles — little different from his version. He came to point seven, and first raised a minor objection. In the second sentence "aggression" should replace "to use force." The article, which Churchill may have recognized as the President's creation, received enthusiastic approval. But he missed any reference to a revived League of Natons. "He inquired . . . whether the President would

not agree to support some kind of 'effective international organization' as suggested . . . in his original draft." Roosevelt's first reaction was negative. He could not agree to those three little words
"because of the suspicions and opposition" at home.[69]

F.D.R. touched on his prejudice against revival of a world organization. He could not support any new "Assembly of the League"
until after a period of transition. During this stage an international
force staffed by the United States and Great Britain would police the
world. Churchill possessed considerable sympathy for this view, but
his concern was with *British* public opinion. "He did not feel he
would be candid if he did not express to the President his feeling
that point seven would create a great deal of opposition from the
extreme internationalists." Roosevelt would not budge. He came
back to his conviction that "the time had come to be realistic and
that . . . the main factor in the seventh point was complete realism." [70] Churchill had no choice but to accept the President's decision.

The Prime Minister remarked that he did not intend to leave until
at least 5:00 P.M. the next day. He attached so much importance to
reaching "a complete meeting of minds" that he was willing to stay
an additional twenty-four hours. Welles feared the Prime Minister's
cordiality, and attempted to convince F.D.R. to use this extra time to
American advantage. He urged him "to see whether Mr. Churchill
might not be induced to cut corners and expedite his communications with the Dominions' governments." If pressure of time were
removed, the President would stand behind his Department — and
Welles. The fourth point as Churchill intended to rewrite it would
mean nothing. F.D.R. seemed to agree, or so Welles believed.[71] He
knew Churchill was using the President's desire for an immediate
declaration to force a disastrous compromise; but there was little he
could do.

Churchill had great confidence in this maneuver. On returning to
his quarters, he cabled Attlee a full summary of the morning's session. He described the President's desire for a declaration of ideals
and enclosed the American draft. Attlee would note it "is not free

from the difficulties attaching to all such declarations . . . The fourth condition would evidently have to be amended to safeguard our obligations contracted in Ottawa and not prejudice the future of Imperial Preference." He assured Attlee he had "little doubt" Roosevelt would accept the British changes "for the sake of speedy agreement." The seventh point was "most remarkable" for realism, and, encouragingly, the President contemplated complete disarmament of "guilty" nations. Maintenance of British and American armed forces "for a long and indefinite period" opened intriguing vistas.[72]

In view of English attachment to some international organization, Churchill intended certain amendments to point seven. As a minimum he would insist on the phrase, "pending the establishment of a wider and more permanent system of general security." Roosevelt might not be "very happy" but the Prime Minister was confident he would accept it for the sake of dispatch. In turn, the Cabinet must not raise "unnecessary difficulties." They should approach the declaration "as an interim and partial statement of war aims designed to assure all countries of our righteous purpose, and not the complete structure which we should build after victory." [73] Attlee was to summon the full War Cabinet for immediate discussion of the declaration, and send along their views. Churchill seems to have desired an evaluation from men not submerged in the emotional atmosphere of Argentia, but he was anxious that the Cabinet approve the declaration without serious emendations. "I fear," he wrote, "the President will be very much upset if no Joint Statement can be issued, and grave and vital interests might be affected." [74]

Churchill finished dictating this cable at 2:00 P.M. Within the next hour difficulties over article four were settled, just as he had predicted. A meeting of Welles, the P.M., and Cadogan had been arranged for 3:00 P.M. Just a few minutes before the hour a messenger from *Augusta* handed Welles a surprising but not entirely unexpected note. At 2:30 the President had written out his decision on point four. "Dear Sumner: Time being of the essence I think I can stand on my own former formulas — to wit: access to raw materials. This omits entirely the *other* subject which is the only one in conflict: discrimination in trade. The fourth paragraph would then read 'of access to the raw materials of the world,' etc. For *me* that is consistent." [75] Welles thought it was not at all consistent. He was shocked and deeply disappointed by Roosevelt's defection — but there was nothing he could do. A few words from the President destroyed his hopes and those of the Department that Argentia would bind the British to trade liberalization. The Under Secretary blamed Harry Hopkins; probably he was right.[76]

The meeting with Cadogan (the Prime Minister did not attend) was anticlimactic. Welles had no further reason to delay an agreement — on British terms. His English colleague asked him to read a summary of the morning discussion, and Welles passively approved. Cadogan stated that the Prime Minister had dispatched to London a text of the joint declaration, which incorporated certain "modifications" of points four and seven. The revised fourth article read: "They will endeavor, with due respect for their existing obligations, to further the enjoyment by all States, great or small, victor or vanquished, of access on equal terms to the trade and to the raw materials of the world." The article did refer both to commerce and raw materials, and Welles accepted this minor concession. Welles explained that "inasmuch as the Prime Minister's draft of point four was far broader and more satisfactory than the minimum which the President had instructed me . . . to accept" nothing would be gained by raising objection.[77]

The Under Secretary bestirred himself to approve the changes in point seven. Perhaps he reasoned that he could salvage something of value. The two diplomats engaged in frank exchange about the President's and Prime Minister's attitudes on international organization. Cadogan said the Prime Minister "felt very strongly — perhaps exaggeratedly — the opposition which would be created on the part of a certain League-of-Nations element to the contents of point seven." He believed this sentiment received undue importance; but it would be tragic "to place sole emphasis upon the transition period after the war." Some reference to an agency to function after the transition stage was essential. Welles was in sympathy, but stressed that, "as recent experience had shown," only the President could decide the matter. While the British draft of point seven was completely satisfactory, he "had no idea what the President's decision might be." It was now Welles' turn to play the role of marionette.[78]

The Under Secretary subsequently took these revisions to his master. F.D.R. accepted the redraft of point four as "better than he had thought Mr. Churchill would be willing to concede." He accepted Churchill's version of the seventh article without question, since it conveyed the idea of a transition period before the creation of any international organization.[79] If Welles had doubted the Prime Minister's cards before, these words removed any question.

He made bold to pose several questions before withdrawing and allowing the President to contemplate achievement of his desires. In Welles' opinion isolationists at home would react violently to that portion of point seven which declared it "essential" to disarm aggressors. "If a great Power like the United States publicly declares that something is essential, the inference is that that Power is going to do something about it." Welles said it was more than likely that "the isolationists will insist that this public statement by the President meant that the United States would go to war in order to disarm not only Germany but even possibly Japan and theoretically at least even the Soviet Union."[80] Basking in his success, the President shrugged off this prophetic statement. The intent of the seventh article, as he interpeted it, "was to make clear what the objective would be if the war was won." He believed the American people would look at it in this way, another example of his peculiar attitude about public opinion. The "realism" would be apparent to the enormous majority of Americans and they would support disarmament.

Roosevelt's breezy response begged the question his assistant had raised. Even if interpreted as an aim "if the war was won," the seventh point implied American participation in the disarmament of aggressors.[81] The declaration was, of course, to register America's resolve to take a part in the postwar world.

Welles asked if he could learn more about F.D.R.'s "realist" approach to international politics. He had been surprised "and some-

what discouraged" by a casual remark the President had made that
"nothing could be more futile than the reconstitution of a body such
as the Assembly of the League of Nations." The paternalistic tone of
this statement was troublesome. If the President viewed the immediate postwar era as one requiring world police powers by America
and Britain, Welles argued that "it would be enormously desirable
for the smaller Powers to have an Assembly in which all would be
represented and in which they could make their complaints known."
Roosevelt agreed — as long as the work of the transition period was
accomplished. He did not object to "ostensible" participation by
small countries.[82] His blindness on this issue was astonishing.

Welles could not avoid showing his bitterness about British duplic-
ity. He pointed out that, since the declaration had turned out to
everyone's satisfaction, there was no reason to delay the Prime Minister's departure. Churchill had assured him the War Cabinet would
approve his recommendations. All that remained was preparation of
the announcement which was to preface the joint statement. Welles
thought everything "could be definitely agreed upon and cleared up"
by next afternoon; there was "no practical reason" for waiting another day. Roosevelt agreed and promised to bring it up when the
Prime Minister came to dinner Monday night.[83]

X. Goodbye, Columbus

C HANGES IN ATMOSPHERE are noticeable in a conference of such short duration as the one at Argentia. There were peaks of activity, valleys of relaxation, and, after Monday, a declining slope to conference's end. Monday was eventful, the busiest day of the meeting. By late afternoon, as will be recalled, Roosevelt and Churchill and their staffs had dealt with most problems. From that time until the meeting concluded late Tuesday afternoon the participants relaxed.

As described earlier, Churchill returned to *Augusta* Monday night to dine with the President, and here transpired the most intimate and probably most informal of their dinner meetings. It was a comfortable, unstrained occasion. Both men were satisfied. Churchill had won the warning to Japan he had striven for so doggedly; it was not the commitment he had hoped for but he believed it a giant step in that direction. On other matters he and the President had resolved the difficulties between them. The United States was to undertake measures in the Atlantic which amounted to a limited, undeclared war against Germany. The awkward portions of the joint declaration had been hedged to Churchill's satisfaction. Roosevelt believed he had obtained most of his objectives. One desire, that idealistic statement of war and peace aims which was to bring important results, was in the bag. Its formulation apparently had not weakened Roosevelt's relations with the British or with his own Department of State.

The tone of the entire conference was pleasing to F.D.R., for it recognized American leadership in the informal alliance. Churchill had come to Argentia in the manner of a suppliant and not as a competitor for the mantle of world leadership. President Roosevelt appreciated the Prime Minister's yeoman service in attempting to calm the aggressive, single-minded American military leaders — even though the success of his efforts would become known only later. With the exception of the one incident, he was pleased with Churchill's restraint in not pleading for United States intervention.

The one decision known to have been made at the affair on Monday night was agreement on ending the conference. Roosevelt pointed out, in consonance with Welles' lecture of Monday afternoon, that there was no reason for Churchill to delay his departure. The finishing touches on the declarations could be completed by Tuesday morning. The Prime Minister said in that case he would return to his original itinerary. He did not mention that he had modified his original plans in anticipation of devoting more time to bringing the President around to the British viewpoint.[2] Since the President's "flexibility" had removed this rationale, there was no reason to remain.[3] Hopkins explained later that "the conferences ended when Churchill and Roosevelt decided that further talk would be useless — that nothing more definite could be agreed upon by both sides." [4] The Prime Minister left *Augusta* at 11:30 and hurried back to speed up the sailing.

In the midst of these activities, which Churchill — always in top form after midnight — personally directed, the reply to his cable about the declaration came in from London. Attlee had not received the message until after two in the morning, London time. He recalled, "I was still up — never got to bed very early. I called a Cabinet at three o'clock in the morning, and by four we were able to send our reply." [5] Their cable gave word-for-word reaction to the proposed statement. The rapidity of the response was a remarkable example of the efficiency of the British system. During the conference more than thirty messages passed between *Prince of Wales* and Whitehall and, as Robert Sherwood has written, "the speed of communication thereon was astonishing to the Americans." [6] It amazed members of Churchill's staff as well. They were prepared to wait a day or longer for a reply from the Cabinet.

The cable arrived shortly after one o'clock, Argentia time. Colonel Hollis took it up to the Prime Minister's cabin near the bridge. Churchill was just emerging from a voluminous, gaudy, dragon-figured dressing gown, and he was preparing to climb into bed while talking animatedly with Cherwell. When he heard that the telegram was the War Cabinet's reaction to his and the President's decisions, he asked fearfully, "Am I going to like it?" Hollis assured him the Cabinet had raised very few objections and that all was well.[7] The cable suggested a somewhat altered version of point four. Churchill disregarded this since the problem had been worked out to his satisfaction late Monday afternoon — after the draft had gone to London. He did adopt another of the Cabinet's suggestions. In line with British emphasis upon national economic planning, the Cabinet proposed the insertion of a new article dealing with social security.[8]

The morning was spent in preparations for departure, launches being hoisted on board and lashed to davits, skylights being dogged down, all the myriad details of going to sea being completed. Churchill and Roosevelt held their final meeting at noon Tuesday. The Prime Minister visited his host to put the declaration in its final form and, what was perhaps more important, to express gratitude for the chance to meet the President. He showed Roosevelt the War Cabinet's "revised version" of point four but implied that he did not place much importance in it. F.D.R. said he preferred "to adhere to the phrasing already agreed," and Churchill refrained from pressing the matter.[9] The new paragraph received Roosevelt's enthusiastic approval, because it embodied one of his four freedoms. It became article five. Both leaders were later to regret they did not think to include another of the four freedoms — that of religion. Its exclusion from the eight-point statement was quickly noted and proclaimed as proof of Roosevelt and Churchill's sellout to "godless" Russia.[10]

After verbal alterations (which did not affect the meaning of any point), the joint declaration was complete. In final form, a preamble and eight points, it read,

Joint Declaration by the President and the Prime Minister

August 12, 1941

The President of the United States of America and the Prime Minister, Mr. Churchill, representing His Majesty's Government in the United Kingdom, being met together, deem it right to make known certain common principles in the national policies of their respective countries on which they base their hopes for a better future for the world.

First, their countries seek no aggrandizement, territorial or other.

Second, they desire to see no territorial changes that do not accord with the freely expressed wishes of the peoples concerned.

Third, they respect the right of all peoples to choose the form of government under which they will live; and they wish to see sovereign rights and self-government restored to those who have been forcibly deprived of them.

Fourth, they will endeavor, with due respect for their existing obligations, to further the enjoyment by all states, great or small, victor or vanquished, of access, on equal terms, to the trade and to the raw materials of the world which are needed for their economic prosperity.

Fifth, they desire to bring about the fullest collaboration between all nations in the economic field, with the object of securing for all improved labor standards, economic advancement, and social security.

Sixth, after the final destruction of the Nazi tyranny, they hope to see established a peace which will afford to all nations the means of dwelling in safety within their own boundaries, and which will afford assurance that all the men in all the lands may live out their lives in freedom from fear and want.

Seventh, such a peace should enable all men to traverse the high seas and oceans without hindrance.

Eighth, they believe that all the nations of the world, for realistic as well as spiritual reasons, must come to the abandonment of the use of force. Since no future peace can be maintained if land, sea, or air armaments continue to be employed by nations which threaten, or may threaten, aggression outside of their frontiers, they believe, pending the establishment of a wider and permanent system of general security, that the disarmament of such nations is essential. They will likewise aid and encourage all other practicable measures which will lighten for peace-loving peoples the crushing burden of armaments.[11]

Welles and Cadogan had done their work well, and little more can be said about this final draft. The eight points, especially articles four and eight, were a compromise between American and British delegates. From the perspective of Argentia they appeared to be a successful compromise.

The President and Prime Minister also confirmed the language of the statement which was to preface the joint declaration. To F.D.R. this was, naturally, a matter of much concern. He wanted it vague. There could be no suggestion of alliances or secret commitments. It should not weaken the effect of the declaration of ideals by revealing the scope of the meeting. The leaders had worked out a satisfactory form for the announcement at their meeting Monday morning. It was felt necessary to insert a paragraph taking cognizance of the arrival of an important English official at the meeting. Lord Beaverbrook, the Minister of Supply and a leading figure in the War Cabinet, came aboard *Prince of Wales* at 6:00 Tuesday morning after a harrowing journey. Churchill had invited "the Beaver" soon after embarking on the westward voyage. Though he was a lone wolf and at times "pretty erratic," the Prime Minister thought Beaverbrook a genius at getting things done, and the two men maintained a relationship based on deep admiration and fondness through a lifetime of political differences, injured feelings, and clashing egos.[12] The Minister of Supply had been keen to accept the invitation to Argentia. It was arranged that he fly into Newfoundland for the final days of the conference, perhaps because of his galloping hypochondria. Lord Moran has written of Beaverbrook's exaggerated preoccupation with his health: "For Max there is no comfort in a sniff of danger. If he makes himself fly the Atlantic, he fears for his life, although, he says, he prefers 'one night of terror' to 'a week of boredom' in a ship."[13] The Prime Minister convinced him that he must risk the trip. The Canadian-born Beaverbrook was a more staunch Imperialist than Churchill, and his powerful newspapers echoed his views. He would prove a bulwark if the Americans made difficulties about supply matters — or about the Ottawa Trade Agreements.

As it happened Churchill had no need of his support. Beaverbrook's arrival on the last day was anticlimactic. His trip, however, almost vindicated his dread of flying, for it narrowly missed tragedy. Churchill also had asked Sir Arthur Purvis, head of the British Purchasing Mission in the United States, to stop off at Argentia on his way back to Washington.[14] Beaverbrook and Purvis traveled together from London to Prestwick and then boarded different planes for the transatlantic flight. "It was an even chance who went in either plane." Just a few minutes after takeoff Purvis' aircraft crashed into a hill and all aboard were killed. Churchill wrote of this respected and admired Canadian: "Purvis was a grievous loss, as he held so many British, American, and Canadian threads in his hands, and had hitherto been the directing mind in their harmonious combination." News of his death cast a pall, but the English representatives (including Beaverbrook who only learned what had occurred when he got to Argentia) accepted it stoically. "It was wartime," the Prime Minister observed.[15]

Lord Beaverbrook had experienced difficulty getting from St. John's to the conference site. Finally he made himself known "with accustomed vigor" and hired a special train. The journey on this rickety, wood-burning conveyance did nothing for his state of mind.[16] Accompanied by his personal physician and valet, Beaverbrook boarded *Prince of Wales* in a state verging on physical and emotional exhaustion. His first reaction to the joint declaration was outrage. Point four, even with the qualifying phrase Churchill had inserted, seemed a direct challenge to the Empire's system of preferential tariffs. Beaverbrook had fought for the Ottawa Agreements nine years before, and "he was now prepared to wade in and fight for them again."[17] He later claimed to have rescued them from destruction by insisting on new wording for article four. "I found the Four Freedoms under preparation, one of which, in effect, abolished imperial preference," Beaverbrook asserted in a confused memorandum to himself after the meeting. "The British Cabinet had accepted the document. I protested at once and claimed that there must be a modification, protecting our Ottawa Agreements. It would be impossible to take any other course. Apart from the political issues in Great Britain, it would be an offence to the Dominions engaged in the war. It could not be contemplated or tolerated by them." [18] Despite the evidence Beaverbrook manufactured to justify his claims as the savior of imperial preference, it is clear that Churchill convinced him that the clause, "with due regard for their existing obligations," offered guarantees for the present.

As the most vehement advocate in the Churchill government of all-out aid to Russia, Beaverbrook was happy with decisions on this issue. Earlier discussion had brought agreement about the diversion of large amounts of raw materials and munitions to the Soviet Union. Roosevelt had strongly favored the arrangement, because of desire to keep Russia in the war and because it reinvigorated his arsenal of democracy thesis. American and British military authorities — familiar with the love-hate aspect of supply between the United States and the United Kingdom — could not view with enthusiasm the seating of another guest, this one the most voracious yet, at the production table. Nonetheless, they accepted it as inevitable. The Prime Minister had determined before coming to Argentia that he must share with the Russians. He had decided to support an Anglo-American-Russian supply conference, and while en route he set in motion preparations for such a meeting.[19]

Roosevelt and Churchill concluded that Lord Beaverbrook's presence was too important to ignore in the announcement — especially as the ostensible purpose of the conference was production and supply priorities. Reference to his participation went into the prefatory statement. "Lord Beaverbrook, the Minister of Supply of the British Government," this announced, "has joined in these conferences. He is going to proceed to Washington to discuss further details with appropriate officials of the United States Government. These conferences will also cover the supply problems of the Soviet Union." [20] Glory-hungry members of the two staffs undoubtedly resented the special mention of a man who had arrived at Argentia a few hours before the conference adjourned. The President's desire that Lend-Lease arrangements appear as the principal reason for and result of the meeting was the decisive factor. A statement to that effect occupied a strategic place in the announcement.

As soon as Beaverbrook had eaten breakfast Tuesday morning, the

Prime Minister took him for a walk along the shoreline. He informed the Minister of Supply that he was to proceed to Washington and then would go to Moscow for the three-power supply conference. Even though Churchill assured his friend that he would be given a free hand, "with power to act for all British departments," Beaverbrook was not eager to take on these assignments.[21] Harry Hopkins witnessed the conversation and wrote: "There was Beaverbrook talking earnestly, gesticulating. Churchill, his face grim, would stoop and pick up pebbles and shells and skim them across the water as he listened." Beaverbrook argued that he should return to London with the Prime Minister. Hopkins told him later in the morning that he must come to Washington so that "he might tell the President in detail all he knew about Britain's present and coming air power. Moreover, he could learn first hand just what might be expected of our American production — now and in the future." [22] Together, the Prime Minister and Hopkins beat down Beaverbrook's reluctance. When he was informed of their success, the President said that he would probably appoint Averell Harriman as the leading American representative to the Moscow meeting, since Hopkins' health was too precarious to allow him to undertake a second journey to Russia.[23]

To set up the conference the two leaders addressed a joint communication to the Russian Premier. It was couched in extremely friendly language. Asserting that their discussions "as to how best our two countries can help your country in the splendid defense that you are making against the Nazi attack" stemmed from Hopkins' report, they assured Stalin that the "very maximum" of supplies urgently needed was being sent. "Already many shiploads have left our shores, and more will leave in the immediate future." Roosevelt and Churchill did point out that Allied resources, "though immense were limited," and decisions must take into account the most productive use of raw materials and manufactured goods. The message continued: "The needs and demands of your and our armed services can only be determined in the light of the full knowledge of the many factors which must be taken into consideration in the decisions that we make. In order that all of us may be in a position to arrive at speedy decisions as to the apportionment of our joint resources, we suggest that we prepare for a meeting to be held at Moscow, to which we would send high representatives who could discuss these matters directly with you. If this conference appeals to you, we want you to know that, pending the decisions of that conference, we shall continue to send supplies and materials as rapidly as possible." [24] Here was pointed reference to need for complete and frank knowledge of the military and economic resources of the associated powers. That last sentence seemed to threaten that aid might cease if information about Russia's position were not forthcoming. Still, the message was a remarkable commitment. "This pledge of American resources to a common pool of the three powers," Raymond Dawson has written, "for the purposes of a combined effort against Hitler's Germany, was by far the most sweeping declaration made to that date regarding the policies to be followed in support of the Soviet Union." [25] Reference to the decisions upon assistance for Russia also went into the preface of the announcement.

One final inclusion was made. Churchill's political difficulties in Great Britain made requisite some reference to the fact that the meeting was directed against flesh and blood enemies. The joint declaration committed the United States in principle to defeat the Axis Powers. Accordingly, Churchill insisted emphasis be given to his and the President's agreement upon this subject. He got a compromise. The last paragraph of the preface was revised to read: "They have considered the dangers to world civilization arising from the policies of military domination by conquest upon which the Hitlerite government of Germany and other governments associated therewith have embarked, and have made clear the steps which their countries are respectively taking for their safety in the face of these dangers." [26] F.D.R. earlier had amended Churchill's fiery draft to avoid any reference to common action. It is noteworthy that he was able to keep this manifesto out of the declaration proper.

These matters were decided while Roosevelt, Churchill, Hopkins, and Beaverbrook lunched in the President's quarters. As they

reached agreement, the decisions were passed on to other members
of the staffs who were waiting and having lunch in the Admiral's
cabin. This business took little time, and the four men were able to
enjoy their meal and some stimulating conversation. Robert Sherwood writes that this was the most satisfactory of all the sessions.
"There was no business to be transacted. Both Roosevelt and
Churchill were relaxed and amusing and amused. This was Hopkins'
ambition as a catalyst or marriage broker: to prove to Roosevelt that
it was possible to be utterly at ease with Churchill and vice versa.
Beaverbrook, whom Roosevelt had known of old, helped considerably in this process." [27] One may doubt whether the two men were
ever "utterly at ease"; yet this luncheon, at which formality and pos-
turing were notably absent, was of benefit in bringing understanding. While still under the influence of the luncheon atmosphere on
Tuesday afternoon, Churchill wrote: "I am sure I have established
warm and deep personal relations with our great friend." [28] The
President was more reserved but also believed he and the Prime
Minister now understood each other.

The warmth of the luncheon did not last, for sometime Tuesday
afternoon news came of the shockingly close vote in the United
States House of Representatives upon the bill to renew the Selective
Service Act. One commentator said, "The news . . . dropped like
enemy bombs on the decks of the *Augusta* and the *Prince of
Wales*." [29] The closeness of the margin (203–202) was more distress-
ing because it was so unexpected. The struggle over extension of the
draft had been going on since late June, when Secretary of War
Stimson and General Marshall had taken the responsibility of recommending an additional eighteen months' service for draftees. There
was tremendous opposition to the proposal resulting from personal
antipathy to the President and, more important, from fear of political repercussions. The Selective Service Act obligated draftees to
twelve months' service. Many of these men and their families were
insistent that the government honor this commitment even though
this would destroy the battle-readiness of almost every Army unit.
By early summer the morale of draftees was plummeting and the

ominous letters "O.H.I.O." (over the hill in October) were being chalked on barracks and latrines.[30]

By early August, after a bitter fight in and out of Congress, victory seemed assured. When the American delegation left for Argentia, legislative leaders were confident they had easily the support needed for passage. It was clear that Republican votes were necessary; but the manner in which the bill's sponsors were able to turn back attempts to modify key provisions made it appear that the measure would pass by a comfortable margin.[31] On August 6, however, Speaker Sam Rayburn and Majority Leader John W. McCormack took another nose count. McCormack reported that not only had a number of Republicans reneged but also some forty-five Democrats were definitely opposed. About thirty-five Democratic congressmen were shaky. For these men it was a matter of political survival. Forrest Pogue has written: "Mindful of next year's elections, members from strongly isolationist areas of the country were weighing their desire to back the Army against their chances of returning to Washington. In most cases Washington won." [32]

F.D.R. knew what was happening, having received a full report from Steve Early soon after McCormack's tabulation. He told Early that the best strategy was to carry on, relying upon appeals to undecided members by the House leadership. He gave permission to say that the President had expressed an "urgent hope" the bill would go through. Early should stress the serious dangers to hemispheric security "if Europe and Africa and Far East are wholly controlled by aggressor nations leaving United States with a weak army composed of very new recruits." In the end administration strategists decided not to risk further defections by using the President's message.[33]

The return of a few Democrat fence-sitters and the votes of Representative James W. Wadsworth's faithful band of Republicans carried the day. The bill squeaked through the House in the late evening of August 12.[34] It is clear that overconfidence, a breakdown of communication, and failure to ensure that Democratic congressmen stay in line (and in town) contributed to the paper-thin margin. The vote did not indicate that the administration's policy teetered precariously upon a majority of one in the lower chamber. The vote in March on Lend-Lease was more representative of the true alignment of power in Congress.[35]

The British did not see the vote in that perspective. They automatically equated the House of Representatives with the House of Commons and a majority of one for a government-backed measure with a near vote of no confidence. British delegates, Churchill included, were shocked and badly frightened by the House's action. "Such an extremely narrow vote on a matter which concerned the life or death of the Army was a potent warning of the continued power of isolationism," has commented a British military historian.[36] Harry Hopkins, who had risen from his sickbed to attend the final luncheon, reported that the news had "a decidedly chilling effect" upon all present, but upon the British especially. "The psycological [sic] effect of that minimum vote of confidence in the President was not wholly happy up there in the North Atlantic," Hopkins said.[37] Marshall and his colleagues perhaps found grim comfort in British reaction. If Churchill and the British Chiefs were shocked into better understanding of the administration's handicaps, they might refrain from demanding the impossible of the United States.

This last meeting broke up sometime before three o'clock. The President and Prime Minister came out on *Augusta*'s quarterdeck to say formal goodbyes. United States Army and Navy representatives, in full regalia, had assembled on the deck in front of the airplane hangar — close to shelter in event that the weather turned foul again. *Augusta*'s officers and men stood massed in the rear. "Aided by both sons, F.D.R. walked to a spot directly in front and facing his Chiefs of Staff. Pound, Dill, and Freeman shook hands with the President and then went down the line of U.S. officers, saying goodbye. Then the Prime Minister came down, said goodbye to the impassive line, and shook hands once more with the President." [38] Always conscious of the dramatic potential of any event, Churchill brought the meeting to a close with a pleasing little ceremony. He produced illuminated copies of Longfellow's verse, "Sail on, Oh Ship of State," which the President had sent him eight months before.

Both men signed these copies, Roosevelt keeping one and the Prime Minister another. They also exchanged autographed portraits.[39] Pomp and circumstance then reappeared. An honor guard and band paraded, other honors were rendered. The Prime Minister turned to offer a last farewell and then, preceded by his staff, he stepped into a motor launch. As the British party left *Augusta* for the last time, her band struck up "God Save the King."

Although the meetings were finished, Roosevelt spent his remaining hours at Argentia reading and replying to messages from *Prince of Wales* and other British warships expressing appreciation for his gift parcels. One of these notes had special meaning. Captain Leach gave Franklin, Jr. for his father a medallion reproducing the insignia on the gun muzzles of *Prince of Wales*. The President was to refer to this gift in a letter of condolence to Mrs. Leach in March, 1942.[40] Churchill maintained a frantic pace, and while the British ships were being readied for departure he dashed off a cable to Whitehall which summarized the results of the final meeting.

The War Cabinet had expressed further misgivings about the fourth part of the declaration in a second message Tuesday morning.[41] This reached Churchill just after his return to *Prince of Wales*. In reply the Prime Minister assured his colleagues that the qualifying words, "governing as they did the whole paragraph, sufficiently safeguarded our position." The President had not wanted to change the phrasing in favor of Whitehall's first alternative, and Churchill saw no hope for this second, more restrictive version.[42]

The cable to London revealed the Prime Minister's confidence that he had won the struggle for a strong warning to Japan. The final version relied on his original draft ultimatum. "We have laid special stress upon the warning which constitutes the teeth of the President's communications," he noted. "One would always fear State Department trying to tone it down; but President has promised definitely to use the hard language."[43] Churchill soon learned his confidence had been misplaced. However, Roosevelt's attitude on the question — when the Prime Minister left him — justified optimism.

In this message supply matters also received attention. Churchill urged that the Cabinet press for review and expansion of production. He said, "President welcomes Beaverbrook's arrival at Washington and I am convinced this is the needful practical step." He ordered the Cabinet to "see also the Roosevelt-Churchill message to dear old Joe." The proposed three-power supply conference, if held in an open atmosphere, would be valuable. This final statement also revealed he believed that Roosevelt had been converted completely to strategic air power, as witnessed by the decision to step up production of heavy bombers and tanks. *In toto,* the message showed Churchill to be rather satisfied.[44]

At 4:45 P.M. Beaverbrook left *Prince of Wales* and two minutes later she got under way. "The gangway came in; the anchors came up. The battleship began to vibrate. On the stroke of five she turned and passed slowly from the bay." [45] The clouds had closed in again and there was a slight drizzle. As *Prince of Wales* moved alongside *Augusta,* passing honors were rendered and the battleship's band played "Auld Lang Syne." The President and his full staff came back on deck to watch Churchill's little fleet stand out of the harbor. Those with sharp eyes noticed there had been an addition to the British complement. Probably at Roosevelt's behest, Admiral King had ordered Destroyer Division Sixteen, less U.S.S. *Trippe* and U.S.S. *Sims,* to proceed "in company but not in formation" with *Prince of Wales* to Iceland. They were to refuel and to accompany the British flotilla to a point 150 miles east of Iceland and then return to Argentia. By that time Churchill's party might have air cover. One of these American destroyers was *Mayrant,* whose executive officer was Franklin D. Roosevelt, Jr. The President's son was to go on to England with Churchill.

These arrangements almost miscarried at the beginning. Colonel Jacob remarked that as the battleship moved out into the bay, "one by one of the destroyers which are to escort us joined us in our wake, led by two American destroyers. When we had gone about a mile we increased speed to 20 knots, but shortly afterwards we had to reduce speed again as we were passing near an anchored destroyer. Apparently the two American destroyers . . . did not notice the fact that we were reducing speed until the leading ship was within a hundred yards of our stern. They then woke up and both turned violently to port and left the line . . ." There was yet another "excitement" an hour later when the U.S.S. *Reading*, which was keeping pace on the port bow, suddenly swerved and headed straight across *Prince of Wales'* bow. The *Reading's* helm had jammed over and, temporarily, she was completely out of control. Captain Leach ordered "full speed astern" and the runaway destroyer safely crossed the great battleship's path, missing a collision by some forty to fifty yards. "It had been a narrow squeak," was Jacob's only comment. The British probably were happy to reach the open sea.[47]

When the British vessels had passed from sight into the far reaches of Placentia Bay, the Americans completed their own preparations for the return. F.D.R. had decided to retrace his itinerary at a leisurely pace. He wanted no premature discovery of the activities of the past four days to endanger the Prime Minister — or to detract from the impact of the joint declaration. It was necessary for several of the party to get back to Washington quickly. Admiral King made arrangements. Arnold, Burns, Sherman, and Bundy were to fly back immediately. They were to take off in a Navy PBY, the "Dolphin," early Tuesday evening but bad weather prevented immediate departure. Harriman and Lord Beaverbrook also flew out of Argentia. Under Secretary Welles transferred to *Tuscaloosa*, where he, Stark, and Marshall were to be quartered for part of the return trip. Arrangements were to have air transportation awaiting them when the ships reached Maine.[48] That left the President, his personal staff, and Harry Hopkins with free run of *Augusta*.

The President's cruiser got under way minutes after the British ships disappeared. The ship's band struck up "God Save the King," as was proper when leaving British waters. Bands on *Tuscaloosa* and *Arkansas* followed suit, and the men and officers of the old battleship stood at attention for a last salute to the President. The echoes of the British anthem fled across the spacious anchorage to be replaced by blasting steam and the whine of anchor winches as the U.S. warships began to move. F.D.R. stayed on the bridge for a final look at the scene where so much had occurred in the past four days. Almost at once the two heavy cruisers, with Destroyer Division Seventeen, plus *Madison,* following in line to the rear, disappeared into heavy fog. Save for a couple of destroyers, *Arkansas,* a tanker, and a lone Navy amphibian rolling in the wake of the departing ships, Argentia harbor was deserted. The low stone hills were silent, brooding over gray harbor waters where, after two centuries, human history briefly had centered once again.

XI. Homeward Bound

THE PRESIDENT'S FLAGSHIP set a course for Blue Hill Bay, Maine, and a rendezvous with *Potomac* and *Calypso*. On this slow run through gray Atlantic waters, the passengers gratefully settled into shipboard routine. For Churchill and party the first leg of the voyage, except for the two near collisions, was also uneventful. What might have happened if submarines had attacked *Prince of Wales* in the presence of American destroyers offers interesting speculation. There may have been calculation that the Germans would not organize an interception until after broadcast of the joint declaration. Still, everyone's guard was up. Through direction-finding apparatus the Admiralty on August 12 identified the location of numerous U-boat radio transmissions in the North Atlantic. Three or more submarines were in the vicinity of 60° North, 23° West, and several more were in the area between 45° and 55° North and 13° and 20° West.[1] Next day the British informed U.S. Naval Operations that they believed thirty German submarines to be operating in the Atlantic — at least one half of which were in or close to the *Prince of Wales'* path.[2] Their presence was particularly worrisome because the force escorting the battleship could not maintain tight formation. The two United States destroyers stayed five or six miles in the lead, and the Commonwealth escorts had difficulty in keeping up when the battleship zigzagged at twenty knots. As a result, late Tuesday night, Captain Leach ordered abandonment of the zigzag maneuver and from then on *Prince of Wales* steamed straight ahead toward the northeast. A few hours later he announced to the ship's company that there was to be a stopover in Iceland. He also said, "The Germans no doubt know we had been to Newfoundland and were probably aware of our having sailed." Leach asked the crew to be particularly "on their toes" against possible submarine and aircraft attacks.[3] H. V. Morton wrote that everyone was anticipating "with some pleasure" a battle during the return trip. "Some thought U-boats would lie in wait for us; others thought long-range bombers; a few enthusiasts thought U-boats and long-range bombers, and I was inclined to throw in the *Tirpitz* and a few cruisers as well." Churchill did not see fit to relieve Morton's anxiety about the *Tirpitz,* and the English writer dutifully continued to practice with his "Mae West" life preserver.[4]

The Prime Minister continued, in his turn, to send out a flood of messages. Before leaving Argentia he had dispatched to London the final text of the announcement and the joint declaration. Attlee replied that he personally would make the broadcast. On August 13 Churchill thanked the Lord Privy Seal for his "kind message" and expressed delight with arrangements for the announcement. Following the President's wish he asked a "definite break" between the preliminary statement and reading of the joint declaration. No further comment would be necessary "as announcement itself sufficient to fill the newspapers." A certain "guidance" might be given to the press, "but they will surely see the Joint Declaration proposing final destruction of Nazi power and disarmament of aggressive nations while Britain and the United States remained armed is an event of first magnitude." Churchill's conception of the Atlantic Charter is obvious. "It would be well," he continued, "to let this soak in on its own merits on friend and foe." Perhaps he would broadcast to the nation Sunday night (August 17) "when reaction in United States to our meeting and Joint Declaration will be apparent." He was interested and, perhaps, concerned "to know how it is all taken" in England.[5] The radio soon answered this question.

The *Times* reported prominently on August 14 that the Lord Privy Seal was to make "an important announcement today on behalf of the government." It was to be broadcast over the BBC at 3:00 P.M.[6] Intentionally, the British public had only a short time to wonder about the content of the announcement after reading about it in their morning papers. In that marvelous combination of Oxonian and Labour Party accents, Attlee slowly and unemotionally read the statement at the appointed hour. At the same time, of course, Stephen Early was making a similar announcement in Washington.

Announcement came too late in London for most of the evening editions. A small number, which apparently had penetrated Whitehall's security measures, gave some attention to it. The *Evening Standard* wrote that this statement of "previously expressed aims" would awaken new faith in the Allied cause.[7] The *Evening News* and the *Star* emphasized the drama of the meeting, and offered no editorial comment.[8] Friday morning all London newspapers blazoned the news. The *Daily Telegraph* captioned its feature story: "Meeting For Which History Knows No Parallel," and the text compared the conference with the meeting of Napoleon and Czar Alexander on the Niemen. This account, typical of the British reaction, made wild guesses about the conference. "It is rare that an epoch throws up two figures of the first caliber who are so sympathetic in outlook, political instinct, and historic purpose," the *Daily Telegraph* effused. "When they met it was as close friends who see completely eye to eye and whose singleminded concern is to render an already established union of aim and ideals still more productive of practical results."[9] This stretched journalistic license; but it reflected the hope by the British public that its headstrong leader was able to cooperate with the American President.

Other accounts ran the gamut of interpretation. The *Times* gave emphasis to the joint declaration. It stated under a subhead: "America Faces Economic Realities." "Britain and the U.S. United for the Peace," proclaimed the masthead of the *Daily Telegraph*. The *Express,* Beaverbrook's chief organ, gave emphasis to the message to Stalin, a "new deal for the world." The *Daily Mail* concentrated on the Meeting and the fact that the "U.S. war fleet" stood guard. "New Deal for the World" was also the headline of the *Chronicle*. Its page-one column termed the declaration a message of hope, a turning point. The next step for the U.S. was entry; and it inquired, "Is this Mr. Winant's idea?"[10]

The *Daily Herald* was apparently first to describe the joint statement as the Atlantic Charter. In a prominent editorial August 14 there was the phrase, "This is the Atlantic Charter, a prelude to peace aims not a complete statement." [11] The label seemed to capture the purpose of the document. The world press and public took it up. During this "honeymoon" period only the *Daily Sketch* and *Daily Mirror* printed critical or unenthusiastic comments. Asserting that Roosevelt had provided the initiative for the declaration, the *Sketch* insisted that these disappointing terms concealed important commitments. The *Mirror* stressed the message to Stalin and dismissed the declaration as "merely a restatement" of war aims. [12]

In the first days after the news broke, London tabloids devoted most space to speculation about the conference site and arrangements. They complained that the story had been suppressed with greater determination in England than elsewhere. "Churchill's meeting with Roosevelt was the world's best-kept secret in Britain," growled the *Daily Sketch*. "Germany, however, knew it early — but could get no details." [13]

The august *Times* was moderate in praise and in speculation. "Mr. Churchill Meets the President; Joint Declaration of Peace Aims; Freedom From Fear and Want; New Survey of Munitions Supply," announced its banner. The supporting story observed that "the secret of the P.M.'s journey to meet the President at sea has been well kept, though for some days rumor had been busy all over the world." A special editorial, "A Historic Meeting," declared that the conference concerned urgent problems as well as "the principles of a more distant peace settlement." The value of the declaration was "immense," even though it contained nothing not in speeches by British and American statesmen. It cited the four freedoms, Churchill's statements, Eden's Mansion House Address, and the Allied Governments Proclamation of June. Nonetheless the *Times* believed "the world now knows beyond a doubt what we are fighting for and what the enemy is fighting against. No one will call for terms in greater detail. The eight clauses are full enough and they deserve and must receive close study." [14]

On succeeding days the *Times* amplified these statements. On August 16 there appeared an obituary for Sir Arthur Purvis — with a vague explanation that he had been killed in the crash of an Atlantic Ferry Command plane.[15] A *Times* editorial of August 19 commented on the Prime Minister's return to England. "It may be too early to speak of the Atlantic conferences as a turning point in the war. But they hold that promise, and its fulfillment must lie in the decisions and exertions of the coming weeks and months." Not even the exceedingly polite *Times* could refrain from joining the chorus which asked proof of American involvement.[16]

These reactions filtered back to Churchill as *Prince of Wales* approached the midpoint of its journey. Attlee's broadcast was as much news to most of Churchill's staff as it was in Britain and America. If one accepts Morton's account of the reception of the announcement by those aboard the ships, it paralleled that coming from England. "I have since been told," Morton related, "that in clubs, and places where men gathered to hear the broadcast, faces grew long with disappointment as Mr. Attlee proceeded, and the exciting rumours set about by Mr. Churchill's Atlantic journey were all deflated in an atmosphere of anticlimax. Curiously enough, precisely the same scene took place in the wardroom of the *Prince of Wales*. What we had all subconsciously hoped for, and not perhaps entirely subconsciously, was a declaration that America was coming into battle with us; the only thing that seemed to us to justify the dramatic encounter . . . between the two statesmen. In comparison with that, words, no matter how admirable, were a disappointment." Morton gave a moving description of reaction in *Prince of Wales*' wardroom. "We sat looking at one another, remembering the launches going to and from the *Prince of Wales*, the staff meetings, the air of bustle and excitement; and this was all they meant! We were not, of course, statesmen. We knew nothing of the difficulties . . . We knew that, sooner or later, somehow, and in some way, America would come in with us and fight; then we asked ourselves, why not now?" Morton recounted that, when the radio was switched off, a senior officer commented: "Well, I expect there was far more to it than just that!" Someone suggested the conference was "like one of the icebergs encountered in the Atlantic, the largest part of which remains invisible." [17]

The Prime Minister did not confirm, nor did he deny such speculation. He followed a routine similar to that of the trip across — cable writing, ladder climbing, moviegoing. A slight cold and a pulled leg muscle (from clambering up and down the battleship's passageways) cut down his exercise; but Churchill attended almost all the nightly motion pictures. During the voyage the company saw diverse fare. *Ghost Breakers* was presented the first night at sea, and a double feature — *Foxhunting*, with Donald Duck, and *Saps at Sea*, a Laurel and Hardy comedy was shown Wednesday night. On Thursday *Power Dive*, a propaganda-crammed war film was scheduled, and Churchill elected not to attend. Perhaps because he anticipated being wrapped up in monitoring the wireless, nothing was presented on August 15. He did come Saturday for another comedy, *Caught in the Draft*, starring Bob Hope. The last night the company watched *Love Crazy*, a romantic American comedy, "which all liked very much." [18]

The Prime Minister dispatched messages, orders, and memoranda by the dozen. Cables to the King, Menzies (the Prime Minister of Australia), the First Lord of the Admiralty, and Attlee headed the list.[19] The cable to Menzies was to inform the head of a Dominion perilously close to Japanese ambitions of the developments at Argentia, and it therefore bears special importance. Churchill believed the President would give the warning to Japan in the terms agreed upon at Argentia. Then England and the Dominions "should range ourselves beside him" and make clear the solidarity of the British Empire and Commonwealth with the United States. The Dutch and perhaps the Soviets would lend support. "If this combined front can be established, including China, I feel confident that Japan will lie quiet for a while. It is, however, essential to use the firmest language and the strongest combination." [20] There was no disputing Roosevelt's determination to help in the Atlantic, as proved by the decision to institute convoying. Churchill believed the President had mustered a similar determination to deal with the Far East. In the midst of these weighty matters the Prime Minister somehow found time to dash off a message about the new *Lion* class battleships. He was fanatically interested in naval design and had made use of the conference to question Admiral Stark on the *North Carolina* class battleships. When he learned they possessed triple sixteen-inch turrets, a message went to the Admiralty reopening the debate on battleship construction.[21]

During this, thought to be the most dangerous leg of the journey, neither U-boat, Messerschmitt, nor surface units offered a challenge. The great battleship pounded through heavy seas, and low cloud cover shielded her. The flotilla sighted only one fellow traveler, a convoy (HX-173) of seventy-three ships bound for England with Lend-Lease material.[22] The dingy vessels carried Texas oil, Kansas wheat, tanks and armored cars from Detroit, crated aircraft from southern California, and foodstuffs from nearly every state. They were escorted only by eight corvettes, although three merchant ships carried Hurricanes on catapults.[23] Churchill ordered *Prince of Wales* to pass through the convoy. This maneuver, by which the distinctive figure of the Prime Minister was recognized, brought messages from every kind of signaling device on the merchant ships. Churchill asked that *Prince of Wales* reply, giving the convoy his personal best wishes. Since there was no signal for "Prime Minister" in the International Code, an ingenious signal officer put together a flag for church and a flag for hill to spell out "Good Voyage, Churchill." [24] The Prime Minister was so impressed by the sprawling convoy that he had Captain Leach take the battleship through a second time before consenting to a resumption of course. He watched the convoy until dusk and distance overtook his view. "A delectable sight," he said.[25]

Early on August 16, a beautiful, warm day, *Prince of Wales* anchored in Hvalsfiord, Iceland. The Canadian destroyer, *Assiniboine*, transported Churchill's party along the red volcanic rock-strewn inlet to Reykjavik, the capital and largest town with some 30,000 inhabitants. To the surprise of the British garrison, the Prime Minister received a "warm and vociferous welcome" from the Icelanders.[26] He visited the national parliament, the Althingishus, and proceeded to a review of British and American occupation forces. "I took the salute with the President's son standing beside me," Churchill wrote, "and the parade provided another remarkable demonstration of Anglo-American solidarity." [27] First to pass the reviewing stand was a large contingent of United States Marines. "Quite a good-looking body of men in their olive-green khaki with fawn-colored spats and steel helmets." [28] Many British officers missed this ceremony to concentrate on shopping in Reykjavik. Schofield was overjoyed to be able to buy four pounds of butter, which he knew his wife would consider the "most welcome present of all." [29] Jacob and "Jo" Hollis each purchased a large cheese and one of the junior officers found them several pairs of silk stockings. "We carried the cheese rather shamefacedly aboard the destroyer," Jacob confessed, "but were determined to get it home somehow." [30] The Prime Minister finished his tour in late afternoon and returned to the quay to be met by a Guard of Honor and another large crowd. A little girl offered shyly a huge bunch of flowers which Churchill reluctantly accepted and handed to his bodyguard. As the Prime Minister boarded the destroyer, H. V. Morton recalled, "He appeared to be very happy, and behind him, looking oddly bridal, walked Inspector Thompson carrying an enormous bouquet of carnations." [31] *Prince of Wales* had shifted higher up the fiord and now lay at anchor near two battleships, H.M.S. *Ramillies* and U.S.S. *New Mexico*. Churchill boarded *Ramillies* and made a short speech to the crew. As night was falling, "with the sun going down and throwing a pinkish light on all the hills," the British flotilla steamed out of Hvalsfiord for Scapa Flow.[32]

Although the weather soured and the sky darkened, *Prince of Wales* drove ahead steadily at twenty-five knots. The overcast was welcome, as it hid the warships from enemy aircraft and, Jacob commented, "no doubt was a handicap to any submarines which might have been lurking in our path." Early Monday morning, August 18, after a display of target shooting and a photographic session on the forecastle, the great battleship ended its dangerous journey. All ships saluted with their main armament as they passed into the safety of Scapa Flow.[33]

The Prime Minister and party transshipped at once to the mainland and boarded his special train, still waiting at Thurso, for London and return to the war. The trip south was uneventful. Churchill was still bothered by a cold and slept much of the time. Others watched the stark loveliness of the Highlands roll by, and after night fell played bridge and poker to pass the time.[34] Churchill's train pulled into King's Cross Station at 9:30 A.M., Tuesday. A crowd of reporters, officials, and curious commuters was waiting far up the platform. When the Prime Minister stepped from a car near the tail of the train, there was a stampede down to him "with the Press photographers easy winners." [35] An attempt to stage a formal ceremony of greeting proved impossible in the confusion. Churchill posed for photographs alone, with his wife, and with cabinet ministers. In these pictures the Prime Minister's gleaming face radiates confidence and satisfaction. Robert Sherwood has written: "Back in England, Churchill seemed so bursting with confidence — he gave the new 'V for Victory' sign with such exuberant assurance — the British people delightedly assumed, like the American isolationists, that perhaps there *had* been some secret agreements at the Conference, the results of which would become apparent in due course." [36] Winant echoed these sentiments, cabling to President Roosevelt that the Prime Minister "was in great form" at the station.[37] Churchill realized that first impressions were critical if the meeting was to raise British morale, and he put extra effort into the cocksure grin and easy salute for that reason. His happy, relaxed appearance was not pretense. He believed he had achieved most of those aims he had set at departure two weeks before. He could do no more. The initiative rested with Roosevelt and those of his advisers who were waiting in Washington. It was up to the Americans to transform the paper agreements of Argentia into substantial action.

1

The President paid close attention to Churchill's return. Events showed that his own enforced tardiness in coming back to Washington was unnecessary; but it would have been difficult to convince

Roosevelt of that. The vicarious exposure to danger may have given him a sense of involvement in the war. His carefully timed return arose from other reasons as well. Roosevelt desired the bewilderment about his whereabouts to lend mystery and importance to the joint declaration. As noted, only the most necessary information went out and both the American press and official Washington were not entirely sure what was going on until August 14.[38]

A few minutes before 9:00 A.M. on August 14, the press room in the White House had filled with a sleepy, jostling, rather puzzled crowd of newspapermen and network radio technicians. These men were present at what most believed an ungodly early hour to receive a news release from President Franklin D. Roosevelt's press secretary. This genial southerner, Stephen T. Early, had informed press and radio staffers in confidence late the previous night that he would have something of interest. He alerted them to stand by for a release the next morning.[39]

The group answering this summons, now drinking coffee and complaining in the press room, awaited Early's entrance with undisguised eagerness. Stephen Early, who had borne journalistic pressure since Roosevelt abandoned him ten days before, also awaited the hour of his deliverance. He had attempted to relieve some of the pressure by arranging for White House correspondents to move to Swampscott, Massachusetts, where the President was scheduled to come ashore. There they could grouse where Early did not have to listen. This decision had just been carried out when he learned what F.D.R. had been doing.

Sometime during the afternoon of August 12, Early received a cablegram from the President through Navy communications. It confirmed the wildest of the rumors. F.D.R. and Churchill, with high-ranking diplomatic, military and naval officials of the two nations, had been conferring somewhere at sea. Early was to expect an "important statement" which he was to give out "without comment" exactly at 9:00 A.M. EST Thursday. He was to inform the press and radio "in confidence" late Wednesday night that a bulletin was coming. The next paragraph ordered him to read the bulletin to Secre-

tary of State Cordell Hull. Just a few hours after this directive, the
text of the "important statement," which included the Atlantic Charter, came through the naval communications net.[40]

In accord with instructions Early faced at the appointed hour an
assembly of reporters (those who were not at Swampscott) and
broadcasters who were carrying the announcement live to the entire
country. The Press Secretary read the statement in his slow drawl
and then, cuttting off a clamor of questions, indicated the press conference was over. Reporters rushed off to telephones to file the
leads for their stories. They were thankful but hardly surprised that
the timing of the announcement allowed for full coverage in early
afternoon editions.

The scene on *Augusta,* when the broadcast of Early's announce-
ment came, was similar to that far to the east on *Prince of Wales.*
The time of day differed, position of dials on "radio" and "wireless"
was different, as were the voices — Attlee's clipped tones, and
Early's southern drawl — which vibrated through the wardrooms.
Words were the same. But American reaction was more diverse.
Roosevelt and Hopkins were satisfied. Welles less so. Marshall and
Stark did not react as had senior officers on *Prince of Wales,* and may
not have registered opinions. Such matters were the concern of civil
leaders; the declaration did not offer guidance for their immediate
problems.

In contrast with August 13, when *Augusta* and her sister ships had
steamed slowly through dense fog, Thursday was extremely active.
The radio was monitored all day for reaction. Evening radio broad-
casts were excited about the conference, but reaction to the joint
declaration was unenthusiastic. Albert L. Warner, a Washington
news analyst, stated for CBS that interest in these questions "had
already passed a peak," that, coming at this time, the declaration
begged the question. "The question arose some time ago as to
whether such an American and British conference as this would produce a platform of war aims . . . Frequently voices have been
raised in Congress . . . calling upon Britain to tell what kind of a
world it was fighting for. In the last year these demands have not

risen in the same volume. As Hitler extended the scope of the invasion and conquest . . . there was apparently a growing body of opinion which held that the first necessity . . . was to stop him." [41] This evaluation was disappointing, for F.D.R. disliked criticism of his sense of timing. From London, Edward R. Murrow broadcast a similar opinion. There was noticeable lack of enthusiasm in England. "The meeting and the announcement have not caught the public imagination," Murrow said. [42]

Meanwhile, F.D.R. had gone on deck to watch a demonstration of naval air power. Admiral King had made special arrangements for this display the previous day. The U.S.S. *Long Island*, a "converted" aircraft carrier, launched an air strike against hypothetical targets on the coast of Maine. Planes went up by catapult and conventional means. Five returned safely but the sixth, which lost its engaging hook, was directed to a landing field on shore. One doubts whether this demonstration impressed the President. King was disturbed by some aspects and elaborated on them in strong terms to his subordinates, but said nothing to Roosevelt at luncheon. [43]

During or just after lunch *Augusta* anchored in Blue Hill Bay, Maine. *Potomac* and *Calypso*, having finished their diversionary cruise through the Cape Cod Canal, anchored close by. *Potomac* moved alongside the heavy cruiser, and transfer of baggage and other gear began. Accompanied by McIntire, Watson, Beardall and Hopkins, the President crossed to his yacht. Other members of the party left the cruise at this point. Marshall, Stark, and Welles, plus one stenographer, clambered aboard a PBY. The ungainly amphibian flew to Quonset Point, Rhode Island, where the Chief of Staff's plane picked him up along with Welles and the secretary. They landed at National Airport the same day. Stark kept the PBY to make an informal inspection of the Newport area, and did not return to the Navy Department until Sunday or Monday. The naval complement, *Augusta*, *Tuscaloosa* and the destroyers departed southward. King dissolved "Task Force 11" next day. [44]

A few minutes after two o'clock Thursday afternoon *Potomac* and *Calypso* left Blue Hill Bay. The last portion of Roosevelt's epochal voyage truly was a pleasure cruise. F.D.R. ordered several stops in Eggemoggin Reach in search of good angling — but the fish refused to cooperate. Early in the evening the little flotilla dropped anchor for the night in the same stretch of water. No effort was made to conceal the President's presence in the area. In fact, the White House some days later received letters from several irate fishermen, who complained that Roosevelt's yacht had torn their nets during the day's whimsical cruising.[45]

Friday was equally uneventful, given to rest and relaxation. F.D.R. tried his hand once more at fishing with indifferent success. Happily, L. R. Betts of Deer Island, Maine brought a large bucket of lobsters, and this provided the main course at dinner Friday night. F.D.R. wrote to thank Betts next day, saying in tribute to the meal, "It quite surpassed the fine reputation that Maine lobsters have enjoyed so long." [46] By nightfall *Potomac* had moved only as far south as Pulpit Harbor, Maine. The President decided this was a pleasantly obscure berth. He and his shipmates planned to spend the evening going over summaries of American press reaction, and they did not wish to be disturbed.

First reports were disappointing. The mixup over release of the announcement, by which several British newspapers had received the story before the official release, had angered White House reporters. The President could soothe away journalistic pique; however, the tone of the stories was disturbing, as they expressed a view of the conference contrary to that F.D.R. had anticipated. The tenor of press reaction in America was stated concisely in a Los Angeles *Times* headline: "Roosevelt, Churchill Form Entente; Lay Down World Peace Program; Leaders Reach Accord For Crushing Hitler." Its feature story admitted in dark hues of disappointment that "there does not exist any binding commitment beyond possibly the pledged individual word of Mr. Roosevelt and Mr. Churchill." The Los Angeles *Times*, a champion of preparedness and an aggressive foreign policy, found that insufficient and demanded: "Splendid, Mr. President — but what else?" [47] The St. Louis *Post-Dispatch* agreed with the Los Angeles *Times*' conclusion that "there is big stuff in the

background." It asked in a suspicious editorial, "Have we heard all
there is to hear from this . . . declaration? Is a statement of war
aims all the President and the Prime Minister drew up? If they
talked about peace did they not also talk about the war and its conduct? What precisely is the present state of American relations with
the British and their struggle against Hitler? These graver questions
remain unanswered." The *Post-Dispatch* printed a cartoon on the
editorial page which pictured a buoy labeled "8-point declaration"
over the caption, "The largest part of a buoy lies below the
surface." [48]

These suspicions were found in newspapers which offered staunch
support to the administration. The Chicago *Tribune*, bible of the
isolationists, differed with them only in its bluntness and vitupera-
tive language. A banner headline on August 15 proclaimed: "Pact
Pushes U.S. Near War; F.D.R. Alliance With Churchill Rocks Capital." It compared the conference to Tilsit, when Napoleon and Alexander II "met to divide up the world." The Chicago *Tribune* read
English reaction as evidence that Roosevelt was preparing a war
message and that the eight points were merely a cover-up. This
anglophobic paper saw in the meeting conclusive proof of Roosevelt's slavish obedience to the English. An editorial cartoon for August 15, which bore the caption, "Taking On The Pilot," portrayed
the Prime Minister being helped aboard *Augusta* by an obsequious
President Roosevelt. A subsequent story charged: "Information
leaking out of the Roosevelt entourage leaves no doubt that the conference . . . was engineered and managed by the British government from start to finish and that Mr. Roosevelt was merely a necessary instrument to accomplish a very definite purpose." [49] This
amazing piece made the President of the United States seem like an
idiot dupe of a foreign power.

Few "isolationist" newspapers indulged in the Chicago *Tribune's*
brand of character assassination. Some, like the New York *Daily
Mirror,* approached the issue tangentially by questioning the President's wisdom in committing the country to defeat of the Axis before he untangled "the shocking muddle that has hog-tied this na-

tion's defense effort." [50] Although the *Wall Street Journal* avoided name-calling, its lead editorial bluntly asserted: "Mr. Roosevelt has joined . . . in a statement of postwar aims, a performance which has always been the role of an active belligerent and which is bound to raise the question of how we can share in a peace if we do not share in the fighting." [51] It is notable that most newspapers reached similar conclusions. They assumed that the conference and joint declaration placed America at the side of the United Kingdom.

F.D.R. could ignore views such as the New York *Daily News* summation: "We have small doubt that Mr. Roosevelt . . . envisions . . . a world with himself as President of the whole layout and Mr. Churchill as his Prime Minister." The New York *Sun's* judgment that "far more important than the things Mr. Roosevelt and Mr. Churchill actually say are the things about which . . . they are keeping silent" could be written off as isolationist paranoia. Yet the American press generally agreed with the *Sun* and with the opinion of the highly-respected St. Louis *Post-Dispatch* that action of a "decisive nature" was in the offing.[52] Even the *New York Times,* most prestigious and widely quoted newspaper in the country, stressed this side of the conference. Tall black headlines on August 15 set the pattern of *Times'* coverage: "Roosevelt, Churchill Draft 8 Peace Aims Pledging Destruction of Nazi Tyranny." A front-page feature stated that official Washington expected the Atlantic Charter to be followed by "further declarations and actions setting forth definitive Anglo-American policies . . . and making clear the exact extent of Anglo-American cooperation." Also on page one was a piece from the *New York Times'* English correspondent, entitled: "London Expects More From Talks; British Believe Discussion of War Aid, Still Secret, Will Prove Important." This reporter frankly admitted that few people in England believed the Prime Minister had crossed the Atlantic "at great personal risk and inconvenience" to approve such euphemisms as contained in the joint declaration. Rather, "the measure of disappointment apparent in London tonight can perhaps best be judged in the light of what the statement left unsaid." [53]

These sentiments were excluded from the editorial page of the

Times, perhaps from deference to the President's sensitivities. A *Times* editorial writer thought the method chosen to dramatize Anglo-American solidarity was brilliant. "The dictators in their armored trains at the Brenner Pass are dwarfed into actors on a local circuit by this bold encounter on the Atlantic battlefield." [54] Next day Hanson Baldwin put into words what was implied in the editorial. "It is still . . . up to the United States — strategically, militarily, industrially, even psychologically! The burden of any defeat of Germany rests mainly upon us." [55] These were words Roosevelt had hoped to escape after Argentia; but the sum of the flood of verbiage in editorials, news stories, and signed columns was that he had taken the devious route once too often.

The President returned to "civilization" — in the guise of irritated, news-hungry reporters — Saturday, August 16. *Potomac* and *Calypso* swung at anchor in Pulpit Harbor until early Saturday afternoon, while Roosevelt received a flock of callers, mostly old friends of Campobello Island days. Under overcast skies the little fleet then began the final leg of the cruise. It ran through fog and rain squalls during the ten mile jaunt to Rockland, Maine. [56] *Potomac* moored at Tilson's Wharf, Rockland, just after three o'clock P.M. Waiting on the damp, musty dock were some fifty men: newsmen, cameramen, radio announcers, technicians, and "bottleholders." As *Time* described their attitude: "They had been waiting a long time — two weeks at Swampscott, Mass., two days at Rockland, Me. They were angry as a bunch of bears with sore haunches." [57] This was the reception committee for Franklin Roosevelt, who was returning from "the greatest fishing trip that any President of the U.S. had ever undertaken." A press conference had been arranged aboard the yacht and as soon as the wharf slip was cranked up to deck level the horde of "sweating, shoving" newsmen rushed down to the President's quarters. [58] He welcomed them aboard with the casual observation, "Well, all of you got here all right." Roosevelt was on close terms with several of these men — particularly M. E. Hennessy of the Boston *Globe.* After pointing out Harry Hopkins, "just back from Moscow," who was leaning wearily against the wardroom bulkhead, he indicated he was ready for questions. [59]

Responding to the first of these queries — where the conference was held — the President said he could not give that information "for obvious reasons." He laid down guidelines for the press conference. "I had better make one or two things clear in the beginning. Names of ships are out . . . The Prime Minister was there on the *Prince of Wales* and I was there on the *Augusta*, but outside of that, nothing about ships, nothing about times, dates, and nothing about locations. All those for perfectly obvious reasons, which I don't have to explain. Things of that kind cause trouble if you make known the exact location on the high seas of the President and the Prime Minister." He assured the audience there had been no German attacks, perhaps because of foggy weather. "While it's open season out there," he said with careless exaggeration, "no submarine fired a torpedo at us as far as we could see, and we are here safely." [60]

The President gave a summary of the meeting — with stress on the "very remarkable religious service" of Sunday morning, August 10. He confirmed names of other participants. To a question about who was responsible for calling the conference, he replied: "The thing has been talked about since last February, and would have taken place a good deal earlier, had it not been for the campaign in Greece and the campaign in Crete." Desire and suggestion for the conference had been a joint idea.[61] Perhaps he said this to prevent isolationist speculation about motives if either he or Churchill had been identified as the originator.

He refused point-blank to elaborate on the joint declaration. He instructed the reporters to label the meeting "an interchange of views relating to the present and the future — a swapping of information, which was eminently successful." He complained that in commentary about the conference one important purpose had been "overlooked": "the need for an exchange of . . . views relating to what is happening to the world under the Nazi regime, as applied to other nations." The press should emphasize this point of propaganda, for "it's a thing that needs to be brought home to all of the democracies more and more." [62] F.D.R. was not averse to managing the press.

When asked if the press "might assume" that the President and

Churchill had reached an understanding on all aspects of the world situation, "including the Far East," F.D.R. fended the question smoothly. "I don't suppose there is a single section or a single continent that was not discussed at one time or another, in all the conferences you ever heard of." He refused to be drawn into comments about the Far East or the French situation, pleading lack of knowledge because of his enforced isolation. He did say he planned to see Secretary Hull for a briefing shortly after returning to Washington. This did not satisfy one reporter, who asked whether the Roosevelt-Churchill meeting had brought the United States closer to war. F.D.R. replied flatly that, no, it had not — but he refused to antagonize his new friend Churchill by allowing direct quotation of this remark.[63]

Questioners next turned to the effects of the meeting on the Russian situation. Roosevelt admitted that the Soviet Union was not bound to the "eight-point program" and avoided any suggestion that aid to Russia would be contingent. "Nobody suggested it until you did," he said. He indicated he had acquired faith in Soviet powers of resistance, and sharp ears did not miss this note of confidence. The direct query — whether Russian resistance would continue into the winter — brought a typical Roosevelt response. "I guess . . . there is a sort of assumption in there," he said. The President admitted that Lend-Lease would not extend to the Soviet Union at present.

Reporters naturally were interested in the President's plans about further revelations — on the radio or through a message to Congress. F.D.R. replied, only half in jest, "that depends on you fellows . . . If you give the country an exceedingly correct picture, I probably won't go on the radio." The reporters accepted this suggestion with good humor. "You can rely on us, sir," some wag shouted.[64]

Roosevelt refused to make the press conference a platform from which to call for greater sacrifices from America. Questions from his auditors repeatedly invited F.D.R. to describe England's desperate situation as the Prime Minister had presented it to him and then frankly to spell out the actions he had decided to take to rescue the United Kingdom. No grim call to battle was forthcoming. Each time the door opened the President slammed it shut. He demonstrated that he was more concerned about reestablishing good relations with American newspapermen. F.D.R.'s rapport with the working press — especially the White House contingent — was due largely to his frankness and sense of fair play. He bolstered this friendship by an honest description of the conference press arrangements, confessing that unintentionally he had done harm to American coverage. To a question as to whether any Americans had recorded the sights and sounds of Argentia, the President replied,

"I will have to talk off the record — not for use, literally not for use. There is no reason why you fellows shouldn't know. The reason I can't use it is that it would be discourteous. The whole point of the original arrangement was, as you know, secrecy, for perfectly obvious naval reasons, and I didn't take any newspapermen. Neither did I take any cameramen. But when we got there we found that there was a moving-picture man who goes around with Mr. Churchill, and he says he is very different from ours. Mr. Churchill travels with no newspapermen whatsoever, but he does travel with a regular Ministry of Information man . . . and I think he is a Government employee and not a press association, and nearly all the moving pictures that you see of myself and Mr. Churchill were taken by Government men and then given to the press. We found that he had this man who customarily travels with him and I was able to find, from Navy personnel, one or two people who took some pictures which were sent down to Steve and have been released.

On the question of writing, why, I never assumed for a minute that there would be an official historian, and the Ministry of Information in England, at the last minute, had sent two gentlemen who they insisted were not newspaper men, they were people who wrote books. I said, "Good God, I've got a whole lot of people who are not only newspapermen, but have written books too!" If I had known, I would have done it too. So they are two gentlemen who were literary gentlemen. They were told very definitely by me, and they acceded to it, if these two literary gentlemen ever wrote anything over there inside of a year about this conference, that they were to give it to the three American press associations in London, free of charge. That was about the best I could do. If they do write anything, the three press associations will get their stuff . . . . I have protected you the best I could, having been taken by surprise.

I think on the three press associations, there is no particular reason
why you shouldn't let your London offices know that you are aware of
the fact that there were two literary gentlemen who were put on board
by the British Ministry of Information, and that they have agreed with
me that any release from the pens of either of those gentlemen goes to
our three press associations. I couldn't think of any better way to cover
it. I can't say *"Mea culpa,"* because it was the other fellow's *"culpa."* [65]

The press accepted this appealing if sophistical explanation. During the next few days irritation evaporated as supplementary information about the conference was diverted to Americans. Newspapers in the United States even achieved a belated scoop when Navy pictures were flown down to New York and the British had to beg for copies.[66] The President's promise that recompense would be made eased the atmosphere. The reporters filed out happily when the President indicated the conference was at an end and trooped back to the wharf to phone their stories. F.D.R. had instructed William D. Hassett to hold the train for thirty minutes so they could file. News photographers used this interlude to take still and moving pictures of the smiling, bronzed President on the upper deck of his yacht. There had been for this photogenic President a long drought of such pictures. F.D.R. and his staff left *Potomac* at 4:00 P.M. for the brief trip across town to the railroad station. "Comparatively large crowds" lined the streets along his route and he responded breezily to their applause.[67]

The train pulled out of Rockland station at 4:30 P.M. en route to Washington. Roosevelt, Hopkins, McIntire, Beardall, Hassett, and most of the newsmen were on board. Adlai Stevenson, Special Assistant to the Secretary of the Navy, met the train at Portland for a short conference with Roosevelt on shipbuilding problems. The train arrived at Union Station, Washington, exactly on the dot, 10:30 A.M., EST. A small crowd of onlookers, including the Secretary of State, was present. Pausing only for a few pictures, the presidential party, joined by Hull, entered limousines for the short drive to the White House.[68]

XII. The Aftermath

THE PRESIDENT'S ARRIVAL IN WASHINGTON, to be attended at the train by Cordell Hull, the deliberate, dignified Secretary of State, was in a way anticlimactic. His safe return ended a period without precedent of personal, secret diplomacy. For ten days the President of the United States had absented himself from public view, his whereabouts unknown, his intentions a mystery, to fulfill a unique and dangerous mission. Only F.D.R., one is inclined to think, could have carried it off; yet the President was denied an opportunity to relax, to savor the country's shocked admiration as the extent of his daring became known.

Sea- and sun-bronzed, more relaxed than the infuriated White House staff had found him for many months, the President immediately was caught up in duties. Reports of ominous Soviet reverses in the Caucasus were handed him as he entered the White House. Hull undoubtedly summarized the most recent Anglo-Russian warning to Iran, and discussed the British claim that 3000 German "tourists" had been spotted in Teheran. Awaiting F.D.R.'s signature was the draft extension bill, passed with such difficulty on August 12. There was even a labor dispute to complicate this homecoming. Four federal agencies, he was informed, had recommended that the President authorize seizure of the huge Kearny, N.J., shipyard.[1]

No hiatus was to follow the meeting at Argentia. Actions taken there added their weight — great or infinitesimal — to the momentum of events. F.D.R. might hope as he had on an earlier occasion that the nation would "take time out . . . and compare past attitudes with present needs; to compare the pronouncements of a year ago with trends today."[2] If so, it was in vain, for the aftermath of

Argentia afforded neither him nor the country time for contemplation.

During the next two weeks certain of the decisions were carried to conclusion. Others were modified under pressure from colleagues. Still other problems for which solutions appeared necessary at the time of Argentia were allowed to drift because reasons for immediate steps to resolve them disappeared. The meeting even generated difficulties which no one had anticipated.

Secretary Hull's first words to the President regarded problems from the conference. Hull had been deeply wounded by the decisions concerning Far Eastern policy and trade liberalization, decisions he had learned only upon Sumner Welles' return — the previous Thursday. Embittered by his subordinate's apparent perfidy, Hull later poured out his feelings to Breckinridge Long. Had he been asked to select a Department of State representative, he said, he would have named the Under Secretary; "but he resented not being asked for suggestions and being kept in the dark about it all — and he was mad that the incident should have come close to wrecking his work for settlement." [3] He confessed that Welles' constant contacts with the President were upsetting to him and, more important, to his wife. Hull accused his Under Secretary of publicity-seeking and of openly challenging his position. On one occasion, he recounted, he had informed Welles of some new development, and the man "could hardly wait to get out of my room to rush over there and tell him [the President] something important. Of course I did not interpose an objection when he displayed such anxiety to do it." [4] It appears that Hull held his emotions in check during the Sunday interview with President Roosevelt; but his forebearance did not extend to his much-maligned Under Secretary. Indeed, personal antagonism between Hull and Welles exerted great influence on policy toward Japan.

During the flight from Portland, Maine, on August 15, Welles likely thought of the ordeal which lay before him. He expected that Hull would object to some parts of the joint declaration, but he could hope the Secretary would come to understand that Welles was not at fault, that he had upheld the Department's policy until over-ruled. The proposed warning to Japan, a matter of much greater immediate importance, was also not easily explained. Welles was the bearer of this agreement to issue an ultimatum to Japan, and the Secretary of State, he realized, would link his subordinate with the message, whatever Welles might say.

The draft statement which Welles carried away from his final meeting with Sir Alexander Cadogan, and which he had rewritten during the flight to Washington, was to be the source of much con-troversy. Much of it was historical review of Japanese-American re-lations, but the crucial last paragraph read,

> The Government of the United States, therefore, finds it necessary to state to the Government of Japan that if the Japanese Government undertakes any further steps in pursuance of the policy of military domination through force or conquest in the Pacific region upon which it has apparently embarked the United States Government will be forced to take immediately any and all steps of whatsoever character it deems necessary in its own security notwithstanding the possibility that such further steps on its part may result in conflict between the two countries.[5]

The most notable aspect of the message is its moderation. Welles had attempted to ameliorate the ominous final paragraph by devot-ing most of the statement to renewal of negotiations, one of Hull's projects.

The Secretary of State reacted predictably on receiving the state-ment. He feared the last sentence would destroy any hope of peace. It would result in war at a time when the United States was entirely unprepared for war. "Hull and his staff," Herbert Feis has written, "looked over this sea-born statement with a worried gaze, with a sense that the President, away, had forgotten the divisions at home." [6] At an emergency meeting in Hull's office the Secretary, Jo-seph W. Ballantine, Stanley K. Hornbeck, and Welles examined the draft statement. His advisers concurred with the Secretary's reaction that the draft "needed toning down." [7] Any revision had to be with care, for Welles pointed out that the President had promised that "the American and British Governments would both say to the Japanese substantially what appeared in the last paragraph of that draft." Coming from Welles, cautionary words had no effect. Hull said that he was alarmed by what might follow the statement in its present form. He brought up "for discussion" the nature of United States action should the Japanese accept the "dare" embodied in the declaration.[8]

Emasculation of strong declarations was the kind of challenge to which the Department of State responded eagerly. Machinery for the operation began to move on Friday afternoon, August 15, and ground away Friday night, Saturday, and Sunday morning. On each day there was "discussion and drafting and redrafting."[9] It was decided to "recommend" to the President that he give the Japanese Ambassador two documents. One would contain a statement "designed to make it unmistakably clear . . . although in a manner which could not well be exploited by the extremists in Japan . . . that we could not be expected to remain passive in the presence of a continued expansion of Japanese aggression."[10] This classic example of "State Departmentese" offered only the vaguest suggestion of military action by the United States.

The second document, in the guise of a formal note, then listed the conditions "in a more expanded form than contained in the draft brought back by Mr. Welles" for resumption of conversations. Hull liked the method of two communications, "one which would contain a warning and the other in the nature of an olive branch."[11]

By Saturday afternoon the drafters and redrafters had drawn up what they hoped was an acceptable emendation of the Roosevelt-Churchill declaration. Marked "final" and "long warning" and dated August 16, this document reposes with other discarded compromises in the National Archives.[12] If it differed from Welles' draft in purpose, the language was markedly similar. For the original phrase in paragraph one, "concur in a joint declaration," the Saturday version had: the United States — speaking for itself — "makes a binding and solemn declaration." In the same paragraph Department editors took out another "joint," which had escaped the President's scrutiny.

In place of "threats of force in the Pacific" in the sixth paragraph, there was American opposition "to threats of force of Japanese control of areas outside the Japanese Empire." The warning was expanded and diluted. The last and most important paragraph was changed to remove open reference to possible military conflict. It then read: "If the Japanese Government takes any further steps in pursuance of a policy or program of military domination by force or threat of force of neighboring areas of the Pacific, including the mainland of Asia, the Government of the United States will be forced to take immediately any and all steps of whatsoever character it may deem necessary in its own security." [13] Hull found this version still unacceptable. The concluding paragraph was "too strong" and still threatened war. He demanded another draft.[14]

Ballantine was responsible for the final wording of the oral warning. Only unimportant problems were encountered in writing the "olive branch" message. On Sunday morning final touches were put on both statements and Ballantine took them to Hull's apartment for approval. A few minor objections about phraseology were settled, the two drafts were "approved and adopted" by the Secretary, and tucked away in his briefcase.[15] He took them along to Union Station and, as soon as the party arrived at the White House, showed them to the President.

Roosevelt had not known the Department of State was taking liberties with his commitment to Churchill.[16] He had only a short time to examine the statements before Ambassador Nomura arrived for a 4:30 appointment. If F.D.R. was disturbed by the tone of the revised message, actually two messages now, he did not show it. Perhaps he did not realize how much the statements differed from Welles' draft. He had not seen the Under Secretary's explication and had not paid close attention to Welles' and Cadogan's conversations. Yet he must have noticed the discrepancies in language and intent.

One must conclude that for once F.D.R. was satisfied with his Department of State's timid ways. The new communication contained almost nothing of the American military commitment for which the Prime Minister had campaigned; and Roosevelt was relieved it did not. The circumstances provided a perfect excuse to postpone the confrontation with Japan. He could claim that the Department of State had tied his hands.

F.D.R. was most affable when Ambassador Nomura was shown in, precisely at 4:30 P.M. Feeling that Nomura, a retired naval officer, would be interested in his excursion, he began by saying that "he had spent some days enjoying life at sea . . . that sailing was fine, and little fog had been encountered to mar the pleasure of the voyage." Adopting a more serious mien, Roosevelt introduced the business of the meeting. According to Nomura, he said that "the Secretary of State, you, and I are continuing our efforts to bring about peace in the Pacific, but no one else is." The Ambassador replied cagily: "There are many among the third powers who desire war in the Pacific." Roosevelt agreed, identifying the United States, Britain, "and probably the Soviet too," as nations which desired peace. He attempted a feeble joke about "our German friend" and his interference in the Far East, but the sally brought no response.[17]

F.D.R. continued in his best folksy manner that "neither you, the Secretary, nor I have come up through the diplomatic ranks and, therefore, do not observe diplomatic conventions." The document he was presenting was not a formal note or *aide mémoire*, "but is merely what we want to say." The President read the statement. Nomura immediately understood that this oral communication was clearly not an ultimatum. The section which reviewed Japanese iniquities and America's patient response followed the Welles draft. The critical last paragraph had shriveled to near invisibility. "This Government," Roosevelt concluded, "now finds it necessary to say to the Government of Japan that if the Japanese Government takes any further steps in pursuance of a policy or program of military aggression by force or threat of force of neighboring countries, the Government of the United States will be compelled to take immediately any and all steps which it may deem necessary toward safeguarding the legitimate rights and interests of the United States and American nationals and toward insuring the safety and security of the United States." [18] The journey to this conclusion had been long and arduous.

The President realized that what he had just read would not deter the Japanese. A statement that the United States would protect its nationals and insure American safety and security was in no sense an ultimatum.[19] It was sufficiently vague as to raise doubts, and might result in a useful, if temporary, pause. Hull agreed wholeheartedly.

There remained the Japanese reaction. F.D.R. had attempted to gain a preview by pumping Admiral Nomura. Asked about the "situation," the Ambassador read a note which stressed Japan's desire for good relations and revived Premier Konoye's project of a meeting with the President. Nomura said Japan had "every confidence" in the President's "exemplary statesmanship and . . . ability to settle matters."[20] F.D.R. displayed considerable interest in a meeting with Prince Konoye. "Geographically speaking," he said, "it is impossible for me to go to Honolulu. I am not permitted to travel in an airplane." The Premier might come to Washington or he and Konoye could meet at Seattle or Juneau. Nomura received the impression that the President was considering the project.[21]

Ambassador Nomura was greatly encouraged by the friendly atmosphere of the interview. Before ending the talk Roosevelt did state, "It is not that I welcome the 'closed door' such as we have today, but, since we have been forced to it by Japan's actions, there is only one country that can open the door. This time it's Japan's turn." Nomura was made to understand that Roosevelt's request to see him before anyone else except the Secretary of State underlined the "graveness" with which the President viewed the situation. Yet also he detected encouraging signs. Roosevelt interrupted himself to provide a softening gloss of certain points during his reading. Nomura concluded that the written note "seemed to contain much that was the President's own attitude and opinion"; and he remarked with some satisfaction that Secretary Hull had urged him to call at any time.[22]

Nomura's observations went into the diplomatic bag along with translations of the two messages. The reaction in Tokyo on receiving these communications was relief. The Roosevelt-Churchill meeting might have brought disaster. Undoubtedly, the democratic leaders had arranged to strengthen their forces in the Pacific, and a secret alliance against Japan could not be ruled out; but no open challenge to Japan's status had resulted. Nomura was convinced that the Prime Minister of Great Britain had not been able to draw America into the European conflict by "a Japanese-American war started at the back door." [23]

Tokyo realized the oral statement was open to fearful interpretation, but at least Japanese and American diplomats would talk again. Dimming hopes of settlement meanwhile would not blink out. Probably Konoye and his fellows were as fatalistic about war as was the Roosevelt administration. The aftermath of Argentia did nothing to persuade Japanese leaders their confident course led to national suicide.

A meeting of Roosevelt and Konoye was considered for several weeks more, but never passed the stage of discussion. F.D.R. refused to give a definite answer and most of his advisers, Hull being the foremost, were adamantly opposed. The project, in fact, was illusory, for each side misunderstood the other. "Konoye and his circle were . . . measuring each degree of warmth and coolness shown by the President. He and Toyoda . . . were resting their hopes on the belief that the President's 'statesmanlike way' would prevail over Hull's 'theoretical diplomacy.'" [24] Washington made parallel assumptions regarding Konoye's control over policy.

What might have occurred if F.D.R. had delivered the warning the Prime Minister had written out for him is impossible to say. A Japanese-American clash could have occurred some months earlier, an attack which would have found the United States more unready than at Pearl Harbor. Perhaps proof of American determination would have halted Japan, perhaps an "ultimatum" in August, 1941, would have given force to the doomsayings of liberals in Japan and averted the cataclysm. Most authorities, however, agree that conflict was inevitable after July, unless one side reversed course. [25]

In any case, on August 18 Hull drafted and the President approved a message to Churchill which explained their interview with Nomura. [26] In no sense was this cable an apology for failure to deliver a harsh warning to Japan. Hull had the President say: "On

August 17 I sent for the Japanese Ambassador and the Secretary of State and I received him. I made to him a statement . . . along the lines of the proposed statement such as you and I had discussed. The statement I made to him was no less vigorous than and was substantially similar to the statement we had discussed." [27] This distortion of the Argentia agreement must have enraged Churchill, but he assigned the blame to the old women at State. He would have been even angrier had he known of Roosevelt's easy acceptance of the revisions.

Forced to accept F.D.R.'s feeble statement to Japan, the Prime Minister persuaded himself — and attempted to convince the British people — that at Argentia he had gained the assurance, "more important than any words," that a Japanese move against British or Dutch possessions would bring the U.S. into the fight.[28]

1

Secretary of State Hull was not as successful in rewriting Argentia's patchwork agreement dealing with trade policy, the fourth point of the Atlantic Charter. The Secretary of State's reaction to this section of the joint declaration was profanely unfavorable. Embittered about Welles' role, Hull deduced that the Under Secretary and the President had sold out the program closest to his heart. They had allowed the British, by the hypocritical qualification in Article IV, to betray the trade liberalization program to which he had dedicated his life. "There can be no doubt whatever," Langer and Gleason have written, "that Article IV was a great blow to the Secretary, whose health in general left much to be desired. A full month later one of his associates found him discouraged and resentful over what had happened, very tired and without fight." [29] In retrospect, this emotional commitment to free trade and faith in its benefits seems naïve, but in 1941 not just Hull but almost all American diplomats viewed it as a universal panacea.

Hull's perturbation increased with each question by reporters about Article IV. Their cynicism strengthened his belief that a vital American position had been surrendered.[30] The declaration could not be withdrawn but the Secretary resolved to repair its weakest point. As soon as the President returned, the Secretary confronted him with a list of necessary improvements. They were delivered, if not with recriminations, then certainly with reproachful looks. Hull indicated his displeasure at the Sunday conference, and next day F.D.R. received a memorandum of the Department's objections.[31] The Secretary insisted some "clarifying statement" was essential. Roosevelt, who had convinced himself at Argentia that he could smooth things over, discovered that on this issue the Secretary was unaffected by words. The result was permission for Hull to renew the campaign for a British commitment on postwar economic policy.

After brooding about the perfidious act for a week, Hull dispatched a cable to Ambassador Winant, which ominously began: "The press in London and here seems uncertain about the meaning of the words 'with due respect for their existing obligations.' . . . One interpretation is that these words mean that the Ottawa agreements and the American tariffs are to remain unchanged." He insisted that such a gloss was intolerable. "Indeed, unless the right sort of official interpretation is immediately given wide publicity, the whole purpose, especially of this portion of the joint statement itself, may be defeated." He suggested that release of an "explanation" of Article IV "would meet the requirements of the situation," and included such a statement. This proposed release, of course, bound Great Britain to postwar "reduction of trade barriers and . . . elimination of preferences and discriminations." [32] Hull was prepared to issue his statement with or without British approval. He instructed Winant "to take the matter up" with the Prime Minister but only for his information. He hoped Churchill would provide a parallel explanation; but it did not matter, for "the President has seen and approved this telegram." [33]

The proof of presidential support impressed Winant; but as the representative on the ground he knew the message was explosive, and he believed Anglo-American harmony of far greater importance than any idealistic promise. Four days after he received Hull's blockbuster Winant reported he had discussed the matter with both

Churchill and Eden. The Prime Minister had expressed sympathy with the "underlying principles" of the statement but insisted he needed time to consult with the Cabinet.[34]

Hull consented to withhold release and thus gave Winant time to cable a full explanation of the British position. Winant's chief fear was that a public debate in Parliament on a postwar issue involving the United States would get out of control. What he termed "the growing restlessness" in England, which arose from Churchill's failure to produce an American declaration of war, might find voice in criticism of the U.S. for its gall in demanding postwar concessions while refusing itself to take part in the war. "A lot of people here would like to get on with the war and they are beginning to feel that we are slow about coming in," Winant said. "A debate in the Parliament which might be critical of the United States could not lift opinion at home."[35] He asked the Secretary of State to postpone the statement until a calmer opinion prevailed in England.

Hull had to recognize the weight of this argument.[36] He dropped the project — but not without a show of disappointment and poorly concealed anger. He insisted that Winant take the first opportunity "and every suitable occasion that may present itself in the future" to press for a trade liberalization agreement.[37] Obviously, his failure to use the Charter as a vehicle for the program did not spell the end of the endeavor. The Department returned to pressing upon the British its version of the Master Lend-Lease Agreement.

2

Military leaders were also using the transatlantic cable to deliver stern lectures to the British. The gist of their messages was bluntly: you had better agree to fight the war our way or you may not win at all. Of course, the apparent solidity of this position was deceiving, for U.S. military authorities were as divided among themselves regarding strategy for winning the war as were American and British diplomats with regard to policy for preventing future wars.[38]

Marshall, Stark, and their staffs engaged in exhaustive debate about the proper strategy for the United States during and after the return from Argentia. They had an opportunity to argue this question without White House intervention since military and naval figures returned to Washington several days before the President. Secretary Stimson noted in his diary on Thursday night that the men who had been at the Atlantic Conference "began to drift in. The first one that came in to me was General Arnold — very furtively, without letting anyone know he was there. He came into my room and I kept him for about an hour, or a half hour, telling me about the high points of the situation as far as the air force was concerned." [39] Marshall, who was unfailingly courteous, telephoned the Secretary to give notice of his return. He received an invitation to come out to Stimson's house, "Woodley," after dinner Thursday night, and he and Stimson sat out on the lawn under the trees while Marshall recounted his adventures. These interviews convinced Stimson the meeting had been useful. He thought the Atlantic Charter would "do good," but feared the President might be using noble words to avoid a strong stance. "If it is not followed by action, which is what most people are thinking about, it will not do much good," he said. From Arnold and Marshall the Secretary learned that the "practical" British wanted action, and were ignorant "of how far the cupboard was bare" with regard to production and training of American forces. "All they want now is great big 4-engine bombers, regardless of the fact that we are behind in the bombers mainly because they knocked them so hard in the beginning." He was resentful that the British, who had taken so many airplanes from the Army Air Corps, dared ask for more.[40] Still, to his subordinates' relief, the Secretary accepted the fact of the conference and the decisions reached. Arnold and Marshall expressed belief that the meeting had been "well-worthwhile" and that the chance to talk to British military authorities, hopefully to reach a "meeting of the minds," was important. The Army Air Corps chief said he believed that British and American delegates had reached agreement upon six questions: aid to Russia; seizure of the Azores; reinforcement of the Philippines; "handling of Japan" if she moved further southward; Iceland's defense; occupation of the Canaries and Cape Verdes. He thought differences remained only about the response to possible German penetration of North and West Africa.[41]

Marshall was hardly as optimistic about the "pluses" from the meeting, and he added one unresolved difficulty which Arnold had failed to mention. This was the conflict over grand strategy — the dependence of Britain on strategic bombing, as opposed to the American belief that a mass confrontation of armies was necessary. The Chief of Staff could not know that the strategic conflict uncovered at Argentia was to remain between the two nations all through the war.[42] If American representatives failed to make clear at Argentia their doubts regarding British strategy, their official commentary, sent to London on September 25, erased all doubt. Marshall submitted the British paper to the War Plans Division as soon as he returned to his office. This group unanimously opposed the British argument. Their memoranda, and parallel responses by the Navy planning staff were the basis of the Joint Board's reply, signed by both Marshall and Stark, and flatly stating that the strategic decisions of ABC-1 were correct. It rejected the whole theory of strategic air power. The proposal for a land offensive only after naval and air offensives should have beaten down German resistance was unacceptable. The covering letter scolded the British for their heresy. "It should be recognized as an almost invariable rule that wars cannot be finally won without the use of land armies." The Joint Board also rejected the British appeal for American intervention. "Involvement of United States Army forces," the letter stated, "would at best involve a piecemeal and indecisive commitment of forces against a superior enemy under unfavorable logistic conditions."[43] This did not entirely preclude naval or air forces.

The Joint Board response demonstrated also the differences between American military and naval strategists. Both supported the primacy of the European theater; both opposed acts in the Pacific which might lead to war with Japan. But in late summer and early autumn they disagreed about when to enter the war and what to do once American participation was a fact.[44] Stark and most of his advisers desired swift intervention. They believed that Germany's preoccupation with Russia offered opportunity for the Allies to win the battle of the Atlantic and ultimate victory. Army planners, however, wished to use the breathing space to build American forces for an invasion in 1942 or 1943. This conflict was clear in the pages of the "Joint Board Estimate of United States Overall Production Requirements" — the so-called Victory Program presented to the President on September 11. The report assumed America would take part in the war. It was "out of the question" for the United States and its allies in the near future to launch a sustained land offensive. Other methods must be used — economic blockade, attacks on "distant regions" of the Axis empire, air and sea strikes against Germany, and subversive activities. Similar techniques could be applied against Japan.[45]

The Army saw these measures as expedients; the Navy apparently regarded them as sufficient to bring about an Axis collapse. Because the Army view, masterfully carried forward by Marshall, was realized in *Operation Overlord*, one is tempted to think of it as the majority opinion. That may have been not at all accurate in September, 1941, or for some time thereafter. In the "minority" were the British, the U.S. Navy, and apparently Franklin D. Roosevelt. The President had sympathy for a strategy of air and sea power. At the time he was a convert to strategic bombing; he refused to accept the prospect of ordering millions of Americans to fight and die on European soil. Preference for the "minority view," first revealed at Argentia, may be the cause of his suggestion in September, at the height of the controversy, that the Army reduce its ground forces.[46] Stunned Army leaders bitterly attributed Roosevelt's proposal to continuing British preachings about air power.[47]

The British Chiefs of Staff woud have pleaded not guilty. They may have known the Prime Minister was writing to President Roosevelt about the unlimited vistas opened by strategic air power.[48] Dill, Pound, and Freeman stayed clear, fearing further to antagonize the Americans. Having shared impressions about the conference during the homeward voyage, they had concluded that the U.S. Chiefs had been, if anything, less generous with aid than at any time during the previous year: The Joint Board's reaction to their strategic review merely confirmed earlier estimates of the American position.[49] The night the conference ended Colonel Jacob commented, "The only unsatisfactory feature of the whole business has been the realization that neither the American Navy nor the Army go much on the heavy bomber." Each service was too immersed in immediate problems, the Navy needing patrol planes for reconnaissance and convoy protection, the Army selfishly holding back planes for the Air Corps, "to realize the value of a really heavy and sustained aerial offensive on Germany."[50] A week later Jacob expressed the second lesson pounded home to the British Chiefs of Argentia. The Americans were militarily and psychologically unprepared to come in. "The general opinion in our party would be that the Americans have a long way to go before they can play any decisive part in the war," he wrote. "Their Navy is further along . . . both in thought and in resources. Both are standing like a reluctant bather on the brink, but the Navy are being forced to dip a toe at a time into the shark-infested water. Their ideas, however, have not yet got beyond how to avoid being bitten; they have not yet reached out to thoughts of how to get rid of the shark."[51] Had they read this assessment American military authorities would have been forced to admit it was a fair statement of their position. Indeed, they would have been overjoyed to see evidence that the British had gained a degree of understanding about the U.S. Army and Navy positions.

In spite of the above one must conclude that the staff conversations at Argentia were of limited significance. They were exploratory and, as events revealed, conditional; yet to say, as did Robert Sherwood, that "the only development of really lasting importance . . . was beginning of the friendship between Marshall and Dill" is misleading.[52] U.S. forces did not go to combat in Europe, Army Air Corps bombers flown by American crews were not sent into action, the Pacific Fleet did not sail to Singapore; but absence of decision can be a kind of commitment.

✻

3

In the aftermath of Argentia, American military leaders were preoccupied with directing the rapid expansion and reorganization of
the armed forces which the draft extension made possible. British
manpower and resources were stretched to the limit in the desperate
struggle for Egypt and the Near East. Both sides, therefore, were
probably relieved that those military operations in the Atlantic
which had been the subject of so much discussion at the conference
were not carried forward. Certain of these problems still were being
debated two years later. Occupation of the Azores did not take
place as planned in autumn, 1941; the project was not resolved as
late as May, 1943.[53] A similar fate encompassed the two leaders'
deliberations about Vichy France. With the exception of convoy escort, postponement and gradual extinction was the fate of all the
bold measures F.D.R. and Churchill proposed for the Atlantic.

These schemes had depended on German encroachment — into
North Africa, Iberia, the Atlantic Islands. Roosevelt and Churchill
miscalculated badly in assuming that a meeting of his two greatest
democratic opponents would cause the Führer to speed up such
movements. During this period Hitler's attention was on the Eastern
front and not on minor annoyances England and the United States
might arrange. He believed the war against Russia was reaching its
triumphant climax, which would force the democracies into a Ger-
man-dictated peace. When, even before Argentia, German observers informed Berlin that measures such as occupation of the Azores
and Canaries should be expected, the German government failed to
register much interest.[54]

Indifference marked German and Italian reaction to the meeting
and to the Atlantic Charter. Hitler's regime interpreted it as part of a
propaganda campaign to seed dissension among the conquered peoples of Europe. Nazi leaders claimed the meeting was a confession
of weakness, of Roosevelt's and Churchill's inability to launch military operations against occupied Europe. Von Ribbentrop asserted
in a "Brief for the Führer" that Churchill had demanded "early

entry" of America in the war and that the President "evidently" spurned the entreaty. Lack of "really positive results" had led to Roosevelt and Churchill "beating the propaganda drum." The projected meeting in Moscow was another propaganda trick. "Undoubtedly Roosevelt's policy at present lacks any real basis of power," von Ribbentrop concluded.[55]

Hitler and Mussolini referred to the conference only in passing during their conversations a week later at Hitler's field headquarters. The Duce did observe that the "Potomac meeting" had resulted in a plunge of Roosevelt's political stock; but, he said, "however that might be, the attitude of the United States was now clear enough and, as matters stood, it was preferable to avoid any useless polemics." Hitler dismissed the conference with a few sarcastic remarks. After a detailed analysis of "the Jewish clique" which surrounded Roosevelt and exploited the American people, the Führer said passionately: "I would not for anything live in a country like the United States, which had a concept of life inspired by the most vulgar commercialism and had no feeling for any of the most sublime expressions of the human spirit, such as music." [56] Someday, perhaps, he would turn to purification of the Western Hemisphere. There was no urgency, for a thousand-year Reich could not be created in a day.

One must not overemphasize the exploratory side of the meeting. It was more a time for debating alternatives than for decision, but the conference did have results. One was the three-power supply conference. From talks with Stalin, Hopkins had returned as a powerful advocate of this project. Western diplomats in Moscow cabled support for such a meeting, while *Prince of Wales* was in mid-ocean. It offered a means of penetrating the secrecy surrounding Russia's military situation. A meeting of this type also forced the United States and the United Kingdom to make decisions about production and distribution.

Their joint message to Stalin arrived in Moscow on August 13. Texts received by Steinhardt and the British Ambassador, Sir Stafford Cripps, differed in wording and sequence. Cripps' version arrived garbled and Steinhardt was unable to read his because the Department of State had used a code not available to the Moscow Embassy. Finally the Embassy staffs worked out a compromise text, and the two diplomats presented the statement to Stalin at 6:00 P.M., August 15.[57] The Russian Premier scanned the message intently and immediately asked the American and British Ambassadors to transmit his great appreciation "for the readiness of President Roosevelt and Prime Minister Churchill to render help to the Soviet Union in its war of freedom against Hitlerism." He was ready to arrange a meeting of American, British, and Soviet representatives to study the supply situation.[58]

Without consulting anyone Stalin dictated a full reply, copies were made and handed to Steinhardt and Cripps, and they were informed this constituted the text "of a communiqué to be issued by the Soviet Government as nearly simultaneously as possible." The conference would begin as soon as American and British delegates could go to Moscow.[59] Steinhardt added the humorous observation that "at the last moment, with a smile, he [Stalin] changed his signature from Comrade Stalin to Mr. Stalin." [60] In his report of this interview the American Ambassador expressed his belief that the Russians would hold out, and this bolstered Roosevelt's opinion. The President, Langer and Gleason have commented, "evidently felt confident enough about the situation to publish the joint message to Stalin, which was released on August 16." [61] He expressed his faith in Soviet powers of resistance at the Rockland press conference, and three days later reiterated this opinion to Congressional leaders. Of this development Raymond Dawson has written that "in brief, aid to Soviet Russia had ceased to be a temporary expedient and had become a long-term project." [62] Notably, F.D.R. stayed with the policy in spite of the anathema it called forth from the isolationists.

4

President Roosevelt watched these developments with interest and took an active part in preparations for the supply conference, convoying, and in the debate over military policy. Whatever else the meeting had achieved, it allowed F.D.R. to shake off the lethargy and dispiritedness which had gripped him. He worked hard all week before going up to Hyde Park for several days. He even carried out social obligations, a tea for the Duke of Kent, receptions for Beaverbrook and others, which had been shunted aside during the period of isolation. Associates believed he had regained energy and confidence. On a visit to the White House on August 27, Breckinridge Long found him "keen, well, and in high spirits." [63] If the return to his old form lasted, Long and others decided, the meeting with Churchill would go down as a great event. The focus of Roosevelt's attention in the weeks following Argentia showed, however, that resurrection of the aggressively confident image did not mean that he had determined upon comparably bold action. He worked hard not to prepare the country for war but rather to exploit the conference to gain a measure of support which would permit intervention without full commitment.

In spite of slurs by isolationists (and because of their potency), F.D.R. maintained the line of interpretation he had established at the press conference aboard *Potomac*. He worked to shore up weaknesses in his glittering propaganda victory, the Atlantic Charter. This was difficult, particularly because of embarrassing statements originating in London. Attempts to push acceptance of the view that the meeting had not resulted in secret agreements and did not move the United States to the brink of war were not aided by loud hints to the contrary by British officials.

The immediate reaction of English newspapers that important commitments had been made at Argentia was given support after Churchill's return by "high officials" of the government. Roosevelt suspected that the Prime Minister himself was firing this awkward speculation. He soon had proof. Even though his contemplated Anglo-American-Dutch warning was now impossible, the Prime Minister decided to proceed with a radio broadcast over the BBC on August 24. England would follow the American lead "when and if Japan took further violent action and Roosevelt made known his policy"; but Churchill never found a passive stance congenial.[64] If he could not align his country with a presidential ultimatum to Japan, the Prime Minister could reassure his countrymen that America was on the march toward full intervention.

His broadcast revealed Churchill at oratorical best. He began by describing the meeting, held "in a spacious, landlocked bay," as the first mobilization of the forces of good against evil. The prime importance of the conference was symbolism, expression of "the deep underlying unities which stir and at decisive moments rule the English-speaking peoples throughout the world." The Argentia meeting marked "for ever in the pages of history" acceptance by the English-speaking nations "of guidance of the fortunes of the broad toiling masses in all the continents." After he had labeled Hitler's "methodical, merciless butchery" in Eastern Europe "a crime without a name," the Prime Minister turned to evil on the other side of the world:

> For five long years the Japanese military factions, seeking to emulate the style of Hitler and Mussolini . . . have been invading and harrying the five hundred million inhabitants of China. . . . Now they stretch a grasping hand into the southern seas of China; they snatch Indo-China from the wretched Vichy French; they menace . . . Siam; menace Singapore, the British link with Australasia; and menace the Philippine Islands under the protection of the United States. It is certain that this has got to stop . . . The United States are labouring with infinite patience to arrive at a fair and amicable settlement which will give Japan the utmost reassurance for her legitimate interests. We earnestly hope these negotiations will succeed. But this I must say: that if these hopes fail we shall of course range ourselves at the side of the United States.[65]

This final sentence was an oratorical triumph. In a few phrases Churchill combined the allegiance of the United Kingdom to American policy with the virtues of peaceful settlement, both enshrouded in implications that the United States would go to war with Japan.

When he was certain the audience had a picture of American and British flags waving over the Pacific, he returned "to the quiet bay somewhere in the Atlantic where misty sunshine plays on great ships which carry the White Ensign or the Stars and Stripes." He proceeded to clarify the meaning of the Atlantic Charter and reassure England and the empire by claiming joint responsibility for it. The declaration was "a simple rough and ready wartime statement of the goal towards which the British Commonwealth and the United States mean to make their ways." Its most important clause, to which Churchill gave abundant emphasis, was in the preamble: U.S.-U.K. efforts to work the "final destruction of the Nazi tyranny." He promised — speaking for himself and the President — that this was a "solemn and grave undertaking. It must be made good; it will be made good." To encourage interest about secret agreements he said offhandedly: "And, of course, many practical arrangements to fulfill that purpose have been and are being organized and set in motion." [66]

The Prime Minister had undertaken the broadcast to relieve pressure on the government, and he did silence violent criticism by the press. Defenders of the empire also were mollified by his stress on the preliminary, nonbinding nature of the joint declaration of war aims. Whether the broadcast salved his pride — and faith in the President's sincerity — is doubtful. Churchill's government faced the fact that American entry was becoming urgent, especially from a standpoint of morale.[67] The Prime Minister unburdened himself in a letter to Hopkins a few days later. "I ought to tell you," he began, that there had been "a wave of depression" throughout the Cabinet and informed circles "about President's many assurances and no closer to war, etc." Churchill feared this depression would appear in Parliament and endanger his position. If the year 1942 opened with Russia knocked out of the war and Britain alone again, "all kinds of dangers may arise." The note ended with the awkward words that Churchill "would be grateful if you could give me any kind of hope." [68]

Churchill's pessimism was strengthened by no less a personage than Lord Beaverbrook. When it was decided that the "Beaver" should fly to Washington for preliminary discussions before the Moscow supply conference, Churchill asked that he sound out American

public opinion. A shrewd observer, Beaverbrook saw through the
hosannas heaped on the Roosevelt-Churchill meeting. His conclusions were entirely negative. "There isn't the slightest chance of
the U.S. entering the war until compelled to do so by a direct attack
on its own territory," he reported to colleagues in London, "and it
seems that this could not happen until Britain and Russia have been
defeated." [69]

The President was not worried or did not voice his concern. Apparently, the meeting gave him confidence that the British Prime
Minister, whose political mastery he now recognized as equal to his
own, was in no danger of being dismissed from his post. Since he
had witnessed the performances at Argentia and had become aware
of the British leader's ingrained habit of dramatizing every situation,
F.D.R. was able to take this gloomy prediction by Churchill calmly.
He now knew firsthand how emotional Churchill could become.
This knowledge gave added impetus to F.D.R.'s first reaction that
the wisest response was to say nothing. Insofar as was possible,
deeds were made to answer the Prime Minister's appeal. Hundreds
of tanks and planes were sent to the Middle East; more U.S. merchant shipping was turned over to Great Britain; and on September
11 the President issued the long-awaited announcement of convoying in his dramatic "shoot-on-sight" speech. Privately, Churchill accepted these actions, proof that growth of understanding was mutual.

The most significant aspect of the meeting clearly was the confrontation between President Roosevelt and Prime Minister Churchill.
Theirs had been a meeting "devoutly wished and gladly consum-
mated." There had been great anxiety that the two leaders, whose
peoples were linked in so many ways, might find themselves unable
to work together harmoniously. Harry Hopkins once predicted:
"Bringing together Roosevelt and the Prime Minister on a ship
would cause the biggest explosion ever seen." [70] He was fortunately
mistaken: Roosevelt and Churchill reached an amicable truce and
even friendship of sorts. F.D.R. later told his wife he believed this
meeting "had broken the ice." He had been shown that Churchill,

who he earlier assumed "was typical of John Bull," was a man with whom he could work.[71] Thus was launched the adventurous alliance between the two men which brought assurance of victory in the struggle against the Axis.

5

In one sense the aftermath of Argentia comprehended the history of the Second World War. Long after the site of the first conference between Roosevelt and Churchill had been forgotten, when the discussions with Japan and Vichy and Premier Salazar were remembered only by file clerks in the Department of State and Foreign Office archives, the Atlantic Charter was a live issue. Subsequent problems with regard to each of the eight points were great. The history of these conflicting interpretations is outside the scope of this study. It is sufficient to understand how much a part of national desires and anxieties were the "peace aims" contained in the joint declaration. The Charter somehow survived identification with the crisis of 1941, and, in truth, of the period 1941–45. It comprised principles, not policies. There is a direct connection between the eight-point declaration and establishment of the United Nations. Seen as a goal for those nations which fought the Axis, the Charter became the beacon toward which the Allied nations were to strive. As Cordell Hull was to write, "It is a statement of basic principles and fundamental ideas and policies that are universal in their practical application." [72]

The joint declaration attained multilateral sanction by action of the Inter-Allied Meeting in London, September 24, 1941, when representatives of the United Kingdom, Canada, Australia, New Zealand, South Africa, the governments-in-exile of Belgium, Czechoslovakia, Greece, Luxembourg, the Netherlands, Norway, Poland, and Yugoslavia, and representatives of the Free French signed a resolution "adhering to the common principles of policy set forth in the Atlantic Charter and expressing their intention to cooperate in giving them effect." [73] The delegation from the U.S.S.R. expressed qualified agreement. In an address before the conference Ambassador

Maisky stated: "Considering that the practical application of these principles will necessarily adapt itself to the circumstances, needs, and historic peculiarities of particular countries, the Soviet Government can state that a consistent application will secure the most energetic support on the part of the Government and peoples of the Soviet Union." [74] The Inter-Allied Meeting's decision preceded approval by the legislative organs of most signatory states, and endorsement by national and international agencies such as the International Labor Organization — and even by the moribund League of Nations. [75] Representatives of twenty-six nations on January 1, 1942, signed the United Nations Declaration. By this act each subscribed to the Atlantic Charter and pledged cooperation in achievement of its principles. The Roosevelt-Churchill statement became the approved vehicle of Allied war aims, the ideal basis for the war and the peace.

In practice the Charter's influence was severely limited. More important were national ambitions and fears, and the changes in them as the fortunes of war fluctuated. One is tempted to claim that the primary relevance of the Charter during the Second World War lay in its usefulness in justifying the policies of one or another parties. The Polish leader Stanislaw Mikolajczyk based his objections to Teheran and Yalta on the Charter. On occasion Churchill was not averse to finding in the joint declaration an excuse for avoiding commitments, "secret or public, direct or implied," which were not in England's immediate interest. Soon after the meeting he claimed that it was never intended that the eight points be applied to the British Empire. [76] The sad history of the Charter is best expressed by the rapid shift of Russia from support to denigration. "I thought that the Atlantic Charter was directed against those people who were trying to establish world dominion. It now looks as if the Charter was directed against the U.S.S.R.," exclaimed Stalin in December, 1941, to Sir Anthony Eden. [77] Ideals, of course, became increasingly burdensome to the Russian leadership as the war progressed.

The Roosevelt-Churchill statement was the embodiment of a real yet informal alliance between the two men and their countries. It was a tentative compromise statement of their credos. As such the Charter possessed whatever force was inherent in the power and determination of Roosevelt and Churchill to influence international affairs. One has to conclude that the exact legal position of the joint declaration is, as President Roosevelt was fond of saying, an "iffy" question.

XIII. Epilogue

ABOVE ALL ELSE, the reaction of the American public to the conference dominated President Roosevelt's attention. When popular support stalled, as it had in the summer of 1941, Roosevelt believed his duty was to pull "forward" public opinion. As we know, success in this endeavor was not always to come from frank description of the problem. Blunt speaking was not one of the President's dominant traits.[1] Rather, Rooseveltian leadership made use of indirection, of devices such as a dramatic secret meeting with Winston Churchill.

What F.D.R. expected from the conference is not entirely clear. He may have hoped that his spectacular encounter with a belligerent Prime Minister and the idealistic statement of war aims might galvanize opinion at home and abroad — thereby relieving him of the necessity of aggressive leadership. Toward what goal popular attitudes might be precipitated, one is not sure; but neither, it appears, was President Roosevelt. Was Argentia the propaganda blockbuster that F.D.R. anticipated? Did the conference obscure or postpone the nexus of problems which clamored for decision?

It was clear that the meeting had not changed in any important way current views about the war, except to make interventionists and isolationists more vociferous in their demands. The public's easy acceptance of this meeting with the leader of a nation at war was encouraging; it was plain that Argentia represented the comfirmation of an informal alliance with Great Britain. Still, of proof that Roosevelt's planning of the past eight months had wrought a startling transformation of American opinion there was none.

Far from easing his difficulties, the meeting pinned F.D.R. tightly between the horns of isolationist denunciation and interventionist outcry. He chose to ward off accusations that the conference meant war. This, of course, sacrificed a large part of the impact. How the American people might have responded had Roosevelt frankly confessed that the meeting was arranged to deal with a desperate crisis, and then proclaimed that the country must endure whatever sacrifice was required will never be known. Such a risky act of leadership was precisely what the President expected the meeting to avert.

Had the White House hoped for an accretion of support in Congress it suffered additional disappointment. Congressional reaction followed the now familiar pattern — enthusiastic approval by supporters, cautious then violent criticism by opponents and speculation about hidden commitments in both camps. If anything, the brief flare-up in Congress following announcement of the meeting hardened the battle lines.

Newspaper editors represented personal opinions, even though these views had wide distribution. Congressmen claimed to represent the public will; but usually their own views, not any carefully surveyed attention to the voice of the people, governed their responses. A useful assessment of public reaction is well-nigh impossible.

Perusal of correspondence filed in President Roosevelt's papers gives an inkling of public feeling. Notably, disapproving letters from John Q. Citizen are few. The letters follow the pattern established in press reports: the meeting and the Atlantic Charter were tremendous steps forward; and now that the President had jarred opinion he must continue his aggressive leadership. Only occasionally does a letter, such as the resolution from the America First Committee, Pasadena Chapter, condemning the conference, strike an antagonistic note.[2]

The various responses to Argentia could have taken F.D.R. and his advisers on a roller coaster ride — from euphoria to depression and back — had they been able to afford such luxury. More immediate matters occupied the President's attention and prevented him from scanning editorial clippings and reading the stacks of mail piled on

White House secretaries' desks. He apparently was content to wait for the one barometer upon which he placed most reliance, the public opinion polls. For some time the White House had been receiving summaries of the major polls. In fact, before the Princeton Institute of Public Opinion released its findings, the information was sent to Anna Rosenberg, Social Security Administrator in New York City, who then transmitted it to the President.[3] Results of the Daniel Roper surveys also were provided the White House prior to publication.

Roosevelt's dependence on polls was not a one-way street. It was not coincidence that both Roper and Gallup in late July surveyed popular feelings about American participation in some future international organization, and that the results were published less than two weeks before announcement of the Atlantic Charter.[4] The subject matter of this poll, and others evidently, was suggested by the White House. Roosevelt was not averse to staging these surveys. He was well aware that polls, which revealed the state of public opinion, also could influence opinion.

Despite these careful preparations, despite all that had been done since Hopkins' first mission to England, the polls betrayed the President. They indicated that in the United States the meeting was a propaganda bust. A Gallup Poll, taken immediately after news of Argentia broke, revealed no change in attitude toward entering the war. According to this information, published August 19, response to the question — How would you vote today on the question of the United States entering the war now against Germany? — showed that 20% of those polled supported entry, 74% voted to stay out, and 6% registered no opinion. This was almost identical with the Gallup Poll released on August 5 when 20% voted for war, 75% were opposed, and 5% undecided. The same question two weeks after news of the meeting, returned an almost exact response: 21% voting to go in, 74% to stay out, and 5% no opinion.[5]

Every other index supported the judgment that the administration had won little if any accretion of support from the conference. Asked, "Which of these two things do you think is the more impor-

tant — that this country keep out of war or that Germany be defeated, even at the risk of our getting into the war" — 38% voted to
stay out, 57% to defeat Germany, and 5% had no preference. This
survey came out on July 9. When the Gallup people posed the same
question in late September, opinion was dramatically if temporarily
reversed — with 68% desiring avoidance of war in all eventualities
and only 32% voting for defeat of Germany whatever the risk.[6] Even
the increment of support for aid to Great Britain, which Roosevelt
certainly expected from the meeting, was minimal.

The meeting at Argentia offered no solution for F.D.R.'s crisis in
leadership. The American people continued to hang in midair between the precipice of all-out aid to England and Russia and the
rocks of war which lay below. Secretary of War Stimson captured
the administration's and country's dilemma through a less flamboyant metaphor. While on vacation during late July Stimson noted
in his diary:

> I have been reading while at St. Hubert's Carl Sandburg's first vol-
> ume on Lincoln and I have been reading the portion about the period
> between Lincoln's actual inauguration and Fort Sumter and the terrific
> trouble that they had there in the vacillations and the pulling back and
> forth, trying to make the Confederates fire the first shot. Well, that is
> what apparently the President is trying to do here. The difficulty is
> that the danger now to the country is very much greater than it was
> then, though not so palpably apparent, and a great deal depends on
> our not having this delay give Hitler a chance to jump us.[7]

There is one important difference between Lincoln's actions before
Fort Sumter and those of Franklin Roosevelt in the months before
Pearl Harbor. Lincoln admitted that his decisions were likely to result in a bloody war and went ahead to carry them out. It appears
that F.D.R. rejected any such conclusion and, in fact, seemed unable
to face the possibility of total American involvement.

Notes

Bibliographic Essay

Index

Notes

I. INTRODUCTION

1 *New York Times*, August 3, 1941.
2 Rexford Tugwell, *The Democratic Roosevelt* (Garden City, N.Y., 1957), 572.
3 William L. Langer and S. Everett Gleason, *The Undeclared War* (New York, 1953), 436.
4 See the Prime Minister's telegram of May 4, 1941, to Roosevelt in Winston S. Churchill, *The Second World War* (6 vols., Boston, 1948–53), III, 235–36. Hereafter cited by title of volume.
5 Robert E. Sherwood, *Roosevelt and Hopkins* (New York, 1948), has written that Missy LeHand told him the President really suffered from a case of "sheer exasperation," 293.
6 J. M. A. Gwyer, *Grand Strategy* (London, 1964), III, Part I in J. R. M. Butler, *History of the Second World War*, United Kingdom Military Series, 113.
7 Harold L. Ickes, *The Secret Diary of Harold L. Ickes* (3 vols., New York, 1953–54), III, 311. Ickes admitted that if he could have looked "this far ahead and seen an inactive and uninspiring President, I would not have supported Roosevelt for a third term."
8 Quoted in Langer and Gleason, *The Undeclared War*, 456.
9 Stimson Diary, June 30, 1941, Henry L. Stimson Papers, Yale University.
10 Tugwell, *The Democratic Roosevelt*, 577.
11 John M. Blum, *From The Morgenthau Diaries* (3 vols., Boston, 1959–67), II, 264. Stimson described how the President had "pranced in" and tied into him for the Department of War's failure to assist the the Russians, Stimson Diary, August 1, 1941.
12 *Time*, August 11, 1941.
13 Log of the President's Cruise aboard *Potomac* and *Augusta*, August 3–16, 1941, OF 463-C, Conference At Sea folder, Roosevelt Papers, Hyde Park, N.Y.
14 Grace Tully, *F.D.R.: My Boss* (New York, 1949), 248.

15 Log of the President's Cruise, August 3–16, 1941.
16 Memorandum by the President, August 23, 1941, PSF, Box 2, Roosevelt Papers; *New York Times*, August 3, August 4, 1941.
17 Memorandum by the President, August 23, 1941; Roosevelt remarked in cabinet meeting in late 1940 that he "had had his fill of entertaining Crowned Heads and ex-Kings and Queens," Stimson Diary, October 25, 1940.
18 The President had participated in the conversion of *Potomac* from the beginning and had inspected and approved each step, Elizabeth B. Drewry, Director of Franklin D. Roosevelt Library, to author, January 30, 1967.
19 *Ibid.; Newsweek*, August 18, 1941.
20 They could get no answer. Early would say only that the President's plans were indefinite, *New York Times*, August 5, 1941; a *Newsweek* article claimed that never had there been "dizzier stories" about a presidential vacation than regarding this one, August 11, 1941.
21 Memorandum by the President, August 23, 1941; Stimson Diary, August 6, 1941.

II. "SAIL ON, OH SHIP OF STATE"

1 Churchill, *The Gathering Storm*, 440.
2 Lewis Broad, *Winston Churchill: The Years of Achievement* (New York, 1963), 131.
3 Jay Pierrepont Moffatt once said: "To such a degree our foreign affairs centralize with the President that no one here knows what is going on," Nancy H. Hooker, ed., *The Moffat Papers: Selections from the Diplomatic Journals of Jay Pierrepont Moffat* (Cambridge, Mass., 1956), 93. Advisers feared this led to the President's being given advice by irresponsible men, and if they were the last to see him, the acceptance of their silly ideas.
4 Langer and Gleason, *The Undeclared War*, 237.
5 Churchill, *The Finest Hour*, 360, 362–67.
6 Sherwood, 230.
7 *Ibid.*
8 *Ibid.*
9 Other presidential advisers could understand parts of Hopkins' appeal to F.D.R.; they were baffled by it nonetheless, as Ickes and Morgenthau show.
10 Marquis W. Childs, "The President's Best Friend," *The Saturday Evening Post* (April 19, 1941), 64.

11 Sherwood, 2–3. He claims the "half-man" epithet referred to Hopkins' physical frailty. The President likely intended another connotation.

12 Stimson Diary, March 13, 1941; for similar reaction by Marshall, see Forrest C. Pogue, *George C. Marshall* (2 vols., New York, 1963–66), II, 25.

13 Sherwood, 4.

14 Morgenthau Diaries, February 17, 1941, quoted in Langer and Gleason, *The Undeclared War*, 663.

15 Roosevelt to Ickes, January 4, 1941, in Elliott Roosevelt, ed., *F.D.R.: His Personal Letters, 1928–45* (2 vols., New York, 1950), II, 1100.

16 Sherwood, 234.

17 Louis W. Koenig, *The Invisible Presidency* (New York, 1960), writes: "The poor man . . . motionless in his seat midway in the plane. His face, or what could be seen of it beneath a battered fedora pulled forward against the light, was cadaverous. His eyes, which opened now and then to reproach his untoward circumstances, were two glazed black beads," 300.

18 Sherwood, 236. The British were to exhibit similar feelings on experiencing Hopkins' optimism and determination.

19 Department of State, *Foreign Relations of the United States* (Washington, D.C., 1862–), 1941, I, 341. Hereafter cited as *FR*.

20 If this correctly described F.D.R.'s feelings, it was a substantial commitment. There is doubt it did. Hopkins repeated these sentiments before a gathering of newspapermen at Claridge's, hosted by Lord Beaverbrook. Sherwood gives a full summary of his address, 248–50.

21 Sherwood, 248.

22 *Ibid.*, 236.

23 Former Naval Person to President, January 26, 1941, Churchill, *The Grand Alliance*, 26.

24 Ickes, III, 387–88.

25 *Ibid.*, 388.

26 Sherwood, 243; it is also printed in *FR*, 1941, I, 346. In a call paraphrasing this cable Hopkins said he realized "telegraphed or written words . . . inadequately express my deep conviction that the time to help Britain is now," Hopkins to Roosevelt and Hull, January 28, 1941, Decimal File 740.0011 European War 1939/8071 11/12.

27 Hopkins to Roosevelt and Hull, February 2, 1941, Decimal File 121.841 Hopkins, Harry/10 1/7.

28 Sherwood, 259–60.

29 Roosevelt to Churchill, January 19, 1941, Elliott Roosevelt, ed., *F.D.R.: His Personal Letters, 1928–45*, II, 1109.

30 Churchill to Roosevelt, January 28, 1941, Churchill, *The Grand Alliance*, 25–26.

31 Hopkins to Hull for Roosevelt, January 30, 1941, D.F. 121.841 Hopkins, Harry/11.

32 Memorandum by President Roosevelt, August 23, 1941, PSF, Box 2, Roosevelt Papers.

33 He had laid down conditions for visits with foreign leaders sometime before. The essential condition was that the meeting place must not be more than a twenty-four hour train ride from Washington, Elliott Roosevelt, ed., *F.D.R.: His Personal Letters, 1928–45*, II, 1038. At the same time reinforcement of Caribbean bases proceeded under presidential writ, Memorandum for President from Secretary Stimson, April 7, 1941, PSF: War Department, Box 37. Roosevelt wrote on this, "O.K., but hurry Bermuda. That is necessary priority."

34 Ickes, III, 470–73.

35 Memorandum by the President, August 23, 1941, PSF, Box 2.

36 *Ibid.*

37 *Ibid.* Exclusion of the Canadian Prime Minister was justifiable on several grounds, some of which Roosevelt mentioned. However, his willingness to make King the dupe for a cat-and-mouse game with the press is disturbing. Documentation of the correspondence between Roosevelt and King regarding a visit is in PPF 3089 and PSF: Canada, Box 2.

38 James M. Burns, *The Lion and the Fox* (New York, 1956), 459–60.

39 Roy Howard to Alf M. Landon, March 17, 1941, Roy Howard folder, Landon Papers, Kansas State Historical Society, Topeka, Kansas.

40 Burns has written that Roosevelt "anxiously examined public opinion polls during 1941 . . . once again . . . failing to supply the crucial factor of his own leadership," 458.

41 Recent research on the domestic political history of the 1930's has tended to raise the importance of Congress' initiative and to downgrade the President's role.

42 William Allen White, *Autobiography* (New York, 1946), 642.

43 He often spoke of the possibility of impeachment in this period. See Sherwood, 299.

44 The author believes this to be a peculiar approach to the relations between the Presidency and the electorate — and an unwarranted reading of the circumstances of spring-summer, 1941. There exists evidence, which may or not be convincing, that Roosevelt lagged behind public opinion in important respects. If that view is accepted, a major thesis of this study will be supported.

45 Samuel I. Rosenman, ed., *The Public Papers and Addresses of Franklin D. Roosevelt* (13 vols., New York, 1948–50), X, xvi.

46 Mrs. Ogden Mills Reid to Roosevelt, May 23, 1940, PPF 897.

47 He concluded bitterly: "When a section of the press can bring itself to such extravagant falsification it becomes necessary to resort to other media in order to give the people of the country the facts they are entitled to have concerning what their government is doing." Roosevelt to Mrs. Ogden Mills Reid, June 6, 1940, PPF 897.

48 Burns, 459–60.

49 Stimson Diary, May 7, 1941. The Secretary of War supported the suggestion because of longtime belief that Great Britian would be reduced to desperation and Roosevelt "should be thinking of some dramatic way of restoring their morale," Stimson Diary, January 2, 1941.

50 Ickes to Roosevelt and reply, June 13, 1941, D.F. 740.0011 European War 1939/12470 1/3.

51 Ernest J. King and Walter M. Whitehill, *Fleet Admiral King* (New York, 1952), 329–31.

52 *Ibid.*, 329.

53 *Ibid.*, 330. With customary thoroughness Admiral King had compiled and sent to the President complete data on ice conditions in the suggested routes, April 22, 1941, Roosevelt Papers, PSF, Box 2.

54 *Ibid.*, 330; Memorandum by the President, August 23, 1941, PSF, Box 2.

55 King and Whitehill, 330.

III. FINAL PREPARATIONS

1 Memorandum by the President, August 23, 1941, PSF, Box 2, Roosevelt Papers.

2 Sherwood, 308.

3 Welles to Winant, July 12, 1941, D.F. 121.841 Hopkins, Harry/25A.

4 Winant to Welles for President, July 13, 1941, D.F.121.841 Hopkins, Harry/35.

5 Sherwood, 308.

6 *Ibid.*, 311.

7 There is some question about the President's trust in Winant's ability. James B. Conant has said that F.D.R. told him at a White House visit in February: "I am going to appoint Winant as Ambassador. I'm not sure he is really up to it, but I'm going to send another man along — Harriman — who will keep him straight." Transcription, William Tuttle Interview with James B. Conant, June, 1967. For contradictory

views of Winant's ambassadorship, see Walter Thompson, 217; James
Leasor, 157; John Connell, *The 'Office'* (London, 1957), 285; and
Breckinridge Long Diaries, June 4, 6, 1941, Breckinridge Long
Papers, Library of Congress.

8 This issue is discussed at greater length in chapter eight.

9 Sumner Welles, *Where Are We Heading?* (New York, 1946), 18–20.

10 Welles to Winant, July 14, 1941, *FR*, 1941, I, 342.

11 Winant to Hull, July 16, 1941, *FR*, 1941, I, 343.

12 Arthur Krock Oral History Memoir, 76, Columbia Oral History Project.

13 Hamilton Fish Armstrong to F.D.R., May 6, 1941, PPF 6011, Roosevelt Papers.

14 Rexford Tugwell has written: "Those closest to him felt that . . . if
the nation was rearmed and resolute, and if all possible aid was sent
to Britain, our intervention might be avoided. There is indeed
reason to believe that the last vestige of this optimism was not squeezed
out of his mind until the news from Pearl Harbor came over the
White House wires," *The Democratic Roosevelt*, 485.

15 Charles Eade, compiler, *The War Speeches Of The Rt. Hon. Winston
S. Churchill* (3 vols., London, 1955), I, 256.

16 For instance, Sumner Welles told Breckinridge Long of his fear about
England. "He said he thought the next three months were *the* critical
months. If London had many more experiences like it had last night,
he was afraid the morale of the British people might break." Long
Diaries, May 12, 1941.

17 R. Davis to Joseph E. Davies, August 6, 1941, Davies Papers, Library
of Congress.

18 *Newsweek*, August 11, 1941.

19 "We Must Fight," *American Magazine*, September, 1941, 9.

20 He made this clear to Hopkins at the Admiralty Liaison Conference
on July 23 and on other occasions, Sherwood, 317.

21 Langer and Gleason, *The Undeclared War*, 690.

22 Sherwood, Broad, and others assert that Churchill imbibed the principles of American government "at his mother's knee"; the author remains unconvinced. Randolph Churchill's first volume of *Winston S.
Churchill* (Boston, 1966) offers support by revealing how rarely the
young Winston saw his mother.

23 By this time Hopkins was so convinced of the need for full involvement by the United States that in his talks with Churchill he may not
have given faithful expression to F.D.R.'s feelings.

24 Welles to Hopkins from President, July 19, 1941, D.F. 121.841 Hopkins, Harry/25B.

25 Churchill, *The Grand Alliance*, 427.

26 There is indirect evidence that Roosevelt first hoped that the meeting would begin several days earlier and conclude in time to have influence upon the vote over Selective Service renewal. Churchill set the date in a cable of July 25, *The Grand Alliance*, 427.

27 The choice came apparently at the last minute, for Hopkins believed that he was to travel to Argentia on *King George V*. He may have thought he *did* travel to Argentia on that warship. See the draft article on the conference by Hopkins, Box 303, Hopkins Papers.

28 This was Roosevelt's idea, Memorandum by the President, August 23, 1941.

29 Churchill, *The Grand Alliance*, 427.

30 Sherwood, 350; as Sherwood points out the agreement Churchill desired was not the Atlantic Charter but an ultimatum to Japan — perhaps even a U.S. declaration of war.

31 Churchill, *The Grand Alliance*, 427.

32 Hopkins to F.D.R., July 26, 1941, Box 303, Hopkins Papers. This cable was not sent but it represented Hopkins' assessment.

33 Sherwood, 317.

34 Memorandum by the President, August 23, 1941, PSF, Box 2.

35 H. H. Arnold, *Global Mission* (New York, 1949), 247.

36 Stimson Diary, August 4, August 6, 1941; Long Diaries, August 31, 1941.

37 Arnold, 247.

38 *Time*, August 11, 1941; Robert Bendiner, *The Riddle of the State Department* (New York, 1942), 205.

39 *Time*, August 11, 1941; *New York Times*, August 3, 1941; Hooker, ed., *Moffat Papers*, 332; William C. Phillips Oral History Memoir, 130, Columbia Oral History Project; Memorandum by the President, August 23, 1941, PSF, Box 2.

40 Welles, *Where Are We Heading?*, 6. No copy of Welles' draft has come to light.

41 Churchill said, "I had the keenest desire to meet Mr. Roosevelt, with whom I had now corresponded with increasing intimacy for nearly two years," *The Grand Alliance*, 427.

42 Sherwood, 317.

43 Raymond Dawson, in *The Decision to Aid Russia* (Chapel Hill, N.C., 1962), has written: "The original suggestion of this special mission has been variously ascribed to Churchill, to Winant, and to Hopkins himself. It is suggestive that Joseph E. Davies had already urged both Hopkins and the President to 'get word to Stalin direct,'" 173.

44 Sherwood, 317.

45 The Prime Minister insisted that Hopkins accompany him to Argentia, mission to Moscow or no. Hopkins to Roosevelt, July 26, 1941, Box 303, Hopkins Papers.

46 United States Congress, *Joint Committee on Investigation of Pearl Harbor Attack, Hearing Pursuant to S. Con. Res. 27, Authorizing Investigation of Attack on Pearl Harbor* (79th Cong., 1st and 2nd sess., Washington, 1946, 39 parts), Part 20, 4384–85. Hereafter cited as *Pearl Harbor Attack.*

47 *Ibid.*, Part 20, 4373.

48 John G. Winant, *Letter From Grosvenor Square: An Account of A Stewardship* (Boston, 1947), 207–208.

49 Welles to Hopkins, July 26, 1941, D.F. 740.0011 European War 1939/1348A.

50 Winant, 208.

51 Harriman reported all kinds of problems, ranging from British tyranny over the native populations to the overlong tea breaks of English workmen.

52 Sherwood, 315.

53 Captain Tracy S. Kittredge, "United States-British Naval Cooperation, 1939–42," unpublished historical monograph of the Office of Naval History, Naval Archives, Washington, D.C., Section V, Part A, 525. Hereafter, this invaluable source will be referred to as "Kittredge MS."

54 Hopkins to Roosevelt, July 26, 1941, Box 303, Hopkins Papers.

55 *Ibid.*

56 Sherwood, 320.

57 Quentin Reynolds, *By Quentin Reynolds* (New York, 1963), 223.

58 H. V. Johnson (London) to Hull, July 31, 1941, D.F. 740.0011 European War 1939/13922.

59 *Ibid.*

IV. DOWN TO THE SEA IN SHIPS

1 John M. Blum, Morgenthau's biographer, states that Roosevelt sent Hopkins to Russia to get "the details of Russian requirements," and that aid was being sent anyway, II, 262; see also Hopkins' draft article on Roosevelt-Churchill conference, Box 303, Hopkins Papers.

2 Sherwood, 321.

3 *Ibid.*, 324–25; Sherwood takes his description of the trip from Hopkins' article, "The Inside Story of My Meeting With Stalin," *American Magazine* (December, 1941), 14–15, 114–117.

4 Steinhardt to Hull, August 1, 1941, *FR*, 1941, I, 815.

5 Hopkins, "The Inside Story of My Meeting With Stalin," *American Magazine* (December, 1941), 15.

6 Sherwood, 326.

7 Hopkins "gathered" the Soviet leader "would have felt the same about the State Department if he had been asked," Memorandum, October 30, 1941, Box 303, Hopkins Papers.

8 He refused to tell reporters whether Lend-Lease was to go to the Soviets, PPF 1-P, XVII, Roosevelt Papers.

9 Dawson, 122.

10 Stimson wrote the President on June 23 that the Army believed Germany would win within one to three months. Knox stated Navy opinion that it would take "anywhere from six weeks to two months for Hitler to clean up on Russia," quoted in Herbert Feis, *The Road to Pearl Harbor* (Princeton, N.J., 1950), 220; the next conclusion was, as Admiral Leahy wrote from Vichy on June 30, that the completion of the German campaign against Russia (within two months) "will be followed by peace proposals that Great Britain will accept," Leahy to Welles, June 30, 1941, D.F. 740.0011 European War 1939/13688.

11 The polls showed a majority of Americans continued to oppose extension of Lend-Lease aid to Russia.

12 Elliott Roosevelt, ed., *F.D.R.: His Personal Letters, 1928–45*, II, 1177.

13 Dawson, 139.

14 Memorandum by Welles of conversation with Soviet Ambassador, June 30, 1941, FR, 1941, I, 779–81; Dawson, 145ff.

15 *Ibid.*

16 John M. Blum, *From the Morgenthau Diaries* (3 vols., Boston, 1959–67), II, 264–65.

17 Richard Lukas, "Air Force Aspects of American Aid to the Soviet Union: The Crucial Years, 1941–42," unpublished dissertation (Florida State University, 1963), 373.

18 Sherwood, 327.

19 *Newsweek*, August 11, 1941; see cable from Steinhardt to Hull cited in note 34.

20 Joseph Davies' journal, Notes of a conversation with Hopkins on September 8, 1941, Davies Papers, Library of Congress.

21 Memorandum by Hopkins of conference with Premier Stalin, July 30, 1941, FR, 1941, I, 802–05.

22 *Ibid.*

23 James Leasor, *War At The Top* (London, 1961), 156. This interesting book is based upon the diaries and recollections of General Sir L. C. Hollis.

24 Colonel Hollis said that Cripps was undoubtedly a brilliant man but that "he was a goose politically," *ibid.*

25 This statement was essentially the same as the cable to Stalin dispatched from Argentia two weeks later, Sherwood, 331.

26 Memorandum of conversation between Hopkins and Mr. Molotov, July 31, *FR*, 1941, I, 880–82.

27 *Ibid.*, 882.

28 Memorandum by Hopkins of conference with Mr. Stalin, July 31, 1941, *FR*, 1941, I, 805–14.

29 *Ibid.*

30 *Ibid.*

31 *Ibid.*

32 *Ibid.*

33 Sherwood, 343.

34 Steinhardt to Hull, August 1, 1941, *FR*, 1941, I, 815.

35 John Cassidy, *Moscow Dateline* (New York, 1944), 126.

36 Steinhardt to Hull for President, August 1, 1941, I, 814.

37 Sherwood, 347.

38 Charles C. Eade, ed., *Churchill By Contemporaries* (London, 1952), 91.

39 British newspapers naturally could not carry detailed reports of the Prime Minister's movements. They had no information anyway.

40 London *Daily Telegraph*, July 30, 1941. The outcry against Cherwell was markedly similar to antagonism in America toward Hopkins' intimacy with Roosevelt.

41 Eade, ed., *Churchill By Contemporaries*, 91.

42 The Ministry of Information had been caught in the crossfire between press and government since the outbreak of the war. For all his charm and highly placed friends, Bracken was no more successful than predecessors in resolving the conflict between the regime's insistence upon censorship and the demand that the public be fully informed. See Francis Williams, *Press, Parliament, and People* (London, 1946), for an interesting description of the issue.

43 H. V. Morton to author, March 8, 1967.

44 *Ibid.*

45 Williams, 192–94.

46 H. V. Morton, *Atlantic Meeting* (London, 1943), 5. This book was read and approved by Churchill and also warmly lauded by the President. It must be considered the authoritative account of the externals of the meeting; see letter of H. V. Morton to author, March 8, 1967.

47 Vice Admiral Brian B. Schofield, unpublished memoir, n.d., 236.

48 Morton, 9.

49 General Sir Ian Jacob, manuscript diary, "Operation Riviera," August 3–19, 1941, August 3, 1941; hereafter cited as Jacob Diary.

50 Schofield memoir, 236.
51 Jacob Diary, August 3, 1941.
52 *Ibid.*
53 Walter M. Thompson, *Assignment: Churchill* (London, 1952), 224–25.
54 Schofield memoir, 237.
55 Jacob Diary, August 3, 1941; Morton had been forced to go AWOL from Home Guard duties, since he was forbidden to explain his sudden departure.
56 *Ibid.*
57 Leasor, 69.
58 Thompson, 225; Lord Moran and James Leasor provide descriptions of this incident which differ in detail from Thompson's account.
59 Jacob Diary, August 4, 1941.
60 Sherwood, 348–49.
61 Winant to Welles, August 2, 1941, D.F. 740.0011 European War 1939/13620 1/2.
62 Hopkins wrote later: "Churchill, an old man in the terms of today's world, was fresh, dynamic, clear-minded, certain in every move and word," Hopkins draft article, Box 303, Hopkins Papers.
63 These items joined a "goodly supply" of caviar and vodka brought by Hopkins from Russia as a gift from Ambassador Cripps.
64 Churchill, *The Grand Alliance*, 428.
65 Morton, 35.
66 *Ibid.*, 33
67 Hopkins draft article, Box 303, Hopkins Papers.
68 Reports from Naval Operations were based on "scanty, unreliable information," but claimed that German submarines were quiet. On August 2 the intelligence people said six German and twelve Italian submarines were known to be between Madeira and Portugal. The British estimated twelve in the general area 48°–57° North and 20°–30° West, and some four in the region about 30° North between 20° and 30° West, northbound, OpNav to all Task Force Cmdrs, August 2, 1941, CinclAnt File, Naval Archives.
69 H. H. Arnold journal, July 31, August 1, 1941, Conference folder, Box 271, Arnold Papers, Library of Congress.
70 Pogue, II, 141.
71 Arnold, *Global Mission*, 247.
72 Stimson Diary, August 4, 1941.
73 Arnold journal, August 3, 1941. The military were so obsessed with the necessity of secrecy that when a newspaperman came into the New

York airport restaurant they left their lunches unfinished and fled by a rear door.

74 Arnold, *Global Mission*, 247.

75 Arnold journal, August 3, 1941.

76 Log of President's Cruise, August 3–16, 1941; Michael Reilly, *Reilly of the White House* (New York, 1947), 19.

77 Memorandum by the President, August 23, 1941.

78 Elliott Roosevelt, *As He Saw It* (New York, 1946), 19–20.

79 For instance, the communiqué for August 9 stated: "Ships anchored in fog. Prospects for fishing appear very poor. Everything quiet on board. No news." OF 463-C, Conference At Sea folder, Roosevelt Papers.

80 *Jane's Fighting Ships, 1940*. A major reason for selection of *Augusta* was that she had been fitted with radar.

81 Arnold journal, August 4, 1941.

82 He refused to allow Welles to let others in on the secret. The blackout stretched all the way to London. As late as August 2, Winant still believed Roosevelt was going to Ottawa. He cabled that it was urgently necessary he be informed of the date of F.D.R.'s arrival there, Winant to Welles, August 2, 1941, D.F. 740.0011 European War 1939/13620 1/2. Welles replied that the President personally requested him to say that he was not going to Ottawa, but did not enlighten Winant further, Welles to Winant, August 3, 1941, D.F. 740.0011 European War 1939/13621. F.D.R. refused to tell Mackenzie King until August 4, King to Roosevelt, August 15, 1941, PPF 3089.

83 Tugwell, 543.

84 This is Sherwood's magnificent phrase.

85 The best source of these views is Secretary of War Stimson's Diary. Stimson once said that trying to follow the President's thinking was like chasing a vagrant beam of sunshine. Even Hopkins was concerned about the President's accessibility to advice from almost any source.

86 Menu of dinner aboard *Augusta*, August 6, 1941, OF 463-C, Conference At Sea folder; Arnold journal, August 6, 1941.

87 Arnold, *Global Mission*, 250.

88 *Ibid.;* it is worth noting that military talks at Argentia conformed to these principles.

89 Tully, 263; the President's respect for Arnold was of recent vintage. He blamed the airman for mishandling the Chmedlin disaster and only after Arnold's trip to England in early spring, 1941, was he fully accepted into the presidential circle, Stimson Diary, May 6, 1941.

90 Arnold journal, August, 1941.

91 After its destruction by a British raiding squadron, Plaisance was to be taken over by the British and to serve as a center for activities against privateering. Its military value was constant from the eighteenth through the mid-twentieth century. Only knowledge of the Newfoundland harbor and settlement lessened. See Morton's colorful description, 21ff.

92 ComTaskForce 1 to ComTaskUnit 1.3.3, action, August 5, 1941; on August 8, CinclAnt ordered ComTaskGroup 1.1.3 to watch for a "non U.S. battleship." CinclAnt File, Naval Archives.

93 Elliott Roosevelt, *As He Saw It*, 17.

94 Arnold, *Global Mission*, 250.

95 Elliott Roosevelt, 16.

96 Memorandum by the President, August 23, 1941.

97 The Smithsonian collection of "large ugly fish" grew considerably because of F.D.R.'s sea vacations, Log of the President's Cruise, August 3–16, 1941.

98 Mark I. Watson, *Chief of Staff: Prewar Plans and Preparations* (Washington, D.C., 1950), 398; Arnold, *Global Mission*, 248–49.

99 Arnold, *Global Mission*, 249.

100 *Ibid.*, 250.

101 Sherwood, 308.

102 Watson, 401.

103 Elliott Roosevelt, 22.

104 Arnold, *Global Mission*, 250.

105 Log of the President's Cruise, August 3–16, 1941.

106 King and Whitehill, 333.

107 Log of the President's Cruise, August 3–16, 1941.

108 Hopkins' draft article, Box 303, Hopkins Papers.

109 Sherwood, 351.

110 The events of the first day of the meeting demonstrated that Roosevelt also was aware of this distinction.

111 Jacob Diary, August 4, 1941.

112 *Ibid.*

113 W. M. Yool to author, March 8, 1967.

114 Churchill, *The Grand Alliance*, 429.

115 Jacob Diary, August 5, 1941; Schofield wrote, "The Prime Minister had ordered a Map Room to be fitted up onboard, similar to the one we had in the Admiralty and on which the movements of all shipping in the Atlantic was shewn by coloured tags, appropriately marked," Schofield memoir, 240.

116 Jacob Diary, August 5, 1941.

117 Hopkins' draft article, Box 303, Hopkins Papers.

118 Sherwood, 350.

119 At first opportunity he cabled Oliver Lyttelton, Minister in Cairo, who had given him the book, "I find *Hornblower* admirable." Middle East Hdq., knowing Churchill's penchant for odd code names, queried London for the plans of "Operation Hornblower," Churchill, *The Grand Alliance*, 429.

120 Howard Spring, *In The Meantime* (London, 1942), 209–10.

121 Jacob Diary, August 5, 1941.

122 Churchill, *The Grand Alliance*, 429.

123 Jacob Diary, August 8, 1941; Howard Spring noted: "Before breaking up they stood there for a little while longer than they were accustomed to stand, clearly touched to the quick by that simple sentence which had so unerringly linked them with the immortal moments of this English people," 210.

124 See the Prime Minister's memorandum on the supply question, *The Grand Alliance*, Appendix C, Book Two, 848–49.

125 Sherwood, 350.

126 Churchill, *The Grand Alliance*, 431.

127 *Ibid.*, 430.

128 Sherwood, 351.

129 London *Times*, August 3, 1941

130 Winant to Hull, August 5, 1941, *FR*, 1941, I, 343.

131 *Ibid.*, 343–44.

132 Hull to Winant, August 6, 1941, *FR*, 1941, I, 344–45.

133 Churchill, *The Grand Alliance*, 430.

134 Morris to Hull, August 8, 1941, D.F. 740.011 European War 1939/13794.

135 Hopkins' draft article, Box 303, Hopkins Papers.

136 Jacob Diary, August 9, 1941.

137 Thompson, 234.

138 Jacob Diary, August 9, 1941; Morton, v.

V. THE MEETING BEGINS

1 Log of the President's Cruise, August 3–16, 1941.

2 Jacob Diary, August 9, 1941.

3 Sherwood, 352.

4 Hopkins' draft article, Box 303, Hopkins Papers.

5 Hopkins to Churchill, August 9, 1941, Box 303, Hopkins Papers. This resolved confusion about arrangements for the first meetings. Jacob had noted on August 8, "the programme is quite unknown at present," Jacob Diary, August 8, 1941. Churchill had invited Roosevelt to

be his guest Saturday night. He did not receive an answer until Beardall came over. The Prime Minister willingly adjusted to F.D.R.'s wishes.

6 Morton, 95–96; Schofield gives a similar, though more philosophical, description in his regrettably unpublished memoir: "The American ships looked very spic and span with their glossy paint and shining brass work compared to the dull war paint worn by the Prince of Wales. Did we envy them? I think not. We knew by that time the measure of the evil with which we had to wrestle," Schofield memoir, 241.

7 The British were much impressed by the dress and bearing of the U.S. Marines, "looking extremely smart in their dark blue coats and light blue trousers and white caps," Jacob Diary, August 9, 1941.

8 Morton, 98.

9 King George VI to Roosevelt, August 3, 1941, PSF, Great Britain, 1941–42, Roosevelt Papers. What words of greeting passed between the two men is not known. Just as Churchill handed over the King's letter, the only sound camera aboard (operated by a member of the Prime Minister's entourage) broke down and the brief exchange was lost. It is a doubtful tragedy, Thompson, 232.

10 Schofield memoir, 244.

11 Elliott Roosevelt, 21.

12 H. V. Morton to author, March 8, 1967.

13 Elliott Roosevelt, 26.

14 Sherwood gives an excellent description of the relationship established between Roosevelt and Churchill at Argentia, 363–65.

15 "This . . . was a somewhat sore point with Roosevelt," Sherwood wrote. "When he was Assistant Secretary of the Navy in the First World War, he had gone to London and had met Churchill at a banquet. Churchill, already an eminent statesman, had apparently failed to take much notice of the young American official and had promptly forgotten this encounter, but Roosevelt remembered it clearly," 350–51.

16 The best evidence for the President's pique is the transparent effort Churchill made in his memoirs to convince all and sundry that he *had* remembered the meeting at Gray's Inn.

17 General Sir Ian Jacob to author, March 12, 1967.

18 "The political and military sides of the discussions were quite distinct," affirms Sir Ian Jacob.

19 The material in this section is taken mainly from Under Secretary Welles' memorandum of his conversation with Sir Alexander Cadogan, written at sea, August 9, 1941; it is published in *FR*, 1941, I, 346–54.

20 Thompson, 271.
21 *Time*, August 2, 1941.
22 Welles' memorandum, August 9, 1941, *FR*, 1941, I, 346.
23 *Ibid.*, 347.
24 *Ibid.*, 350.
25 *Ibid.*
26 *Ibid.*
27 Later in the meeting F.D.R. was to say that even thirty days more of postponement of war with Japan was useful and desirable.
28 Welles' memorandum, August 9, 1941, *FR*, 1941, I, 350.
29 *Ibid.*
30 *Ibid.*
31 *Ibid.*
32 *Ibid.*
33 Quoted in Paul Hasluck, *The Government and the People, 1939–41* (Canberra, 1952), 526; "It seems to us entirely feasible that . . . an indication of the United States' attitude will certainly appear . . . We consider it vital, however, that the question should be raised in one form or another."
34 Hasluck, 527.
35 Welles' memorandum, August 9, 1941, *FR*, 1941, I, 351.
36 *Ibid.*
37 Defenses of this decision and of the course of U.S. policy toward Vichy are William L. Langer, *Our Vichy Gamble* (New York, 1947), and Langer and Gleason, *The Undeclared War*. See also Hull's *Memoirs*, II, and William D. Leahy, *I Was There* (New York, 1950). A devastating review article of Langer's study of Vichy policy is Louis Gottschalk, "Our Vichy Fumble," *Journal of Modern History*, XX, no. 1 (March, 1948), 47–56.
38 Sumner Welles, *Seven Decisions That Shaped History* (New York, 1950), 33.
39 Louis Gottschalk dismisses the argument as "ingratuitous" and stupid. He has written: "We now know (and if our intelligence from our 'Vichy friends' had been good, we should have been so persuaded at the time) that if Pétain and Darlan were sincere in anything it was in their declarations that they would rather scuttle the French fleet than surrender it to the Germans. In short, no real need existed to continue recognition of the Vichy government for the purpose of cajoling it into preserving its navy." Gottschalk, "Our Vichy Fumble," 54.
40 The President's consciousness of Africa's strategic importance is well documented in such works as Sherwood, 124ff, and Forrest Davis, *The Atlantic System* (New York, 1942), 315. Notably, Charles de Gaulle

was aware of Roosevelt's interest and attempted repeatedly to have the United States base its invasion strategy on North and West Africa rather than on the United Kingdom.

41 This tradition went back at least to the London Economic Conference of 1933.

42 Robert Murphy, *Diplomat Among Warriors* (New York, 1964), 84.

43 Roosevelt to Churchill, May 1, 1941, D.F. 740.0011 European War 1939/10485 1/2.

44 Memorandum of telephone conversation between Hull and Welles, July 29, 1941, D.F. 740.0011 European War 1939/423.

45 Murphy (Algiers) to Welles, August 2, 1941, *FR*, 1941, II, 406–07.

46 Winant to Hull, August 6, 1941, D.F. 851.00/2319.

47 Murphy to Hull, August 12, 1941, *FR*, 1941, II, 411–12.

48 Winant once commented: "I have not yet been able to discover here the basis of a constructive diplomatic policy in relation to the Vichy Government, particularly as it affects French Africa . . . From a naval standpoint it is to maintain the blockade," Winant to Hull, March 3, 1941, D.F. 740:0011 European War 1939/10623.

49 Stimson Diary, April 8, 1941.

50 Murphy, 100.

51 *Ibid.*, 95.

52 Welles' memorandum, August 9, 1941, *FR*, 1941, I, 352.

53 *Ibid.*

54 Log of the President's Cruise, August 3–16, 1941.

55 *Newsweek*, August 18, 1941.

56 See the poignant account of these differences in Morton, 23–28.

57 Jacob Diary, August 11, 1941.

58 Air Vice-Marshal W. M. Yool to author, March 9, 1967.

59 Morton, 27.

60 Log of the President's Cruise, August 3–16; Hopkins' draft article, Box 303, Hopkins Papers.

61 Morton, 27; Thompson, 233; an "ear-witness" quoted the Prime Minister as waving his cigar at the group and crying, "More tooth!," Kay Halle, *Irrepressible Churchill* (New York, 1966), 185.

62 Thompson, 233–34.

63 Arnold journal, August 10, 1941.

64 Dinner menu for *Augusta*, August 9, 1941, PSF, Box 2, Roosevelt Papers. The menu is autographed by all present.

65 For this question see Dawson, 178.

66 Memorandum by Hopkins of conversation with Molotov, July 31, 1941, *FR*, 1941, I, 802–05.

67 Churchill, *The Grand Alliance*, 433.

68 Churchill, *The Grand Alliance*, 433.

69 Elliott Roosevelt, 29.

70 *Ibid.*, 29–30; Arnold, *Global Mission*, 250.

71 Sherwood, 364.

72 Their eagerness was limited to entry in the European war; *e.g.*, Stark's letter to Admiral Husband E. Kimmel, January 13, 1941, *Pearl Harbor Attack*, Part 5, 2111. It is clear also that Marshall, as the difficulties of arming, equipping, and training the American forces mounted in 1941, became more and more fearful of the destructive effects of premature intervention; see Pogue, II, for full discussion of this attitude.

73 Churchill attempted to convert the President through his advisors, telling them at Argentia that he would rather have an American declaration of war immediately and no supplies for six months than double the supplies and no declaration. When this reached Roosevelt, "he thought it a hard saying," Churchill to Smuts, November 9, 1941, *The Grand Alliance*, 593.

74 Watson, 400.

75 The works by Watson, Arnold, Sherwood, and Gwyer, and materials in the Roosevelt and Stimson papers support this judgment; there is contrary evidence, naturally.

76 Arnold journal, August 9, 1941.

77 Sherwood, 314–16; Memorandum of August 18, 1941, from Comdr. Forrest Sherman to Chief of Naval Operations, containing notes on Staff Conferences, 11–12 August, 1941, Kittredge MS, Section V, Part B, Appendix B.

78 Arnold, *Global Mission*, 252.

79 *Ibid.*

80 Elliott Roosevelt, 29.

81 Watson, 401.

82 Log of the President's Cruise, August 3–16, 1941. Dean Acheson, in *Sketches From Life* (New York, 1963), suggests another reason. He writes Hopkins told him during the war: "The President's strong competitive instinct . . . led him to try to keep up with Mr. Churchill in everything. But in one contest he was definitely outclassed, as became evident as the after-dinner hours passed. Sometimes during these evenings the Prime Minister would produce a slip of paper and suggest that he and President Roosevelt initial conclusions reached earlier in the day. On these occasions Harry would pocket the memorandum for more mature consideration," 61.

VI. UNITED IN PURPOSE

1 Jacob Diary, August 10, 1941.
2 Morton, 87.
3 Jacob Diary, August 9, 1941.
4 Arnold journal, August 10, 1941.
5 Air Vice-Marshal, W. M. Yool to author, March 9, 1967.
6 Churchill, *The Grand Alliance*, 431.
7 Order of Divine Service, August 10, 1941, OF 463-C, Conference At Sea folder, Roosevelt Papers.
8 *Ibid.*
9 Churchill, *The Grand Alliance*, 432.
10 Memorandum by the President, August 23, 1941, PSF, Box 2, Roosevelt Papers.
11 Elliott Roosevelt, 33.
12 Churchill, *The Grand Alliance*, 431. Others reacted similarly. Captain Schofield looked back to write: "It was the first of many meetings between the men on whose shoulders would lie the task of forging victory out of disaster and what could have been more fitting than that they should seek God's blessing on their endeavors. '. . . that we being armed with Thy defence may be preserved evermore from all perils to glorify Thee, who art the only giver of victory . . .' As that combined chorus of British-American voices echoed across the still waters of the bay it was impossible not to feel deeply moved and spiritually uplifted." Schofield memoir, 243.
13 Morton, 114, 122.
14 King and Whitehall, 335; Jacob Diary, August 10, 1941.
15 Welles' memorandum of conversation with Cadogan, At Sea, August 10, 1941, *FR*, 1941, I, 354.
16 *Ibid.*, 354–55.
17 Welles' memorandum for Roosevelt, May 22, 1941, *FR*, 1941, IV, 208.
18 Roosevelt to Ickes, July 1, 1941, in Elliott Roosevelt, *F.D.R.: His Personal Letters, 1928–45*, II, 1173–74. This statement was in reply to a letter from Ickes urging an embargo upon oil.
19 See memorandum by Assistant Chief of Division of Far Eastern Affairs (Adams), June 25, 1941, *FR*, 1941, IV, 278–80.
20 Translation, *Pearl Harbor Attack*, Pt. 20, 4018–19.
21 Feis, 219–20.
22 Leahy, 44; Inaction was justified by the mirage created by the fall of another cabinet in Japan. See also memorandum by Welles of conversation with the British Minister, Mr. Butler, July 16, 1941, *FR*, 1941, V, 213.

23 Memorandum of conversation by the Chief of the Division of Far Eastern Affairs (Hamilton), July 17, 1941, *FR*, 1941, IV, 325–26.

24 Feis, 235.

25 Washington *Star*, June 5, 1941.

26 Memorandum by Welles of conversation, July 24, 1941, *FR, Japan, 1931–41*, II, 527ff.

27 Feis, 239.

28 The Dutch were especially anxious, since the embargo opened the way to Japanese invasion of the East Indies. See memorandum of conversation by Welles, July 29, 1941, *FR*, 1941, IV, 350–51; E. N. van Kleffens, Netherlands Foreign Minister, said on July 25: "If, and only if, the Japanese had reason to believe they would burn their fingers by advancing in any given direction, they would not move," Biddle to Hull, July 25, 1941, *FR*, 1941, V, 232–33.

29 Feis, 239.

30 Sherwood, 319–20.

31 Grant (Bangkok) to Hull, July 28, 1941, D.F. 792.93/135. See memorandum by Willys R. Peck, July 30, 1941, for recommendation there be no reply to this request, *FR*, 1941, V, 238.

32 Memorandum by Cecil W. Grey, July 31, 1941, *FR*, 1941, V, 241.

33 Memorandum by Welles, August 4, 1941, *FR, Japan, 1931–41*, II, 543.

34 Menu of Luncheon, August 10, 1941, on *Prince of Wales*, OF 463-C, Conference At Sea folder, Roosevelt Papers.

35 Morton, 124; Schofield memoir, 242.

36 *Ibid.*; it was traditional in the British Navy to serve turtle soup at a dinner of this kind aboard ship.

37 List of musical selections by Royal Marine Band, n.d., OF 463-C, Conference At Sea folder, Roosevelt Papers.

38 Elliott Roosevelt, 37.

39 On the back of his menu, which he passed to Roosevelt, Hopkins wrote that Churchill had told him the following story "apropos of yours and the P.M.'s speech about the men and the tools." The King [sic] of Abyssinia (Haile Selassie) had cabled Churchill in bafflement: "I have the men. What shall I do with the tools?" There is no record of the President's reaction. PSF, Box 2, Roosevelt Papers.

40 OpNav for CinclAnt, August 9, 1941, 082359.

41 Jacob Diary, August 10, 1941.

42 Log of the President's Cruise, August 3–16, 1941.

43 Thompson, 235.

44 Memorandum by Welles, At Sea, August 10, 1941, *FR*, 1941, I, 355–56.

45 Jacob Diary, August 10, 1941.
46 Thompson, 234–35.
47 *Ibid.*, 235.
48 Schofield memoir, 246.
49 Arnold journal, August 10, 1941.
50 Elliott Roosevelt, 34.
51 *Ibid.*, 35.
52 *Ibid.*, 35–37.
53 Lord Moran, *Churchill: Taken From the Diaries of Lord Moran* (Boston, 1966), 33.
54 Tugwell, 592.
55 Memorandum, F.D.R. to Eleanor Roosevelt, August 21, 1941, OF 48-H, Roosevelt Papers.
56 Lloyd C. Gardner, *Economic Aspects of New Deal Diplomacy* (Madison, Wis., 1964), 178.
57 See Hull, *Memoirs*, 1482–83, for discussion of India during the Arcadia Conference. State cabled the American Consul at Calcutta (Wilson) in June, 1941, for detailed information on the Indian war effort. The Department also urgently desired "information . . . concerning extent to which *satygraha* and anti-British sentiment are actually impeding war effort." Secretary to American Consul, Calcutta, June 20, 1941, D.F. 740.0011 European War 1939/12365. Wilson replied that "the Indian contribution is much greater than in the corresponding period in the last war; that administrative mistakes by Europeans have probably retarded progress more than Indian ineptitude"; and he asserted that "*satygraha* has not impeded war effort; preoccupation with future status giving way to realization of menace to India itself." Wilson to Secretary, July 8, 1941, D.F. 740.0011 European War 1939/12942.
58 Churchill, *The Grand Alliance*, 800.

VII. HYPOTHETICAL QUESTIONS

1 Jacob Diary, August 12, 1941; Arnold journal, August 14, 1941; Schofield stated that these personal contacts "were to prove of inestimable value in the difficult and testing years to come," 247.
2 Jacob Diary, August 9, 1941.
3 *Ibid.*
4 Schofield admitted that "beneath his grim and sour look he had a sense of humor but many a tussle did we have . . . with this hardbitten old man of the sea," 242.
5 After he became Chief of Naval Operations, Admiral King had opportunities to give vent to these prejudices. He seized them.

6 Jacob Diary, August 11, 1941.

7 Stimson Diary, October 12, 1940, May 6, 1941; Pogue, II, 125; F.D.R. said when Stark became C.N.O. that he was pleased because "we think alike," Roosevelt to Stark, March 22, 1939, PPF 166, Roosevelt Papers.

8 Jacob Diary, August 11, 1941; Turner was widely reputed to be America's most brilliant strategist.

9 Francis Williams, *A Prime Minister Remembers* (London, 1961), 50.

10 Pogue, II, 270.

11 Schofield memoir, 242.

12 Vice-Admiral B. B. Schofield to author, March 4, 1967.

13 Arnold journal, August 10, 1941.

14 *Ibid.;* the statement ascribed to a U.S. Navy officer after this meeting, "Love us . . . All they want is our birthright," is apocryphal since no naval officers attended; it is also evocative, Elliott Roosevelt, 38.

15 Jacob Diary, August 9, 1941.

16 Pogue, II, 16.

17 Harvey H. Bundy Oral History Memoir, 152–53, Columbia Oral History Project.

18 Moran, 22; Hopkins told Secretary of War Stimson that Marshall had been the "outstanding figure" at the conference, Stimson Diary, August 19, 1941.

19 Moran, 21.

20 Pogue, II, 271–72.

21 Jacob Diary, August 11, 1941; Arnold journal, August 9, 1941.

22 Jacob Diary, August 9, 1941. This paper is summarized in Watson, 403–13.

23 Arnold journal, August 9, 1941; the Army Air Corps chief was so preoccupied with thoughts about the British airplane program that he was unable to pay attention to the Prime Minister.

24 Gwyer, 129; Pogue, II, 142.

25 Sherman memorandum, Kittredge MS; see also Gwyer, 127.

26 This directive was approved in July, 1940, Ray S. Cline, *Washington Command Post* (Washington, D.C., 1953), 44.

27 Army leaders would have agreed with Breckinridge Long's statement, made in June, 1941, that the United States was preparing to take "a big leap—almost overseas—to islands in another hemisphere" but this did not mean the President wanted to get into the war. It was part "of the 'fog' we are now entering upon" and nobody could see through the fog to any great distance, Long Diaries, June 4, 1941.

28 See Roosevelt's speech before the Teamster's Union Convention, September 11, 1941, reported in the *New York Times*.

29 Rosenman, ed., *F.D.R. Public Papers and Addresses,* IX, 514ff.
30 Kent R. Greenfield. *Strategy in World War II* (Chicago, 1957), who stated: "The concept underlying his guidance of American strategy was that . . . America was from first to last to serve as 'the arsenal of democracy' and that its proper contribution to victory was to confront its enemies with a rapidly growing weight of material power," 74.
31 Gwyer, 142.
32 The special position which Marshall occupied in the White House circle was largely responsible for this fact, Cline, 6–7.
33 This analysis, a gold mine of information about Roosevelt's strategic views, is summarized in Maurice Matloff and Edwin M. Snell, *Strategic Planning for Coalition Warfare, 1941–42* (Washington, D.C., 1953), 13–14.
34 Tugwell, 487.
35 Trumbull Higgins, *Winston Churchill and the Second Front* (New York, 1957), 48.
36 Quoted in Gwyer, 27.
37 Arnold, *Global Mission,* 235.
38 Stimson Diary, February 8, 1941.
39 Long Diaries, February 29, 1941.
40 Higgins, 48.
41 Stimson commented: "The old principles of the conversations between the Staffs of the two countries which took place last winter seem to be departed from by what the President is doing and both Marshall and I are worried about the situation," Stimson Diary, May 26, 1941; Pogue, II, has an excellent discussion of this point.
42 Jay Pierrepont Moffat to James Dunn, Political Advisor, July 16, 1941, D.F. 740.0011 European War 1939/13577.
43 Churchill, *The Grand Alliance,* 806–07; Trumbull Higgins has observed: "Here the skilled British historian and parliamentarian's language must be considered with extreme care; every word meant exactly what it said but it all added up to something very different indeed from what was implied at first sight," 62.
44 Watson, 401.
45 Arnold, *Global Mission,* 252.
46 Jay Pierrepont Moffat to James Dunn, July 16, 1941, D.F. 740.0011 European War 1939/13577.
47 Jacob Diary, August 10, 1941.
48 Watson, 403.
49 Arnold journal, August 10, 1941.
50 Jacob Diary, August 10, 1941.

51 Watson, 403; this can be taken as a restatement of the Prime Minister's plea to F.D.R., Churchill, *The Grand Alliance,* 593.

52 *Ibid.;* Gwyer has described how the British Chiefs concluded that without immediate United States entry "it is difficult to see how or when we can pass from a grim defence to a resolute offensive," 16.

53 Watson, 403.

54 Sherman memorandum, Kittredge MS, Section V, Part B, Appendix B.

55 Arnold journal, August 10, 1941.

56 Arnold, *Global Mission,* 253.

57 Elliott Roosevelt, 33–34.

58 And, it appears, gladly; the P.M. wrote Attlee that Russia was "a welcome guest at a hungry table," Churchill, *The Grand Alliance,* 446.

59 Memorandum, Conference file, Box 181, Arnold Papers.

60 Arnold journal, August 10, 1941.

61 Langer and Gleason, *The Undeclared War,* 665.

62 Gallup Poll, May 28, 1941, Indianapolis *Times.*

63 Kent R. Greenfield, *Command Decisions* (Washington, D.C., 1960), 40.

64 Watson, 587.

65 *Ibid.*

66 Long Diaries, April 17, 1941.

67 Kittredge MS, Section V, Part B, 539–40.

68 Long Diaries, May 12, 1941.

69 Churchill reprimanded the First Sea Lord for allowing this gloss to get about. "Who has been responsible for starting this idea among the Americans that we should like their destroyer forces to operate on their own side of the Atlantic rather than upon ours?" he growled. "Whoever has put this about has done great disservice and should be removed immediately from all American contacts," *The Grand Alliance,* 776.

70 Kittredge MS, Section V, Part B, 541.

71 American forces were to "destroy or capture" any and all enemy units sighted.

72 Langer and Gleason, *The Undeclared War,* 579.

73 *Ibid.*

74 Kittredge MS, Section V, Part B, 547.

75 *Ibid.*

76 The presence of Commander M. G. Goodenough, an expert on convoy routing, and Admiral Sir Percy Noble showed that the British expected a decision, *ibid.,* 556.

77 W.P.L.-51, Handwritten appendix (detailed instructions for the operations of convoys and escorts), Naval Archives.

78 Samuel Eliot Morison, *History of United States Naval Operations in World War II* (14 vols., Boston, 1946–59), II, 73.

79 Arnold journal, August 10, 1941.

80 Jacob Diary, August 11, 1941.

81 Air Vice-Marshal W. M. Yool to author, March 9, 1967.

82 Describing this conversation, Jacob said: "We also had a useful discussion on our Chiefs of Staff organization and theirs, and tried to pave the way toward the acceptance of our idea that the ultimate requirements for winning the war should be worked out . . . on the basis of our Future Strategy Paper," Jacob Diary, August 11, 1941.

83 Sherman memorandum, Kittredge MS.

84 Transcript of Admiral Stark's statement at CofS meeting, August 11, 1941, Box 271, Arnold Papers.

85 Sherman memorandum, Kittredge MS.

86 *Ibid.;* Jacob recorded that Marshall argued for reinforcement of the Philippines "so as to constitute a serious check to Japanese southward expansion," Diary, August 9, 1941.

87 *Ibid.;* the British, knowing how weak were such reinforcements, took little consolation from Stark's statement.

88 After the blowup in cabinet meeting on August 1, F.D.R. had ordered that airplanes already created for shipment to England be reassembled, flown across the country and Siberia, to be presented to the Russians, Stimson Diary, August 17, 1941.

89 Churchill, *The Grand Alliance,* 426.

90 Mattloff and Snell, 53.

91 Jacob Diary, August 9, 1941.

92 Sherman memorandum, Kittredge MS.

93 Jacob Diary, August 11, 1941.

94 This appears a complete reversal of roles, but London gladly would have accepted Hopkins' proposal — had it included increased deliveries of bombers, Sherman memorandum, Kittredge MS.

95 *Ibid.*

96 *Ibid.*

97 Pogue, II, 306.

98 Sherman memorandum, Kittredge MS; sympathy from American compatriots — the Navy leaders — was not forthcoming. They had their own problems.

99 *Ibid.*

100 Reports from the United States Consul at Dakar (Wasson) were without exception pessimistic regarding an easy occupation; see also

the letter of William C. Bullitt to Roosevelt, May 21, 1941, PPF
1124, Roosevelt Papers.

101 Report of Comdr. Goodenough at Admiralty Liaison Meeting, August 22, 1941, Kittredge MS, Section V, Part B, 585.

102 Dawson, 43.

103 *Pearl Harbor Attack,* Part 14, 1346–47; Part 16, 2183.

104 Sherman memorandum, Kittredge MS.

105 Arnold journal, August 11, 1941.

106 Jacob Diary, August 11, 1941; Pogue rebuts this statement by writing: "At a time when Marshall was trying to find enough troops to replace the Marine brigade in Iceland, the question of whether he
would send a large or small force to Europe was completely unrealistic," II, 144.

107 Arnold journal, August 11, 1941.

108 Jacob Diary, August 11, 1941; this lively party is described more
fully in Morton's book.

109 Jacob Diary, August 12, 1941.

110 Arnold journal, August 12, 1941.

111 Jacob Diary, August 12, 1941.

112 Arnold journal, August 12, 1941.

113 Jacob judged it "the best meeting of all those which have taken place
over here," Diary, August 12, 1941.

114 Sherman memorandum, Kittredge MS.

115 This arose from U.S. complaints about the lack of coordination between the British service missions. The British Chiefs confessed to
ignorance of many of the problems and promised that the missions
"would be overhauled and reorganized," *ibid.;* see also letter from
Air Chief Marshal Portal to Arnold, September 3, 1941, Special
Official File, 1941–45, Aircraft Allocation folder, Box 38, Arnold
Papers.

VIII. THE THIRD CLIMACTERIC

1 *New York Times,* August 11, 1941; London *Daily Telegraph,* August
10, 1941.

2 *New York Times,* August 11, 1941.

3 Leahy to Hull, August 10, 1941, D.F. 740.0011 European War 1939/
13830.

4 Nobutaka Ike, *Japan's Decision For War: Records of the 1941 Policy
Conferences* (Stanford, Calif., 1967), 113.

5 See the discussion of this message and its implications in chapter four.

6 Ike, 118.

7 Los Angeles *Times,* August 9, 1941.

8 Hull to Grant (Bangkok), August 7, 1941, D.F. 740.0011 Pacific War/428a; memorandum by Hull of conversation with Halifax, August 9, 1941, D.F. 740.0011 Pacific War/460.

9 Waldo Heinrichs, *American Ambassador: Joseph C. Grew* (Boston, 1966), 339–40. Heinrichs writes: "The Japanese had indeed miscalculated the severity of the American reaction. The stoppage of trade, particularly oil, presented the appalling prospect of slow immobilization of Japan's land, sea, and air forces. A sense of finality settled over the Japanese consciousness: their nation would have to solve its problems with the United States or resort to war."

10 Ike, 24.

11 Memorandum by Dooman and Grew, August 18, 1941, *FR, Japan, 1931–41*, II, 559–64; for a fascinating but questionable report of this interview, see Arthur Krock Oral History Memoir, Columbia Oral History Project.

12 Long Diaries, August 31, 1941.

13 *Newsweek*, August 18, 1941.

14 Long Diaries, August 11, 1941.

15 Stimson Diary, August 7, 11, 1941.

16 *Newsweek*, August 18, 1941.

17 *Ibid.; New York Times*, August 6–13, 1941.

18 Log of the President's Cruise, August 3–16, 1941.

19 Memorandum by Welles of Meeting, August 9, 1941, *FR, 1941*, I, 356.

20 *Ibid.*, 357. Churchill stated that the islands were heavily fortified and that German officers were engaged in training the Spanish garrison.

21 Langer and Gleason, *The Undeclared War*, 669.

22 *Ibid.*, 669–70. Another interpretation of *Pilgrim* is that of Trumbull Higgins, who asserts: "Probably the motive for this bold British policy lay . . . in Winston Churchill's . . . inveterate hopes of involving the United States more actively in the war through President Roosevelt's special interest in French North and West Africa," 64.

23 See, for example, Fish to Hull, May 26, 1941, D.F. 740.0011 European War 1939/11327; Fish to Hull, June 13, 1941, D.F. 740.0011 European War 1939/11364; and Fish to Hull, May 9, 1941, D.F. 853B.014/13.

24 CinclAnt File, A16-3 (6834), May 10, 1941, Naval Archives.

25 Welles' memorandum, August 11, 1941, *FR, 1941*, I, 357. Brazil was considered by American military planners of critical importance.

26 *Ibid.*

27 *Ibid.*

28 These messages are printed in *FR, Japan, 1931–41*, II, 546–50.

29 Welles memorandum, August 11, 1941, *FR*, 1941, I, 358.

30 *Ibid.*

31 *Ibid.*

32 *Ibid.*

33 Churchill, *The Grand Alliance*, 595.

34 Welles' memorandum, August 11, 1941, *FR*, 1941, I, 358; if this were not possible, Roosevelt hoped war could be held off "for at least thirty days."

35 The President cabled Hull on August 12 that "it seems highly desirable that you and I should see Nomura as soon as I get back," and asked that the Japanese Ambassador be ready to come to the White House Saturday or Sunday, *Pearl Harbor Attack*, Part 14, 1254.

36 Welles' memorandum, August 11, 1941, *FR*, 1941, I, 358.

37 Churchill, *The Grand Alliance*, 439.

38 Welles' memorandum, August 11, 1941, *FR*, 1941, I, 358.

39 His concern is understandable; but the assertion that he lacked authority to do so is not.

40 Welles' memorandum, August 11, 1941, *FR*, 1941, I, 360.

41 Log of the President's Cruise, August 3–16, 1941.

42 Thompson, 238.

43 Roosevelt to King George VI, August 11, 1941, PSF: Great Britain folder, 1941–42, Roosevelt Papers.

44 Arnold, *Global Mission*, 255.

45 Churchill to Eden, August 11, 1941, Churchill, *The Grand Alliance*, 439.

46 *Ibid.*, 440; Eden was to have a difficult time persuading the Dominions' leaders that the President's statement comprised a "great advance."

47 Churchill to Attlee, August 11, 1941, Churchill, *The Grand Alliance*, 441.

48 Elliott Roosevelt, 40.

49 *Ibid.*, Morton provides a less flamboyant account of the Prime Minister's afternoon amusement.

50 Morton, 124–27; Jacob Diary, August 11, 1941.

51 Memorandum by Welles of conversation with Cadogan, August 11, 1941, *FR*, 1941, I, 364–65.

52 Log of the President's Cruise, August 3–16, 1941; Arnold journal, August 11, 1941.

53 Elliott Roosevelt, 41.

54 Sherwood, 370.

55 Elliott Roosevelt, 41.

IX. THE ATLANTIC CHARTER

1 Welles, *Seven Decisions*, 178.

2 Knoxville, Tennessee *Clarion*, April 13, 1913, quoted in Frank Freidel, *F.D.R.: The Apprenticeship* (2 vols., Boston, 1952–54), I, 173.

3 Louis Wehle, *Hidden Threads of History: Wilson Through Roosevelt* (New York, 1953), 227.

4 Elliott Roosevelt, ed., *F.D.R.: His Personal Letters, 1928–45*, II, 1175; the President had stated this view even more graphically earlier, writing Sir Arthur Willert: "After all . . . armament is the real root of the world disease — and the other difficulties are resulting symptoms. When everybody goes a little more bankrupt there will be war or disarmament," Roosevelt to Sir Arthur Willert, June 16, 1937, PPF 4715, Roosevelt Papers.

5 Nancy H. Hooker, ed., *The Moffat Papers*, 388. A more complete discussion of this point is provided later in this chapter.

6 Welles, *Seven Decisions*, 136.

7 This is a reflection of Roosevelt's faith in personal diplomacy, for he assumed he would be present to dominate the "universal" peace conference.

8 Dawson, 136.

9 H. G. Wells to Roosevelt, October 29, 1940, PPF 1041, Roosevelt Papers.

10 Hadley Cantril to Anna Rosenberg for the President, March 20, 1941, PPF 1820, Roosevelt Papers.

11 Stimson Diary, April 8, May 20, 1941.

12 "Memorandum Concerning the Meeting of May 3, 1941," May 31, 1941, PPF 1820. This fascinating document would be of great significance if the names of the participants could be determined; unfortunately, the author's efforts to solve the mystery have been unsuccessful. It is notable that a good many of the phrases in the "Memorandum" recur in the Atlantic Charter.

13 *Ibid.* One of the participants asserted: "During and after hostilities the United States has an immediate concern for the future of the British Empire — if Hitler should smash England this summer it will be our job to pick up the pieces."

14 *Ibid.*

15 [Harley Notter], *Postwar Foreign Policy Preparation, 1939–45*. Department of State Publication 3580, General Foreign Policy Series 15 (Washington, D.C., 1949), 22.

16 Long Diaries, January 13, 1942.
17 *Department of State Bulletin,* May 7, 1941.
18 Rosenman, ed., *F.D.R. Public Papers and Addresses,* IX, 672.
19 Gardner, *Economic Aspects of New Deal Diplomacy,* 262–63.
20 See the cable of Halifax to Hull, May 16, 1941, *FR,* 1941, III, 119–20.
21 Memorandum on Master Lend-Lease Agreement, May 22, 1941. Uncataloged except for notations, "Pasvolsky file," Department of State Records, National Archives.
22 Langer and Gleason, *The Undeclared War,* 678–79.
23 Gardner, 276.
24 *Ibid.* Morgenthau claimed that there was good reason for the President's reticence. "And Keynes was indiscreet," he said. "One evening at the home of Justice Frankfurter . . . Keynes had criticized Roosevelt. He had seemed, in his talks with Morgenthau and Hopkins, overgenerous with advice, often supercilious," Blum, II, 246.
25 Hull to Halifax, May 21, 1941, *FR,* 1941, III, 121.
26 Langer and Gleason, *The Undeclared War,* 678.
27 Nancy H. Hooker, ed., *The Moffat Papers,* 374.
28 Hull to London Embassy for Welles, March 2, 1940, D.F. 121.840 Sumner Welles, 106A.
29 Johnson to Hull, February 10, 1941, D.F. 740.0011 European War 1939/9103.
30 Welles to Roosevelt, February 3, 1941, PPF 1820, Roosevelt Papers; also in D.F. 740.0011 European War 1939/8176a.
31 Louise Holborn, *War and Peace Aims of the United Nations* (Boston, 1943), 42.
32 Memorandum by Pasvolsky for Hull, June 7, 1941, D.F. 840.50/232 1/2. Hull's assistant observed that "these ideas are obviously important in proportion to the extent to which the Labor Party will dominate British reconstruction policy."
33 Johnson to Hull, July 11, 1941, D.F. 740.0011 European War 1939/13118.
34 Memorandum by Pasvolsky for Hull, June 7, 1941, D.F. 840.50/232 1/2.
35 Churchill, *The Grand Alliance,* 433.
36 Memorandum of Welles-Cadogan conversation, August 9, 1941, *FR,* 1941, I, 351.
37 Kittredge MS, Section IV, Part C, 420.
38 See Hull to Winant, June 13, 1941, D.F. 740.0011 European War 1939/11970; Johnson to Hull, June 13, 1941, *FR,* 1941, I, 170–72; and Dawson, 132.

39 Memorandum by Welles, June 15, 1941, *FR*, 1941, I, 759–61; Welles threatened Halifax in the only way open to him: "I asked whether Lord Halifax believed that American public opinion would continue to have faith in the validity of the moral issues involved in this struggle if such steps were taken by the British Government."

40 The Foreign Secretary confessed privately: "The spectacle of an American President talking at large on European frontiers chilled me with Wilsonian memories," Eden, 273.

41 For an example, see Johnson to Hull, June 17, 1941, D.F. 740.0011 European War 1939/12157.

42 Memorandum of Welles-Cadogan conversation, August 9, 1941, I, 351.

43 *Ibid.* For evidence that Cadogan was misinformed or lying diplomatically see the memorandum of a conversation between Adolf A. Berle and Ralph C. S. Stevenson, British Minister to Uruguay, September 15,1941. Stevenson admitted that London had given a "half promise" to support Russian political domination in Eastern Europe, *FR*, 1941, I, 188. Eden's word, which contradicts this view, properly should be given more weight.

44 These are in *FR*, 1941, II, 6–17.

45 Memorandum of Welles-Cadogan conversation, August 9, 1941, *FR*, 1941, 351. Article VII was the center of the controversy. It provided for the abolition of discrimination in U.S. and U.K. against the importation of any product of the other country — thus abolishing imperial preference.

46 *Ibid.*

47 Welles later testified that he and F.D.R. had been talking about the crisis for some weeks before the conference, and that the President had said: "Nothing would be more valuable from the standpoint of keeping alive some principles of international law, some principles of moral and human decency, than for him to make some kind of public statement of the objectives in international relations in which the Government of the United States believed," *Pearl Harbor Attack*, Part 2, 536ff.

48 Sherwood, 350.

49 Churchill, *The Grand Alliance*, 434.

50 Churchill's draft, with corrections in his handwriting, is reproduced in *The Grand Alliance*, 435.

51 Welles, *Where Are We Heading?*, 9.

52 *Ibid.*, 7.

53 Elliott Roosevelt, 35–37.

54 The reason for this intemperate statement again is India. There is no

intention here to deny the depth of the gulf which separated the views of Roosevelt and Churchill on "Empire." Rexford Tugwell, Lord Moran, innumerable others, statements of Roosevelt in press conferences — all support the existence of the difficulty. Its divisiveness at Argentia, however, is not demonstrated by extant evidence.

55 Welles, *Where Are We Heading?*, 10.
56 *Ibid.*, 7.
57 *Ibid.*, 7–8.
58 *Ibid.*, 9.
59 Welles considered that this change was a matter of phrasing only, *ibid.*, 9–10.
60 *Ibid.*, 10–11.
61 Memorandum by Welles of conversation, August 11, 1941, FR, 1941, I, 360.
62 *Ibid.*, 360–61.
63 One may point to this statement as further evidence of the President's expectations for large propaganda benefits from the joint declaration.
64 Memorandum of conversation, August 11, 1941, FR, 1941, I, 361–62.
65 It may be admitted that the Prime Minister was emotionally committed to a mystique of "free trade," but these emotions belonged to a world which no longer existed; certainly he was able to overcome them when the Empire was in danger.
66 Memorandum by Welles of conversation, August 11, 1941, FR, 1941, I, 362.
67 *Ibid.*
68 *Ibid.* One wonders whether Hopkins had passed a note to the President suggesting this idea. It must be noted that Sherwood places a different gloss upon Hopkins' intervention.
69 *Ibid.*, 363.
70 *Ibid.*
71 Welles, *Where Are We Heading?*, 15.
72 Churchill, *The Grand Alliance*, 441.
73 *Ibid.*, 442.
74 *Ibid.* This implied that Churchill had arranged a *quid pro quo* — Roosevelt's joint declaration of ideals for his joint declaration with regard to Japan. It is a plausible idea that nowhere else are the two proposals linked directly.
75 Welles, *Where Are We Heading?*, 16. The President's note is published in facsimile in the frontispiece to this book, a comment on the importance Welles gave it.
76 *Ibid.*

77 Memorandum by Welles of conversation with Cadogan, August 11, 1941, *FR*, 1941, I, 364.
78 *Ibid.*
79 *Ibid.*, 365. The President went so far as to term point seven "entirely desirable."
80 *Ibid.* Roosevelt was confronted by such an interpretation. He consistently denied its validity, except for an implication of American involvement in the message transmitting the joint declaration to Congress on August 21. See *Documents on American Foreign Relations*, IV, 13.
81 *Ibid.*, 365–66.
82 *Ibid.*, 366.
83 *Ibid.*, 367.

X. GOODBYE, COLUMBUS

1 Memorandum by Welles of conversation, August 11, 1941, *FR*, 1941, I, 364–67.
2 The British had believed until late Monday morning that the meeting was to end that night, Jacob Diary, August 11, 1941. Apparently the Americans believed this also, Memorandum by Captain Beardall, outlining arrangements for departure early Tuesday, after the Prime Minister had gone, August 10, 1941, Conference File, Box 271, Arnold Papers.
3 Churchill, *The Grand Alliance*, 447.
4 Hopkins' draft article, Box 303, Hopkins Papers.
5 Francis Williams, *A Prime Minister Remembers* (London, 1961), 54.
6 Sherwood, 361.
7 His demeanor was "rather like a small boy about to take medicine," Jacob Diary, August 12, 1941.
8 Churchill, *The Grand Alliance*, 442.
9 The Prime Minister seemed to want the Cabinet to believe that Roosevelt only reluctantly had accepted the reservation to Article IV — and that his powers of persuasion were responsible, *The Grand Alliance*, 442.
10 The explanation which first occurs follows the isolationist argument: that reference to religious freedom would anger the Soviets and cause needless complications. However, F.D.R.'s later actions suggest that failure to bring in all "four freedoms" was an oversight.
11 *FR*, 1941, I, 367–69.
12 Churchill, *The Grand Alliance*, 430; Moran, 28.
13 Moran, 10.

14 The Canadian had provided the glue by which the rickety vehicle of British supply moved forward. The system was improved upon but no one replaced Purvis.
15 Churchill, *The Grand Alliance*, 446.
16 Morton, 128.
17 Sherwood, 360. Sherwood stated that Lord Beaverbrook was present all through the conference and that he doggedly upheld Conservative economic views. He got this, apparently, from Hopkins' notes, which had Beaverbrook arriving early Monday morning. A recent book, Kenneth Young's *Churchill and Beaverbrook* (London, 1966), perpetuates this error.
18 This *aide mémoire* by Beaverbrook contradicts a mass of other evidence. He wrote that *he* had caused the qualifying phrase in Article IV to be inserted; which matter had been thrashed out at luncheon between he, Roosevelt, Hopkins, Welles, and Churchill. "Welles objected to the insertion of the words. Churchill persisted and Roosevelt gave way," Young, 322–25. This "document" is inexplicable.
19 Churchill, *The Grand Alliance*, Appendix C, Book Two, 848–49.
20 *FR*, 1941, I, 367; *Time* observed that Beaverbrook was coming to the U.S. "to see if the British had left anything," August 25, 1941.
21 Churchill, *The Grand Alliance*, Appendix C, Book Two, 849.
22 Hopkins explained that Beaverbrook's reluctance arose from desire to take part in the dangerous voyage home! Hopkins' draft article Box 303, Hopkins Papers.
23 Sherwood, 359.
24 *FR*, 1941, I, 822–23.
25 Dawson, 180.
26 *FR*, 1941, I, 368.
27 Sherwood, 363.
28 Churchill, *The Grand Alliance*, 447.
29 Sherwood, 367.
30 Pogue, II, 146–52. Roosevelt had thought it best not to bring up the issue in Congress. "He was again afraid of fear itself," Sherwood said, 367. As a result the chore of putting across the measure devolved upon military leaders, especially Marshall.
31 Pogue, II, 152.
32 *Ibid.*
33 Roosevelt to Early, delivered orally by Admiral Ingersoll, August 7, 1941, OF 463-C, Conference At Sea folder, Roosevelt Papers; Stimson Diary, August 8, 1941.
34 *New York Times*, August 13, 1941.

35 The President apparently recognized this fact and was not much discouraged by the August 12 vote, Tugwell, 581.

36 Gwyer, 129.

37 Hopkins' draft article, Box 303, Hopkins Papers.

38 Jacob Diary, August 12, 1941.

39 Morton, 143.

40 Roosevelt to Mrs. John C. Leach, March 12, 1941, OF 463-C, Conference At Sea folder, Roosevelt Papers.

41 Churchill, *The Grand Alliance*, 444.

42 *Ibid.*

43 *Ibid.* The solidity of Roosevelt's "promise" was the crux. Langer and Gleason have written: "Just how explicit the President's promise to use 'hard' language may have been, it is impossible to say . . . Churchill's messages do not suggest that Mr. Roosevelt bound himself in any formal way to employ the wording of the British draft," *The Undeclared War,* 677.

44 Churchill, *The Grand Alliance*, 446–447.

45 Morton, 144.

46 CinclAnt to ComDesDiv 16, August 10, 1941; CinclAnt to OpNav, action, August 11, 1941, 131720.

47 Jacob Diary, August 12, 1941.

48 Log of the President's Cruise, August 3–16, 1941; CinclAnt to OpNav, August 11, 1941, 131720.

XI. HOMEWARD BOUND

1 OpNav to CinclAnt, August 12, 1941, 132037.

2 OpNav to CinclAnt, August 13, 1941, 132046.

3 Jacob Diary, August 13, 1941.

4 Morton earlier had feared being set adrift at sea — when the Americans discovered his presence at the meeting. He mourned that "if we had been cast adrift in a ship's boat it might have been easier to bear," 83.

5 Churchill, *The Grand Alliance*, 448.

6 London *Times*, August 14, 1941.

7 London *Evening Standard*, August 14, 1941.

8 London *Evening News, Evening Star*, August 14, 1941.

9 London *Daily Telegraph*, August 15, 1941.

10 London *Daily Telegraph*, London *Express*, London *Daily Mail*, London *Chronicle*, August 15, 1941.

11 London *Daily Herald*, August 14, 1941.

12 London *Daily Sketch, Daily Mirror*, August 15, 1941.

13 London *Daily Sketch,* August 15, 1941.

14 London *Times,* August 15, 1941.

15 The story was then released for publication. His death was announced in the *New York Times* on August 17.

16 London *Times,* August 19, 1941.

17 Morton, 149–50.

18 *Ibid.,* Jacob Diary, August 12–17, 1941; W. M. Yool confessed that "by the time we got back to England I felt I had seen enough films to last me a long time. (Perhaps that is why I have only seen about half-a-dozen films in all since then.)," W. M. Yool to author, March 9, 1967.

19 Churchill, *The Grand Alliance,* 447–49.

20 *Ibid.,* 448–49.

21 Glancing reference to C's conversation with "Betty" Stark on this subject is in Kittredge MS, Section V, Part B, Appendix B; the Admiralty's rebuttal is in Churchill, *The Grand Alliance,* 868–69.

22 S. E. Morison, I, 73; Schofield "was delighted to have the opportunity of seeing one of my convoys at close quarters . . . I regret to say that the first thing sighted was a column of smoke, which is one of the most tell-tale advertisements of its presence which a convoy can give to a prowling U-boat," Schofield memoir, 244.

23 *Ibid.,* 245; Jacob Diary, August 15, 1941.

24 Morton, 156–57; Jacob states that the steam whistles on the merchant ships sputtered ineffectually the first time; but they blasted out the Morse Code for "Pleasant Voyage, Churchill" with a vengeance on the second pass, Diary, August 15, 1941.

25 Morton, 157.

26 Jacob Diary, August 16, 1941. This was unexpected because of the unconcealed dislike of the Icelanders for the British occupation forces.

27 Churchill, *The Grand Alliance,* 449.

28 Jacob Diary, August 16, 1941.

29 Schofield memoir, 247.

30 Jacob Diary, August 16, 1941.

31 Thompson, 243; Morton, 152.

32 Jacob Diary, August 16, 1941.

33 *Ibid.,* August 17, 1941; Schofield memoir, 247.

34 Jacob Diary, August 18, 1941.

35 *Ibid.*

36 Sherwood, 365.

37 Winant to Roosevelt, August 19, 1941, D.F. 740.0011 European War 1939/14148. Winant also saw Brendan Bracken, Minister of

Information, who gave him his word that the two British news-papermen on board "would do no reporting whatsoever."

38 Both were prepared to make well-informed guesses, Tully, 251.

39 Roosevelt to Early, August 11, 1941, PSF, Box 2, Roosevelt Papers.

40 Roosevelt to Early, August 12, 1941, PSF, Box 2, Roosevelt Papers.

41 Albert L. Warner, *Analysis of Roosevelt-Churchill Meeting At Sea,* Broadcast over CBS, August 14, 1941, William Lindley, "Press Re-action to the Atlantic Charter," *Journalism Quarterly* (Summer, 1964), 378.

42 Edward R. Murrow, *The World Today,* August 14, 1941, *ibid.,* 380.

43 CinclAnt to OpNav, August 11, 1941, 131720.

44 *Ibid.*

45 August 19, 1941, OF 463-C, Conference At Sea folder, Roosevelt Papers.

46 Roosevelt to L. R. Betts, August 15, 1941, PPF 7685, Roosevelt Papers.

47 Los Angeles *Times,* August 15, 1941.

48 *Ibid.;* St. Louis *Post-Dispatch,* August 14, 1941.

49 Chicago *Tribune,* August 15, 17, 1941.

50 New York *Daily Mirror,* August 16, 1941.

51 *Wall Street Journal,* August 15, 1941.

52 St. Louis *Post-Dispatch,* August 15, 1941.

53 *New York Times,* August 15, 1941.

54 *Ibid.*

55 *Ibid.,* August 16, 1941.

56 Log of the President's Cruise, August 3–16, 1941.

57 *Time,* August 25, 1941.

58 *Ibid.*

59 Press Conference, August 16, 1941, microfilm reel 10, University of Kansas Library. The microfilm transcript shows that the published version deletes certain of Roosevelt's responses.

60 *Ibid.*

61 Roosevelt's concern that it not become known who arranged the con-ference is reflected in a covering letter attached to the Hopkins draft article on the meeting, Walter Davenport, to Hopkins, October 7, 1941, Box 303, Hopkins Papers.

62 Press Conference, August 16, 1941.

63 The reservation meant precisely nothing, as headlines on August 17 showed; *ibid.*

64 *Ibid.*

65 Morton writes of this: "And, of course, he was right. He had gone to

the meeting without his usual Press escort and naturally expected
that Churchill would have done the same. Looking back on things,
it seems to me strange that Churchill, who was no novice in writing
and newspaper affairs, should have allowed Brendan Bracken to put
over a fast one like this; for such it was," H. V. Morton to author,
March 8, 1967.
66 *Newsweek*, August 25, 1941; Hull to Winant, August 14, 1941, D.F.
740.0011 European War 1939/13965a.
67 Log of the President's Cruise, August 3–16, 1941.
68 *Ibid.*

XII. THE AFTERMATH

1 *New York Times*, August 17, 1941.
2 Roosevelt to Mrs. Ogden M. Reid, May 31, 1940, PPF 2219, Roosevelt Papers.
3 Long Diaries, August 31, 1941; Hull also complained to Stimson,
saying that Welles "habitually" conferred with the President without
the presence of or communication with him. "This reached its apex
in the recent Atlantic Conference where the President invited Welles
to go instead of Hull," Stimson Diary, August 19, 1941.
4 Long commented that the episode had to be exaggerated — since he
had never seen the imperturbable Welles in a state of excitement, Long
Diaries, August 31, 1941.
5 Draft statement, dated August 15, 1941, and "brought to the Department by Mr. Welles following conference between the President and
Mr. Winston Churchill," but "not given to the Japanese Ambassador,"
FR, 1941, IV, 370–72.
6 Feis, 256.
7 Second Memorandum by Joseph W. Ballantine, June 12, 1944, *FR*,
1941, IV, 376.
8 Memorandum by Stanley K. Hornbeck, June 12, 1944, *FR*, 1941, IV,
376.
9 *Ibid.*
10 First Ballantine Memorandum, *FR*, 1941, IV, 373.
11 *Ibid.*
12 Draft Statement, August 16, 1941, D.F. 740.0011 European War
1939/in folder of series of memoranda compiled for President but not
sent him, August 29, 1941.
13 *Ibid.*
14 Second Ballantine Memorandum, *FR*, 1941, IV, 375.
15 Hornbeck Memorandum, *FR*, 1941, IV, 376.

16 Second Ballantine Memorandum, *FR*, 1941, IV, 375.
17 Nomura (Washington) to Tokyo, August 18, 1941, *Pearl Harbor Attack*, Part 17, 2749–54.
18 *FR*, 1941, IV, 369–70.
19 It is difficult to understand how this shadow of the statement pressed for by Churchill could be termed an ultimatum; but Hull, in testimony before the Joint Congressional Committee investigating Pearl Harbor, and others, including some historians, have flattered the August 17 message by terming it an ultimatum.
20 *Pearl Harbor Attack*, Part 17, 2753.
21 *Ibid.*, Part 17, 2755.
22 *Ibid.* Langer and Gleason state that this second communication offered "an economic program for the Pacific area which, if adopted, would give Japan everything it needed," *The Undeclared War*, 695.
23 *Pearl Harbor Attack*, Part 12, 17.
24 Feis, 260.
25 "Within and without," Feis has written, "Konoye's project of persuasion was encircled with vetoes," *ibid.*
26 Hull to Winant, August 18, 1941, *FR*, 1941, IV, 380. Hull's draft was returned from Hyde Park, initialed, "OK, FDR."
27 *Ibid.*
28 Sherwood, 357.
29 Langer and Gleason, *The Undeclared War*, 689.
30 *Ibid.*, 688.
31 Hull Memorandum for Roosevelt, August 18, 1941, PSF, Box 86, Roosevelt Papers.
32 Hull to Winant, August 25, 1941, *FR*, 1941, I, 369–70.
33 *Ibid.*
34 Winant to Hull, August 29, 1941, *FR*, 1941, I, 370.
35 Winant to Hull, September 1, 1941, *FR*, 1941, I, 370–71.
36 *Ibid.* Also influential was a memorandum by Herbert Feis, advisor on international economic affairs. Feis wrote he had initialed the proposed statement "with uneasiness," and argued that it was not possible to demand more "than an expression of intention . . . without risking a crisis either in Anglo-American relations or relations between the United Kingdom and the Dominions or both," Memorandum by "H. F.," September 1, 1941, D.F. 740.0011 European War 1939/ 14570.
37 Hull to Winant, September 9, 1941, *FR*, 1941, I, 372; finally, in February, 1942, the President was persuaded to intervene directly and Great Britain signed a Lend-Lease Agreement which embodied the

Department's position. There was no guarantee that the United Kingdom (or the United States) would carry out these promises; but Hull
believed he had attained a great victory. Perhaps it was a substitute
for his exclusion from the Argentia meeting.

38 See the "Joint Board Estimate of United States Over-All Production
Requirements," summarized in Sherwood, 410–18, and Watson, 406–
10. The conclusion revealed a division between American strategists
of large proportions.

39 Stimson Diary, August 14, 1941.

40 *Ibid.*, August 16, 1941; Stimson was alluding to English skepticism
about the combatworthiness of the B-17 when it was first sent into
action in 1940.

41 Arnold journal, August 14, 1941; Colonel Jacob mentioned only one
military decision (the promise by Roosevelt to send immediately
150,000 rifles for the British Home Guard) when he listed the meeting's achievements, Jacob Diary, August 12, 1941.

42 Higgins, viii.

43 Memorandum, Joint Board to Special Army and Navy Observers, London, approved September 25, 1941, quoted in Watson, 406–10.

44 Matloff and Snell, 55.

45 Watson, 356; Sherwood termed this "one of the most remarkable
documents of American history, for it set down the basic strategy of a
global war before the country was involved in it," 415.

46 According to Marshall, the President was convinced that American
participation was to be "Navy, Air, and manufacturing." The War
Plans Division attributed Roosevelt's views to continuing British pressure, Watson, 362.

47 See Churchill's General Directive on the forthcoming U.S.-British-
Russian supply conference, September 22, 1941, *The Grand Alliance*,
Appendix D, Book Two, 851–52.

48 *Ibid.*; an interesting question is the effect of this pressure upon Army
leaders. During the fall of 1941, Marshall, Stimson, and others did
come to believe in application of strategic air power theories *to the
Pacific*. The springs of Atlantic and Pacific strategies require more
investigation; see Pogue, II, 76–79, 186ff.

49 Report of Comdr. Goodenough at Admiralty Liaison Meeting, August
22, 1941, Kittredge MS, Section V, Part B, 585–87.

50 Jacob Diary, August 12, 1941.

51 *Ibid.*, August 19, 1941.

52 Sherwood, 358.

53 Churchill to Roosevelt, September 1, 1941, D.F. 740.0011 European War 1939/14536; see the discussion of the Azores problem in Eden, *The Reckoning*, 390–93.

54 *Documents on German Foreign Policy, 1918–45*, Series D, XIII, 1941 (Washington, D.C., 1964), 131.

55 *Ibid.*, 324.

56 Record of the Duce's conversation with the Führer, August 25, 1941, *ibid.*, 387.

57 Steinhardt to Hull, August 15, 1941, *FR*, 1941, I, 819–22.

58 *Ibid.*

59 The Russian dictator said this, although he was aware of Churchill's desire to wait until October 1, when Soviet military chances would have become more clear.

60 Hull to Roosevelt, At Sea, August 16, 1941, D.F. 740.0011 European War 1939/13649j.

61 Langer and Gleason, *The Undeclared War*, 668.

62 Dawson, 247.

63 Long Diaries, August 27, 1941.

64 Feis, 258.

65 Winston S. Churchill, *The Unrelenting Struggle* (London, 1942), 230–34.

66 *Ibid.*, 234.

67 See Churchill's speech before the House of Commons, September 9, 1941, *ibid.*, 247.

68 Churchill to Hopkins, August 29, 1941, D.F. 740.0011 European War 1939/14536 2/4.

69 Sherwood, 368.

70 Sir John Kennedy, *The Business of War* (London, 1957), 183.

71 Eleanor Roosevelt, *This I Remember* (New York, 1949), 226.

72 Hull, *Memoirs*, II, 975.

73 [Notter] *Post War Foreign Policy Preparation*, 52.

74 World Peace Foundation, *Documents in American Foreign Relations*, IV, 215.

75 [Notter] *Post War Foreign Policy Preparation*, 52.

76 Churchill, *The Grand Alliance*, 630; he specifically excluded Burma and India (and by implication all British colonies) from its purview in the September 9 address before the House of Commons, London *Times*, September 10, 1941.

77 Eden, *The Reckoning*, 296.

XIII. EPILOGUE

1 As one last contribution to this argument, it can be said that even the President's wife admitted that he had not been entirely frank and that Churchill was more blunt with the English people, Eleanor Roosevelt, 167.

2 OF 463-C, Conference At Sea folder, Roosevelt Papers; examples of the "need for action" letters are Grenville Clark to Roosevelt, August 21, 1941, PPF 1958, and letter in memorandum from E. M. Watson to Roosevelt, August 21, 1941, PSF: Speech Material, Box 56, Roosevelt Papers.

3 Hadley Cantril to Anna Rosenberg for President, n.d., PPF 1820, Roosevelt Papers.

4 Roper Survey, *Fortune*, August, 1941; Gallup Poll, Indianapolis *Times*, August 4, 1941.

5 Indianapolis *Times*, August 19, 1941; lest it be thought that the failure of Argentia to mobilize public support extended only to the European war, a Gallup survey on opinion toward Japan is given. When a national sample was asked on August 5 whether the U.S. should go to war immediately with Japan, 78% were opposed and only 22% favored war; the same on October 22 showed that only 12% approved of war against Japan — a drop of 9%.

6 *Ibid.*, September 23, 1941.

7 Stimson Diary, July 21, 1941.

Bibliographic Essay

I. GENERAL WORKS

Students of international affairs in the period, 1939–41, must render obeisance to the monumental achievement of William L. Langer and S. Everett Gleason. Their two-volume history, *Challenge to Isolation, 1937–40* (New York, 1952) and *The Undeclared War, 1940–41* (New York, 1953), combines scholarship, insight, and effective organization. Certain of their conclusions have been and will be corrected, but the work itself will not be easily superseded. Donald F. Drummond, *The Passing of American Neutrality, 1937–41* (Ann Arbor, Mich., 1955), is a shorter survey. As do the Langer and Gleason tomes, Drummond approves of Roosevelt's foreign policy. Of that group of books which register emphatic disapproval, the only one deserving of attention is Charles A. Beard's two-volume polemic, *American Foreign Policy in the Making, 1932–40* (New Haven, 1946), and *President Roosevelt and the Coming of War, 1941: A Study in Appearances and Realities* (New Haven, 1948). Unlike his imitators Beard argues from an intellectually tenable position; it is the method of his argument which is objectionable. Basil Rauch, *Roosevelt: From Munich to Pearl Harbor* (New York, 1950) is uncritical.

Herbert Feis, *The Road to Pearl Harbor* (Princeton, N.J., 1950), remains the most comprehensive survey of Japanese-American relations. It relies on impressive research and on Feis' experience as a Department of State official. His *Churchill, Roosevelt, Stalin: The War They Waged and the Peace They Sought* (Princeton, N.J., 1957) glances at pre-Pearl Harbor contacts. British foreign policy receives full exposition in E. L. Woodward, *British Foreign Policy in the Second World War* (London, 1962). See also Sir C. M. Webster, *et al.*, *United Kingdom Policy, Foreign Strategic and Economic* (London, 1950). William H. McNeill, *America, Britain, and Russia: Their Cooperation and Conflict, 1941–46* (London, 1953), in the three-volume *Survey of International Affairs* edited by Arnold J. Toynbee, is a balanced treatment.

Several theoretical studies require attention for a study of this kind.

Robert Osgood, *Ideals and Self-Interest in America's Foreign Relations* (Chicago, 1953), challenges traditional definitions. Kenneth N. Vines and Morton Gordon, eds., *Theory and Practice of American Foreign Policy* (New York, 1955), is convenient for theories of idealism and realism. *Power Through Purpose* (Baltimore, Md., 1954), by Thomas I. Cook and Malcolm Moos, serves the same function.

II. SPECIAL WORKS

A. Monographs

Forrest Davis and Ernest K. Lindley, *How War Came* (New York, 1942), is a contemporary defense of Rooseveltian foreign policy which offers a point of departure for later studies. In one direction there are found the "revisionist" books, as Charles C. Tansill, *Back Door to War: Roosevelt Foreign Policy, 1933–41* (Chicago, 1952), and William H. Chamberlain, *America's Second Crusade* (Chicago, 1950). The spectrum of revisionism is presented in Harry Elmer Barnes' anthology, *Perpetual War for Perpetual Peace* (Caldwell, Idaho, 1953). *Roosevelt's Road to Russia* (Chicago, 1959), by George N. Crocker, is the most recent revisionist work. Crocker terms the Atlantic Charter a declaration of war.

A good survey of relations with Russia is the McNeill book. The outstanding work on American policy toward the Soviet Union in this period is *The Decision to Aid Russia, 1941: Foreign Policy and Domestic Politics* (Chapel Hill, N.C., 1961), by Raymond H. Dawson. H. L. Trefousse, *Germany and American Neutrality, 1939–41* (New York, 1951), is still the best analysis of German-American relations. Joachim Remak, "Hitlers Americapolitik. Das Auswartige Amt dachte Anders," *Aussenpolitik*, no. 11 (1955), discusses Nazi evaluation of the United States. Two recent books, Alton Frye's *Nazi Germany and the Western Hemisphere, 1933–41* (New Haven, 1967) and James V. Compton's *The Swastika and the Eagle* (Boston, 1967) study German attitudes toward the United States. Frye's analysis is especially impressive. John L. Snell, *Wartime Origins of the East-West Dilemma Over Germany* (New Orleans, 1959), contains information relevant to Argentia. *Allied Wartime Diplomacy: A Pattern in Poland* (New York, 1958), by Edward J. Rozek, is of limited value.

Herbert J. Feis, *The Spanish Story* (New York, 1948), follows the twists of Franco's policy. Carlton J. Hayes relies heavily on his experience as wartime ambassador to Spain in *The United States and Spain: An Interpretation* (New York, 1951). Comparable studies of U.S.-Portuguese relations are lacking. In *Our Vichy Gamble* (New York, 1947) William L. Langer justifies administration policy toward Vichy as the only one practical under the circumstances. There is no similar analysis of American "relations" with the Free French. Dorothy S. White's *Seeds of Discord: De Gaulle, Free France and the Allies* (Syracuse, N.Y., 1964) is sketchily researched and certain of its conclusions are unsubstantiated. Milton Viorst, *Hostile Allies: F.D.R. and De Gaulle* (New York, 1965), presents a stronger argument.

Studies of Japanese-American relations continue to pour forth. A most interesting book, which emphasizes the centrality of the Tripartite Pact, is Paul W. Schroeder, *The Axis Alliance and Japanese-American Relations, 1941* (Ithaca, N.Y., 1958). Still worth reading is *Japan's New Order in East Asia: Its Rise and Fall* (New York, 1954), by F. C. Jones. Most studies of Japanese leaders lie beyond the purview of this work, but Robert J. C. Buto's *Tojo and the Coming of War* (New York, 1957) should be mentioned. An article by Buto, "The Hull-Nomura Conversations: A Fundamental Misconception," *American Historical Review*, LXV (July, 1960), shows how serious was the misunderstanding about the possibility of settlement by negotiation. Joseph W. Ballantine, "Mukden to Pearl Harbor," *Foreign Affairs*, XXVII, no. 4 (July, 1959), is an insider's view. Thomas A. Bisson, *Shadow Over Asia: The Rise of Militant Japan* (New York, 1941), provides a revisitation of the "yellow peril" viewpoint.

A massive attack on American policy toward China is Tang Tsou, *America's Failure in China, 1941–50* (Chicago, 1963). He makes a convincing case. More sympathetic is Herbert Feis, *The China Tangle* (Princeton, N.J., 1953).

For American views on economic foreign policy one must consult Lloyd C. Gardner's *Economic Aspects of New Deal Diplomacy* (Madison, Wis., 1964). Daniel R. Fusfeld, *The Economic Thought of Franklin D. Roosevelt and the Origins of the New Deal* (New York, 1956), contains some information about Roosevelt's ideas on international economics. There are numerous contemporary articles on this subject. Some are Herbert Feis, "On Our Economic Relations with Britain," *Foreign Affairs Quarterly*, XXI (April, 1943); "Restoring Trade After the War," *Foreign Affairs Quarterly*, XX (January, 1942); and "Economics and Peace," *Foreign Policy Reports*, XX (April, 1944). A popular discussion is Harry Hopkins' "What Victory Will Bring Us," *American Magazine*, CXXXVIII (January, 1944). Similarly, there is Herbert Whidden's "Reaching a Lend-Lease Settlement," *Foreign Policy Reports*, XX (April, 1944). Feis wrote an interesting study of Lord Keynes, the great English economist: "Keynes in Retrospect," *Foreign Affairs Quarterly*, XXIX (July, 1951).

Several studies of the State Department were helpful. Graham H. Stuart, *The Department of State: A History of Its Organization, Procedure and Personnel* (New York, 1949) is a full if mechanical treatment. *The Riddle of the State Department,* by Robert Bendiner (New York, 1942), is a caustic discussion of the "striped pants boys" — and intriguing. A much different book is Gordon Craig and Felix Gilbert, eds., *The Diplomats* (Princeton, N.J., 1953), a superb dissection of diplomats and diplomacy, 1919–39.

Special works on the personal diplomacy which typified the period are Elmer Plischke, *Summit Diplomacy: Personal Diplomacy of the President of the United States* (College Park, Md., 1958), and Arthur Kemp, "Summit Conferences During World War II As Instruments of American Diplomacy," in George L. Anderson, ed., *Issues and Conflicts* (Lawrence, Kansas, 1959). For discussion of presidential power in the crisis, the reader is referred to E. S. Corwin's able summary, "The War and the Constitution: President and Congress," 37 *American Political Science Review* (February, 1943), and to the full analysis in his *The Presidency: Office and Powers* (4th ed., New York, 1957). Also informative is Louis W. Koenig, *The Presidency and the Crisis* (New York, 1944).

The struggle for public support is limned by Walter Johnson, *The Battle against Isolation* (Chicago, 1944), Selig Adler, *The Isolationist Impulse* (New York, 1957), and Wayne S. Cole, *America First — The Battle against Intervention, 1940–41* (Madison, Wis., 1953). For the influence of opinion on foreign policy there is Thomas A. Bailey's pioneering study, *The Man in the Street* (New York, 1948). More methodical — but less interesting — are H. H. Lasswell and H. H. Cummings, *Public Opinion in War and Peace* (Washington, 1943), Lester Markel, ed., *Public Opinion and Foreign Policy* (New York, 1949), J. S. Bruner, *Mandate From the People* (New York, 1944), James N. Rosenau, *Public Opinion and Foreign Policy* (New York, 1961). Elmer E. Cornwell, Jr.'s *Presidential Leadership of Public Opinion* (Bloomington, Ind., 1965), which uses materials at Hyde Park, shows how tentative must be conclusions about F.D.R. and public opinion. Two other books, Nicholas Halasz, *Roosevelt through Foreign Eyes* (Princeton, N.J., 1961), and Maurice Stael, *Mr. Churchill and the Opinion of America* (London, 1941), supplement the above works.

Much of the literature on postwar issues and establishment of the United Nations is relevant to study of the Atlantic Charter. Ruth B. Russell's *A History of the United Nations Charter: The Role of the United States, 1940–45* (Washington, 1958) is excellent. See also Redvers Opie *et al., The Search for Peace Settlements* (Washington, 1951). Julius Stone, *The Atlantic Charter: New Worlds for Old* (Sydney, Australia, 1945), is a brief analysis of the joint declaration. Less useful is *The At-*

lantic Charter and Africa from an American Standpoint (New York, 1942), published by the Committee on Africa, the War, and Peace Aims. Walter Gollwitzer, *Die Atlantik Charta: Ihre Stellung und Bedeutung in Politik und Volksrecht des Zweiten Weltkrieges* (Munich, 1947), and Gustav Kafka, *Freiheit und Anarchie* (Munich, 1949), offer interpretation by German scholars. Hallet Abend's *Pacific Charter* (Garden City, N.Y., 1943) applies the Roosevelt-Churchill points — with any compassion for the vanquished removed — to the Far East. The Woodrow Wilson Foundation published a short (4 pp.) comparison, *Woodrow Wilson's Fourteen Points: The Atlantic Charter's Eight Points* (New York, 1942). Robert A. Divine's *Second Chance: The Triumph of Internationalism During World War II* (New York, 1967) became available too late to be of value for this study; cursory reading showed that it promises to be a definitive analysis of the victory of internationalism within the United States.

Percy E. Corbett, *Post-War Worlds* (New York, 1942), brings together contemporary evaluations. In absence of official British publications, one must rely on such reports as C. R. Atlee et al., *Labour's Aims in War and Peace* (London, n.d.). Louis H. Pink, *Freedom From Fear* (New York, 1944), analyzes the relation of Roosevelt's domestic and international programs. A brilliant comparative study is J. L. Brierly's *The Covenant and the Charter* (London, 1945). E. S. Corwin, *The Constitution and World Organization* (Princeton, N.J., 1944), also deals with constitutional questions.

Contemporary evaluation of the Charter is voluminous. See Julia E. Johnson, *The 'Eight Points' of Post-War World Organization*, XV, no. 5 in *The Reference Shelf* (New York, 1942), and League for Industrial Democracy, "Atlantic Charter: A Bibliography and Some Comments," *News Bulletin* (January, 1942), for surveys of this reaction. George R. Schwartzenberger, *Power Politics: An Introduction to the Study of International Relations and Post-War Planning* (London, 1941), presents the English side.

Herbert Hoover and Hugh Gibson, *Problems of Lasting Peace* (Garden City, N.Y., 1942), deal with these issues from a Republican viewpoint. A helpful work is Percy E. Corbett, *War Aims and Post-War Plans* (Princeton, N.J., 1941). *The Atlantic Charter, The War and Christian Responsibility*, Bulletin no. 105 of the Anglican Council for Social Service (February, 1942), is revealing of English response. Francis J. McConnell et al., *Basis for the Peace to Come* (New York, 1942), presents an interesting article by Leo Pasvolsky, a State Department expert. Notably, an article by George Peel, "Atlantic Charter No. 2," *Contemporary Review* (May, 1942), termed Article VII of the Master Lend-Lease Agreement a second joint declaration. Also worth attention is Bernadotte E. Schmitt's "Roosevelt-Churchill Declaration and the Terms of a Future Peace," *Social Education* (February, 1942).

Vice-President Henry A. Wallace, in "Beyond the Atlantic Charter," *New Republic* (November 23, 1942), saw it as a step toward world government. W. Arnold-Foster, "Atlantic Charter," *Atlantic Quarterly*, XIII (April, 1942), offers a more cautious interpretation. An unfavorable view is that of Emery Reves, "Wanted: A Declaration of Interdependence; the Fallacy of the Atlantic Charter," *American Mercury* (March, 1943). See also Viscount Sir H. L. Samuel, "Thoughts on the Atlantic Charter," *Contemporary Review* (January, 1942); Julian S. Huxley, "Peace Aims as War Weapons," *Common Sense* (June, 1942); and Rene Albrecht-Carrie, "War Aims and Peace Proposals," *South Atlantic Quarterly* (January, 1942).

Special studies are Adam Ciolkosz, "Atlantic Charter (Article V) and East-Central Europe," *New Europe and World Reconstruction* (June, 1942); R. H. Crofton, "Atlantic Charter: Its Colonial Applications," *Crown Colonist* (March, 1943); and Emile Cammaerts, "Future of the Small Nations," *Contemporary Review* (January, 1942). See also Alfred Cobban, *National Self-Determination* (Chicago, 1944), for application of Articles II and III.

Military affairs and grand strategy have undergone close inspection by historians. Some books are of the "what went wrong" variety; but most, including studies by various government departments, are of the highest quality. It is notable that so many scholars involved in the United States Army's historical writing projects have attained distinguished reputations. *The United States Army in World War Two* is a basic source for military affairs at the time of Argentia. Individual volumes are generally outstanding — marred only by the stylistic blandness seemingly demanded by the Department of the Army. Mark S. Watson's *Chief of Staff: Prewar Plans and Preparations* (Washington, 1950) is excellent for strategic thought before Pearl Harbor. *Strategic Planning for Coalition Warfare, 1941–42* (Washington, 1953), by Maurice Matloff and Edwin M. Snell, also has information about prewar strategy. Louis Morton's *Strategy and Command: The First Two Years* (Washington, 1962) was of little value to the present study because of its focus. Ray S. Cline, *Washington Command Post: The Operations Division* (Washington, 1951), analyzes the General Staff, especially valuable for military operations in the Atlantic before Pearl Harbor. The relation of production, supply, and grand strategy is in R. M. Leighton and R. W. Coakley, *Global Logistics and Strategy, 1940–43* (Washington, 1955). Most striking is the dependence of planning on production and "material allocation" — a favorite jargon phrase and the bane of American military leaders' existence. The operations and contemplated moves, done in the name of hemispheric security, are in Stetson Conn and Byron Fairchild, *The Framework of Hemispheric Defense* (Washington, 1960).

In contrast with the Army's many-handed approach, one man has chronicled the part of the United States Navy in the Second World War. Samuel Eliot Morison's monumental study, *History of United States Naval Operations in World War II* (14 vols., Boston, 1946–59), offers unsurpassed narrative. The pertinent volumes for this subject, *The Battle of the Atlantic*, I, and *The Rising Sun in the Pacific*, II, do not offer much information for special studies. It is fortunate that some portion of the naval archives are open for the prewar period. An unpublished manuscript by Captain Tracy B. Kittredge (see below) was invaluable; it formed the basis of his article, "United States Defense Policy and Strategy," *U.S. News and World Report* (December 3, 1954).

For development of military aviation — and supporting strategy — there is Wesley Frank Craven and Hames L. Cates, *The Army Air Forces in World War II* (7 vols., Chicago, 1948–58). Volume I, *Plans and Early Operations: January, 1939 to August, 1942*, is a necessary source.

The History of the Second World War, United Kingdom Civil and Military Series, covers Britain's army, navy, and air forces. The accuracy and objectivity of these studies is more difficult to judge, and one does observe the commitment of almost all "official" military historians to British strategy. The volumes do not suffer from any literary comparisons with their American counterparts. H. Duncan Hall, *North American Supply*, U.K. Civil Series (London, 1955), is a superb study of a complex subject. Questions at Argentia received extensive treatment in *Grand Strategy* (6 vols., London, 1955–62), edited by Roland M. Butler. Volume III, Part I, by R. M. A. Gwyer, is concerned specifically with the period; his characterization of American strategy as confused is in part justified. For naval history see Captain S. W. Roskill, *The War At Sea, 1939–45* (4 vols., London, 1954–61). A one-volume abridgment, *The White Ensign: The British Navy at War* (London, 1960), provides an excellent introduction to the subject. Sir Charles Webster and Noble Frankland, *The Strategic Air Offensive Against Germany* (4 vols., London, 1961), is the least satisfactory of the British official histories.

A small number of contemporary books on military affairs were used. Oswald Garrison Villard's *Our Military Chaos: The Truth About Defense* (New York, 1939), presents an interesting thesis. "The War Department," *Fortune* (January, 1941), describes military affairs at a time of tremen-

dous expansion. Alexander de Seversky, *Victory Through Air Power*
(New York, 1942), exemplifies the dogma of strategic bombing. Edgar
Snow, writing in *Fortune* (June, 1941), "How America Can Take The
Offensive," demonstrates how widespread were ideas which surfaced at
Argentia. *Strategy for Victory*, by Hanson Baldwin (New York, 1942),
was informative.

F.D.R.'s actions as Commander in Chief remain a cause of argument.
Ernest R. May, ed., *The Ultimate Decision: President as Commander-in-
Chief* (New York, 1960), places more importance on Roosevelt's part
than the evidence warrants. An article by May, "Development of Politico-
Military Consultation in the United States," *Political Science Quarterly*
(June, 1955), is more convincing. Kent R. Greenfield, in two books,
Command Decisions (Washington, 1959), and *American Strategy in
World War II* (Baltimore, 1963), offers balanced judgment on these ques-
tions. See also Samuel Eliot Morison's outstanding treatment, *Strategy
and Compromise* (Boston, 1958).

British participation in the war is skillfully narrated by Chester A.
Wilmot, *Struggle for Europe* (New York, 1952), who summarizes and
defends the arguments of Winston Churchill. A corrective is Arthur M.
Schlesinger, Jr., "Wilmot's War, or 'Churchill Was Always Right,'" *Reporter* (April 29, 1952). The demolition of Churchill's military genius is
gleefully carried out by Trumbull Higgins, *Winston Churchill and the
Second Front* (New York, 1957). Lt. Col. Alfred Burne, "The Development of British Strategic Thought," *Army Quarterly*, volume 52 (April,
1956), is an able summary. Surveys of the military operations are A. Russell Buchanan's *The United States in World War II* (2 vols., New York,
1964), and the excellent work by Louis L. Snyder, *The War: A Concise
History, 1939–45* (New York, 1960).

B. Biographies and Autobiographies

The present study relies largely on biographies and especially on memoirs. Fortunately, the memoirs of high officials are abundant, and many of
these pertain to the meeting at Argentia. H. V. Morton, journalist and
travel writer, has set down an eyewitness account of the conference, *Atlantic Meeting* (London, 1943), which is invaluable for the atmosphere
of the conference.

F.D.R. had no time to write an autobiography although it appears such
was his intent. Earlier books, *Whither Bound?* (Boston, 1926) and *On
Our Way* (New York, 1934), deal almost exclusively with domestic problems. One must rely on memoirs by Roosevelt's subordinates and confi-
dants for understanding his mind, that "heavily-forested interior." Grace

Tully, *F.D.R., My Boss* (New York, 1949), recounts the experiences of a presidential secretary. *Reilly of the White House* (New York, 1947), a Secret Service agent, accompanied F.D.R. to Argentia. His boss at the time, Edmond W. Starling, in *Starling of the White House* with Thomas Sugrue (New York, 1946), says nothing about the conference and, indeed, little about the Roosevelt administration. Frances Perkins, *The Roosevelt I Knew* (New York, 1946), suggests some novel explanations of the Roosevelt personality. *Affectionately, F.D.R.: A Son's Story of a Lonely Man* (New York, 1959), by Franklin Roosevelt, Jr. and Sidney Shallett, concentrates on the period before 1933 and contains nothing about Argentia. The President's physician, Admiral Ross T. McIntire, was present at the meeting and set down his observations in *Twelve Years With Roosevelt* (London, 1948). See also Samuel I. Rosenman, *Working With Roosevelt* (New York, 1952); Donald Richberg, *My Hero* (New York, 1954); and Charles Michelson, *The Ghost Talks* (New York, 1944).

Cordell Hull, *Memoirs* (2 vols., New York, 1948), is informative though in the Secretary's colorless style. Three books by Sumner Welles, the brilliant Under Secretary of State, are essential sources: *The Time for Decision* (New York, 1944), *Where Are We Heading?* (New York, 1946), and *Seven Decisions that Shaped History* (New York, 1951). Welles edited *The World of the Four Freedoms* (New York, 1943), a collection of speeches of which several bear directly on the joint declaration. Henry L. Stimson and McGeorge Bundy, *On Active Service in War and Peace* (New York, 1947), is a lively record of Stimson's half-century of public service. Another useful autobiography is H. H. Arnold's *Global Mission* (New York, 1949). In certain respects it dovetails with Ernest J. King and Walter M. Whitehill, *Fleet Admiral King: A Naval Record, 1900–45* (New York, 1952). This is a warm, surprisingly humorous account.

I Was There (New York, 1950), by Fleet Admiral William D. Leahy, discusses his ambassadorship to Vichy and his relations with the President. The American Ambassador in Tokyo, Joseph C. Grew, fills lacunae about U.S.-Japanese relations in two memoirs: *Turbulent Era*, edited by Walter Johnson (2 vols., Boston, 1942), and *Ten Years in Japan* (New York, 1944). One wishes that John G. Winant, *Letter From Grosvenor Square: An Account of a Stewardship* (Boston, 1947), had more about day-to-day developments and less of trivia; nonetheless, his account is informative.

Other memoirs, by men not directly involved in the conference, are worth reading. *The Secret Diary of Harold Ickes* (3 vols., New York, 1954), is an inside view of the Roosevelt circle. Its conclusions should be approached carefully. *Lend-Lease: Weapon for Victory* (New York,

1944), by Edward R. Stettinius, Jr., provides statistical data about Lend-Lease. See also Joseph E. Davies, *Mission to Moscow* (New York, 1941); William C. Bullitt, *The Great Globe Itself* (New York, 1946); and William Phillips, *Ventures in Diplomacy* (Boston, 1952). Of great interest is the autobiography of a diplomat, Robert D. Murphy, whose *Diplomat among Warriors* (New York, 1964) adds impressive information about policy toward Vichy.

In a category all its own is Elliott Roosevelt, *As He Saw It* (New York, 1946). Elliott's observations are as fascinating as they are prejudiced; were the anglophobism removed the book would lose much of its appeal. Harry Hopkins wrote a colorful account of his trip to Russia, "The Inside Story of My Meeting with Stalin," *Amerian Magazine* (December, 1941). Jay Pierrepont Moffat set down in his private diary observations on practically every subject, and the Atlantic Charter is no exception. A sample is in Nancy H. Hooker, ed., *The Moffat Papers: Selections from the Diplomatic Journals of Jay Pierrepont Moffat, 1919–43* (Boston, 1956). It may be that the journals of Breckinridge Long will win a comparable reputation. All the important entries have been published as *The War Diaries of Breckinridge Long* (Lincoln, Neb., 1966), a model of historical editing by Fred L. Israel.

Winston Churchill left an enduring monument in his memoirs, *The Second World War* (6 vols., Boston, 1948–53). These felicitous volumes are the first assignment for every student of the war. Colin Coote and Danzil Batchelor, eds., *Maxims and Reflections* (Boston, 1949), bring together some of the most (and least) memorable of Churchill's sayings. Elizabeth Nel, *Churchill's Private Secretary* (London, 1946), describes the Prime Minister's methods during working hours. See also Walter M. Thompson, *Assignment Churchill* (London, 1952), by his bodyguard-valet-factotum.

Autobiographies by English officials are fewer in number but no less important than those by Americans. Arthur Bryant, *Turn of the Tide, 1939–43* (New York, 1957), is based on the diaries of Viscount Alanbrooke, but is mostly irrelevant to a study of Argentia. Lord Moran, *Churchill: Taken from the Diaries of Lord Moran* (Boston, 1966), is by far the most intriguing and informative view of the Prime Minister to emerge. A recent publication, *The War Years, 1939–45* (New York, 1967), the second volume in *Diaries and Letters of Harold Nicolson*, edited by Nigel Nicolson, is a humorous, mocking, tragic, always compelling memoir of England and her leaders during the war. Clement R. Attlee, *As It Happened* (London, 1954), is a superficial record of his public career. His *The Prime Minister Remembers*

(London, 1961), concentrating on the war and postwar period, is not much more helpful. Important for working out the "pecking order" in Churchill's regime is John Kennedy, *The Business of War* (London, 1957). Useful memoirs about military affairs are: Air Marshal Sir Arthur Harris, *Bomber Offensive* (London, 1957); Sir John Slessor, *The Central Blue: Recollections and Reflections* (London, 1956); and the autobiography of Viscount Cunningham, Admiral of the Fleet, *A Sailor's Odyssey* (2 vols., London, 1947).

Sir Anthony Eden's *The Reckoning* (London, 1965) heads the diplomatic memoirs. This book, dealing with 1940–45, contains a tremendous store of information. It is unfortunate that Eden could not attend the conference. Lord Halifax described his Washington ambassadorship in a stuffy book, *Fulness of Days* (London, 1957). See also Sir Edward Marsh, *A Number of People* (London, 1957). *India and Democracy* (London, 1941), by Leo S. Amery, is not a formal memoir, but is revealing of views of a leading Conservative — and imperialist — spokesman.

Jan Ciechanowski, *Defeat in Victory* (Garden City, N.Y., 1947), by the Polish Ambassador to the United States, has an interesting interpretation of the meetings' purpose. See also Charle de Gaulle, *War Memoirs* (3 vols., New York, 1955–57), and Maxime Weygand, *Recalled to Service* (Garden City, N.Y., 1952), the old general's defense of his actions.

No biographer has captured the convolutions of Roosevelt's foreign policy, and such a feat may be a long time in coming. Frank Freidel's *Franklin D. Roosevelt* (3 vols., New York, 1952–56) has not reached the President's submersion in foreign affairs. James M. Burns, *The Lion and the Fox* (New York, 1956), is the best one-volume biography, but also slights foreign affairs. See also John Gunther, *Roosevelt in Retrospect* (New York, 1950); Rexford G. Tugwell, "The Compromising Roosevelt," *Western Political Quarterly*, VI (June, 1953), and his *The Democratic Roosevelt* (Garden City, N.Y., 1957). Uncritical is Edgar E. Robinson, *The Roosevelt Leadership, 1933–45* (Philadelphia, 1955). John T. Flynn, *The Roosevelt Myth* (New York, 1948), is a piece of character assassination.

A superb example of biography is Robert E. Sherwood's *Roosevelt and Hopkins: An Intimate History* (New York, 1948), an analysis of Roosevelt as well as of his close friend. Two other portraits of Hopkins are Louis W. Koenig, *The Invisible Presidency* (New York, 1960) and Marquis W. Childs, "The President's Best Friend," *The Saturday Evening Post* (April 19, 1941). Julius W. Pratt's study of Cordell Hull (2 vols., New York, 1964), in Robert H. Ferrell, ed., *The American Secretaries of State and Their Diplomacy*, is the only satisfactory treatment of Hull's long tenure. See also the essay in Norman A. Graebner, ed., *An Uncertain*

Tradition: American Secretaries of State in the Twentieth Century (New York, 1961). John M. Blum's multivolume biography of Henry Morgenthau, Jr. promises to be an important contribution. The second volume, *From the Morgenthau Diaries: Years of Urgency, 1938–41* (Boston, 1965), broadens understanding of military and economic developments. Two biographies of Henry L. Stimson, the Secretary of War, are notable. Richard N. Current's *Secretary Stimson: A Study in Statecraft* (New Brunswick, N.J., 1954) is "acidly critical." A more balanced exposition is Elting E. Morison, *Turmoil and Tradition: The Life and Times of Henry L. Stimson* (Boston, 1960). Of the military leadership only Marshall has attracted biographers. Early studies are Robert Payne, *The Marshall Story* (New York, 1951) and William Frye, *Marshall: Citizen Soldier* (Indianapolis, 1947). Forrest C. Pogue's *George C. Marshall*, of which the first two volumes, *Education of a General* (New York, 1963) and *Ordeal and Hope, 1939–42* (New York, 1966) have been published, should be definitive.

As yet no one has dared tackle Winston Churchill the man — and the myth — in a full, scholarly biography. The best short study is Alan Moorehead's *Winston Churchill: In Trial and Triumph* (Boston, 1955). Interesting is Olivia Coolidge, *Winston Churchill and the Story of Two World Wars* (Boston, 1960). Emrys Hughes, *Winston Churchill: British Bulldog* (New York, 1955), carries out the promise of its title. Violet Bonham Carter's sympathetic memoir and biography of Churchill's early career is required reading. The most ambitious biography thus far, Lewis Broad's *Winston Churchill*, is disappointing. His second volume, *Years of Achievement* (New York, 1963), is almost a travesty of a biography.

The Prof in Two Worlds (New York, 1964), by the Earl of Birkenhead, traces the career of Lord Cherwell, Churchill's scientific adviser and sometime confidant. See also Birkenhead's *Halifax: The Life of Lord Halifax* (London, 1965). Roy F. Harrod, *The Life of John Maynard Keynes* (London, 1951), studies the great economist. J. W. Pickersgill, *The Mackenzie King Record* (Toronto, 1960), writes of the Canadian Prime Minister at the time of Argentia.

III. NEWSPAPERS AND PERIODICALS

The *New York Times* provides magnificent coverage for the complex events of summer, 1941. A selection — one hopes it is representative — of other American papers was consulted for reaction to the meeting: the Chicago *Tribune*, Los Angeles *Times*, St. Louis *Post-Dispatch*, Denver *Post*, Indianapolis *Times* and *Star*, and the New York *Herald Tribune*. The author was fortunate in having an opportunity to use the newspaper library of the British Museum. Located at Colindale, a pleasant forty-minute train ride out of London, this repository brings together magnificent files of English newspapers.

Useful periodicals were the *American Journal of International Law*, historical journals, and *Foreign Affairs*, together with periodicals such as *Fortune, The Saturday Evening Post, Contemporary Review, American Magazine*, and *New Republic*.

IV. PRINTED SOURCES

A convenient source for agreements to which the United States was a party is the World Peace Foundation's *Documents on American Foreign Relations*, IV (Boston, 1942), edited by Leland Goodrich. Louise W. Holborn, *War and Peace Aims of the United Nations* (Boston, 1943), brings together documents relating to Allied goals.

Several publications of the Department of State are essential. *Foreign Relations of the United States* (Washington, 1861–) is a selection of official documents which has no peer. The six volumes for 1941 maintain the series' high standard. They add to two compilations published earlier: *Peace and War: United States Foreign Policy, 1931–41* (Washington, 1943), and *Foreign Relations: Japan, 1931–41* (2 vols., Washington, 1943). See also *Soviet Supply Protocols* (Washington, 1948). *Documents on German Foreign Policy, 1918–45*, Series D, XIII (Washington, 1964) is a remarkable source, selected from captured German archives. *The Department of State Bulletin* carries press releases and speeches by administration leaders, a good source for current policy. Harley Notter, *Postwar Foreign Policy Preparation, 1939–45* (Washington, 1949), traces the Department's interest in these questions.

Useful for military policy is Generals Marshall and Arnold and Admiral King, *War Reports of the Joint Chiefs of Staff* (New York, 1947). See also Department of Navy, *Fuehrer Conferences on Matters Dealing with the German Navy, 1939–41* (5 vols., Washington, 1947). The massive *Hearings Before the Joint Committee on the Investigation of the Pearl Harbor Attack* (39 vols., Washington, 1946), is essential. Committee members in their zeal for the "truth" about Pearl Harbor requisitioned thousands of documents and interrogated high officials regarding the background of the tragedy.

Documents on British Foreign Policy, 1919–39, ends with the Nazi invasion of Poland. One of its editors, E. L. Woodward, has written *British Foreign Policy, 1939–45* (London, 1962), based on archives but no substitute for a documentary publication. See also *Report of Proceedings, Inter-Allied Meeting Held in London at St. James' Palace on September 24, 1941* (London, 1941).

Parliamentary materials consulted were the *House of Commons Debates* and *Congressional Record,* as well as Senate and House hearings on subjects such as Lend-Lease, Selective Service renewal, and convoying.

Charles Eade, comp., *The War Speeches of the Rt. Hon. Winston S. Churchill* (3 vols., London, 1951) is helpful. Churchill's *Secret Session Speeches,* compiled by Eade, were published separately (New York, 1946). Samuel I. Rosenman, ed., *The Public Papers* and *Addresses of Franklin D. Roosevelt* (13 vols., New York, 1938–50), brings together presidential addresses, proclamations, and press conferences. With only a few reservations the quality of this publication is excellent. Somewhat less representative of Roosevelt's views, but still valuable, is the edition of his correspondence by Elliott Roosevelt — *F.D.R.: His Personal Letters* (4 vols., New York, 1947–50).

V. MANUSCRIPT SOURCES
A. Archives

Although the present study was undertaken as a multinational investigation of the meeting at Argentia, government regulations regarding use of archives played a large part in making it largely a study of American participation. English archives for this period are closed, and the author's efforts, feeble at best, to penetrate into them were unsuccessful.

Fortunately, the American situation presents an embarrassment of riches. Not only does the student have the *Foreign Relations* series, but he can obtain access to the voluminous unpublished files of the Department of State. Through 1937 these files are completely open; records are "open with restriction," that is, examination of notes, through 1943. For the present subject the most important file is D.F., 740.0011 European War 1939/, an agglomeration of messages, memoranda, and miscellany, much of which has only a tenuous connection with Europe or the war. Also valuable were: 121.841 (the Harry Hopkins file); 840.50 (interdepartmental discussions); 711.94; 123 Winant, John G.; and 740.0011 Pacific War.

An attempt to use records of the Office of the Chief of Staff of the United States Army, located at Alexandria, proved futile. The Department of the Navy was more cooperative, and research in the archives at Washington Navy Yard was of great benefit. The unpublished monograph by Captain Tracy B. Kittredge, "United States-British Naval Cooperation, 1939–42," now available for scholarly examination, proved a gold mine for such topics as convoying. Background studies for the various war plans, and some operational messages were consulted.

B. Personal Papers

The papers of Franklin D. Roosevelt, located in the presidential museum-library at Hyde Park, N.Y., offer both blessings and frustration. The researcher can lose himself happily in mountains of letters, memos, and so-called background papers. But this student, at least, emerged with a feeling of bafflement. Neither Roosevelt the man nor Roosevelt the President really resides in these tons of paper. One is tempted to curse Alexander Graham Bell, perhaps to excuse one's own defects. Certainly, F.D.R. found the telephone a useful invention. Examination of the correspondence file with the Secretary of State — dominated by "Thank you for the black umbrella, Cordell," and "I deeply appreciate your remembering our wedding anniversary, Mr. President" letters — is proof of this contention.

Nonetheless, Roosevelt's papers contain a tremendous amount of information. The Official File, President's Secretary File, and over 100 subclassifications of the President's Personal File for this period were searched. The President's Personal File, especially PPF 463–C (materials about the conference) and PPF 1820 (speech material and documents about public opinion) was extremely valuable. The Hopkins Papers are at Hyde Park of course, and though still in partial disorder have considerable information. Also at the Roosevelt Library, but unavailable in varying degrees, are the papers of Henry Morgenthau, Jr., Henry A. Wallace, William D. Hassett, Samuel I. Rosenman, Myron C. Taylor, and John G. Winant.

The Henry L. Stimson MSS are at the Sterling Library in Yale University. They are open without any important restrictions. Stimson's diaries, conveniently bound and typewritten, form a marvelous source. Also useful was his correspondence (Boxes 372–91), a small collection of War Department Papers (503), and news clippings. The papers of Robert Patterson, one of Stimson's lieutenants, are in the Library of Congress; because of Patterson's later posts only a small part is open. The Frank Knox papers in the Library of Congress are few in number (8 ft.) and of little value. One does get the impression that Knox was the most ardent interventionist in the cabinet.

The Cordell Hull papers, also on deposit in the Library of Congress, are available with permission. The Secretary of State apparently was as uncommunicative in private as in public, and his papers are disappointing regarding matters dealt with here. I saw Hull's correspondence and sub-classifications in the Subject File, 1921–46. Container 62 has a thin folder on the Atlantic Charter. Papers of other State Department officials are of varying usefulness. Breckinridge Long kept journals which are unrivaled for the inner workings of the Department — and of Cordell Hull. They are located in the Library of Congress, as are the papers of Leland Harrison, whose letters to friends at posts in occupied Europe in 1940–41 are revealing. The bulk of the Harrison papers, however, relates to the Paris Peace Conference of 1919. A good source for foreign affairs, especially attitudes toward the Soviet Union, is the Joseph E. Davies MSS also in the Library of Congress. Particularly interesting are the notes Davies made during preparation of *Mission to Moscow*. The papers of George Fort Milton were disappointing. Milton was a special assistant and friend to Hull, but with rare exceptions his correspondence concerned financial matters — in particular the difficulties of a historian who was trying to make a buck from his craft. Pierrepont Moffat's journals in the Houghton Library, Harvard University, compare with those of Long for insight and detail. Unfortunately for the historian of policymaking, Moffat accepted an appointment as Minister to Canada in summer, 1940. Herschel V. Johnson was Minister of the American Embassy in London at the time of Hopkins' visits. His papers (15 ft.) are in the Harry S Truman Library in Independence, Mo., but have little of value for the present study.

The interviews of Arthur Krock, Royal Ingersoll, William Phillips, Harvey H. Bundy, Admiral Thomas C. Hart, Joseph Ballantine, H. Kent Hewitt, and Alan G. Kirk, deposited in the Columbia Oral History Collection, were used. The Krock, Hart, and Ballantine memoirs were most informative.

An attempt was made to elicit reactions to individually directed questions from some twenty-five persons who were present at Argentia or took part in the preparations. Of the replies, the more helpful were from British participants: General Sir Ian Jacob, General W. M. Yool, Vice-Admiral B. B. Schofield, and H. V. Morton. Sir Ian Jacob generously allowed me to use his fifty-five-page diary of the meeting. It was invaluable, a shrewd, humorous, informative account of the journeys to and from Argentia and of the conference itself. Almost equally helpful was the extract from an unpublished autobiography provided me by Admiral Schofield, who is a distinguished naval historian in his own right. Comments by these officers, by General Yool, and by Mr. Morton, cleared up several questions for which I had found no answers.

Index

ABC-conversations, strategy discussions, 135, 142, 147, 154, 161–162, 183–184, 251
ABCD powers, 157
Acheson, Dean, 185
Advisory Committee on Problems of Foreign Relations, 178, 180
Africa, *see* North Africa; South Africa; West Africa
Air power, 133–136, 216; and English strategy, 105, 134–136, 139, 149, 251–252; and Beaverbrook, 210; theory rejected by Marshall and Stark, 251; and F.D.R., 252
Alison, Lieutenant J. R., 43
America First Committee, Pasadena Chapter, 265
American Magazine, Beaverbrook's article in, 30
Amery, L. S., 124
Anglo-American relations, 19, 20, 30, 111, 226, 232, 233–234; policy vis-à-vis Soviet Union, 33, 36–37, 50, 102; policy for Japan, 89–93, 103, 112–116, 163–169, 224; and naval supremacy, 94; and joint declaration, 112, 174–202; and convoy policy, 143; and *Operation Indigo*, 162–163; and postwar policy, 175, 177–179, 186; and trade policy, 248
Anglo-Soviet relations, 27, 43, 184; and warning to Iran, 239
Anticolonialism, *see* Colonialism
Antisubmarine operations, Western

Atlantic, 136. *See also* Submarines
Arcadia conference, 129
Argentia, Newfoundland, vii–viii; obstacles to meeting at, 8, 24–25; F.D.R.'s preferred site, 26, 33; Roosevelt arrives at, 66–67; security precautions at, 67–68; Churchill arrives at, 80–81; principals leave after conference, 204–205, 214–218. *See also* Atlantic Conference
Arizona, U.S.S., 66
Arkansas, U.S.S., 67, 217–218
Armament, reduction of, *see* Disarmament
Armstrong, Hamilton Fish, 28
Arnold, General Henry H., 7, 32, 34, 71, 85, 121; departs for Argentia, 61–63; on opulence of the *Augusta*, 64–65; anxiety before conference, 66; and conference banquets, 101–102, 104–105, 145; and British counterparts, 125–126, 130; advocate of air power, 134, 136; and strategy talks, 137, 139; and aid to Russia, 140; at first full staff conference, 147, 152, 153; returns to Washington, 217, 250; reaction to Charter, 250–251
Assiniboine, H.M.C.S., 100, 225–226
Astrid, Princess, 6
Atlantic, 36, 92; Anglo-American

Cape Saint Mary Light, 66
Cape Verde Islands, 121, 149–150, 161, 162, 250
Caribbean, obstacles to meeting in, 18
Casablanca Conference, vii
Catalinas (PBY's), 149
Caucasus, 239
Caught in the Draft (film), 224
Censorship, 53, 78–79
Chamberlain, Joseph, 196
Chequers, Churchill's estate, 15, 40–41, 43, 54, 57
Cherwell, Lord (Professor Frederick Lindemann), 54, 57, 58, 60, 205; at banquets, 101, 121; explores beaches with Churchill, 120
Chicago, U.S.S., 64
Chicago *Times*, 159
Chicago *Tribune*, 232
Childs, Marquis, 11
China, 114, 163, 164, 169, 170, 258. *See also* Far East
Chronicle, London, 221
Churchill, Lady Clementine, 56
Churchill, Major John Spencer, 155
Churchill, Winston S., vii, 2, 7, 211; and obstacles to meeting with F.D.R., 8, 18–19, 25; reveals Britain's plight (1940), 9–10; meets with Hopkins, 10–11, 15, 26, 31, 38; hopes for U.S. intervention, 29–30, 89–93; staff, 31–33, 54, 131–132; and agenda, 36; concern for Soviets, 36–37, 43, 48, 75; secrecy concerning trip, 53–54, 78–79; departs for Argentia, 54–63; anxiety over meeting, 65–66, 80; en route to Argentia, 72–81; meets F.D.R., 82–87; banquet honoring, 101–102; informal talk on war, 103–107; and postwar peace organization, 105, 136, 198, 199; and air power, 105, 134–136; hosts

church service, 108–111; seeks anti-Japanese entente, 113, 119, 163–167, 203, 215; hosts banquet for presidential party, 117–119; explores coastal beaches, 120–121, 169; argues with F.D.R. about colonialism, 122–124; admiration for Pound, 127; modification of views, 148; F.D.R.'s admiration for, 166–167; and statement of peace aims, 181–183, 187; balks on Article IV of declaration, 195–198, 248–249; cables draft declaration to War Cabinet, 198–199, 204, 215–216, 220; and Beaverbrook, 207; shocked by Congressional action in Selective Service Act, 214; summarizes results of meetings for Whitehall, 215; voyage home, 216, 219, 223–227; interest in naval design, 224–225; salute to convoy en route, 225; arrives in London, 226–227; and statement to Japan, 247; describes meeting on BBC, 257–259; and morale, 259; shift in attitude toward Charter, 262. *See also* Roosevelt-Churchill correspondence
Citizen X (film), 75–76
Clark, Grenville, 176
Clive, Robert, 123
Colindale newspaper library, British Museum, ix
Collier's Weekly, 99
Colonialism, 122–124, 187, 189–190
Colossus, British battleship, 127
Columbia Oral History Project, ix
Combined Chiefs of Staff, 154
Commonwealth nations, *see* British Empire
Comtaskforce 1, 67–68
Congress, U.S., 1, 23; and Lend-Lease Act, 2, 10, 22, 214; reac-